THE I TATTI
RENAISSANCE LIBRARY

James Hankins, General Editor

PONTANO

DIALOGUES

VOLUME 2

ITRL 91

GIOVANNI GIOVIANO PONTANO

◆ ◆ ◆

DIALOGUES

VOLUME 2 ◆ ACTIUS

EDITED AND TRANSLATED BY

JULIA HAIG GAISSER

THE I TATTI RENAISSANCE LIBRARY
HARVARD UNIVERSITY PRESS
CAMBRIDGE, MASSACHUSETTS
LONDON, ENGLAND
2020

Series design by Dean Bornstein

First printing

Library of Congress Cataloging-in-Publication Data

Pontano, Giovanni Gioviano, 1429–1503.
Dialogues / Giovanni Gioviano Pontano ;
edited and translated by Julia Haig Gaisser.
volumes. cm. — (The I Tatti Renaissance library ; 53)
Latin and English on facing pages.
ISBN 978-0-674-05491-2 (v. 1)
ISBN 978-0-674-23718-6 (v. 2)
ISBN 978-0-674-24846-5 (v. 3)
I. Gaisser, Julia Haig. II. Pontano, Giovanni Gioviano, 1429–1503.
Dialogues. English. 2012. III. Pontano,
Giovanni Gioviano, 1429–1503. Dialogues. Latin. 2012.
IV. Title. V. Series: I Tatti Renaissance library ; 53.
PA8570.P5D53 2012
871′.04 — dc23   2012007924

Contents

ॐ§?ॐ

Introduction

൫ട൫

Giovanni Gioviano Pontano (May 7, 1429–September 17, 1503)
served five kings of Naples as a courtier, official, and diplomat, and
earned even greater fame as a scholar, prose author, and poet.[1]
Pontano was Umbrian by birth, but in 1447, at the age of eigh-
teen, he joined the entourage of the king of Naples, Alfonso I,
who was then campaigning in Tuscany. In 1448 he accompanied
Alfonso to Naples, and there he spent the next fifty-five years, almost all of them in the service of the Aragonese kings. He saw the
apogee of the dynasty under Alfonso, its defeat by the French under Ferrandino (1495), and its final collapse under Federico (1501).
From his first days in Naples Pontano participated in the social
and intellectual gatherings of his fellow humanists; ultimately he
led the sodality. (Modern scholars generally call the group the Accademia Pontaniana, but the name is first attested in the 1480s
and came into general use only after Pontano's death.)[2] Throughout his public career Pontano was always actively and productively
engaged in scholarly and literary activity, transcribing and annotat-
ing ancient texts, and writing poetry, histories, and treatises on
various subjects. He also wrote five dialogues: *Charon, Antonius,
Actius, Aegidius,* and *Asinus. Charon* and *Antonius* appeared in volume 1.[3] *Actius* is the subject of the present volume. *Aegidius* and
Asinus appear in volume 3 (ITRL 92).

The Neapolitan sodality is central to the content and preserva-
tion of Pontano's dialogues. Its interests are reflected in all the dialogues, and its members appear as interlocutors in all but one —
Charon, whose speakers are denizens of the underworld of classical
mythology. After Pontano's death members of the sodality preserved his literary legacy, publishing many of the works not printed

in his lifetime, including *Actius, Aegidius,* and *Asinus,* edited by Pietro Summonte and printed in 1507.[4] (*Charon* and *Antonius* were printed under Pontano's supervision in 1491.)[5] The sodality evolved over the years. Originally it met in the royal library; after Alfonso's death (1458) the humanists gathered under an arcade near the house of their leader, Antonio Beccadelli (Panormita), and called both meeting place and sodality the *Porticus Antoniana.* When Pontano became head of the sodality on Panormita's death (1471), the group kept the name *Porticus,* although it now met in various places.[6] It is generally called *Porticus* as well as *conventus, consessus,* or *consessio* (assembly or gathering) in the dialogues.

Pontano's dialogues were composed over a thirty-year period, from *Charon* (around 1469) to *Aegidius* (1501).[7] *Asinus* was probably written between 1488 and 1492, but it has been printed at the end of the collection since the first edition of *Actius, Aegidius,* and *Asinus* in 1507, and the sequence in the I Tatti volumes follows that tradition.[8] The five dialogues are diverse in subject but share certain fundamental similarities. Each has its starting point (but not its principal subject) in a contemporary event, each is concerned (whether seriously or satirically) with moral or religious questions of current interest, each is deeply interested in language — its rules, history, and artistic effects. Three of the five (*Antonius, Actius,* and *Aegidius*) reflect but do not replicate the discussions and procedure of the sodality. *Charon* deals with similar topics, but its speakers belong to the classical underworld, while *Asinus* is a satirical comedy with Pontano himself as the protagonist and several members of the sodality in the cast.

Actius is named after one of its principal interlocutors, Azio, the renowned poet Jacopo Sannazaro, whose academy name was Actius. Its numerous exchanges demonstrate the variety and depth of the philosophical, philological, and literary interests of the sodality and especially those of Pontano himself. Moving with formal courtesy from topic to topic, the interlocutors talk about the de-

cline of true religion, the immortality of the soul, the nature of dreams, small points of Latin orthography and syntax, astrological influences, and etymology and the history of language. The principal subjects of the dialogue, however, are poetry and history — specifically, the qualities of the Latin hexameter and the nature and purposes of historical writing. These are treated at length in two distinct but closely related sections. Azio is the principal speaker of the first, Gabriele Altilio of the second.[9] The dialogue has usually been studied for its relevance to Renaissance historiography, but it is at least as important for its perceptive and highly technical discussion of the Latin hexameter. The poet Azio is the speaker, but the analysis is all Pontano's, the fruit of his long study of the rhythmical and sound effects of ancient poetry and the application of his findings to his own poetry. The historiographical discussion attributed to Altilio balances and complements Azio's treatise on the hexameter. It falls into two sections separated by an intermezzo. In the first, Altilio notes that the ancients called history a kind of poetry written in prose — an analogy that he explores and justifies by comparing the purposes, methods, styles, and rhythms of the two genres in various passages of Livy and Sallust, whom he deems "the princes of history." The intermezzo turns to other interlocutors and to grammatical topics, but the focus is still historical; the subjects of discussion are etymology and the development of human language. In the second section, Altilio discusses the elements of good historical writing, using passages from Livy and Sallust as examples. He mentions clear structuring of events, a style attentive to both brevity and speed, appropriate description of places, events, and characters, and above all, objectivity on the part of the historian, who must consider himself a judge and teacher rather than a partisan.

The metrical and historiographical discussions in *Actius* are both landmarks in the history of scholarship, for each is the first of its kind. Pontano's Azio claims that no one before him has

delved into his subject: "no one has yet written about them," he says in section 34.[10] And his claim is correct; the discussion should be regarded as the first full treatment of the hexameter in the history of philology, as Guido Martellotti observed in an important article.[11] Altilio's account of historiography is also presented as lacking predecessors (section 61); here too, modern scholars have agreed.[12] The conception and analysis in both discussions are original, the products of understanding gained directly from close study of the methods and techniques of the ancient authors and not from treatments by previous scholars.

NOTES

1. For a fuller introduction to Pontano's life and works, see Pontano 2012, vii–xxvii, with earlier bibliography, and Bruno Figliuolo, "Giovanni Pontano," *DBI* 84 (2015): 729–40. Short references to works cited in this Introduction and in the Notes to the Translation are given in full in the Abbreviations or the Bibliography.

2. Furstenberg-Levi, *The Accademia Pontaniana*, 70–75; Furstenberg-Levi, "The Fifteenth-Century Accademia Pontaniana," 40–42.

3. Pontano 2012.

4. For Summonte see Appendix II. Some details of the efforts of Pontano's friends are given in Summonte's dedications to the dialogues. For his dedication to *Actius*, see Appendix I. For his dedications to *Aegidius* and *Asinus*, see Appendix I in volume 3. For publication as a project of the group, see Furstenberg-Levi, *The Accademia Pontaniana*, 135–43.

5. Pontano, [*Dialogi qui Charon et Antonius inscribuntur*] (Naples: Mathias Moravus, January 31, 1491).

6. Furstenberg-Levi, *The Accademia Pontaniana*, 70–75.

7. Monti, "Ricerche sulla cronologia."

8. The dialogue can be dated between the marriage celebration of the son of Pope Innocent VIII mentioned in *Asinus* 10 (January 20, 1488)

and Innocent's death (July 25, 1492); Monti, "Ricerche sulla cronologia," 821–22.

9. For Azio and Altilio see Appendix II. For the dialogue, see Tateo, "La poetica"; Deramaix, "*Excellentia et Admiratio*"; Gray, *History and Rhetoric*.

10. See also Puderico's comment in section 57: "This is a subject that I see has been omitted by our literary men or rather has been unknown to them."

11. "L'*Actius* del Pontano è sfuggito per lo più all'attenzione dei classicisti, eppure esso presenta, per la prima volta nella storia della filologia, una trattazione coerente e completa dell'esametro latino." Martellotti, "Critica metrica," 366 n. 29.

12. For the significance of Pontano's contribution to the theory of historical writing, see Black, who calls him "the first author of a substantial *ars historica*": "The New Laws of History," 131. See also Grafton, *What was History?*

ACTIUS

ACTIUS

Caeparius Notarius, Pascutius et Segnitius[1]

1 *Caep.* 'Pascutius Caulita, Pasculli Caulitae filius, Sarnensis, sarcularius,[2] cum Pignatia Nigella, quae viro suo nunc hic adest, et
suo et uxoris nomine, vendit Segnitio Funestillo, Acerrano viatori, qui ipsus emit sibi, liberis, nepotibus, pronepotibus abne-
potibusque suis cum omni posteritate domunculam.'

Segn. Adde illud: 'et anteritate'; utraque enim parte, anteriore ac
posteriore, domus constat.

Caep. Caute agito, mi Caulita; ea domuncula . . .

Segn. Mater eius Macronilla non domunculam, sed democulam
verbo suo nominabat; quo enim die Sueratus, Pasculli pater, in
illam ab harula demigravit cum familia et sue, oculum male
auspicato ingressus amisit.

Caep. Scite, caute, averuncate! ammones; pergam: 'Sita est Sar-
nensi in suburbio secundum flumen.'

Segn. Atqui vetuverbio[3] cavetur secundum flumen emundum non
esse.

Caep. Rivum volui, non flumen dicere; evincet tamen illam tibi
cum omni quoque posteritate Pascutius.

Segn. Et anteritate quoque memor uti fuas facito.

Caep. 'Tribules ac vicinos bonos habet, Pilutium Rufillum.'

Segn. Grex mihi suillus venum si daretur, pilus hic nequaquam
placeret.

ACTIUS

The Notary Caeparius, Pascutius, and Segnitius[1]

Caeparius. "Pascutius Caulita, son of Pascullus Caulita, of Sarno,   1
hoer, with Pignatia Nigella, who is now present with her husband, both in his own name and in that of his wife, sells a cottage to Segnitius Funestillus, traveling official from Acerra, who
himself buys it for himself, his children, grandchildren, great-
grandchildren and great-great-grandchildren, with the entire
posterity."[2]

Segnitius. Add this point: "and the anterity."[3] For a house consists
of both parts, anterior and posterior.

Caeparius. Be careful, Caulita, my friend: "this cottage . . ."[4]

Segnitius. [*Interrupting*] His mother Macronilla used her own word
for it—not "cottage" but "eye-catcher"; for on the day that Sueratus, Pascullus' father, moved into it from the little pigsty
with his family and hog, he had the bad luck to lose his eye on
the way in.[5]

Caeparius. You recall this cleverly, prudently, and prophylactically.[6]
Ward off the evil! I will continue: "This cottage is located in the
outskirts of Sarno beside the river."

Segnitius. But the old saying warns us not to buy beside the river.[7]

Caeparius. I meant to say "stream," not "river." In any case, Pascutius will make it over[8] to you and with the entire posterity, too.

Segnitius. And make sure to remember "and also with the anterity."

Caeparius. "He has excellent kinsmen and neighbors, like Pilutius
Rufillus [*Red Hair*] . . ."

Segnitius. [*Interrupting*] If someone was selling me a herd of hogs,
hair [*pilus*] like this wouldn't suit me at all.

Caep. Senex est et cassus iam sanguine institutusque illi est haeres Hordeatius Panicocta et quidem bene auspicata successio; pergam: 'Cocleatium quoque Surriponem.'

Segn. Quid (malum!) istud est et nominis et cognominis? quasi cochlea bonam anni partem domi inclusus succo se suo pascat, mox prodiens rapto ac surrepto vivat. Apage a me vicinos tam male nominatos!

2 *Caep.* Hoc vide, Segniti, quod nec tibi nec patri tuo Funestillo nomen satis bene ominatum est. Audibis reliquum: 'Itemque Lardatium Fabaronem, probum virum, agricolam bene unctum abundeque triticatum. Neque tibi verendum est illud, vicini ne moires fame atque inopia impulsi tuam in crumeram[4] nocturni irrepant. Proba est domuncula tota, proba contignatio, probus paries, tectum ipsum probe canteriatum asserculatumque[5] quaernis etiam scandulis Averunconis fabri, proba cisterna, sine ullo stillicidii vitio aut latrinae servitute, fundamenta bene iacta, volutabrum lutulentum, in quo viciniae totius sordes desideant, harula ad solem medidianum exposita firmiterque quaternata.' Age igitur, argentum e vestigio dinumera deo cum bono et illud vide, confestim eo uxor uti traducatur; est enim domus ipsa foecunda cupioque mirandum in modum egnatum iri ex te quamprimum qui et cognato nomine et pascendi gregis solertia patrem tuum Sueranum referat Funestillum. Unicabis itaque praepropere digitulatimque pecuniam; unciolae tres pretium est.

Segn. Duillabo illas potius; binatim enim quam singulatim e vestigio magis numerabitur pretium.

Caeparius. He is an old man, already bloodless, and Hordeatus Panicocta has been appointed as his heir; and to be sure, the succession is very fortunate.[9] I will continue: "Also Cocleatius Surripo [*Snaily Thief*] . . ."

Segnitius. [*Interrupting*] What kind of first and last name is that, damn it? As if a snail [*cochlea*] shut up in its shell for a good part of the year were to feed on its own juice, and then come out and live on what it has snatched and stolen! Spare me such ill-named neighbors!

Caeparius. Consider this, Segnitius, that neither you nor your fa- ther Funestillus [*Funereal*] has a name of good omen. You will hear the rest: "And likewise Lardatius Fabaro [*Porky Bean*], an excellent man, a farmer well oiled and with plenty of bread.[10] You won't have to be afraid that nearby mice[11] driven by hunger and need will creep by night into your purse.[12] The whole cot- tage is sound; the flooring of beams and joists is sound; the wall is sound; the roof itself is soundly raftered and timbered also with the carpenter Averunco's oak slats; the cistern is sound, without any problem of water dripping from the eaves or of be- ing used as a latrine; the foundations are well laid, the hog wal- low is muddy, since the filth of the whole neighborhood settles in it; the pigsty faces the noonday sun and is made secure on four sides." Come then, count out the money at once for God's sake, and make sure that your wife moves in immediately. The very house is fecund, and I have a remarkable desire for a son to be begotten of you as soon as possible to resemble your father, Sueranus [*Piggy*] Funestillus, both in his family name and in his care for feeding his herd.[13] And so count out the money quickly one by one on your fingers — the price is three little ounces.[14]

Segnitius. No, I'll do it two by two.[15] The price will be counted out at once better by twos than by ones.

3   *Caep.* 'Tu, Pascuti, accepisse argentum omne et numeratum et perpensum probe. Tibe vero, Segniti, ea domuncula solenni more est a Pascutio evincunda.'

   Segn. Ab ipsis etiam fundamentis tota, cum tecto, asseribus, canteriis, claviculis, scalis, foribus, culinae volutabrique decursibus. Quid enim si quispiam aedificandum inferius superius ve curaverit, tentaverit ve? Quid? inquam. Evinci mihi summum etiam coelum et ipsum terrarum soli profundum volo caveoque.

   Caep. Haud iniuria, hoc ipsum ago. 'Pascutius Caulita, Pasculli Caulitae filius, domunculam ipsam evicturum spondet ab infimo solo ad usque coeli subsellium, cum ipso etiam coelo cumque terrae imis ac perimis infernisque, Segnitio Funestillo, Acerrano viatori, eiusque posteritati.'

   Segn. Tute et viatorem interrogato et illud caveto, anteritatis bene memor uti sies, et item furni, qui est sinistrum ad latus, triangulum enim domicilium ipsum est, piscationis quoque diurnae nocturnaeque, hamariae ac retiariae.

   Caep. 'Sistet autem in omni foro et causa, festis profestisque, fastis nefastisque diebus, Segnitioque ac Segnitii posteris evincet, adversarios vero vinciet. Pro quo praestando praedia supelectilemque suam et cum ea bacem,[6] cofinos, riscum ac rete triplumbatum obligat seque staturum in praetorio ad iudicem.' Tu, Pascuti, fuste illum investito, tu, Segniti, fustem ipsum manu capito. Haecce uti vera sunt, sciens volensque suaeque spontis atque ex convento utque inter bonos decet uterque agitis meque ut scribam rogatis iureque iurando cuncta haec confirmatis

Caeparius. "You, Pascutius, take the money all properly counted 3
and weighed. To you, indeed, Segnitius, this cottage is to be
formally signed over by Pascutius."[16]

Segnitius. The whole thing, starting with the foundations, along
with the roof, joists, rafters, keys, stairs, doors, and drains of
the kitchen and hog wallow. Why, if anyone undertakes or at-
tempts to build below or above, what then, I say? I require and
stipulate that the heights of heaven and the depths of the earth
also be bound over to me.

Caeparius. Quite correct. I will do it. "Pascutius Caulita, son of
Pascullus Caulita, pledges to bind over the cottage itself, from
the lowest depths of the ground to the throne of heaven, together with the sky itself and the lowest and very lowest and
infernal regions of the earth, to Segnitius Funestillus, traveling
official from Acerra, and his posterity."

Segnitius. You shall also take the advice of the traveling official and
certify that you will be mindful of the anterity and likewise of
the oven, which is on the left side, for the habitation is a trian-
gle, and also mindful of the rights of fishing by day and night
with hooks and nets.

Caeparius. "Moreover, he will present himself in every court and
proceeding, on holidays and working days, on both lawful and
unlawful days for doing business, and he will make it the property of Segnitius and the posterity of Segnitius, but will restrain opposing parties. By virtue of this guarantee he makes
himself liable for the farm and his furniture, including the
bedstead,[17] hampers, chest, and triple-weighted net, and pledges
to stand up in court before the judge. Do you, Pascutius, put
him in possession of the rod; do you, Segnitius, take the rod in
your hand. And inasmuch as the aforesaid things are correct,
you each act with knowledge and intent and voluntarily and by
agreement and as is proper between good men and you require
me to write; and you confirm all these things by oath in the

7

verbis conceptis, quae ego praeeo. Dice tu, Segniti: 'Per Pedia-
num deum, qui noctu primus iter ivit primusque cauponam est
cauponatus.' Sequere tu, Pascuti: 'Per et Verronem, quem pastores colimus, primus sues maiales qui fecit primusque et fabam
torruit et glandem deglubivit.' Haecce acta sicce sunt.

4   'Testes assunt de more acciti rogatique viri utique probi Actius Sincerus,[7] Franciscus Pudericus, Ioannes Pardus, Gabriel
Altilius, Petrus Compater, Paulus Prassicius, Petrus Summontius.[8] Haecce sicce convenere hisce verbis, hisce conditionibus,
acta et transacta sunt hosce inter, assentiente uxore Pignatia, ut
par est viros inter bonos bene agier. Memores actorum estote,
perinde uti ab utroque adhaec ipsa arcessiti et rogati estis. Vobis
enim arbitris ita testabor actum Kal. Quintilibus, praetore
Gallo.'

Act. Atqui, o bone Caepari, ut nostrum tibi omnium nomine re-
spondeam, negocium profecto rebus tuis maximum maximeque
periculosum comparasti a sacerdotibus, dum in illorum iura ir-
rumpis, contemptis ac despectis legibus, iure deorum prorsus
adempto. An ignoras sacerdotibus dumtaxat ut deum ministris
licere fasque esse venale coelum facere iisdemque etiam solis de
intimis terrae locis permissum esse agere, quippe cum in eorum
manu sit ablegare quos voluerint ad inferna loca? Qua igitur
lege scito ve decreto ve senatus ve consulto de coelo stipulatus
fueris deque infernis locis etiam atque etiam vide. Nos abimus
bene conventorum memores.

formula that I dictate. Segnitius, you say: 'By Saint Pedianus, who first went on his way by night and first kept an inn.'[18] Pascutius, you go next: 'And by Verro, whom we herdsmen worship, who first made his hogs into barrows and first toasted the bean and stripped the acorn.'[19] In this way the aforesaid things have been accomplished."

"Men of integrity are present as witnesses, having been sent 4
for and requested in the customary manner: Azio Sincero, Francesco Puderico, Giovanni Pardo, Gabriele Altilio, Pietro Compatre, Paolo Prassicio, Pietro Summonte.[20] Thus, the aforesaid things have been agreed upon in the aforesaid words, on the aforesaid terms; they have been carried out and concluded among the aforesaid men, with the agreement of the wife Pignatia, as it is right for things to be well done among good men. Be ye mindful of what has been stipulated, according as you have been sent for and requested to this business by each party. With you as witnesses I so testify that the contract has been made on the first of July in the magistracy of Gallus."

Azio. And yet, good Caeparius, to reply to you on behalf of all of us, you have certainly made a lot of trouble for your affairs from the priests, and very dangerous trouble at that, when you trespass on their rights, defying and ignoring their laws, completely annulling the authority of the divinities. Or don't you know that the priests in their capacity as agents of the divinities have the legal right to put heaven up for sale, and that they alone also have a license to act in relation to the deepest places of the earth since it is in their power to consign anyone they please to the infernal regions? Therefore, consider again and again by what law or by what resolution or decree or recommendation of the senate you have made stipulations about heaven and the infernal regions. We depart, mindful of what has been legitimately contracted.

5   *Act.*[9] Divi boni, vestrum ego utrumque, Petre ac Paule, appello, quonam, quo abiit gentium Christianae religionis tanta illa simplicitas? Locorum ubi delituit summa ac peculiaris Christianorum innocentia atque integritas? Audet scrofarius pastor in emunda casula coelestem illam dei sedem evinci sibi deposcere praetoriumque ipsum humanarum actionum ac divinae iustitiae, non timet rusticanus notarius scripto etiam testatum hoc posteritati relinquere! Tedet[10] me pudetque temporibus his, tempestate tam corrupta editum luceque impurissima oculos contaminasse nascentem.

Iure igitur quotidieque magis etiam ac magis desiderio angor Ferrandi Ianuarii eiusque oratio me vehementius in dies commovet, quam ille paucis antequam e vita decederet diebus apud se mecum habuit, cum adesset una Franciscus hic Pudericus quem videtis et Robertus Bonifatius quam honoris causa absentem nomino.[11] Cum enim ab Innocentio Octavo Pontifice Maximo abbas[12] creatus nuper esset Ferrandus paucisque ante diebus e Roma pontificisque e conspectu Neapolim in patriam regressus, in eo sermone qui tum de religione est ab eo habitus, exorsus ipse a primis illis pontificibus tum provincialibus tum Romanis, divi boni, divi, inquam, boni, quam multa, quam etiam memoriter de illorum simplicitate, paupertate, innocentia rerumque humanarum contemptu et retulit et disputavit! Ac ne videretur veterum illorum patrum exemplis tantum solaque antiquitatis auctoritate inniti, plurima de Francisco, de Dominico deque illorum sectatoribus qui tum quoque viverent summa etiam cum admiratione audientium ita disseruit, uti qui aderant commiseratione omnes horum temporum in lacrimas verterentur. Nam et Ferrandus apprime disertus erat et indignationis maior ipsa vis commiseratioque indignationi haud indecenter coniuncta verba quidem ipsa mirificamque illam verborum

Azio. Good gods! I call on both of you, Pietro and Paolo, where,   5
O where in the world has that great simple faith of the Christian religion gone?[21] In what hiding place has the supreme and
singular innocence and integrity of Christians taken refuge? To
think that a swineherd in the purchase of a hut dares to demand that God's heavenly seat and the very court of human
actions and divine justice be made over to him and that a rustic
notary is not afraid to leave this to posterity actually certified in
writing![22] I am disgusted and ashamed to have come into existence in these times in such a corrupt period and to have pol-
luted my eyes with the foulest light at birth.

   With good reason, then, every day I am more and more tor-
mented by grief for Ferrante Gennaro and each day I am more
strongly moved by what he said to me at his house a few days
before his death, when Francesco Puderico whom you see was
there too, and Roberto Bonifacio whom I mention for the sake
of honor although he is not here.[23] Ferrante, having recently
been ordained as abbot by Pope Innocent VIII, had returned
home to Naples a few days earlier from Rome and his audience
with the pope. In the discourse on religion he delivered on that
occasion, he began with the famous first bishops both provin-
cial and Roman. Good gods! good gods, I say, how many things
he recounted and in what detail he presented an examination of
their faith, poverty, innocence, and contempt for human affairs!
And lest he seem to rely only on the examples of those ancient
fathers and on the authority of antiquity alone, he said a great
deal about Francesco and Domenico and their followers who
also lived in those days, and with the greatest admiration of his
audience, in such a way that everyone present was moved to
tears by the moving account of those times.[24] Ferrante was exceedingly eloquent, and the greater power of his indignation
and the appeal to sorrowful compassion not inappropriately
combined with his indignation supplied the words themselves

affluentiam ad dolorem lacrimasque commovendas huberrime excitatissimeque subministrabant, non minore cum animorum nostrorum qui aderamus[13] commotione quam eius ipsius qui disserebat affectu. Qui si conventioni huic paganorum affuisset hominum venumdarique audisset coelum, an putatis, quod Cicero etiam indignanter facit, sola eum illa exclamatione fuisse contentum 'o tempora, o mores'? Christum ipsum ab aula illa (mihi credite) evocasset imprecationibus et manes illos poeticos vociferatu eruisset heiulationeque ab inferis. Sed cum illo bene actum quis non videt, cum eiusmodi praesertim procella paulo post eius obitum ab Alpibus proruperit, quae et Italiam universam concusserit et regnum hoc Neapolitanum exhauserit populis spoliaveritque fortunis, excisis funditus aut incendio vastatis tot urbibus? Itaque cum illo bene actum iam fuerit, desiderio certe consuetudinis orationisque eius viri afficior quotidie magis afficiarque quandiu ipse vixero.

6 *Paul.* E nostro omnium vultu intelligere vel facile quidem, Sincere, potes, quam iucunda nobis fuerit Ferrandi recordatio. Quantum autem, quam etiam valide fixa insideat mentibus nostris illius memoria, consuetudo quidem tam suavis eius nullique non civium ac peregrinorum qui illum noverant probata, docere te oppido abunde potest. Ut autem sermo de veterum patrum castimonia et fide a te tantopere laudatus desiderium in nobis eius renovat, de me ipse ut loquar, non minus fortasse etiam afficit et pene dixerim confirmationis simul atque admirationis magis ac magis implet oraculum illud tibi ab eo in somnis editum; quod mihi quanquam Puderico ab hoc fideliter recitatum, audire tamen ex te ipso coram vel mirifice aveo, cum ad animae immortalitatem confirmandam vel mirandum in modum conferat; et si de ea ita persuasum Christiani habemus omnes, ut

and their miraculous profusion to move us copiously and vehe-
mently to sorrow and tears, with no less agitation of mind of
those of us who were present than with emotion on the part of
the speaker himself. If he had been present at that assemblage
of heathen rustics and heard heaven being put up for sale, do
you think he would have been content with only Cicero's indig-
nant exclamation, "*O tempora, O mores*"?[25] Believe me, he would
have summoned Christ himself from his heavenly kingdom
with imprecations and with his outcry and wail of anguish un-
earthed from the infernal regions the shades the poets talk
about. But who does not see that that it turned out well for
him, especially since a little after his death a storm burst forth
from the Alps that has shaken the whole of Italy and emptied
this Neapolitan kingdom of its peoples and robbed it of its
fortunes, razing so many cities to the ground or laying them
waste by fire?[26] And so, even though it turned out well for him,
I am still moved more every day by longing for the company
and conversation of this man, and the feeling will last as long as
I live.

Paolo. You can easily tell from all our faces, Sincero, how much we   6
enjoyed being reminded of Ferrante. Indeed, his pleasant companionship, which was commended by every citizen or for-
eigner who knew him, can tell you very well how much and
how strongly his memory stays fixed in our hearts. As the discourse you praised so much about the chastity and faith of the
old fathers renews our longing for him (to speak for myself),
perhaps we are also no less affected, and I might almost say,
filled more and more with confidence and wonder at the same
time by that holy utterance he pronounced to you in a dream.
Although Puderico here faithfully reported this to me, I still
want very much to hear it from you in person, since it serves
wonderfully to confirm the immortality of the soul; even though
all of us as Christians are so persuaded of it that we both insist

illorum qui diem obierunt animas sua quandoque redituras in corpora nosque item ipsos, ubi e vita hac discesserimus, statuto quodam tempore resumpturos nobis illa et teneamus et promittamus.

7 *Act.* Memoratu quidem digna res est audituque iucunda e me, Paule, quam requiris, explicatu tamen difficilis. Multa enim somniantes cernimus quae plane referri qualia visa ipsa sunt nequeant, ut figurae quaedam neque ipsae visae alias neque satis per se explicabiles, tum novitate tum complicatione sua; studebo tamen desiderio[14] eorumque qui hic assunt omnium quique mihi idem hoc innuunt tuoque[15] praesertim, Paule, satisfacere.

Illud tamen vobis cognitum vestrosque apud animos testatum volo, qua nocte oraculum, ut ipse appellas, est editum, nullas ea quae noctem antecessit die cogitationes a me initas susceptas ve de animae immortalitate, nullas de reversione eius ad corpora, nullum quam plurimis ante diebus aut sermonem iis de rebus cum doctis viris habitum aut apud me ipsum modo esse aliquo dubitatum. Liber utique curis ab omnibus atque ab iis potissimum cogitationibus vacuus, cum ipse cubuissem solito in lectulo quaeque saepenumero ante cubitum lectio quidam quasi animi cibus sumitur nulla prorsus divinis de rebus praecessisset, ubi diutius quievissem et iam Aurora illa Ioviani nostri, quae coeli postibus affixa est custos, solem excitasset e somno, videre visus sum, quin haec loquens videre ipse iam videor adesse mihi Ferrandum.

Quaeras fortasse unde advenerit mortuus, qua via profectus ac tam repente clausis foribus insinuatus adstiterit; nesciam, nesciam, affuit certe, qualem vivum et videbam pene quotidie et alloquebar congredientem; meque statim desideratissime

and promise that the souls of those who have died will return someday into their bodies and that we too, when we have departed this life, will recover them for ourselves at some appointed time.

Azio. What you ask of me is certainly worth telling and pleasant   7
to hear, Paolo, yet it is hard to explain. In our dreams we perceive many apparitions of a kind that cannot be reported intelligibly — like certain forms neither seen anywhere else nor sufficiently explicable in themselves because of their strangeness and confusion; nonetheless, I will make an effort to satisfy the longing of all those who are present and nodding at me to do the same thing, and your longing especially, Paolo.

In any case I want this point to be known to you and confirmed in your minds, that the night when the holy utterance, as you call it, was pronounced, during the preceding day, I had considered or entertained no thoughts about the immortality of the soul, none about its return to the body; in the many days before, I had held no conversation about these matters with learned men nor had any uncertainty arisen somehow in my own mind.[27] Free of all cares and unconcerned with thoughts like this in particular, when I had gone to sleep on my accustomed bed and after no reading at all beforehand on religious subjects, which is often taken before bed as a kind of food for the soul, when I had slept for a long time and already that Aurora of our Gioviano's, who is placed as a guardian near the doorposts of heaven, had roused the sun from his sleep, I seemed to see him — why, even as I say these things, I imagine that I see Ferrante here with me.

Perhaps you ask where the dead man came from, by what route he came and slipped in so suddenly through closed doors and stood by my side. I know not, I know not. Yet indeed he was there, just as I used to see him almost every day when he was alive and meet and talk to him; and when he had at once

complexus cum esset, ut qui diutius non vidisset, vultu iucundus, risu hilaris, salutatione blandus, et osculo, ut ei mos erat, sane quam familiariter petivisset, 'An, inquit, consuetudinis me nostrae oblitum rebare amicitiaeque tam diuturnae factum tam brevi immemorem? Redeo igitur ad te, et quidem tanquam legatione functus aliqua, ut vivens consueveram confecto munere, maximaque profecto cum voluptate ad te redeo. Reducem igitur ac sospitem ipse me vides atque ante expectatum tibi me et vegetum valentemque et amicorum tuique imprimis memorem tuum apud cubiculum sisto.' Atque his dictis blandiusculum in modum et surrisit et pene sullacrimatus est; quod evenire solet inter viventis, ubi longa e peregrinatione regressi sunt in patriam, exanclatis periculis reduces, quo tempore natura ipsa contrarios una miscere affectus consuevit et praeteritorum periculorum longiorisque absentiae memores et praesentis voluptatis ac letitiae[16] indices.

8   Hoc est autem illud, Paule, vosque, amicissimi viri, hoc inquam illud est quod ne inumbrare quidem suis verbis, nedum figurare queam aut explicare oratione. Cepit[17] eodem me puncto temporis mira voluptas amici iam reducis, cepit admiratio, quod mortuum iam dudum illum esse subiit recordatio; cepit rursum dubitatio, quia vivum illum cernebam et loquentem quidem et vivi hominis munus sermone, vultu affectibusque implentem: num mortuum arbitrarer, an potius illius mihi obitus somnianti esset visus qui re ipsa iam viveret? Itaque, dum ipsi inter se se recursant affectus mentisque in diversum abit cogitatio meque silentii longioris pudet, una et in hilaritatem pariter profusus sum et in lacrimas iam prorupi. Veterem igitur atque desideratum amicum arctius complexus ut peregre redeuntem, ut

eagerly embraced me, like someone who had not seen me for a long time, with a pleasant expression, merry laugh, courteous greeting, and in the most friendly way had sought me with a kiss, as was his custom, he said: "Did you think that I had lost the memory of the bond between us or had so soon become forgetful of such a lasting friendship? Well then, I return to you, indeed as if I had completed some embassy, just as I used to do in life when I had carried out my mission; and certainly I return to you with the greatest pleasure. You see me, then, restored and unscathed; and I present myself unexpectedly in your bedchamber, hale and hearty and mindful of my friends and especially of you." And with these words he smiled in a kindly way and nearly wept a bit, as often happens among the living when they have returned to their homeland from a long journey, restored after going through trials, at a moment when nature herself is accustomed to mingle together opposite emotions, both memories of past dangers and too long absence and signs of present pleasure and happiness.

This is the thing, Paolo and you, my dearest friends, this, I say, is what I cannot even give a shadow of in the right words, much less shape or explain in speech. I was seized at the very same moment by a wonderful pleasure in my friend now restored, seized by amazement, because it came back to me that he was long dead, seized on the other hand by uncertainty because I saw him alive and even speaking and performing the part of a living man in speech, expression, and emotions. Should I think him dead, or rather was it his death that appeared to me in a dream, while the man himself was alive? And so, while these feelings ran back and forth and my thoughts went off in different directions and I was ashamed of being silent too long, at the same time I broke out into giddy delight and burst just as hard into tears. Then I held more closely the old friend I had longed for, as one returning from a foreign

8

sospitem,[18] nec minus etiam subveritus, quae somniantium est consuetudo, ne, quod haud multo post contigit, repente evanesceret, multa quidem proque veteri nostra consuetudine, paucis cum eo tamen, non minus iucunde quam pie domesticeque transegi mutuoque ille mecum peramanter et grate; quodque Ferrandus ipse dum viveret quotidianis in disceptationibus multa saepe de animae immortalitate quaerere esset solitus, subiit tempus esse idoneum interrogandi illius eorum ne de quibus olim dubitasset factus esset iam certior; nec ausus ipse in primo statim orationis vestibulo ac veluti ex abrupto hoc ipsum exquirere, coepi[19] prius sciscitari num ea quae traderentur de mortuis tam acerba, de poenarum magnitudine, de suppliciorum immanitate cruciatuumque perpetuitate vera essent, ut ea ipsa sunt prodita.

Tum ille suo de more, ut quippiam asseverantius erat dicturus, superciliis obductis silentioque paulisper habito, quasi etiam praesagiret quae sciscitanda post a me essent: 'Dicam, inquit, Sincere Acti, dicam vere, fatebor ingenue, asseverabo constanter, nos omnis qui e vita iam migravimus, unum illud solum maxime continenter solicitare, angere, male habere, uno eo desiderio nos teneri, illa una cupiditate eaque postrema affici aut verius cruciari, in vitam illam remigrandi quae animae cum corpore est communis. Haec una nobis omnibus cura est eaque tam assidua et anxia, ut tibi qui haec nunc audis, sit omnino incredibile exuperetque ea viventium cogitationes. Hic autem continuus nobis est acerbissimusque cruciatus poenaque intolerabilis.' Atque his dictis, quasi renovato prioris vitae desiderio cui ferendo par non esset, ne ve me, ut etiam arbitror, dolore ac moerore suo afficeret, deiectis iisdemque conniventibus oculis

country, as safe and sound, and I was equally apprehensive, as
dreamers are, that he would suddenly vanish — a thing that
soon happened. I talked over many things as was our custom,
but in a few words, since it was with him, no less pleasantly
than affectionately and comfortably, and he spoke back to me
lovingly and gladly; and because while he was alive Ferrante often used to raise many questions about the immortality of the
soul in everyday discussions, it occurred to me that it was a
suitable occasion to ask him whether he was now assured of the
things about which he had formerly been in doubt. Since I did
not dare to ask this immediately at first entering into the conversation and out of nowhere, I began by inquiring if those
cruel stories handed down about the dead — about the magnitude of their sufferings, the enormity of their punishments, and
the perpetuity of their torments — were true as they have been
reported.

Then he frowned and kept silent for a moment as was his
custom when he was about to say something rather serious, as
if he had a presentiment of what I was going to ask next. "I will
state, Sincero Azio," he said, "I will state truly, I will admit
frankly, I will declare firmly that all of us who have already departed from life have this one single greatest source of unending
distress, pain, and torment, that we are gripped by this one
longing, that we are afflicted or rather tortured by this one ulti-
mate desire — of returning into that life which the body and
soul have in common. This single grief possesses all of us, so
unremitting and tormenting as to be beyond belief to you who
now hear these things and to exceed the thoughts of living men.
This is our unending and cruelest torment and unbearable
pain." And when he had said these things, as if with renewed,
unbearable longing for his former life, or, as I believe, lest he
afflict me with his own pain and sorrow, he lowered his brows
and half-closed eyes as if (so it seemed to me) he were leaving

ac superciliis, quasi abiens salutaret non summa sine egritudine, ut visus est, discessit.[20] Ego statim somno solutus sum.

9   Habes, Paule, somnium quale meum illud fuerit, plenum, ut opinari te etiam video, divinitatis; ex eo mihi et vita haec habita est suavior, quae perfectio quasi quaedam animae videatur, nec mors futura est tam gravis, postquam suo quidem et statuto tempore membris hisce vernaculis sibique peculiaribus, quorum ministeriis principio ab ipso vitae societatisque est usa, sit iterum quoque usura corporeque in hoc, perinde atque in domo ac patria sua, rursus etiam diversatura. Fungamur igitur eo libentius in hac ipsa animae corporisque societate viventes vitae ipsius muneribus, quodque medii quasi quidam ex anima consistimus ac corpore, mediocritatem sequamur eam quae digna sit homine. Et quanquam degener est corpus, illud tamen ita colamus, uti solertes ac boni agricolae agrum, iis ferendis frugibus quarum anima, utque Ciceroni magis placet, animus sator est idem et cultor. Nihil civi bene instituto patria sua est carius, quoniam in ea honores assequitur ac titulos, remque illic familiarem cumulat, peculiumque omne sibi comparat. Corpus autem hoc nostrum perinde ut proprium illi domicilium et pene[21] patria est; quocirca corporis ipsius non immemores[22] ita quidem erimus, ut hospitium et[23] quasi patriam eam animi ipsius domumque vita in hac[24] existimantes, bene illud constituamus, quo animus ipse honores, magistratus muneraque civilia dignasque homine actiones in illo gerere eiusque etiam opera exercere atque administrare cum dignitate ac decore valeat suo, quamdiu hospitio illius et tanquam[25] patriae utetur beneficio; ac posteaquam ex eo migraverit, quamdiu etiam absens fuerit, ut, illius ipsius memor, desiderio remigrandi ad illud eo vehementius teneatur, quemadmodum cives boni, qui quo sua ipsorum patria est honoratior eo absentes maiore tenentur cupiditate in illam revertendi.

and saying farewell with the greatest distress. He departed. I was immediately released from sleep.[28]

There you have what my dream was like, Paolo, full of divine power, as I see you think, too. As a result of it, I consider this life sweeter, since it seems a kind of completion of the soul, and I think future death not so hard to bear since at its own appointed time the soul will enjoy again these limbs born with and belonging to it, whose services it has enjoyed from the very beginning of its life and association, and it will dwell again in this body as if it were in its home and native land.[29] The more gladly then, living in this association of soul and body, let us perform the duties of this life and because we consist as if half of soul and half of body, let us follow that mean which is worthy of a human being. And although the body is inferior, let us still cultivate it as good and skillful farmers cultivate their fields, in order to bring forth those fruits that the soul, and as Cicero prefers to call it, the mind, both sows and cultivates.[30] To a well brought up citizen nothing is dearer than his native land, since in it he attains offices and authority, there amasses property, obtains everything that belongs to him. But this body of ours is like the proper habitation of the mind and almost its native land; therefore we will be so unfailingly conscious of the body, considering it the lodging and almost the homeland and home of the mind in this life, that we will keep it in good order, so that in it the mind can perform the offices, magistracies, civic duties and activities worthy of a human being and also oversee and direct the body's tasks with its own proper dignity and honor as long as it enjoys the hospitality and kindness of its native place; and so that after it has departed from it, as long as it shall be absent, remembering the body, it shall be the more powerfully gripped by longing to return to it, just as good citizens abroad are gripped by a greater desire of returning to their country the more honorable it is.

9

10 *Paul.* Et oraculum ipsum summa a te cum fide recitatum plenum
est divinitatis et oratio haec ipsa tua teque atque oraculo tali
digna; de ipso autem Ferrando maior in dies apud me futura
est[26] existimatio existimationique coniuncta veneratio cultusque
memoriae ac nominis tanti viri. Inter amicos vero plurimos quibus ille omnibus perfamiliariter utebatur, quod tui praecipue
memor in somno se tibi tam familiariter invisens ostenderit, et
mecum gaudeo plurimum et tibi ex animo gratulor; neque enim
mediocrem tibi excitationem additam video nobisque item aliis
qui haec novimus excolendis animis, vita hac dum fruimur,
quando animi ipsi tanto incenduntur ardore[27] redeundi in corpora; in quibus constituti et quorum etiam ministeriis atque
ope usi id assequentur, uti humanarum divinarumque rerum
naturas, causas potestatesque cognitas ac perspectas habeant.
Quid enim excellentius quam in hoc perexiguo tam vasti aequoris meditullio quae terra dicitur habitantem hominem et
terras et maria et spiritum et coelum omne, tot tantosque stel-
larum orbes ac globos, tantam universi molem, rerum tantam
infinitatem cognitioni suae subiecisse, mortalique in corpore
immortalem subeuntem personam id curare, sciscitari, pervesti-
gare, comprehendere, tandem scire quod deorum est munus
proprium ac peculiare, ab iisque in homines translatum beneficium? Idque ita esse declarare multa quidem possunt, illud vero
cumprimis, quod dii quidem ipsi excellentibus quibusdam viris
visi sunt fuisse praesentiores excellentiaeque illorum et gloriae
permultum studiosi. Neque enim de nihilo opinio illa pervetusta de geniis apud priscos tam constanter esset defensa et
habita, nec apud nos Christianos, ne apud Iudaeos aut Arabes

Paolo. That holy utterance you reported with the greatest convic- 10
tion was full of divine power, and this speech of yours was
worthy both of yourself and of such an utterance. My high
opinion of Ferrante will grow greater every day along with the
respect appropriate to the opinion and the reverence for the
memory and reputation of such a great man. But I greatly rejoice and congratulate you from my heart that among all the
many friends with whom he was on very close terms it was you
he cared for especially and you whom he visited in sleep and to
whom he showed himself in such a friendly fashion; and I see
that you and the rest of us too who have learned of these things
have been greatly spurred on to cultivate our minds as long as
we enjoy this life, since minds are on fire with such ardent desire of returning into bodies; having been established in them
and having employed their services and assistance, they will
achieve knowledge and understanding of the natures, principles,
and properties of human and divine affairs. Indeed, what is
more excellent than the fact that man, dwelling in this tiny
speck that is called earth in the middle of such a vast expanse,[31]
has subjected to his investigation the lands and seas and air and
all the sky, so many and such great circuits and spheres of stars,
such a great mass of the universe, such an infinity of things,
and that the underlying immortal person in the mortal body is
concerned to examine, search out, comprehend, and finally, to
know the proper and particular function of divinities and the
benefit transferred from them to mankind? There are many
possible indications that this is the case, but especially the fact
that certain outstanding men have believed that the divine beings themselves were of very present help and most eager to
promote their preeminence and glory. For there would have
been no basis for that very old notion of guardian spirits held
and defended so constantly among the ancients, or among us
Christians, to say nothing of the Jews and Arabs, unless on

quidem illos, nisi permulta eaque maxime obscura monstrata, perspecta, cognita, his ipsis docentibus, fuissent mortalium generi, quae nunc audiendo ac legendo discimus. Ut autem praetereamus maiora quae sunt, et audisti, Sincere, saepius et audire coram etiamnum potes ex amicissimo viro (cuius familiaritate ac communitate studiorum quis te ipso magis utitur, quanquam et nos quoque valde utimur?) non adolescentem modo se, sed iuvenem, sed aetate iam provectiorem, cum saepenumero interpretandis veterum scriptorum libris haesitabundus non haberet certi quid traderet, in somnis se a genio sub imagine veteris cuiuspiam nunc grammatici nunc aut poetae aut philosophi veritatis admonitum.

11   Quod siquis haec forte contemnat, idem hic quonam ore negaverit maximos quoque duces monentibus in somno diis aut maximas insperatasque sibi comparasse victorias aut evitasse ne victi ipsi essent, copiis profligatis? Adhaec non pauca etiam saepe monstrantur nobis inter dormiendum, quorum antea cogitatio nulla praecesserit nihilque illa privatim ad nos ipsos resque nostras attineant quaeque neque sensus ipsi versandis atque examinandis illis agitati ante, post dormientibus offerunt nosque lacessunt etiam in quiete. Sacerdos equidem ipse sum nec a studiis quibus tantopere delectari te mirifice letor omnino alienus; plena est historia veterum illorum patrum oraculis, plena visionibus, tum adhortantibus ad fortitudinem, ad pietatem, ad contemptum rerum humanarum, tum a vitiis deterrentibus, quibus ego confirmandis his[28] quae dicta sunt commodissime uti possem, verum neque in hoc praesertim conventu necesse esse duco, Christiani enim cuncti sumus solamque pietatem sequimur, teque, Parde, video iam pridem pensitare quid adhaec dicturus sis; itaque te ipsum potius audiamus.

their instruction many hidden matters had been revealed, understood, and known to the race of mortals — things we now learn of by reading and hearing about them. To pass over the more important examples, you have both heard quite often, Sincero, and can hear in person even now from your very close friend (and no one more than yourself has enjoyed his companionship and shared interests, although we greatly enjoy them too) that very often not only as a boy but also as a young man and now as one of advanced years, when he was at a loss in interpreting texts of ancient writers and uncertain what to say, he was informed of the truth in a dream by his guardian spirit in the likeness of some ancient or other, whether a grammarian or poet or philosopher.[32]

But if anyone should discount these things, how would he 11 deny that also through the warnings of divine beings in dreams the greatest generals have both achieved magnificent and unexpected victories and avoided defeat and the destruction of their forces? In addition, many things are revealed to us as we sleep, which we have never thought of before and have nothing to do with us as individuals and our affairs; and our senses, which had not been moved to consider and examine them before, subsequently present them to us as we slumber and worry us in our sleep. I myself am a priest and not altogether unversed in the studies by which I am exceedingly pleased you are so delighted.[33] The history of the ancient fathers is filled with divine utterances, filled with visions, some exhorting to fortitude, to piety, to the contempt of human affairs, others deterring from vice, which I could use very handily to confirm what has been said; but I do not think it necessary especially in the present company, for we are all Christians and use our sense of religious duty as our only guide, and I see that you, Pardo, have been thinking for some time about what you were going to say on this subject. Accordingly, let us listen to you instead.

12 *Pard.* Pensitantem me, Paule Prassici, quae a te dicta non minus
sunt recte quam a nobis grate accepta, subiit Aristotelicum illud, fieri quidem posse ut ob mundi ipsius conversionem, habitu aliquo inducto, quae fera sunt animantium genera, ea ut
mansuescant singula; idque usuvenire in locis non nullis, ut ob
insitam bonitatem, sponte sua, nullo quidem cultu adhibito,
mitiora illic nascantur quam quae alibi summo etiam studio
operaque adhibita diligentiore mitescunt.

In tanta igitur nascentium multitudine, tam varia etiam locorum diversitate mundique ipsius agitationibus tam continuis,
iisdemque tantopere variantibus, cum natura ipsa semper ad
unum aliquod suo in genere perficiendum contendat, quid
mirum, et si rarum, tamen in multis quoque seculis, oriri ali-
quem, cui natura, et studio cumprimis suo et bonitate seminis
stellarumque ipsarum, hoc est mundi ipsius beneficio et opera,
omni e parte genere in illo consulat aut facultatis aut scientiae,
cum nulla virtus corporis, nulla sit animi ingeniique praestantia,
nullus honorum aut externorum bonorum gradus, in quo non,
diversis quamvis temporibus, naturae ipsius summus ille cona-
tus effectu ipso non sit etiam manifesto et cognitus et perspec-
tus, pro temporum videlicet, nationum patriaeque constitutione
et coeli ipsius, a quo cuncta moventur, agitatu? Abstinebo
exemplis, ipsa enim res est per se quam notissima. Verum naturae ipsius opera praesertimque excellentissima quaeque deum
ad ipsum referenda mihi videntur, idque si cuiquam nationi,
genti, sectae par est, Christianae cumprimis religioni convenire
arbitror, quae virtutum omnium, earum dico quae ad animum
referuntur, et fuit et est quam studiosissima. Haec habui quae

Pardo. As I was thinking, Paolo Prassicio, about the words that   12
you have spoken so correctly and we have heard with equal
pleasure, I thought of Aristotle's idea that a condition can be
caused by the rotation of the universe whereby species of animate beings that are wild become tame individually, and that in
a number of places it happens that, because of the good quality
implanted in them, the animals of their own accord, without
the application of any training, are naturally tamer there than
the ones that grow tame elsewhere even with the greatest effort
and the application of diligent care.

In such a multitude of creatures being born, with the diversity of places so various, and the movements of the universe so
unending and these varying so greatly, since nature herself always strives to perfect some one thing in its kind, why would it
be remarkable, though rare, yet also in many periods, for someone to arise for whom nature provides, both especially by her
own zeal and by the excellence of the seed and of the very
stars — that is, through the beneficial agency of the universe itself — making provision in every respect in the area of ability or
skill? It would not be remarkable, since there is no excellence of
the body, no outstanding quality of mind or talent, no degree of
honors or external goods in which, although at different times,
that great tendency of nature herself has not been recognized
and clearly understood by its obvious result — in proportion, of
course, to the nature of times, nations and homeland, and in
accordance with the motion of heaven itself, by which all things
are moved. I will refrain from examples, for the fact in itself is
well known. But the works of nature herself, and especially all
the most excellent ones, I think must be referred to God himself; and I consider that, if to any nation, people, or sect, this is
especially suited to the Christian religion, which has been and
is as zealous as possible for every excellence — for those, I mean,
that are ascribed to the mind. This is what I was thinking

pensitabundus apud vos dicerem, alias fortasse eadem hac de re commodior offeretur quaerendi ac disserendi locus. Quoniam autem, ut scitis, toto sum corpore ac pedibus praesertim imbecillis, considendum hac sub porticu censeo, de more maiorum nostrum; considentibus enim nobis ocio magis tranquillo et quaerere licuerit et disputare et qui praetereunt tum ad sedendi ocium tum ad certamen disserendi invitare honestius multo fuerit.

13   *Comp.*[29] Ego vero, quoniam a consuetudine huiusce porticus meoque ab instituto recessurus non sum, praesertim cum pransi hic consederimus, sequendum illud arbitror quod praestantissimi etiam viri secuti leguntur, uti levioribus de rebus deque grammaticis praecipue post accubitum dissererent, primumque cognoscere ex te, Paule, aveo, quid (malum!) quasi latinitatis oblitus paulo ante dixeris: ʻplena est historia oraculis, plena visionibus.ʼ An non puellulus eructabas Terentianum illud unum ac Ciceronianum alterum: *plenus rimarum sum, et haud magna cum re, sed plenus fidei.* Adde et *stultorum plena sunt omnia.*

Paul. Et de more, Compater, tuo feceris et nobis non ingratum, si quanquam studiis maioribus deditus, tamen meridiani quoque temporis memor ab his ad ea nos advocaris quae cum leviora ipsa sunt, tum iis etiam e studiis, quae pueris nobis prima inhaesere. Quocirca ne diutius te suspensum teneam, et si tentabundum loqui te certo scio, dicas velim sis ne et ipse oblitus Ciceronis tui scribentis ad Tironem: *noctem habui plenam timoribus ac miseriis;* et ad Atticum: *ex tuis litteris plenus sum expectatione de Pompeio, quidnam de nobis velit ut*[30] *ostendat;* et ad Plancum: *sub eas statim recitatae sunt tuae non sine magnis quidem clamoribus; tum rebus enim ipsis essent et studiis beneficiisque in rem publicam gratissimae, tum gravissimis verbis atque sententiis plenae.* Qui si contentus

about to say to you; perhaps on another occasion there will be a more suitable opportunity of inquiring and discoursing on the same matter. But since, as you know, I am infirm in my whole body and especially in my feet, I think we should sit down under this portico as our ancestors did, for if we are seated we could question and discuss in greater peace and quiet, and it would be far more proper to invite passersby both to the comfort of sitting down and to competitive discussion.[34]

Compatre. I agree, but because I will not depart from the custom of this portico and my own way of doing things, especially since we are sitting here after luncheon, I think we should follow the practice we read that the most preeminent men followed, of discoursing on light topics and especially on grammatical ones after a meal; and I want to find out first from you, Paolo, why (horrors!) a minute ago, as if you had forgotten your Latin, you said, "history is filled with divine utterances, filled with visions."[35] Surely as a child you used to regurgitate one line of Terence and another from Cicero: "I am full of cracks" and "not rich but full of loyalty."[36] And add: "the world is full of fools."[37]   13

Paolo. You will have acted according to your custom, Compatre, pleasing us at the same time, if although dedicated to more important studies, nevertheless, mindful of the midday hour, you call us away from them to those that are both lighter and among the first studies that stuck to us as boys. So, in order not to keep you in suspense any longer, although I am sure you are trying to speak, I would like you to say whether *you* have forgotten your friend Cicero writing to Tiro, "I spent a night filled with fear and distress," and to Atticus, "from your letter I am filled with expectation about what Pompey means to profess concerning me," and to Plancus, "immediately after this letter, yours was read out to great applause; for it was not only most pleasing in its subject and in its zeal and service to the state but also filled with important words and sentiments."[38] If you won't

his minime futurus es Tacitique haudquaquam meministi dicentis in *Dialogo de Oratoribus: Illud certe concedet instructum et plenum his artibus animum longe paratum*[31] *ad eas exercitationes venturum;* item[32] in libro *Historiarum* xvii°: *Opus aggredior plenum*[33] *variis casibus, atrox proeliis, discors seditionibus;* et paulo post: *magna adulteria, plenum exiliis mare;* et Plinii in quinto *Naturalis historiae: Polybius, annalium conditor, ab eo accepta classe scrutandi illius orbis gratia circumvectus, prodidit a monte eo occasum versus saltus plenos feris quas generat Africa,* poteris tutemet revocare tibi in memoriam alia quoque Ciceronis loca, in quibus legitur: *plenus officio; plenum vigilantia, celeritate, diligentia.*[34] Poteris auctorum item aliorum meminisse, qui et ipsi principem inter Latinos scriptores locum optinent. Ac nihilominus quoniam in hunc sermonem volens incidisti, potes et de aliis huiusmodi sciscitari, siqua dubium tibi forte animum atque incertum faciunt.

14 *Comp.* Bene profecto a te satisfactum arbitror, nec arcessendis opus est testibus aut comprobatoribus ubi Cicero est ipse auctor. Quo igitur inceptum prosequamur, explicari a te pervelim, Parde, quinam '*maiorum nostrum*' potiusquam '*nostrorum*' paulo est a te ante dictum, cum usurpatissime scriptum legatur '*maiores nostri*'?

Pard. Nec inepte hoc ipsum a te, Compater, quaeritur, nec a me sine magnis quidem auctoribus dictum est, cum etiam a Sallustio scriptum legatur in oratione illa Lepidi:[35] *Clementia et probitas vestri,*[36] *Quirites, quibus per coeteras gentes maximi et clari estis;* tametsi scriptura ipsa, ut iam video, depravata est a litteratoribus, quod in aliis quoque compluribus animadverti, et ab illis praesertim qui nova hac scribendi ratione libros hodie imprimendos curant. Qua in re Sallustius etiam Graecorum loquendi

be satisfied with these, and have no memory of Tacitus' saying in his *Dialogue on Orators*, "let him concede this at least, that the mind instructed and filled with these arts will come well prepared to these exercises," and in book seventeen of his *Histories*, "I begin a work filled with various disasters, savage with battles, riven with insurrections," and a little later, "there were great adulteries, the sea was filled with exiles," and Pliny in book five of the *Natural Histories*, "Polybius, author of the *Annales*, having sailed around in the fleet he had received from him to study that part of the world, reports that beyond that mountain to the west there are forests filled with wild beasts native to Africa," you can also recall other passages of Cicero, among which one reads, "filled with duty," "filled with vigilance, with speed, with diligence."[39] In the same way you will be able to remember other authors who also occupy a foremost position among Latin writers. And in any case, since you fell into this conversation willingly, you can also inquire about other matters of this kind if you happen to get confused about something.

Compatre. I certainly think that you have done quite enough, and there is no need to invoke witnesses or supporters when Cicero himself is the authority. So, to continue our undertaking, I would like to hear you explain, Pardo, why you said "of the ancestors of us" a minute ago, instead of "of our ancestors," although "our ancestors" is most often written.[40]

Pardo. That's not a silly question, Compatre, but in fact I did not speak without the support of great authorities, since one may also read Sallust's words in the well-known oration of Lepidus, "The clemency and honesty of you, fellow citizens, through which you are great and famous among other nations."[41] Yet that passage, as I see now, has been corrupted by scholars, a phenomenon I have also noticed in many other cases — especially by those scholars who nowadays have their books printed in this new method of writing. In this matter Sallust can be

14

morem secutus videri potest; verum ne a Cicerone nostro re-
cedamus, quid si a me ita pronuntiatum est *nostrum* ut sit *nostrorum*, ut *sestertium numum*, ⟨sestertiorum⟩[37] *numorum*, ut *duum
virum*, *duorum virorum*, ut *deum fidem*, *deorum*, ut *praefectus fabrum*, *fabrorum*? Hac enim verborum contractione vetustas illa
vehementer gavisa est; nanque apud eundem Ciceronem leges
veteris poetae dictum: *patris mei meum factum pudet*, pro *meorum
factorum*; item: *cives, antiqui amici maiorum meum*, hoc est *meorum*.
Quae quanquam obliterata magna ipsa e parte iam sunt, tamen
in paucis quibusdam e Ciceronis sententia et plenum verbum
recte dicitur et imminutum usitate.

15 *Comp.* Accipio et rationem et auctoritatem videoque, quod a priscis illis longius deflexerimus, multa recentibus ab his litteratoribus magis damnari ob ignorantiam quam repudiari ob vetusta-
tem. Oblatus est mihi diebus his libellus sane pervetus, in quo
scriptum erat *rhinocerontis*; vetustis enim in codicibus dictiones
has *rhinocerontis* et *Aegocerontis* ubique invenias *n* litteram re-
tinere, quam quidem litteram a grammatista nescio quo, quod
Graecum inodoratus aliquantum esset, atramento oblitam animadverti, videlicet quod recentiores Graeci quique Attice lo-
quantur *Aegoceros Aegocerotis*, et *rhinoceros rhinocerotis* enuntient.
Neque tamen argutulus hic id animipendit,[38] quin ignorare se
confessus est e Graeca fuisse olim gente, ut Siculos, Italicam
nationem, ut Calabros, qui dicerent *Aegoceron* et *rhinoceron* et
Minon atque eiusmodi alia, indeque esse *rhinocerontis*, *Aegocerontis* et *Minonis*, quod Cicero etiam ipse protulit. Accepta igitur a
priscis Latinis terminatio haec Sicula mansit apud nostros;
nec est cur accusetur, siquis morem tot seculorum servatum a

seen to have followed the Greek way of speaking.[42] But not to get away from our Cicero, suppose I said *nostrum* for *nostrorum*, *sestertium numum* for *sestertiorum numorum*, *duum virum* for *duorum virorum*, *deum fidem* for *deorum*, *praefectus fabrum* for *fabrorum*.[43] Antiquity took great pleasure in this sort of verbal contraction; in fact, in the same Cicero you will read the saying of the old poet: "in the presence of my father I am ashamed of my deeds," with *meum factum* for *meorum factorum*, and likewise, "citizens, ancient friends of my ancestors," with *meum* for *meorum*.[44] Although these things have been largely consigned to oblivion, neverthless in a few cases in Cicero's opinion both the full word and the shortened form are spoken correctly in everyday usage.

Compatre. I accept both the explanation and the authority, and I   15
see that as a result of our having turned too far away from the ancient scholars, recent ones are more inclined to condemn things out of ignorance than to reject them by reason of antiquity.[45] Recently I was shown a very old book in which was written the word *rhinocerontis* — indeed, anywhere in ancient books you might find the letter *n* retained in the words *rhinocerontis* and *Aegocerontis* ["Capricorn"] — but I noticed that some grammarian or other, because he had got a little whiff of Greek, had blotted out the letter with ink, evidently because modern Greeks and those speaking Attic say "*Aegoceros Aegocerotis*," and "*rhinoceros rhinocerotis*." And this clever fellow did not stop to think about it; indeed, he revealed his ignorance of the fact that the Italic nation had been of Greek stock once upon a time — for example, the Sicilians, or the Calabrians, who said "*Aegoceron*" and "*rhinoceron*" and "*Minon*" and other things of the same kind, and that is the source of *rhinocerontis*, *Aegocerontis*, and *Minonis*, a word used by Cicero himself.[46] This Sicilian termination, then, which was taken up by the ancient Latins, lived on among our people; nor is there any reason to blame someone

maximis auctoribus et ipse quoque servaverit, quando cognitum ac certum est Graecos quoque auctores, Siculos scilicet ac Brutios, ita esse locutos, cum etiam abunde notum sit quanta inter Graecos est ipsos[39] varietas et terminandorum et flectendorum nominum. Quin etiam Germanicus Arateo in carmine protulit *Aegocerus*, ut cum ait:

Et sedem[40] Aegoceri Cythereius attigit ignis

Item:

Clara Sagittiferi tetigit cum lumina signi
Aegoceri semper coelo levis excidit himber.[41]

Audivi non semel et quidem persancte iurantem eruditum apprime et observantem vetustatis hominem se complures codices et Horatii et Ovidii et aliorum poetarum legisse pene vetustate ipsa consumptos, in iisque scriptum observasse non *Clius*, sed *Clios*, non *Didus*, sed *Didos*, non *Eratus*, sed *Eratos*, quod priscis illis temporibus maiores nostri genitivis casibus Graeco more his in nominibus minime uterentur, cum qui Graece sunt *Didoos, Eratoos, Clioos* contraherent in *o* productum *Didos, Eratos, Clios*, qui casus Attice sunt *Didus, Eratus, Clius*. At nunc quis est e litteratoribus adeo compositis moribus, quin ora sinusque ipsos impudentius conspuat ubi quem aliter locutum senserit? Me ipsum maledictis quoque incessitum, nedum acrius increpitum satis quidem scio, quod *Sapho* uno, idest simplici tantum *p* ac non uti a Graecis scribitur et ipse scripsissem, nec animadvertunt erudituli viri Latinam linguam post *p* statim alterum *p* non admittere, cui tamen insit aspiratio. Itaque dum Graeci nimium esse volunt, Latinum quid velit non vident.

for keeping a usage preserved for so many ages by the greatest authors, seeing that the fact is well known that the Greek authors, too, that is, the Sicilians and the Bruttii, spoke thus, since it is also very commonly known how much variety there is among the Greeks themselves in the termination and inflection of names.[47] Why, even Germanicus mentions *Aegocerus* in his translation of Aratus, as when he says:

And the Cytherian fire (of Venus) has reached the abode of
    Capricorn. [Germanicus, *Aratea* 4.69]

And again:

When he has touched Sagittarius' bright stars,
Gentle rain always falls from Capricorn's sky. [*Aratea* 4.157–
    58]

Often, too, indeed, I have heard a very learned man and one respectful of antiquity solemnly swear that he had read several books of Horace and Ovid and other poets that were almost destroyed by age, and that in them he had noticed that not *Clius* was written but *Clios*, not *Didus* but *Didos*, not *Eratus* but *Eratos*, because in those ancient times our ancestors did not use the Greek forms of the genitive case in these names, since they contracted the Greek *Didoos, Eratoos, Clioos* into a long *o*, *Didos*, *Eratos, Clios*, whereas in Attic the cases are *Didus, Eratus, Clius*. But now what scholar has the good manners not to spit rudely in someone's face or chest when he has heard him speak in a different way? In fact, I know well enough that I myself have been assailed with curses, to say nothing of being sharply rebuked, because I had written *Sapho* with one—that is, with only a single—p and not as it is written by the Greeks; and those pedantically learned fellows[48] haven't noticed that immediately after p the Latin language does not admit a second p that is aspirated. And so in their excessive desire to be Greek they fail to see what Latin requires. For in fact the fathers and

Neque enim patribus ac principibus illis Latinae locutionis cura maior fuit ulla quam ut peregrina lenirentur[42] nomina, utque Palemon[43] usurpat, quam ut Latinitatem musicarent, quo voces lenius illaberentur in aures. Hinc qui Graece est *Odisseus*[44] factus est *Ulisses*,[45] *Achilleus Achilles, Aeas Aiax, Asclepius Esculapius, Polydeuces*[46] *Pollux,* aliaque id genus plurima.

16   Eo autem vecordiae, ne dicam ignorantiae processum est a supinis quibusdam ingeniis, ut inobservato Cicerone, ne dicam contempto, mordicus incursent siquis ita locutus fuerit uti coniunctiones has *et si* et *quanquam,* praeterquam indicativis temporibus coniunxerit, cum et optativis et coniunctivis modis passim coniunctas apud illum invenias. Audite, quaeso, aequo animo Ciceronem tam multis in locis non uni dumtaxat modo, hoc est indicanti, coniungentem; ad Atticum enim ita[47] quadam in epistola: *Sed posteaquam primum Clodii absolutione levitatem infirmitatemque iudiciorum perspexi, deinde vidi nostros publicanos facile a senatu disiungi, quanquam a me ipso non divellerentur.* Alia in epistola: *Rhodum volo puerorum causa, inde quamprimum Athenas, et si etesiae valde reflaverint.*[48] Ad Dolabellam[49] quoque: *Quanquam, mi Dolabella,*[50] *(haec enim iocatus sum) libentius omnis meas, si modo sunt aliquae meae, laudes ad te transtulerim,*[51] *quam aliquam partem exhauserim ex tuis.* Ad Servium Sulpitium: *Accedit eo quod Varro Murena magnopere eius causa vult omnia; qui tamen existimavit, et si suis litteris, quibus tibi Manlium commendabat, valde confideret, tamen mea commendatione aliquid accessionis fore.* Ad Marcum Varronem: *et si quid scriberem non haberem, tamen amico*[52] *ad te eunti non potui*

founders of the Latin language had no greater concern than to
soften the pronunciation of foreign names, and as Palaemon
says, to make Latin musical, so that words might flow more
softly into the ear.[49] Accordingly, the Greek name *Odysseus* became *Ulysses, Achilleus Achilles, Aeas Aiax, Asclepius Aesculapius,
Polydeuces Pollux*, and many others of the same kind.

Moreover, certain negligent geniuses have arrived at such a   16
pitch of silliness, not to say ignorance, that ignoring Cicero —
more than that, despising him — they go after anyone tooth and
nail if he has spoken so as to join the conjunctions *etsi* and
quanquam except to tenses of the indicative, although in Cicero
you might find them joined everywhere with both the optative
and subjunctive moods.[50] Please give Cicero a fair hearing as he
links them in so many places not just to a single mood — that is,
the indicative. So in one letter to Atticus: "But from the time
that I observed first the inconstancy and weakness of the jury in
the acquittal of Clodius, then saw our friends the tax gatherers
easily estranged from the senate, although [*quanquam*] they were
not alienated from me . . ." [Cicero *Epistulae ad Atticum* 1.19.6].
In another letter: "I want to go to Rhodes for the sake of the
boys, and from there to Athens as soon as possible, even if [*etsi*]
the Etesian winds have been strongly blowing the other way"
[*Att.* 6.7.2].[51] And to Dolabella: "Although [*quanquam*], my dear
Dolabella, (indeed, I have made this jest), I would more gladly
transfer all my praises to you — if I really have any — than draw
off any part of yours" [*Epistulae ad familiares* 9.14.4]. To Servius
Sulpitius: "In addition, Varro Murena greatly desires everything
to be done for him, and he thought — although [*etsi*] he had
great confidence in the letters in which he commended Manlius
to you — that something would be added by my recommendation" [*Fam.* 13.22.1]. To Marcus Varro: "Although [*etsi*] I had
nothing to write, nonetheless I could not fail to give something
to a friend on his way to you" [*Fam.* 9.3.1].[52] In the first book of

nihil dare. In primo *Academicorum*[53] libro: *Certe enim recentissima quaeque sunt correcta et emendata maxime, quanquam Antiochi magister Philo, magnus vir, ut tu existimas, ipse negaret.*[54] Item: *Tertia deinde philosophiae pars, quae erat in ratione et in disserendo sic tractabatur ab utrisque. Quanquam oriretur a sensibus, tamen non esse iudicium veritatis in sensibus; mentem volebant rerum esse iudicem.* Et in secundo *De oratore: Erantque multi qui quanquam non ita se*[55] *rem habere arbitrarentur, tamen quo facilius nos incensos studio dicendi a doctrina deterrerent, libenter id quod dixi de illis oratoribus praedicarent.* Item: *se se,*[56] *siquam gloriam peperisse videatur, tamen et si ea non sit iniqua merces periculi, tamen ea non delectari.* Ad hoc Ciceronis testimonium et si aliud nullum abs te requiri certo scio, non praetermittam tamen quae e Sallustio, Livio[57] Tacitoque mihi nunc in mentem veniunt. Sallustii enim verba sunt haec: *Nam vi quidem regere patriam aut parentes, quanquam possis et delicta corrigas, tamen importunum est.* Et Livii libro XXVI°:[58] *Itaque quanquam omnibus omnia deberet, praecipuum muralis coronae decus esse eius qui primus murum ascendisset.* Et libro XXVIIII°: *Mauris inde sicuti convenerat retro ad regem remissis, quanquam aliquanto minore spe multitudinis nec unquam*[59] *tantam rem aggredi satis auderet.* Taciti autem quae sequuntur: *Non numeraverim inter Germaniae populos, quanquam trans Rhenum Danubiumque consederint, eos qui decumates agros exercent.* Item: *Vera statim et incorrupta eloquentia imbuebantur*

the *Academica:* "Indeed, to be sure, all the newest ideas were most improved and corrected, although [*quanquam*] Antiochus' teacher Philo, a great man in your opinion, would deny it" [*Academica* 1.13]. Also: "Then the third part of philosophy, which consisted in reasoning and discussion, was treated by both in this way. They argued that although [*quanquam*] the criterion of truth arose from the senses, it did not reside in the senses; they held that the mind was the judge of matters" [*Academica* 1.30]. And in book two of *De oratore:* "And there were many who, although [*quanquam*] they did not believe that it was so, still willingly promulgated the story I have mentioned about those famous orators in order to deter us more easily from learning when we were on fire with eagerness for oratory" [*De oratore* 2.1]. Also: "If he seems to have won any glory, he does not take pleasure in it, even though [*tamen etsi*] it is not an unfair recompense for his risk" [*De oratore* 2.210]. In addition to this testimony from Cicero, although [*etsi*] I know[53] for certain that you require nothing else, I will not omit the passages that now come to mind from Sallust, Livy, and Tacitus. These are Sallust's words: "For to rule your country or subjects by force, although [*quanquam*] you could correct abuses and might do so, is still tyrannical" [*Bellum Iugurthinum* 3.2]. And in book 26 of Livy: "And so although [*quanquam*] they all deserved every reward, the special honor of the mural crown belonged to the man who first scaled the wall" [Livy 26.48.5]. And in book 29: "When the Moors had been sent back to their king, as it had been agreed, although [*quanquam*] with somewhat less expectation of their number, and he would never quite venture to embark on such a great enterprise" [Livy 29.30.4]. The following words are those of Tacitus: "I would not count those who cultivate the Ten Cantons among the German tribes, although [*quanquam*] they have settled beyond the Rhine and the Danube" [Tacitus, *Germania* 29.14]. Also: "At once they were steeped in real and

et quanquam unum sequerentur, tamen omnes eiusdem aetatis patronos
in plurimis et causis et iudiciis cognoscebant.

17   Tamen haec tolerabiliora; discissum dilaceratumque ab his
iisdem satis scio haud indoctum hominem, quod particulas[60]
nedum ac *ne modo*[61] praeponere sit in scribendo ausus, nec me-
minerunt Ciceronem scribentem ad Atticum, nec Balbum et
Oppium ad Ciceronem; eorum quidem alterum dixisse: *Tu,*
quoniam quartana cares et nedum[62] *morbum removisti, sed etiam gra-*
vedinem, te vegetum nobis in Graecia siste, alteros vero: *Nedum homi-*
num humilium, ut nos sumus, sed etiam amplissimorum virorum con-
silia ex eventu, non ex voluntate a plerisque probari solent. Livius
quoque[63] libro vigesimo nono inquit: *Anno nequaquam satis valido*
ne modo ad lacessendum hostem, sed ne ad tuendos quidem a populatio-
nibus agros, equitatu accepto, id omnium primum egit, ut per inquisitio-
nem numerum equitum augeret.[64] Nec alienum[65] forte fuerit Plinii
quoque verba e nono *Naturalis historiae* libro adducere: *Lolliam*
Paulinam, quae fuit Caii principis matrona, ne serio quidem aut solenni
cerimoniarum aliquo apparatu, sed mediocrium etiam, sponsalium
coena, vidi smaragdis margaritisque opertam.

Haec autem quanquam sunt huiusmodi, movent tamen doc-
tos viros. Indignantur enim non permitti sibi maiorum auctoritate uti tutoque evagari per orationis latinae fines, qui latissimi
quidem sunt. Nam et si possunt conscientia ipsi sua contenti
esse, tamen nescio quomodo praestantibus in ingeniis usuvenit

genuine eloquence; and although [*quanquam*] they were adherents of a single man, they nevertheless got to know all the advocates of the same generation in numerous cases and courts" [Tacitus, *Dialogus de oratoribus* 34.4].

Nonetheless, these things are easier to bear. A not unlearned 17 man of my acquaintance has been shredded and torn to pieces by these same fellows because in writing he dared to show a preference for the particles *nedum* ("not only") and *ne modo* ("not only"); and they fail to remember either Cicero writing to Atticus or Balbus and Oppius writing to Cicero.[54] In the case of the one: "Since you are free of quartan fever, and you have got rid not only [*nedum*] of your illness, but also of your cold, present yourself to me hale and hearty in Greece" [*Att.* 10.16.6]. In the case of the others: "The advice not only [*nedum*] of nobodies like us, but also of the most important men, is usually judged by most people from the outcome, not from the intention" [*Att.* 9.7a.1]. Also, Livy says in book 29: "Since the cavalry Hanno had been assigned were not only [*ne modo*] by no means strong enough to challenge the enemy but not even to protect the countryside from raiding parties, he made it his first priority to increase the number of cavalrymen through a levy" [Livy 29.34.4].[55] Nor will it be out of place to bring up Pliny's words from book nine of the *Natural History:* "I saw Lollia Paulina, the wife of the emperor Gaius, covered with emeralds and pearls — not even at an important occasion or some solemn ceremonial display, but actually at the dinner of an ordinary betrothal party" [*N.H.* 9.117].[56]

These details, trivial as they are, still disturb learned men. They are displeased at not being allowed to profit by the example of their ancestors and to range safely through the territory of Latin speech, which is extremely broad. For although they can be content with their own knowledge of what is correct, still somehow there is the same reaction in the case of

quod in equis generosis, ut nolint pungi, aversentur flagella,[66] ad scuticae sonitum exaestuent; nanque ipsi etiam reges muscas fugitant.[67]

18   Equidem memini, quin videre quidem videor digladiantes grammaticos super Virgiliano versu, qui est:

Instar montis equum divina Palladis arte
aedificant,

dum quid *instar* significet parum intelligunt. Neque enim Ciceronem animadverterunt scribentem ad Atticum: *Mearum epistularum nulla est synagoge; sed habet Tiro instar septuaginta, et quidem sunt a te quaedam sumendae. Eas ego oportet perspiciam, corrigam; tum denique edentur.*[68] Et in *Oratore ad Brutum: Nam invenire et iudicare quid dicas magna illa quidem*[69] *sunt et tanquam animi instar in corpore.*[70] Quid? idem cum dixit Cicero ex ore Antimachi in *Bruto, Plato enim mihi unus instar est omnium,*[71] an sibi vult aliud quam quod Platonis unius audientia idem valeret apud eum tantumque haberet auctoritatis quantum si universus Atheniensis populus ad audiendum convenisset intentusque recitantem spectaret quodque inventio ac iudicium in oratore idem quidem polleat quod in corpore ipso animus? Verum haec a nominis ipsius deductione aliquanto sunt remotiora, cum tamen et Cicero et Virgilius eam innuant, ut quae *instar* aut sunt aut habent, ea quasi oculis ac menti instent illisque perinde ut exemplar quoddam sint proposita. Quod fabris atque artificibus usuvenit, qui propositum ad exemplar fabricantur, ad illudque opus suum dirigunt, id quod Virgilii verba praeseferunt[72]

outstanding intellects as in horses of noble stock, that they dislike the spur, scorn whips, become enraged at the sound of the strap. Indeed, even kings run from flies.[57]

In fact, I remember — why, I even seem to see — grammarians fighting to the death over this verse of Vergil,   18

> A horse the size [instar] of a mountain they built with the
> divine skill of Pallas, [Aeneid 2.15–16]

since they do not understand the meaning of instar ["the equivalent of" or "like"]. Indeed, they have failed to notice Cicero writing to Atticus: "There is no collection of my letters, but Tiro has something like [instar] seventy, and indeed certain ones must be recovered from you. I should look through and correct them; then they will finally be published" [Att. 16.5.5]. And in the Orator to Brutus: "To discover and to decide what to say — those are great things to be sure, and a kind of equivalent [instar] of the mind in the body" [Orator 44]. What about this? When the same Cicero, speaking in the character of Antimachus in the Brutus, said, "For me, one Plato is worth as much as [instar] all the rest" [Brutus 191], did he mean anything other than that the audience of one man, Plato, was worth as much to him and had as much authority as if the whole population of Athens had come together to hear and watched with rapt attention as he recited, and that invention and judgment have the same importance in an orator as the mind in the body? But these points are somewhat too far away from the interpretation of the word, although in any case Cicero and Vergil hint at it: that the things that are "like" [instar] or have the "equivalent" [instar] stand before our eyes and mind, as it were, and are presented to them in the same way as a model. This is what happens in the case of carpenters and artisans who work to the model set before them and guide their work by it, as Vergil's

dicentis equum illum Troianum aedificatum ea vastitate ut quasi vasti imago montis fuisset proposita aedificatoribus, quam et ipsi imitarentur et equus ipse illam referret; quod ipse alibi[73] declarat, cum ait:

Hanc tamen immensam Calchas attollere molem
roboribus textis coeloque educere iussit.

Et Cicero cum respondet Attico *habet Tiro instar septuaginta,* an aliud significat quam quod cum ipse efflagitatarum ab illo epistolarum nullum haberet penes se exemplum, originales quidem epistolae (sic enim hodie non pauci loquuntur) quasque ipse dictasset a Tirone asservarentur quodque de exemplaribus illis utpote archetypis exemplum esset sumendum? Idem Cicero declarat hoc apertius scribens ad Varronem: *Equidem hos tuos Tusculanos*[74] *dies instar esse vitae puto* ac si diceret: 'vitae genus dierum illorum quibus fuisti in Tusculano esse aliis vitae suae exemplum ac specimen debere iudico.' Itaque tum *exemplar* tum *exemplum* videtur *instar* significare, quod et Virgilius[75] confirmat cum dicit: *Quantum instar in illo!*[76] Recentiores tamen, ut Plinius Secundus, alia quadam ratione videntur hac usi dictione, neque improprie tamen, neque indecenter, ut cum ait de Traiano: *Instar refectionis existimas mutationem laboris.*[77] Et alibi: *instar ulctionis videretur cernere laceros artus, truncata membra.* Item: *maximum*

words indicate when he says that the famous Trojan horse was built of such an enormous size that it was as if an image of an enormous mountain had been put before the builders, and that they imitated it and the horse itself replicated it. He makes this clear elsewhere when he says:

> This huge mass Calchas nonetheless ordered them to raise
>   high
> with crisscrossed timbers and build up to the sky. [*Aeneid*
>   2.185–86]

And when Cicero replied to Atticus, "Tiro has something like [*instar*] seventy," did he mean anything other than that, although he had in his possession no copy of the letters Atticus had kept asking for, certainly the original letters (for that is the term used by many today) and those he himself had dictated were preserved by Tiro, and that a copy would have to be taken from those exemplars, inasmuch as they were the originals?[58] Cicero also explains this more clearly in writing to Varro: "I regard these days of yours in Tusculum as an example [*instar*] of life worthy of the name" [*Fam.* 9.6.4], as if he were saying, "I think that the kind of life you led in those days in the Tusculan villa should be an example and model to others for their own life." So *instar* seems to mean both "model" [*exemplar*] and "example" [*exemplum*]; and Vergil confirms this when he says, "What a great example [*instar*] is in that man!" [*Aeneid* 6.865]. Yet more recent authors like Pliny the Younger seem to use this word in a somewhat different way, but neither improperly nor inappropriately, as when Pliny says of Trajan: "You consider a change of work as good as a rest" [*instar refectionis; Panegyricus* 81.1]. And in another place: "It seemed a fitting retribution [*instar ulctionis*] to see the mangled bodies and mutilated limbs" [*Pan.* 52.5]. Also: "The greatest benefit turned into the most

beneficium vertebatur in gravissimam iniuriam civitasque Romana instar erat odii et discordiae et orbitatis.

Pud. Ego vero, Petre Compater, facile sum passus aegreferentem te grammaticorum importunam diligentiam evagatum longiuscule; omnis tamen dicendi oblectatio vacare debet tedio cumprimis audientium ac defatigatione. Quamobrem redeat iam Pardus ad insomnia, quo Horatianum illud *punctum,* dum *iocis miscemus seria,* e dictionibus his nostris ab iis qui audiendi nobiscum hic gratia consederint referamus, sintque posthac res inter nos grammaticae levatio quasi quaedam rerum difficiliorum quae in sermonem venient, non autem disserendi materia.

19 Pard. Revocas me, ut video, Puderice, ad somnia, vel potius aut impellis aut trahis. Atque equidem vereor ne de his disserentem me huberius ad somniandum adigas etiam vigilantem. Dicam tamen quae sentio quaeque ut probentur a multis desiderari quidem potest, utinam vero id consequamur ut a paucis!

Externam quidem esse mentem putat Aristoteles eamque veluti peregre advenientem, ut sentire illum arbitror, in animos hominum illabi idemque animis praestare ipsis officium ad cogitandum pervestigandumque, denique ad iudicandum quod artificibus ipsis ad conficiendum destinatum opus praebeat dextera. Ac mea quidem sententia, perinde ut de luce per orbem a sole diffusa lumen oculis accenditur ad videndum atque discernendum ea quae oculis obiecta sunt (nam et lux, externa idest, coelestis res est, eque coelo a sole diffusa peregre ad nos advenit), sic a coeli ipsius siderumque commotionibus, per eam quae *sympathia* Graece est (Latine *contagionem* fecit Cicero, mihi magis placet appellare *contagem,* quando *contagio* in malam ac

grievous wrong, and the Roman citizenship stood for [*instar erat*] hatred and discord and deprivation" [*Pan.* 37.4].

Puderico. I myself, Pietro Compatre, don't mind your being annoyed with the troublesome pedantry of grammarians and getting a little far off the track, but every pleasing discussion must be free of boredom or weariness, especially for the listeners. So let Pardo go back to the subject of dreams, so that as a consequence of our words, while "we mix serious matters with pleasure," we might carry the "vote" Horace talks about from those who have sat down here with us to listen, and so that afterward grammatical subjects might serve as a kind of relief from the more difficult topics that will come into our conversation, not as the substance of our discussion.[59]

Pardo. You are calling me back to dreams, as I see, Puderico — or rather, you are either driving or dragging me. And indeed I'm afraid that, as I talk about these matters more fully, you will force me to dream even when I am awake.[60] Nonetheless, I will say what I believe, and indeed what can be desireable that many approve — but I hope it may succeed with at least a few!   19

Aristotle believes that there is an external mind [*mens*] and that, coming from outside so to speak, as I think he means, it slips into the minds [*animos*] of men and supplies them with the same function of thinking and investigating, and ultimately of judging, that the right hand provides to artists to complete their intended work. And in my view, just as from the light diffused through the world by the sun a lamp is kindled in our eyes to see and distinguish the things set before our eyes (and indeed the light — I mean the external light — is a celestial substance, and having been diffused from heaven by the sun comes to us from outside), in the same way from the movements of heaven itself and the constellations, through that quality called *sympathia* in Greek (Cicero translated it as *contagio* in Latin, but I prefer *contages* ["influence"], since today *contagio* is taken in a

pestilentem hodie partem accipitur), sic, inquam, a coeli stellarumque agitatu perpetuo animis nostris mens, idest vis illa cogitandi tam acuta et solers tamque etiam sibi constans dono dei infunditur. Nec vero ea quae nunc dico accipi sic velim ut non et ipse de Deo deque animae immortalitate eiusque creatione ea sentiam quae Christiani sint hominis et pii quidem hominis, sed disserentem de somniis par est quaedam tanquam somniantem afferre in medium. Neque vero oblitum te illorum arbitror, quae paulo a me ante dicta sunt de monitis persaepe sanctissimis illis patribus a Deo traditis inter dormiendum.

20   Ne igitur a proposita re discedam longius, quae in somnis offeruntur simulacra et visa, ea partim a cupiditate, studio affectionibusque hominum maioribus excitantur, quod videmus etiam in canibus, et, ut Claudianus ait:

> Venator defessa toro cum membra reponit,
>> mens tamen ad silvas et sua lustra redit. [. . .]
> Furto gaudet amans, permutat navita merces,
>> et vigil elapsas quaerit avarus opes,
> blandaque largitur frustra sitientibus aegris
>> irriguus gelido pocula fonte sapor.[78]

Est enim locum hunc poeta ille luculentissime prosecutus. Partim etiam a quadam tum colluvie humorum, tum malo ab habitu corporis, hique excitantur in corpore cum dormitur; unde etiam visa ac simulacra illa non nisi conturbata videntur et persaepe terrent. Multum quoque adhaec ipsa conferunt tempestates, sincerusne sit an perturbatus aeris ipsius status, anni quoque partes, qualis est autunnus propter inconstantiam ac

negative sense and with disease), in the same way, I say, from the perpetual motion of the sky and the stars, mind [*mens*] — that is, the power of thinking so acute and inventive and even so internally consistent — is poured into our minds [*animis*] by the gift of God. Of course, I would not wish what I am saying now to be taken as meaning that I do not have the sentiments about God and the immortality of the soul and its creation that are proper to a Christian and indeed to a pious person; but it is reasonable for a person discoursing on dreams to make certain pronouncements in public as if he were dreaming. And I certainly do not think you have forgotten what I said a little while ago about the counsel very often imparted by God to those holy fathers while they slept.[61]

Well then, not to depart too far from the subject, the images 20 and visions presented in dreams are set in motion partly by desire, by people's enthusiasm and stronger feelings, as we see even in dogs, and as Claudian says:

When the hunter lays his weary limbs upon his bed,
his mind still returns to his haunts in the woods.
The lover delights in his tryst; the trader markets his wares,
and the miser, alert, looks for riches slipped from his grasp;
and on those sick with thirst a moist savor in vain
lavishes sweet drafts from an icy cold spring. [*Panegyricus de sexto consulatu Honorii Augusti, Praefatio* 3–4, 7–10]

Truly the poet has developed this theme splendidly! Partly, too, dreams arise from both a confluence of humors and a poor condition of the body, and they are set in motion in the body when one sleeps. That is why images and visions inevitably seem disturbed and are quite often terrifying. Weather also contributes greatly to these effects, whether the atmosphere be clear or stormy, and also the seasons of the year, like autumn because of its inconstancy and variety, so that for these reasons

varietatem, ut in somnis quidem contingant ob has ipsas causas pleraque omnia quae nostrorum sunt sensuum, cum et vigilant et exercentur, quippe cum dormientes videmur etiam coenare, potare, Veneris rebus uti, ridere, letari, timere, lacrimari, sequi, fugere, audere, demum quae vegetantis quaeque sentientis sunt animae pleraque inter dormiendum ipsis in visis accipere,[79] ut haec ipsa fere sine[80] sympathia illa coelesti fiant.

At quomodo, inquam, fient, quomodo absque siderum contage et coeli visiones illae divinae quidem ac sanctitatis plenae futurorumque cognitionis atque (ut Christiani dicimus) arcanorum mysteriorum? Quemadmodum igitur mens illa coelitus Sibyllis offertur vatibusque praeclarissimis, per quam remotissimas quoque res nihilque ad se spectantes, ne cogitatas quidem prius nec concupitas vates ipsi et praedicunt et praevident, eundem ad modum coelitus visiones illae offeruntur dormientibus, iis quidem ut nullis occupatis aut curis aut cogitationibus, ipsis vero sensibus ita liberis ac vacuis, ut nihil utique humanum eis inesse videatur, sicuti recte quidem a poetis describitur furor ipse vaticinantium, qui, quod praeter humanos fiat sensus, furor est appellatus.

Qui igitur in vatibus furor est, in dormientibus caret nomine; pie tamen magis quam proprie a bonis quibusdam viris tum visitatio tum apparitio divina dicitur, quasi Deus in somnis illos inviserit aut numen iis aliquod apparuerit quiescentibus; quo factum est ut monita ipsa, perinde ac divino ex *ore* prolata, quidam appellarint *oracula*. Ut autem non omnibus, sed perquam paucis divini illius spiritus concessa est familiaritas visque ad vaticinandum, sic non multis est attributa somniandi veritas, vel, ut rectius loquar, sanctitas atque castitudo.

in dreams almost everything arises that affects our senses when they are awake and active. In fact, in sleep we seem even to dine, to drink, to enjoy sexual activity, to laugh, to rejoice, to be afraid, to weep, to pursue, to flee, to dare, finally to experience in the visions while we sleep most things characteristic of the living and sentient soul, so that these things are generally produced without the celestial *sympathia* I was just talking about.

But how, I say, how will those other visions come about except from the influence (*contage*) of the stars and heaven — those visions that are certainly divine and full of holiness and knowledge of the future and (as we Christians say) hidden mysteries? Well then, just as the mind from heaven is revealed to Sibyls and preeminent seers — the mind through which the seers foretell and foresee very distant events having nothing to do with themselves, things not even imagined before or aspired to, in the same way visions from heaven are presented to sleepers, at any rate to those absorbed by no cares or thoughts but so free and devoid of sensation itself that there seems to be nothing even human in them — so poets rightly refer to the frenzy of inspired seers, which is called frenzy since it comes to pass apart from human consciousness.[62]

The quality called frenzy in seers lacks a name in the case of sleepers. Nonetheless, more piously than correctly some good men call it divine visitation or apparition, as if a god visited them in their dreams or some divine power appeared to them as they slept. Accordingly, it has come about that some have called the counsels themselves *oracles* as if they were brought forth from a divine mouth [*ore*]. But as intimacy with the divine spirit and power to prophesy have not been allowed to all, but to very few, so not to many has been vouchsafed the true nature of dreaming, or to speak more correctly, its holiness and purity.[63]

21   Quam paucissimi vel rarissimi potius existunt poetae, quorum ingenii etiam vis e coelo manare credita est! Quibus itaque divinis cum visionibus haec inest familiaritas et tanquam hospitii ius, et illa quoque eisdem inest a coelo informatio accipiendis apta visis quae de coelo per contagem illabuntur. Qua de re ab illis qui sideralis scientiae quae astrologia Graece dicitur studiosi sunt permulta traduntur, quae nos ad illorum hac in parte disciplinam relegamus. Te ipsum equidem, Paule Prassici, dicentem audivi saepius multum hanc ad rem conferre tum Veneris stellam, tum Iovis, magis autem Veneris, qualem scilicet ea se se in genitura habuerit, praesertim adversus signum illud, qualeque signum illud fuerit quod nonum tunc coeli locum tenuerit aut primum, cum quis in lucem venit. Inter signa vero omnia, cui Virgo nomen est inditum, illud esse divinationi huic quam accommodatissimum; quippe quod eam in constituendo corpore retineat temperationem fermentandis humoribus, qualem fermentationem esse oporteat fabricae illius quae simulacrorum huiusmodi familiaris futura sit atque hospita.

Omnino autem fermentatio illa corporis quae bilis atrae secum habet permultum rei huic est perquam apposita, de cuius natura quaedam etiam admiranda traduntur ab Aristotele. Ea enim ipsa terrenam ob qualitatem, quod atro in vino apparet, ubi concaluit iam, spumam quandam huberiorem excitat, de cuius excitatione spiritus et quidem vehementiores gignuntur. Atqui spiritus quidem ipse aerius cum sit (nam qui Graeco nomine est *aer* Latino dicitur *spiritus*), efficitur ut quemadmodum per aerem a natura ipsa visus, qui oculorum est sensus, exercetur, et qui aurium est auditus, item et olfatus, eundem ad modum contages ipsa coelestis supernaque illa affectio per aerem perque spiritus illos tantopere suscitatos se se insinuans

How very few or rather, how uncommon are the poets the   21
power of whose genius has been thought to emanate from
heaven! Consequently, those who possess this intimacy and a
sort of right of hospitality with divine visions also possess the
predisposition from heaven suited to receive the images that
have flowed down from heaven through influence [*per contagem*].
On this matter those who are devoted to the science of the stars
(which is called *astrologia* in Greek) relate many things that we
ascribe to their teaching on this point. Indeed, very often I have
heard you yourself, Paolo Prassicio, say that very useful for this
are both the planet Venus and the planet Jupiter, but especially
Venus, that is, as she is situated in the horoscope, especially opposite the sign, whatever sign it might be, that occupies the
ninth or the first house of the sky at the time when someone
comes into the light of life. You have said that among all the
signs, the one called Virgo is certainly the most suited of all for
this prognostication, since during the creation of the body it
maintains the kind of balance for the rising humors required for
the concoction of a work that will become friendly and hospi-
table to apparitions of this kind.

In general, exceedingly appropriate for this is the mixture of
the body that includes a quantity of black bile, concerning
whose nature Aristotle has handed down some remarkable information.[64] Because of its earthen quality, which also appears
in dark wine when it has grown warm, it stirs up copious foam,
from whose rising are also produced breaths, and strong ones,
too. And yet since breath itself certainly consists of air (for
what is *aer* in Greek is called *spiritus*, or breath, in Latin), it
happens that just as sight, the sense of the eyes, is naturally
developed through the air, and hearing, the sense of the ears,
and likewise the sense of smell — in the same way, the very influence of heaven and the arrangement of the sky, slipping
through the air and through those breaths roused to such a

exercet mentem in vaticinantibus, plus tamen minus ve pro natura fermentationis ipsius eiusque temperatione; quod item efficitur in dormientibus, pro fermentationis eiusdem ratione et habitu corporisque illorum concretione. Itaque neque Augustinus, tum summa doctrina tum etiam sanctitate vir, neque doctissimi[81] e nostris theologi, neque e philosophis Stoici acutissimi iidemque disputaces homines (utar enim novo hoc nomine, quando eiusmodi Academia quidem fuit) somnia visionesque probare dubitaverunt quaeque in somnis traduntur monita; quae quidem etiam sunt qui vocaverint oracula, neque defuere qui arbitrati sint prophetarum pleraque per somnia eis et oracula divinitus demonstrata; et Syllam, felicissimum tum civem tum imperatorem, consulenti Lucullo in re militari quid servaturus esset potissimum, somnia cumprimis animadvertenda respondisse boni auctores tradunt.

Haec igitur, Puderice, sive suasus a te[82] sive compulsus, quando et Sincero satis iri factum intelligebam, de somniis dixi. Abstinebo a pluribus, ne, quod paulo ante dixi, vel vigilans videar somniare. Quodque poetica vis vaticinantium habetur persimilis, unde poetae et ipsi vates dicuntur, Sinceri ipsius, poeticae quam studiosissimi vel poetae potius et quidem elegantissimi, officium neque indignum fuerit neque ingratum, si et ipse consessu in hoc de poetis afferet in medium aliquid, quo consessores hos dormitantis iam avocet a somno, quando loquens ipse de iis quae inter dormiendum offeruntur somnum iam videor audientibus provocasse. Quam ad rem locus ipse non minus quam oratio haec mea adhortari te debet, Sincere Acti, quem et Panhormita[83] olim Antonius, dum viveret, et senex nunc hic noster dignum uterque vel iudicavere vel fecere ipsi potius in quo de omni disciplinarum genere disputaretur a

high degree, agitate the mind in those making prophetic utterances, depending more or less on the nature of the mixture and its balance; and this also happens in those who are asleep, depending on the structure and condition of the same mixture and on the bodily composition of the sleepers. And so neither Augustine, a man of both the greatest learning and the greatest piety, nor the most learned of our theologians, nor the Stoics, most sagacious of philosophers and also highly argumentatious[65] men (I use the new word, since the Academy was certainly like that), hesitated to commend dreams and visions and the counsels conveyed in dreams. Some people call these counsels oracles, and there have been those who have considered that most utterances and oracles of the prophets were revealed to them by divine influence through dreams. Good authors also relate that Sulla, most fortunate as a citizen and a general, told Lucullus, when he asked what he should most watch out for in warfare, that above all he should pay attention to dreams.[66]

So then, Puderico, this is what I had to say about dreams, whether under your encouragement or your coercion, since I understood that it would also satisfy Sincero. I will say no more, so as not to give the appearance (as I said a minute ago) of dreaming while awake. And because the poetic art is considered a power very like that of prophets (that is why poets are also called bards), the task of Sincero as a great student of poetry, or rather as a poet and indeed a most elegant one, will be neither unworthy nor disagreeable if he himself makes some pronouncement about poets in this gathering to waken these dozing companions from slumber, since while I was talking about the things revealed during sleep I apparently made my audience nod off. This place itself no less than my words should urge you to it, Sincero Azio—the place that both Antonio Panormita, while he lived, and now this old man of ours have either deemed worthy or rather themselves made it so, of being

doctis viris, qui non minus libenter quam ad eum saepe conveniunt.

22 *Act.* Et exuscitasti nos, Parde, a somno, dum de somniorum natura et causis argute non magis quam vere disseris, et nunc me ad dicendum excitas deque iis praesertim studiis quae, quod pace dictum sit vestra, quanquam fateor esse communia, tamen, quod in iis ita laboravi hactenus diesque laboro ac noctis sumque sedulo laboraturus, si mea ea dixerim, videar iure ipso dixisse. Est tamen haec ipsa res maioris ocii curaeque vigilantioris, disserere de poeticae excellentia; quo utar autem hoc verbo senis nostri auctoritas efficit, quem finientem saepius audivi poetae sive officium sive finem esse dicere apposite ad admirationem; nihil autem nisi excellens admodum parit admirationem.

Quod nisi tanta illa moveret Aristotelis me maiestas, vel ausim abdicare a mediocritate poetam, quae tamen in hoc ipso alio quodam modo et requirenda est et laudanda. Quodque admiratio ipsa multis ac maximis comparatur virtutibus, quibus explicandis haud est satis idoneum nunc tempus, cum sit res ipsa multiplex ac laboriosa admodum multaeque animi pensionis,[84] ne non Pardo tamen vel petenti vel iubenti morem geram, eius attingam vel magis seligam eam partem quae tota versatur in numeris. Et si numeri sunt ipsi e verbis quae versum constituunt, quibus inter nostros quidem eminere videtur Virgilius.

Numerus autem ipse cumprimis et movet et delectat et admirationem gignit. Eius autem prima illa laus est quod varietatem parit, cuius natura ipsa videtur fuisse vel imprimis studiosa. Quid enim vel inertius vel, ut ita dixerim, oscitantius quam eodem semper sono ac tenore syllabas et verba compangere? Quo vitio e posterioribus poetis sunt qui laboraverint; quae res

the site of discussion of every sort of discipline by learned men, who meet here gladly and often.[67]

Azio. You awakened us from sleep, Pardo, while you were dis-   22
coursing on the nature and causes of dreams with equal subtlety and truth, and now you rouse me to speak, and on those stud-ies especially, which (let it be said with everyone's permission) although admittedly shared by all of us, I think I could very justly call my own because I have toiled in them up until this moment, and am toiling in them night and day, and will con-tinue to toil unremittingly. All the same, it requires considerable time and alert attention to discourse on the excellence of the poetic art; and indeed, I use the word "excellence" on the au-thority of our old man, whom I have quite often heard say by way of definition that the duty or end of the poet is to speak in a manner suited to inspire admiration.[68] Only what is most ex-cellent, however, produces admiration.

But if I were not influenced by the great majesty of Aristotle, I might even venture to keep a poet away from the middle course, which nonetheless in his particular case is to be sought and praised in some other way.[69] Admiration itself is produced by many very important qualities, which there is not enough time to explain now, since the thing is complex and difficult and requires much deliberation; nonetheless, so as to gratify Pardo's request or command, I will touch on it, or rather I will select the part entirely concerned with rhythm. And yet rhythm itself arises from the words that constitute a verse, and in this Vergil seems preeminent, certainly among Latin poets.[70]

Indeed rhythm by itself especially moves and delights and gives rise to admiration. Its chief merit is to create variety, to which nature herself seems to have been attached more than to anything else. For what is flatter or more listless, so to speak, than always putting words and syllables together with the same sound and accent? Some of the later poets have suffered from

non minus modo illos reddidit admirabiles, verum etiam longe minus graves, siquidem ipsis e numeris, tum collidendis vocalibus tum substinendo ac remorando sono, aut contra vocibus syllabisque praeproperandis, comparatur etiam dicendi quaedam tum gravitas tum ea quae dignitas suo est nomine, quanquam harum utraque artibus etiam aliis comparatur. Hae autem admirationis ipsius praecipuae quidem sunt nunc comites nunc vero et duces.

23   Quae res quoniam exemplo quam dictione fit manifestior, sumam principio ex ipso Aeneidos versum illum:

multum ille et terris iactatus et alto.

Plenus hic quidem est versus, sonorus, gravis, numerosus; quae laus tota existit de collisione vocalium statim repercussa eaque ingeminata. Quod si dictionem eam subtrahas quae est *ille* ac dicas '*multumque et terris iactatus et alto*,' mirum est quantum de versus ipsius dignitate, gravitate, magnitudine detrahatur. Quod quidem ipsum fit etiam ob accentus unius detractionem. Etenim pars ea quae est *multumque* unum tantum secum adducit accentum eumque subinclinatum, at *multum ille* duos, quos utique collisio ipsa et coniungit simul ambos et eos efficit tum pleniores tum etiam magis sonoros.

Videamus et alium, qui est:

multa quoque et bello passus, dum conderet urbem.

Qui si dicas '*multa etiam bello passus*,' tutemet[85] intelliges quanta fiat sonoritatis imminutio et quidam quasi languor[86] ob soni ipsius exilitatem, quam dictio illa *quoque* non solum exterminat,

this fault, a thing that makes them not only less worthy of admiration, but also far less important, since from rhythm, by vowels being clashed together and by sustaining and holding the sound, or the reverse, by hurrying words and syllables along, is produced a certain majesty of speech and what is rightly called greatness, although both these virtues are also produced by other methods. These methods above all, however, are sometimes the companions, sometimes in fact even the leaders of admiration.

Since this becomes clearer with an example than by talking about it, I will take that famous verse from the beginning of the *Aeneid*:

23

> this man, much tossed on land and sea. [Vergil, *Aeneid* 1.3]

Indeed, this verse is copious, resounding, weighty, rhythmical; and its entire merit proceeds from the elision of vowels that is immediately echoed and repeated.[71] But if you were to remove the word *ille* and say, "*multumque et terris iactatus et alto*" (and much tossed on both land and sea), it is remarkable how much would be taken away from the stature, the import, the greatness of the verse. This happens because of the removal of a single accent. This is so because the word *multumque* brings with it only one accent and a weak one at that, but *multum ille* has two, and the elision necessarily brings both of them together at the same time and makes them stronger and more resounding.[72]

Let us look at another example. Here it is:

> and suffering many things also in war, until he should
>   found a city. [*Aeneid* 1.5]

Here if you say, "*multa etiam bello passus*" (many things suffering, too, in war), you will understand yourself how much the melody is lessened and a kind of feebleness arises because of the thinness of the sound itself.[73] The word *quoque* not only

verum ipsum et auget et implet sonum; quem nequaquam etiam implesset si dixisset *'multa quidem et bello passus'*; nam paulo ante cum dixisset *'multum ille,'* in ea quae statim sequebatur copulatione non erat a numeri plenitudine corruendum; dixit igitur *'multa quoque,'* nam tum etiam tum *quidem* sonum faciunt satis exilem, contra dictio *quoque* implet eum. Quocirca vel exquisitissime exigitur in poeta litterarum delectus ac selectio. Habet autem versus tot accentus quot et verba, et si particulae[87] *que* et *ve* non faciunt ipsae per se accentum, sed illum ad se trahunt praecedentibus a syllabis, qua e re a grammaticis dictae sunt inclinativae. Quo fit ut quatuor haec verba *multa quoque et bello* quatuor etiam accentus habeant, at *multa etiam bello* tris tantum. Nam praeterquam quod sonant tenuiter, uno etiam superantur accentu. Hanc ipsam autem soni ac litterae plenitudinem haud multo post, quod locus ipse ab illa esset alienus, Virgilius reiecit, solertissimarum aurium solertissimus subblanditor, dicens: *'tot adire labores.'* Qui si *'obire'* dixisset, in asperitatem quasi quandam et confragosum incidisset sonum, coniungens statim *tot* et *ob*, cum alibi, quod extollenda vox esset, dixerit:

et lituo pugnas insignis obibat et hasta.

Tenuitas enim antecedentis syllabae suffragio egere subsequentis videbatur.

24   Sed omittamus nunc quae tum ad litteras spectant, tum ad syllabas. Quid causae fuit, quid, inquam, causae cur exponere se Virgilius maledicentiae grammaticorum voluerit cum dicere *'fluviorum rex Eridanus'* maluit, quam *'Eridanus fluviorum rex,'* quod

banishes this thinness, but also both amplifies and fills out the sound itself. Also, it would certainly not have filled it out if he had said, "*multa quidem et bello passus*" (for although he had said "*multum ille*" a little earlier, in the combination that immediately followed there was no necessary fall in the fullness of rhythm);[74] and so he said, "*multa quoque*," for both *etiam* and *quidem* make the sound fairly thin, whereas the word *quoque* gives it fullness. For this reason choice and selection of letters are most particularly required in a poet. The verse, moreover, has as many accents as words even if the particles *-que* and *-ve* have no accent by themselves but attract one from the preceding syllables, which is why the grammarians call them enclitics.[75] So these four words, *multa quoque et bello*, have four accents, but the words *multa etiam bello* have only three. Indeed, beyond the fact that they sound thin, they also lack one accent. But a little later, Vergil (the subtlest pleaser of the most subtle ears) rejects this plenitude of sound and letter because the place was inappropriate for it, saying, "*tot adire labores*" (to face so many difficulties; *Aeneid* 1.10). If he had said, "*obire*" here, he would have fallen into a certain harshness and a jarring sound by putting *tot* and *ob* next to each other, although in another place, because the auditory effect was to be increased, he said:

and he marched into battle glorious with trumpet and spear.
[*Aeneid* 6.167]

In this case the thinness of the preceding syllable seemed to need the help of the succeeding one.[76]

But now let us put aside what pertains to letters or syllables. 24 What was the reason, what was the reason, I say, that Vergil willingly exposed himself to the abuse of grammarians when he chose to say, "*fluviorum rex Eridanus*" (of rivers king, Eridanus; *Georgics* 1.482.) rather than "*Eridanus fluviorum rex*" (Eridanus, of rivers king), which was allowed by the verse?[77] Was it because

per versum licebat? An quod aurium pluris faceret voluptatem quam tetricum litteratorum iudicium? Languet enim sic versus sordescitque in ore quodammodo, consideratis praesertim et quae statim praecedunt et quae post sequuntur dictionibus. Quocirca implere illum maluit artificiosa verborum commutatione. At videte quam concinne inter dictiones quae ambae quatuor constarent e syllabis interiecit 'rex,' quae est unius, quippe quae post collocata et structurae ineptitudinem argueret et sonoritatem illam tam suavem auribus ipsis invideret. Hac igitur e commutatione versus ipse redditus est spectabilis, qui aliter ridiculus esset atque abiiciendus.

Claudit saepenumero Virgilius plures versus sustinendo sonum illumque remoratur, ne ipsa aut deliqueat sonoritas aut praecipitetur. At videte, obsecro, quam apposite, quam studiose praestruit tribus e dictionibus versum iisque dyssyllabis[88] et tanquam prima in acie spondeum collocat, solutum quidem ac liberum, indeque, praeterita secunda, alterum atque alterum in tertia et quarta acie. Inter primum autem spondeum ac secundum unum quidem secunda in acie statuit dactylum, et ait:

tantae molis erat Romanam condere gentem

et alibi:

siqua fata sinant, iam tum tenditque fovetque.

At si invertas (*molis erat tantae* et *fata sinant siqua*), omnis illa vocalitas iam exhalat, quod Virgilius ut prohibeat, solutum ab omni connexione spondeum in principio collocat; ut alio in loco cum ait, 'curru iungit Alesus equos.' Potuisset cum dicere: 'iungit Alesus equos curru,' numeris tamen maluit auribusque consulere.

he considered something pleasant to hear more important than the stern verdict of scholars? For in the second version the verse droops and becomes paltry somehow in the mouth, especially when one considers the words that immediately precede and follow. Therefore, he chose to fill it up with an artificial reordering of the words. But see how elegantly he has put *rex*, a word of one syllable, between two words each with four, since if it were placed last it would betray ineptness of structure and also deprive the ears of that very pleasant sound. This reordering, then, makes outstanding the very verse that otherwise would have been absurd and worth discarding.

Vergil often closes several verses by sustaining and holding a sound, lest the resonance either vanish or be rushed. But see, I beg you, how suitably, how carefully he arrays a verse on the foundation of three words, disyllables, and stations a spondee in the front line, so to speak, unconnected indeed and free, and then, passing over the second position, sets another spondee and yet another in the third rank and the fourth.[78] Moreover, between the first and second spondees he stations a single dactyl in the second position, and he says:

so great a task it was to found the Roman nation, [*Aeneid* 1.33]

and in another place:

if somehow the fates should allow it, she already intends and cherishes. [*Aeneid* 1.18]

But if you turn the order around (*molis erat tantae* and *fata sinant siqua*), all that euphony evaporates; to prevent it, at the beginning Vergil positions a spondee unconnected and free, as when he says in another place, "*curru iungit Alesus equos*" (to the chariot Alesus harnesses his horses; *Aeneid* 7.724). Although he could have said, "*iungit Alesus equos curru*," he preferred to pay attention to rhythms and aural qualities. Certainly the sound seems

Dilabi enim videtur sonus et pene fugere cum dicit: '*iungit Alesus equos*,' tali praesertim in loco, apparet enim elegiacus semiversus; contra vero consistit vox et sibi ipsi praesidio est, ne, ut dixi, exhalet ac diffluat cum dicitur: '*curru iungit Alesus equos.*' An se ipsum auresque ignoravit suas Virgilius cum dixit:

bina manu lato crispans hastilia ferro?

Cum enim hac in structura singulisque in dictionibus dyssyllabis primas ad syllabas statuatur accentus, quadrato quasi agmine (quaterni nanque accentus e quaternis illis dyssyllabis dictionibus in aciem simul prodeunt) quaterni simul accentus eodem spatio consonant. At nihil generosum habuerit, nihil selectum si protuleris: '*ferrea cum valida crispans hastilia dextra,*' plebeiusque hic versus fuerit, ille vero Maronianus. Et cum alibi dixit: '*contra tela furit,*' an non poterat: '*tela furit contra?*' Sed noluit esse in accinendo praeproperus. Sic cum dixit:[89] '*Turno tempus erit*' et '*Parcae fila legunt.*'

25   Possem hac in parte excitare e somno aliquos, qui dormitare mihi visi sunt in hoc ipso genere numerorum, a quo quidem consilio longe ipse sum alienus. Sat mihi fuerit, dum Pardo vobisque qui hic adestis morem gero, explicare paucis quae sentiam quaeque a me studio quodam Virgilianae diligentiae fuere observata. Claudit pene iisdem numeris constructionem illam Valerius Catullus:

cum lecti iuvenes, Argivae robora pubis,
auratam optantes Colchis avertere pellem,

to disintegrate and almost to vanish when he says, "*iungit Alesus equos*," especially in such a position, for it seems to be half of an elegiac pentameter.[79] On the other hand, however, the sound remains and, as I have said, keeps itself from evaporating and scattering when one says, "*curru iungit Alesus equos*." Or did Vergil pay no attention to himself and his own ears when he said the following?

in his hand gripping two broad-bladed spears. [*Aeneid* 1.313,
    12.165]

Since in this structure and in the individual disyllabic words the accent is placed on the first syllable, in square battle formation, so to speak (for in fact the four accents from those four disyllabic words come forward into the battle line at the same time), the four accents also sound together at the same interval.[80] But it will have nothing noble, nothing distinctive if you trot out, "*ferrea cum valida crispans hastilia dextra*" (steel-bladed spears gripping with his mighty right hand); this verse will be common, but the other is Vergilian. And when he says elsewhere, "*contra tela furit*" (he rages against their spears; *Aeneid* 9.552), could he not have said, "*tela furit contra*"? Yes, but he did not want to be over hasty in accenting.[81] So too when he said, "*Turno tempus erit*" (for Turnus there will be a time; *Aeneid* 10.503) and "*Parcae fila legunt*" (the Parcae gather up the threads; *Aeneid* 10.815).[82]

I could at this point wake up from their slumber some who 25 have seemed to me to be falling asleep in this very type of rhythm, but I have no intention of doing so. It will be enough for me, while I am gratifying Pardo and the rest of you here, to set out in a few words what I think and what I have observed in some study of Vergil's attention to detail. Valerius Catullus constructs this famous passage with the same final rhythms:[83]

when the chosen youth, the might of Argive manhood,
hoping to win the golden fleece from the Colchians,

ausi sunt vada salsa cita decurrere puppi,
coerula verrentes abiegnis aequora palmis.

Sane quam ridiculum videatur ac despicabile si narrare incipias:
'ausi sunt vada salsa cita decurrere puppi / cum lecti iuvenes.' Ac nihilominus Virgilius et ipse duce tamen dactylo (tanta est in
numero ipso vis) incipit explicationem illam coniunctis statim
quinque vocibus iisque dyssyllabis:

larga quidem semper, Drance, tibi copia fandi,

et si alibi incipit a spondeo, ut,

salve, sancte parens, iterum salvete, recepti.

Adeo ubique consulendae sunt aures. An forte, quod a convicio
exordiretur, remorari vocem magis ac magis numeris illis quin-
quies eodem tenore et spatio ingruentibus voluit? Quod mihi
quidem satis fit probabile. An non idem ipse duce quidem dactylo a crebritate eadem numerorum coepit[90] in enarratione illa
tam eximii apparatus?

Primus init bellum Tyrrhenis asper ab oris
contemptor divum Mezentius agminaque armat.

Quo in loco rem ipsam ut magnam, ut horribilem futuram, quo
adaequaret numeris, talique principio finis quoque ut consonaret, intulit *'agminaque armat;'* parum nanque consumatissimis
aurium eius sensibus visum est si conclusisset *'agmen et armat'*
aut *'agmina cogens.'* Itaque ab ipsis extulit pulmonibus *'agminaque*

dared to run through the salt sea in their swift ship
sweeping the blue waves with oars of fir. [Catullus 64.4–7]

It would certainly seem ridiculous and contemptible if you were
to begin the story: "They dared to run through the salt sea in
their swift ship, when the chosen youth."[84] And nonetheless
even Vergil himself, leading with a dactyl (such power is in that
rhythm), begins this utterance with five words back to back,
and disyllables at that:

Drances, you always have plenty of talk, [*Aeneid* 11.378]

and yet in another place he begins with a spondee, like this:

Hail, sacred father, again hail, [ashes], received [in vain].
   [*Aeneid* 5.80][85]

So true is it that in every circumstance we must consult our
ears. Or, because he was starting with abuse, did he perhaps
wish to slow down the sound more and more with those
rhythms attacking five times with the same accent and at the
same interval?[86] This seems very likely to me. Did not the very
same poet, but leading with a dactyl, start from the same repeated rhythm in the famous narration of such an extraordinary display?[87]

First the savage man from the Tyrrhenian land entered the
   war,
Mezentius, despiser of the gods; and he armed his host.
   [*Aeneid* 7.647–48]

Here, inasmuch as the thing itself will be great and horrifying,
he adds *agminaque armat* (and he armed his host) to make it live
up to the rhythm, and also so that the end might be consonant
with such a beginning. Indeed, it would have seemed inade-
quate to the perfect judgment of his ear if he had ended with
agmen et armat or *agmina cogens*. And so he brought up from the
very source of his breath the phrase *agminaque armat*. See then

armat.' Vide igitur quid collisio faciat suo in loco adhibita, quid artificiosus assultus contundentium se se vocalium.

26   Numerus igitur alibi sedatus esse debet, perinde ut oratio, ut verba e quibus oratio ipsa constat, quales sunt narrationes eae in quibus non exigitur vel magnificentia verborum vel pondus sententiarum, sed paratur tantum audientium attentio, ut rhetores praecipiunt, qualis est illa:

Conticuere omnes intentique ora tenebant.
inde toro pater Aeneas sic orsus ab alto:
infandum, regina, iubes renovare dolorem.

Fluunt verba, labitur oratio, nihil confragosum, nihil caesum aut, ex arte ut videatur, collisum habens. Quid explicatione illa mundius?

Sic fatur lacrimans, classique immittit habenas,
et tandem Euboicis Cumarum allabitur oris.

Quid alia illa sedatius?

At regina gravi iamdudum saucia cura
vulnus alit venis et caeco carpitur igni.

Fluunt itaque numeri ipsi, quibus nihil profecto lenius, ut nulla videatur ars adhibita, nulla ipsi appareant cura temperati. At surrigendum supercilium cum fuerit et magno tonandum ore, numeri ipsi conferti, tanquam conserta in pugna milites esse debent, atque ubi est opus ut et ipsi quoque horrorem incutiant, quin et litterae et syllabae vastiores conquirendae sunt, nonnunquam etiam asperiores aut hiulcae. Age, quaeso, quid tibi hac ipsa de exaggeratione videtur?

the effect of elision applied in the right place, of an artful assault of vowels grinding against each other!

Then in another place the rhythm should be quiet in accordance with the language and with the words of which the language is composed, like the narratives that require no lofty words or weighty sentiments, but only insure the attention of the audience, as the teachers of rhetoric prescribe. For example: 26

> All were silent and eagerly checked their speech.
> Then father Aeneas from his lofty seat began thus:
> Unspeakable, o queen, the grief you bid me revive. [*Aeneid* 2.1–3]

The words flow, the speech glides, having nothing jarring, nothing abrupt or clashing to make it seem to arise from art. What is simpler than the following description?

> So he spoke weeping, and let the fleet run ahead,
> and at length he landed on the Euboean coast of Cumae.
> [*Aeneid* 6.1–2]

What is quieter than this other passage?

> But the queen, wounded by heavy care, for some time
> a wound had fed in her veins and was wasted by a hidden
> flame. [*Aeneid* 4.1–2]

In this way the rhythms flow by themselves (and nothing could be gentler), so that there seems to have been no use of art; they appear to have been put together without effort. But when there is a need for heightened seriousness and a voice of thunder, the rhythms themselves should be close packed like soldiers in combat, and when it is necessary for them also to excite terror themselves, why even more intense letters and syllables should be sought out — sometimes even rough or gaping ones.[88] Come now, I ask, what do you think of this accumulation of effects?

Iam Deiphobi dedit ampla ruinam
Vulcano superante domus, iam proximus ardet
Ucalegon; Sigea igni freta lata relucent.
Exoritur clamorque virum clangorque tubarum.

Quae verborum, quae tum litterarum tum syllabarum selectio, *clamor, clangor, virum, tubarum,* qui accentus pene quaterni tam accommodati, *Sigea, igni, freta, lata!* Quid ille qui e vestigio sequitur duarum dictionum ab eadem littera incipientium convocalis sonus: *arma amens capio?* An est, Parde, quod aures ultra exigant tuae? Sed adhuc adverte, quaeso, admirabilem in iis verborum conquisitionem: voces illae ambae dyssyllabae *clamor* et *clangor* a syllabis incipiunt rigidioribus, desinunt in horridis; illae alterae *virum* et *tubarum,* quae copulationem finiunt, in syllabis desinunt subobscuris. Obscuritas vero omnis horrorem incutit; quod idem poeta servavit in illa tempestate, cum dixit:

clamorque virum stridorque rudentum;

quo in versu singulae dictiones versum constituentes litteram habent asperam, qua multiplicata, horror quasi quidam gignitur loco illi debitus. Ipsae quoque inclinativae particulae, dum accentus ad se rapiunt, horrori etiam ipsi non parum adiungunt: *clamorque, stridorque!*

27   Quando autem properare numerus debeat et quomodo properatio ipsa fiat, docet versus ille:

atque levem stipulam crepitantibus urere flammis.

Cupiens enim poeta artificiosissimus flammarum concremationisque illius celeritatem numeris suis reddere, versum e dactylis struxit coegitque dictiones celeritati perquam accommodatas. Quid quod ut strepitum quoque accensarum referret stipula-

Now the great house of Deiphobus crashes in ruins
overpowered by Vulcan, now next to it burns
Ucalegon's; the broad straits of Sigeum glow with fire.
The shouting of men and blare of trumpets rises in the air.
[*Aeneid* 2.310–13]

What a choice of words, of letters and syllables: *clamor, clangor, virum, tubarum!* Such fitting accents, almost four at once: *Sigea, igni, freta, lata!*[89] And what about the assonance immediately afterward of two words beginning with the same letter: *arma amens capio* [*Aeneid* 2.314]?[90] What more could your ears require, Pardo? But also please notice the wonderful mustering of words in this passage. The two disyllables, *clamor* and *clangor*, both begin with hard syllables and end in harsh ones; the others, *virum* and *tubarum*, which mark off the combination, end in somewhat muffled ones.[91] But every muffled sound excites terror, a fact that the same poet keeps in mind when he says in describing the tempest:

the shouting of men and creaking of ropes. [*Aeneid* 1.87]

In this line every single word making up the verse contains the rough letter *r*,[92] and from its repetition arises the terror required in the passage. The enclitic particles, too, since they pull the accents toward themselves, add greatly to the terror itself: *clamórque, stridórque!*[93]

But this verse shows when the rhythm should be quick and 27
how that quickness is achieved:

and to burn the light stubble with crackling flames. [*Georgics*
1.85]

Indeed, the most artful poet, desiring to make his rhythm reflect the speed of the consuming flames, constructed his verse of dactyls and crowded together words well suited to swiftness. Notice too, that in order to recall the crackling sound of burn-

rum, selegit etiam syllabas interstrepentes, quales sunt primae *stipulae* et *crepitantis*, nulla arcessita collisione aut adhibita inclinativa[91] particula.

Rursus qua via sistendum sit et tanquam standum in acie, habent rei huius instar insequentes versus:

stabant orantes primi transmittere cursum

et:

tum demum admissi stagna exoptata revisunt

et:

extemplo Aeneae solvuntur frigore membra.

Qua etiam ratione servanda sit mediocritas, collocatio quidem ipsa dactylorum mistim alternisque cum spondeis monstrare potest; qualis scilicet est versuum qui sequuntur:

et mulcere dedit fluctus et tollere vento,
gens inimica mihi Tyrrhenum navigat aequor.

talia perstabat lacrimans[92] fixusque manebat.

illa solo fixos oculos aversa tenebat.

talia flammato secum dea corde volutans.

Quo tamen in versu quasi erigere supercilium iam pararet, tris illas dyssyllabicas dictiones in acie quasi media collocavit. Omnis igitur illa sive dignitas sive gravitas magnitudoque numero-

ing stubble, he chose crackling syllables like the first ones in *stipulae* and *crepitantis*, without recourse to elision or using an enclitic particle.

On the other hand, the following verses present a model of how to slow a verse and make it stand its ground, so to speak:[94]

they stood praying to be first to cross the river [*Aeneid* 6.313]

and:

then at last they are let in and revisit the longed-for stream [*Aeneid* 6.330]

and:

at once Aeneas' limbs went slack with chill fear. [*Aeneid* 1.92]

Indeed, the very arrangement of dactyls in a mixed array and alternating with spondees like that in the following verses can show how to observe a middle way:[95]

and he has given you the power to soothe the waves or raise them with wind;
a race I hate is sailing on the Tyrrhenian sea; [*Aeneid* 1.66–67]

weeping like this he stood fast and remained immovable; [*Aeneid* 2.650]

turning away, she kept her eyes fixed on the ground; [*Aeneid* 6.469]

the goddess, turning over such thoughts in her angry heart. [*Aeneid* 1.50]

Yet in this last verse, as if to produce an elevated effect at this point, he places three disyllabic words almost in the middle of the array. Consequently all the dignity or gravity and greatness

73

rum a numerositate ipsa gignitur accentuum, de dictionum collocatione syllabarumque delectu profecta, quippe cum syllabae dictionesque accentum, accentus vero numerum, numerus autem et plenum et generosum et admiratione dignum versum statuat.

Quanquam autem nedum Cicero ipse, eloquentiae pater, accentum vocat, sed etiam litteratores universi, quorum quidem proprium est loqui de litteris, syllabis, dictionibus atque earum qualitatibus, utimur tamen hoc nomine eo libentius quod canere dicuntur poetae et Virgilius exordiens verbo est hoc auspicatus: *Arma virumque cano*. Licet videre in versibus quos paulo post afferam quandam quasi fluctuationem nunc sistentium nunc profluentium dictionum: qua e re necesse est ut accentus quoque ipsi incertitudine ac varietate fluctuent sua invicemque alternentur:

'Quis globus, o cives, caligine volvitur atra?
Ferte citi ferrum, date tela et scandite muros.
hostis adest, eia!'[93] Ingenti clamore per omnis
condunt se Teucri portas et moenia complent.

Alibi:[94]

Sternitur infelix Acron et calcibus atram
tundit humum expirans infractaque tela cruentat.
Atque idem fugientem haud est dignatus Orodem
sternere nec iacta caecum dare cuspide vulnus;
obvius adversoque occurrit seque viro vir
contulit, haud furto melior, sed fortibus armis.
Tum super abiectum posito pede nixus et hasta:

of the rhythm arises precisely from the frequency of the accents that stems from the arrangement of words and the choice of syllables.[96] This is the case since the syllables and words establish the accent, the accent the rhythm, and the rhythm a verse that is full and noble and worthy of admiration.

Not only Cicero himself, father of eloquence, invokes accent, but also the whole body of literary men — at least the ones whose task is to talk about letters, syllables, words, and their qualities. Nonetheless I use the term all the more gladly since poets are said to sing (*canere*) and Vergil opens his work beginning with this phrase: *Arma virumque cano* (arms and the man I sing; *Aeneid* 1.1).[97] In the verses I will present in a moment you can see a certain sort of movement back and forth between words standing still and those that flow readily; as a result, the accents themselves necessarily move to and fro, inconsistent and variable, and by turns change places.

"What is that mass, o citizens, moving in the dark gloom?
Quick, bring arms, issue weapons, and scale the walls.
The enemy is here, come on!" With great shouting
the Trojans take shelter inside the gates and man the
    ramparts. [*Aeneid* 9.36–39]

In another place:

Unlucky Acron was felled, and with his heels drummed
the black earth as he died, and drenched his broken
    weapons with blood.
And the same foe did not deign to cut down fleeing Orodes
or to wound him in the back by hurling his spear;
he ran up to cut him off and brought himself up
face to face, not better by stealth but with his brave arms.
Then planting his foot on the fallen man, and pulling at his
    spear:

'Pars belli haud temnenda viris iacet altus Orodes.'
Conclamant socii letum paeana secuti.
Ille autem expirans: 'Non me, quicunque es, inulto,
victor, nec longum letabere; te quoque fata
prospectant paria atque eadem mox arva tenebis.'
Ad quae subridens mista Mezentius ira:
'Nunc morere; ast de me divum pater atque hominum
        rex viderit.'[95]

Quae igitur vocum varietas accentuumque fluctuatio his sit in versibus ipsi videtis.

28   Dicentem audivi saepius senem hunc nostrum quotiens locus incideret aliquis in quo sordescere posset oratio numerique relanguescere, sustentandum illum esse crebritate accentuum, non minus quam verborum delectu; quibus spondei quidem permuniti essent eosque veluti gravem armaturam primos statui in acie oportere, inde dactylos summitti, qui tristitiam illam exhilararent; quod ipse secutus esset in toto illo loco qui est de Pristice:

Ipsi de rate turrigera aut e puppibus altis
ferratis instant hastis iaciuntque tridentes
pinnigeros. Imo referunt se se icta profundo.

Nec multo post:

Agmina perturbat videasque indagine in una
urgeri armentum vasti aequoris. Ille trucidat
ense ferox, hic sullata secat ossa securi,

"Here lies tall Orodes, a part of the war not to be
    discounted by men!"
His comrades shouted and raised the joyful cry of triumph.
But the dying man: "Whoever you are, victor, you won't
    rejoice long
and with me unavenged; the same fates are facing you,
and soon you too will occupy this same piece of ground."
To this, Mezentius spoke, both angry and smiling:
"Now die. But the father of gods and king of men
will see to me." [*Aeneid* 10.730–44]

You see for yourselves then what a variety of sounds and fluctuation of accents there is in these verses.

Quite often I have heard this old man of ours say that whenever a passage cropped up in which the language could become paltry and the rhythms flabby, it needed to be propped up by close-spaced accents as much as by the choice of words; it was necessary for the spondees to be built up and put in position first like heavy-armed troops and then for the dactyls to be called in to liven up the severity—the course that he himself had followed in his whole passage on the Whale.[98]

The men from a tower-crowned vessel or lofty ships
attack with steel spears and throw winged tridents.
Struck, the monsters take themselves to the lowest depths.
    [Pontano, *Urania* 4.426–28]

And soon after:

The fleet throws the pod into confusion and you might see
    the herd
of the vast sea being penned up in a single enclosure. One
    savagely
butchers with his sword; another cleaves bones with a raised
    ax

28

aut unco trahit ad litus praedaque superbus
ingentis media tauros resupinat arena.

Post etiam subdit:

Hic latis strata in tabulis suffixa ve ad uncos
ferratos, duplici horrescunt pendentia dorso,
et squamosa rigent duris ad tergora pinnis.
Urbs ipsa armentum ad Nerei et spolia effera currit,
ac montana ruit longe ad spectacula pubes.

Extulit idem hic exilem sane rem solis quidem numeris, delectu tamen verborum adhibito conquisitisque rebus aliquanto
remotioribus, imprimisque litterarum sonis, e quibus numeros
et graves et plenos elicuit:

Ast Tingin Bocchique domos, habitataque Mauris
tecta, deosque humeris coelumque Atlanta ferentem,
insignisque auro et pomis radiantibus hortos
Hesperidum ac deserta siti[96] Getula leonumque
arva fame[97] Mars armipotens et Scorpius ardens
inspectant leti coelo et sua iura tuentur,
hic chelis, ille ense potens.

Quid autem exilius quam quod dicturus erat, Getuliam ac Tingitanam[98] subiectas esse Scorpio? Afferam et alium locum huius

or drags to the shore with a hook and proud of his spoil
beats huge bulls to death in the midst of the sand. [*Urania*
    4.434–38]

Later he adds:

Here laid out on broad planks or fastened to hooks
of steel, they are horrible, hanging with backs folded double,
and they grow stiff with their hard fins pressed to scaly
    hides.
The city runs to the herd of Nereus and the fierce spoils,
and youth from the mountains rush a long way for the
    sight. [*Urania* 4.450–54]

In the following passage the same poet has enhanced a very
thin subject with rhythm alone, to be sure, yet also by a dis-
criminating choice of words, a muster of rather far-off things,
and especially by the sounds of letters, from which he has elic-
ited rhythms both weighty and full:

But Tingi and the house of Bocchus and the dwellings
    inhabited
by Moors, and Atlas bearing the gods and the sky on his
    shoulders,
and the gardens of the Hesperides gorgeous with gold and
    gleaming fruit
and the Gaetulian plains deserted because of thirst and the
    hunger of lions —
these Mars powerful in arms and burning Scorpio view
with pleasure from the sky and safeguard as their
    dominions,
the one mighty with claws, the other with sword. [*Urania*
    5.581–87][99]

What was thinner than the point he was going to make, that
Gaetulia and Tingitana were under the control of Scorpio? And

similem, cum dicturus esset Africam ac Numidiam Cancro esse subiectam:

> At Cancer noctisque decus Latonia virgo
> Lotophagum sedes tenet et quos Bragrada saltus
> infidusque secat Cynips[99] et Punica late
> litora quaque vagus se solvit in aequora Triton
> et formidatas olim Carthaginis arces
> ac latebras,[100]Masinisa,[101] tuas cavaque antra leonum.

29   Scimus etiam eundem ipsum fuisse solicitum eo de versu qui est in Andromeda:

> Virginibus praeferre maris se se ausa suumque
> ostentans[102] decus.

Sic enim initio scripserat, verum quod tristem iudicaret ac lugubrem materiam, tarditate potius numerorum quam festivitate prosequendam esse, ab exordio praesertim ipso, commutatis dictionibus, remoratus est celeritatem. Etenim, ut Aristoteles etiam asseverat, celeritas acumen soni gignit, tarditas gravitatem. Itaque, subtracta inde dictione quadrisyllaba ac commutatis locis, collocavit ibi dictiones dyssyllabas quidem duas adiecitque statim monosyllabam ac dixit:

> Ausa maris se virginibus praeferre suumque
> ostentans decus, aequoreas armare sorores.

Quo factum est ut tenor ipse primi pedis, qui uno constabat ex accentu ac fluitabat, altero statim adiecto sustentaretur atque ingravesceret, siquidem e *virginibus* unus tantum consonabat accentus, at *ausa*, cum unum ex se se accentum efflet et quidem circumflexum, *maris* alterum eumque acutum, efficitur ut sonus

I will bring up another place like it, when he wanted to say that
Africa and Numidia were subject to Cancer.

But Cancer and Latona's daughter, ornament of the night,
protect the seats of the Lotus Eaters and the ravines that
    Bragrada
and treacherous Cinyps cleave and the Punic shores
on all sides and the place where wandering Triton flows into
    the sea
and the once dreaded stronghold of Carthage
and your retreats, Masinisa, and the arched caves of lions.
    [*Urania* 5.602–7][100]

We know that the same poet was also concerned about this   29
verse on Andromeda:

To the sea maidens she dared to prefer herself,
and boasting of her beauty. . . . [*Urania* 4.312–13]

This is what he wrote to start with, but because he thought
that the melancholy and mournful subject should be described
with slow rather than rolicking rhythms, especially at the beginning, he changed the words and slowed the speed. Indeed, as
Aristotle asserts, speed produces a high sound, slowness a low
one. And so, by taking away the four-syllable word [*virginibus*]
and changing the order, he placed two disyllables there, immediately added a monosyllable, and said:

She dared to prefer herself to the sea maidens,
and boasting of her beauty, to challenge the watery sisters.
    [*Urania* 4.312–13]

Thereby the movement of the first foot, which used to wobble,
consisting of a single accent, was bolstered with the addition of
a second accent and increased in intensity, for only one accent
rang out from *virginibus,* but with *ausa*—since it emits from itself one accent and circumflex at that, and *maris* has a second

ipse dactylicus duplicetur, qua e re tenor ipse et sistitur et ingravescit. Idem hoc servavit alio in versu, qui primo fuerat:

et de marmoreis guttas stillare columnis.

Cumque iudicaret eo in loco opus esse soni remoratione, usus est eadem commutatione dictionum:

et guttas de marmoreis stillare columnis.

Numerus enim ille e *marmoreis*, quadrisyllaba dictione, constitutus, quod esset ipse festinantior, reddebatur aliquanto fluentior et pene lubricus; at terni illi accentus tribus e dictionibus conflati confertimque assonantes alter alteri quasi manum de proximo sibi porrigunt aciemque ipsam sustinent.

Attulimus hoc praesertim in loco e senis nostri libris exempla, quod consilia eius ex eodem ipso cognovimus. Nam veterum poetarum Virgiliiique ipsius suspicari quidem illa tantum possumus.

Inest et suum quoque numeris decorum, ut cum vel aspera, vel suavis, vel miserabilis, vel iucunda res, vel gravis, vel contra levis versatur in manibus, vel suis aliis affectibus mista et temperata. Vide igitur quibus Virgilius usus est numeris in prognosticatione illa futurae tempestatis:

heu qui nam[103] tanti cinxerunt aethera nimbi.

Ad metum, ad dolorem, ad ducis curam exprimendam coegit tres simul monosyllabas dictiones, summisit deinde dyssyllabam, post alteram atque alteram trisyllabam, iunxitque quatuor simul spondeos. Quid hac aut verborum conquisitione diligentius aut animi conquestione gravius? Nec me quorundam[104]

30

accent, an acute one—the sound of the dactyl is doubled; for this reason the movement itself is supported and gains force.[101] The same poet kept this in mind in another verse, which originally had been:

> And from marble columns drops fall. [Pontano, *Meteororum liber* 1356]

And since he thought that the sound should be slowed in this place, he employed the same change in word order:

> And drops from marble columns fall. [*Meteororum liber* 1356]

The rhythm formed by the quadrisyllabic word *marmoreis*, because it was a little fast by itself, turned out to be somewhat too loose and almost elusive; but the three accents brought together from the three words and resounding in close order one after the other stretch out a hand to each other from nearby and support the line.[102]

We have brought up these examples from the work of our old man especially in this place because we have learned his intentions from the very man himself. In the case of the ancient poets and of Vergil himself we can only infer them.

Rhythms are also suitable for particular effects, as when a difficult matter or a pleasing or pitiful or pleasant one is in hand, or a serious or light one instead, or one mixed and tempered with other emotions. See then what rhythms Vergil uses in this prediction of the coming tempest:

> Oh, what great thunderclouds beset the sky! [*Aeneid* 5.13]

To express the fear, the distress, the concern of the leader, he has assembled three monosyllables at once, then sent in a disyllable, and then two trisyllables one after the other, bringing together four spondees at the same time. What could be more careful than this mustering of words or more serious than this mental anguish? And I will not be moved by the authority of

auctoritas moverit asseverantium a Virgilio scriptum *heu quia*, non *qui*, cum nos iudicemus neque *quia* neque *quid*, sed *qui* fuisse a Virgilio scriptum; nam et littera *d* pleniusculum nescio quid sonat, quod hic ipse numerus nunc renuit, et *quia* brevitate plusculum festinat sua, cum vox ipsa videatur in dolore sistenda. Sed de hoc sit suum cuiusque iudicium, nostra quidem haec est opinio.

Decorandos igitur ad numeros tum litterae tum syllabae, nedum verba integra maximum habent pondus, et, quod non multo ante diximus, in illo versu:

insequitur clamorque virum stridorque rudentum.

nulla ex illis dictionibus asperiore caret littera. Nanque aliarum principium, aliarum finis, aliarum et principium et pausa trahit secum asperitatem litterae rigidioris. Quid quod cum in tempestate obscuritas terrorem augeat, *virum* et *rudentum* ultimae sonant etiam nescio quid subobscurum?

Animipendite, quaeso, versus illius numeros qui est:

Monstrarat,[105] caput acris equi, sic nam fore bello
egregiam et facilem victu per secula gentem.

Qui praecedunt tres versus et huius ipsius dimidium tribus clauduntur accentibus iisque dyssyllabis. Ne igitur a gravitate descisceret sua, conflavit binis e monosyllabis totidemque e dyssyllabis dictionibus accentus quatuor, quodque satis est rarum, octo versum illum locupletavit accentibus, quo fit ut tardius pronuntietur; tarditas autem, ut diximus, gravioris est soni causa, perinde ut acutioris celeritas; acutum autem et grave in iis quae auditus sunt habentur a physicis opposita; qua tamen

those who assert that Vergil wrote *heu quia*, not *qui*, since I believe that Vergil wrote neither *quia* nor *quid*, but *qui*; for the letter *d* makes a sound that is a little too full, which is not acceptable to the rhythm here, and *quia* is a bit too rushed in its brevity, since it seems necessary for the sound itself to be brought to a halt in distress.[103] But let everyone have his own opinion about it; this what I think, at any rate.

Well then, both letters and syllables, to say nothing of whole words, have great value in embellishing rhythm, and as I said a minute ago, in this verse:

insequitur clamorque virum stridorque rudentum, [*Aeneid* 1.87][104]

every one of the words has the rough letter *r*. Indeed, of some words the beginning, of others the end, of others both the beginning and the stopping point bring with them the harsh sound of a hard letter.[105] Furthermore, since terror in a storm is increased by uncertainty, the ends of the words *virum* and *rudentum* make a muffled sound.

Pay attention, if you please, to the rhythms of the next verse:[106]

[which] she had revealed, the head of a spirited horse; for thus would

the nation be eminent in war and prosperous through the ages. [*Aeneid* 1.444–45]

The three preceding verses and the first half of this one are closed with three accented disyllabic words.[107] So that the verse might not deviate from its proper solemnity, he has brought together four accents from two monosyllables and as many disyllables, and — a thing that is pretty rare — he has enriched the verse with eight accents, so that it is pronounced more slowly; moreover, slowness, as we have said, is the source of a lower sound, as speed is of a higher one.[108] Now high and low in matters of hearing are considered opposites by the natural

in re, quo modum retineret, copulavit statim binos dactylos, qui tarditatem illam moderarentur. Sunt autem versus hi:

Lucus in urbe fuit media letissimus umbra,[106]
quo primum iactati undis et turbine Poeni
effodere loco signum, quod regia Iuno
monstrarat, caput acris equi, sic nam fore bello
egregiam et facilem victu per secula gentem.

31   In tertio quoque loco digne idem fit vocalium concursus, ut:

ni faciat, maria ac terras coelumque profundum

ut item:

contigit oppetere, o Danaum fortissime gentis

et ut:

erramus vento, huc et vastis fluctibus acti.

Magnam utique gravitatis partem amiserit si mutaveris: 'Erramus vento et vastis huc fluctibus acti.' Itaque hoc quidem modo erit hiatus ipse copulandi tantum necessitate factus, illo vero implendi ac sistendi sonoris gratia ab arteque profectus. At in quarto et quinto pede quotiens fit atque in sexto et ad pausam, et versus ipse suo cum numero mirifice assurgit quadam etiam cum magnitudine et rara quaedam inde comparatur numeris ipsis dignitas; quod versus illi declarant:

philosophers, yet in the following case, in order to avoid excess, he has combined two dactyls one after the other to keep the slowness in bounds. These are the verses:

> There was a grove in the middle of the city, very rich in
>   shade,
> where first the Carthaginians, tossed by waves and wind,
> dug out the sign, which royal Juno
> had revealed, the head of a spirited horse; for thus would
> the nation be eminent in war and prosperous through the
>   ages. [*Aeneid* 1.441–45]

It is also suitable to run vowels together in the third foot, 31 too.[109] So:

> if he should not do so, seas and lands and vast sky. [*Aeneid*
>   1.58]

Likewise:

> [whose] fate was to perish! O bravest of the race of Danai.
>   [*Aeneid* 1.96]

And like this:

> we went off course with the wind, and here by monstrous
>   waves we were driven. [*Aeneid* 1.333]

This last verse would surely lose a great part of its force if you changed it: "We went off course with the wind and by mon-strous waves were driven here." Accordingly, in the latter version hiatus will have been created only by the need to create a con-nection, but in the former, it has arisen from art to make the sound full and bring it to a halt.[110] But whenever hiatus occurs in the fourth and fifth foot and in the sixth and at a stopping point [*pausa*], the verse itself with its rhythm rises wonderfully, even with a certain abundance, and as a result the rhythms themselves provide an unusual excellence, as the following verses demonstrate:[111]

franguntur remi, tum prora avertit . . . ,

item:

et vera incessu patuit dea. ille ubi matrem,

et:

fundamenta locant, alii immanisque columnas
rupibus excidunt, scaenis decora alta futuris,

et:

Troes te miseri, ventis maria omnia vecti,

et:

omnibus exhaustos iam casibus, omnium egenos,

et:

sevus ubi Aeacidae[107] telo iacet Hector, ubi ingens,

et:

contemptor divum Mezentius, agminaque armat,

item:

aerea cui gradibus surgebant limina nexaeque
aere trabes,

⟨et⟩:[108]

et magnos membrorum artus, magna ora[109] lacertosque
exuit

the oars are broken, then the prow turns . . . [*Aeneid*
1.104][112]

likewise:

and she is revealed by her step as a true goddess; when he
[recognized] his mother [*Aeneid* 1.405][113]

and:

some lay the foundations and cut huge columns
out of the cliffs, lofty adornments for a future theater
[*Aeneid* 1.428–29][114]

and:

[we] wretched Trojans, having sailed all the seas, [implore]
you [*Aeneid* 1.524][115]

and:

by every disaster now exhausted, of everything bereft
[*Aeneid* 1.599][116]

and:

where fierce Hector lies slain by Achilles' spear, where huge
[Sarpedon] [*Aeneid* 1.99][117]

and:

Mezentius, despiser of the gods [entered the war]; and he
armed his host [*Aeneid* 7.648][118]

likewise:

its bronze threshold towered above the steps, and its beams
were entwined with bronze [*Aeneid* 1.448–49][119]

and:

. . . he bared the great sinews of his limbs, his great
countenance
and muscles [*Aeneid* 5.422–23][120]

item:[110]

> iamque[111] iter emensi turres ac tecta Latinorum
> ardua cernebant.

et:

> inseritur vero nucis e foetu[112] arbutus horrida
> et steriles platani malos gessere valentis.

Affert autem raritas haec hiandi cum insequenti versu non sine aurium voluptate etiam dignitatem; nam et novitas delectat ipsa per se et assultus ille hinc versum inchoantis, illinc terminantis vocalis suam quoque vocalitatem auget, qui fit praesertim absque detractione, ut in illis:

> classemque[113] sub ipsa
> Antandro et Phrygiae molimur montibus Idae,

et:

> talem dives arat Capua et vicina Vesevo
> ora iugo.

In horum autem versuum commemoratione non possum non ridere opinionem vel asseverationem potius eorum qui dicunt fuisse a Virgilio scriptum *vicina Vesevo Nola iugo*, mutatum vero post ob denegatam sitienti aquam. Neque enim Virgilius, qui Nolanum plane agrum sterilem nosset minimeque triticum alere, sed milii solius ac secalae feracem, inter fertiles eum numerasset Campanoque coniunxisset, quin vicinam oram nominans campos innuit Acerranos, qui sub ipsum iacent Vesevum occasum versus suntque fertilissimi. Suos igitur numeros

likewise:

> and now having completed their journey, they saw the
>   towers and
> lofty roofs of the Latins [*Aeneid* 7.160–61][121]

and:

> indeed, the rough abutus is grafted from the fruit of the
>   nut,
> and barren plane trees have borne healthy apples.
>   [*Georgics* 2.69–70][122]

And indeed, this rare hiatus with a following verse also adds
distinction, as well as pleasing the ear.[123] The novelty is delightful in itself, and the clash of the vowel beginning the second
verse on the one side, and that ending the first verse on the
other increases the euphony.[124] This happens expecially without
removal of a letter (elision), as in these cases:[125]

> and we toiled to put together a fleet
> near Antandros and the slopes of Phrygian Ida
>   [*Aeneid* 3.5–6]

and:

> Such soil rich Capua tills, and the coast near
> the ridge of Vesuvius. [*Georgics* 2.224–25]

But as I recall these last verses I have to laugh at the opinion, or
rather, insistence of those who say that Vergil wrote: "Nola near
the ridge of Vesuvius," and that it was changed after water was
denied to him when he was thirsty.[126] But Vergil, since he
clearly knew that the soil of Nola is barren and does not produce wheat but bears only millet and rye, would not have
counted it among fertile places and linked it with Campania;
indeed, when he mentioned "the coast nearby," he meant the
fields of Acerra, which lie close by Vesuvius itself on the west
and are extremely fertile. So he was keeping his rhythms and

suorumque concentuum suavitatem sequebatur cum scripsit *vicina Vesevo / ora iugo.*

32 Collisio igitur vocalium, quam et contusionem et concursum a re ipsa vocare possumus, fieri singulis in pedibus eorumque concisionibus potest. (Vocamus autem concisiones ipsas pedum inter se complicationes; Graece nomen habent a numero syllabarum tritimemeris, heptimemeris, enneamemeris.)[114] Eaque duobus fit modis, cum aut eaedem concurrunt vocales aut cum diversae; ubi eaedem se se collidunt extruditurque e versu altera, ea tum ademptio tum extrusio recte vocatur, non minus fortasse proprie explosio. Ipsum autem concursum Cicero hiatum vocat et vocales ipsas dicit hiare; at cum permanent neque truduntur loco boatum sunt e litteratoribus qui vocaverint, rectius utique complosio vocabitur, quod e resultu geminetur sonus, ut in illo:

ter sunt conati imponere Pelio Ossan.[115]

Ipse vero resultus longe minor existit cum e diversis fit vocalibus, ut: *Ionio in magno.* Atque ego quidem, libere vobiscum ut loquar, praeterquam quod Graecam habet imitationem affertque varietatem, quae per se ipsa delectat et naturalis est, non video cur a Latinis complosio magnopere sit probanda, cum vix delectet, nisi in iis quae a Graecis sunt accepta, qualis ille versus: *Glauco et Panopeae et Inoo Melicertae et Dardanio Anchisa* et *in Actaeo Aracyntho.* Raritas tamen ipsa et quam dixi varietas potest reddere illam et venustam et suavem, suo tamen accommodatoque in loco, ac verbis idoneis.

the sweetness of their harmony in mind when he wrote "*vicina Vesevo / ora iugo.*"

Well then, collision (elision) of vowels, which we can also 32 call "crushing" and "running together" from the event itself, can occur in individual feet and in their caesurae. (We give the name caesura to the linkages of feet among themselves; they have Greek names from the number of syllables: trithemimeral, hepthemimeral, enneamimeral.[127]) This comes about in two ways: either when the same vowels run together, or when different ones do; when the same vowels collide and one is thrust out of the verse, the effect is correctly called "taking away" (*ademptio*) and "pushing out" (*extrusio*) and perhaps no less properly, "ejection" (*explosio*).[128] Cicero, however, calls the running together "gaping" (*hiatus*) and says that the vowels themselves gape (*hiare*).[129] But when the vowels stand fast and are not thrust from their place, some grammarians call it a "bellowing" (*boatus*); more correctly, to be sure, it is called "clapping" (*complosio*), because from the rebounding (*resultus*) of the vowels the sound is doubled, as in this example:

Thrice they attempted to place Ossa atop Pelion. [*Georgics* 1.281][130]

This rebounding is much less, though, when it is produced by different vowels, as in *Ionio in magno.*[131] And for my part, indeed, to speak freely to you, beyond the imitation of Greek and the variety associated with it, which is pleasing in itself and natural, I do not see why *complosio* should be greatly approved by the Latins since it is scarcely pleasing except in words taken over from the Greeks, like the verse *Glauco et Panopeae et Inoo Melicertae*, and *Dardanio Anchisa* and *in Actaeo Aracyntho.*[132] Nevertheless, rarity itself and the variety I have mentioned can make it elegant and agreeable, but in an appropriate place and with suitable words.

Cum autem concursus fuerit in primo pede, ea e re numerus ipse fit solidior, cum quadam etiam iucunditate, praesertim ubi eaedem concurrunt vocales, ut *ille ego qui quondam* et *ergo omnis longo solvit se Teucria luctu* et *illi indignantes magno cum murmure montis*. At cum diversae vocales hiant, numerus solidescit ipse quidem, non eadem tamen cum voluptate audientium, ut *credo equidem nec vana fides* et *cuncta equidem tibi rex*. Solidiorem autem stabilioremque numerum inde fieri manifesto apparebit; si dixeris *cuncta quidem tibi rex*, qua e re numerus ipse statim languescet.

Interdum collisione ex ipsa vel extruditur vel exciditur potius integra syllaba vel eius bona pars, idest vocalis cum consonante littera *m*, ut *postquam introgressi*, et *illum expirantem transfixo pectore*; item *illum et labentem Teucri*. Ex hoc si detraxeris *et*, deque altero *ex*, dixerisque *illum labentem Teucri, illum spirantem transfixo pectore*, curtum nescio quid aures statim offenderit. Hoc autem ideo dicimus quod non ubique collisiones ipsae fiunt necessitate carminis, sed arte potius atque aurium obsequio, idest numerorum gratia. Cur autem syllabae ex vocali et *m* compactae deturbentur ubique nunc e versu (nam[116] priscis illis seculis non semper excludi esse solitum versus ille Ennianus docet: *et*[117] *millia militum octo*), videtur causae illud esse, quod syllabae[118] propter *m* terminalem optusum nescio quid ac subobscurum sonent, quod aures vix patiantur in fine vocum.

Itaque nec mirum est si e dictione *sed*, quae olim fuit *sedum*, detruncatio facta est, quando populi quidam finalem *m* compluribus e dictionibus sustulere. Quod ipse aliquot in monumentis summae vetustatis animadverti, ut Beneventi in lapide, in quo scriptum est: *Infelix fatu prior debui mori mater*. Et Telesiae: *Mater*

Well then, when running together occurs in the first foot, it firms up the rhythm in a pleasing way, especially when the vowels running together are the same, as in these cases: *ille ego qui quondam,* and *ergo omnis longo solvit se Teucria luctu,* and *illi indignantes magno cum murmure montis.*[133] But when different vowels gape, the rhythm does indeed become firm, to be sure, but not with the same pleasure of the hearers, as in *credo equidem nec vana fides,* and *cuncta equidem tibi rex.*[134] As a consequence, however, clearly the rhythm will appear firmer and more stable; if you say, "*cuncta quidem tibi rex,*" the rhythm will immediately lose force.

Sometimes the collision results in the expulsion or excision of a whole syllable or a good part of it, that is, of a vowel with the consonant *m.* Thus: *postquam introgressi,* and *illum expirantem transfixo pectore,* likewise *illum et labentem Teucri.*[135] If you take away *et* from the last example, and *ex* from the previous one and say, "*illum labentem Teucri,*" "*illum spirantem transfixo pectore,*" at once something cut off offends the ear. We say this because collisions do not occur in every instance through metrical necessity, but rather through artistry and respect for the ear — that is, for the sake of rhythm. The reason that syllables compounded of a vowel and *m* are now pulled out of the verse in every instance (for Ennius' line *et millia militum octo*[136] shows that they were not always habitually excluded in earlier ages), seems to be that because of the final *m,* the syllables make a weak and indistinct sound that the ear scarcely tolerates at the end of a word.

And so it is not surprising that *sed* has been made as a truncation from the word that was formerly *sedum* since people took away the final *m* from many words. I myself have noticed this in several monuments of the greatest antiquity, like a stone in Benevento, on which is written: "Unhappy fate. I, the mother, should have died first" [*CIL* 9.2045]. And at Telese: "My poor

misera hoc monumentu extruxit Olympias amens. In quibus et *fatum* et *monumentum* sunt absque *m.* Referam verba epigrammatis:

Apollonia quae vocitabar
lapide hoc inclusa quiesco.
Unum sortita maritum,
servavi casta pudorem.
Mater misera hoc monumentu
extruxit Olympias amens.[119]

An non prisci illi fecerunt *gelu* et *cornu,* quae prius erant *gelum* et *cornum,* quorum priori Lucretius non semel utitur? Iidem litteram *s* frequentissime explodebant e versu, ut idem Lucretius testis est. Graeci terminationibus iis carent quae in *m* desinunt, Latinis autem eae sunt familiarissimae et, ut adverti, etiam Ethiopibus. Sed redeamus unde digressi sumus.

33   Eiusmodi quoque litterarum hiatus fiunt in secundo pede sustentandi tenoris atque implendi numeri gratia, etiam cum dignitate, nullam tamen ob necessitatem, ut in illo:

ductoresque ipsos primum capita alta ferentis.

Potuerat enim dicere, *ductores ipsos.* Et in illo:

praeterea aut supplex aris imponet[120] honorem,

videbitur autem tenor ille flaccescere si dixeris, *praeterea supplex ve aris imponet honorem,* cum in illa collocatione non solum hiet *a,* verum alterum *a,* quod est primum elementum in voce *aris,* de proximo loco hiatum ipsum assonando adiuvet. In tertio quoque maiore fit cum vocalitate, ut:

mother Olympias, mad with grief, built this monument" [*CIL* 9.2272.9–10]. In these inscriptions the words *fatum* and *monumentum* lack the final *m*. I shall report the words of the epigram:

> I who was called Apollonia
> rest, shut in by this stone.
> My lot a single husband,
> I chastely guarded my modesty.
> My poor mother this monument
> Built, Olympias, mad with grief. [*CIL* 9.2272.1–2, 7–10][137]

And did the ancients not create *gelu* and *cornu*, formerly *gelum* and *cornum*? Lucretius used the first of these more than once.[138] They also very often ejected *s* from the verse, as Lucretius also attests. The Greeks lack terminations ending in *m*, but these are very familiar to the Latins and — as I have noted — even to the Ethiopians. But let us return to the subject.

Letters are run together like this also in the second foot to sustain the tone and complete the rhythm, excellently indeed, yet not for any necessity, as in this case: 33

> and the leaders themselves first, with heads held high.
>   [*Aeneid* 1.189][139]

In fact, he could have said, "the leaders themselves." And in this one:

> or henceforth will a suppliant put a gift on the altars?
>   [*Aeneid* 1.49][140]

Indeed, the tone will seem flabby if you say: "or a suppliant henceforth — will one put a gift on the altars?" That is so since in the first ordering not only is *a* elided, but also a second *a*, the first letter in the word *aris*, chimes in with the elision and supports it from its position nearby. In the third foot too, elision occurs with an increase in euphony, as in:

97

ni faciat, maria ac terras coelumque profundum.

Sordescet plane numerus si dixeris, *ni faciat, pelagus, terras coelumque profundum.*[121] [At in quarto et quinto pede quotiens fit, in sexto item, et versus ipse mirifice assurgit, quadam etiam cum magnitudine, et rara quaedam inde comparatur numeris ipsis dignitas; quod declarant Virgiliani illi:

haec[122] ait, et dicto citius tumida aequora placat;

fundamenta locant alii, immanisque columnas
rupibus excidunt, scaenis decora alta futuris;

et vera incessu patuit dea; ille ubi matrem
agnovit, tali fugientem est voce secutus;

Troes te miseri ventis maria omnia vecti;

omnibus exhaustos iam casibus, omnium egenos;

sevus ubi Aeacidae telo iacet Hector, ubi ingens.]

Hiatus etiam ille atque complosio quae fit cum insequenti versu, ut dictum est,[123] raritate sua affert etiam cum aurium voluptate dignitatem. Nam et novitas quasi repente edita delectat per se et assultus ille hinc versum inchoantis, illinc terminantis vocalis suam quoque vocalitatem accumulat, ut:

if he should not do so, seas and lands and vast sky.
    [*Aeneid* 1.58][141]

The rhythm will clearly be slovenly if you say: "if he should not do so, sea, lands and vast sky."[142] [But whenever elision occurs in the fourth and fifth foot, and likewise in the sixth, the verse itself rises up wonderfully, even with a certain abundance, and as a result the rhythms themselves provide a certain unusual excellence.[143] These Vergilian lines will demonstrate the point:

he said this, and swifter than his speech, he calmed the
    swollen seas; [*Aeneid* 1.142][144]

some lay the foundations and cut huge columns
out of the cliffs, lofty adornments for a future theater;
    [*Aeneid* 1.428–29]

and she is revealed by her step as a true goddess; when he
    recognized
his mother, with these words he followed her as she fled;
    [*Aeneid* 1.405–6][145]

[we] wretched Trojans, having sailed over all the seas,
    [implore] you; [*Aeneid* 1.524]

by every disaster now exhausted, of everything bereft;
    [*Aeneid* 1.599]

where fierce Hector lies slain by Achilles' spear, where huge
    [Sarpedon]. [*Aeneid* 1.99]]

The hiatus and "clapping" that occurs with a following verse, as I have said, because of its rarity also brings distinction along with pleasure to the ear. Indeed, the novelty produced almost out of the blue is delightful in itself, and the clash of the vowel beginning the second verse on the one side, and that ending the first verse on the other also enhances its euphony.[146] For example:[147]

. . . it clamor ad alta
atria,

et:

expectata dies aderat nonamque serena
Auroram Phaethontis[124] equi iam luce vehebant,

et:

famaque finitimos et clari nomen Acestae
excierat,

et:

in medio sacri tripodes viridesque coronae
et palmae pretium victoribus,

et:

manifesto in lumine vidi
intrantem portus.[125]

34   Verum ego longior forte et ambitiosior explicandis his fui,
feci hoc tamen eo libentius quod scriptum de his adhuc sciam a
nemine, quanquam et multa quoque a me praeterita sunt, quae
post alii et inquirent ipsi acutius et apposite magis explicabunt.
Sat etiam scio esse e vobis longe quam ego sum rerum harum
qui sint studiosiores. Itaque, quod hic convenerimus, te praesertim, Parde, auctore, relinquendus est cuique suus etiam dicendi
locus.

Pard. Mihi quidem, Sincere Acti, si inficias irem satis a te non esse
factum, inique fecerim. Satisfecisti profecto, nec minus docte
quam copiose. Sunt vero etiam qui vultu iam ipso praeseferant
allaturos aliquid, quod se, quod hoc ipso conventu dignum
iudicent quodque locus quidem ipse vel exigit sedentibus nobis,

a cry rose up to the heights
of the hall [*Aeneid* 4.665–66]

and:

the long-awaited day was there and in the fine clear
light the Sun's horses brought in the ninth dawn [*Aeneid*
5.104–5]

and:

and the reputation and name of famous Acestes
had brought out people living nearby [*Aeneid* 5.106–7]

and:

in the middle sacred tripods and green garlands
and palms as the prize of the victors [*Aeneid* 5.110–11]

and:

I saw him in clear light
entering the harbor. [*Aeneid* 4.358–59]

But perhaps I have gone on much too long and insistently in   34
discussing these matters, yet I have done so more freely because
I know that no one has yet written about them—although I
have also passed over many points that others will look into
more acutely for themselves and discuss more suitably. I also
know very well that some of you are far more learned on this
subject than I am. Accordingly, because we are assembled here,
especially on your suggestion, Pardo, each one must be given his
chance to speak.[148]

Pardo. If I were to deny, Azio Sincero, that you have done enough,
at least for me, I would be acting unjustly. You have certainly
given satisfaction, with no less learning than eloquence. Indeed,
some are already showing by their expressions that they intend
to offer something they judge worthy of themselves and of this
assemblage and something that the place itself requires when

vel etiam per se postulat. Atque, ut risu ex ipso praesentio, Summontius[126] hic noster egregium aliquid meditatus iam exurgit verecundiaeque est tuae dare locum dicenti.

Sum. Ego vero, Parde, arbitror Sincerum nostrum multa nos celare velle, quo post, ut mercatores consuevere, longe pluris vendat quod in arca sepositum est, viliori merce iam divendita. Explicasti vel enucleasti potius nobis, Acti, et quidem non iucunde minus quam memoriter, hiatus et explosiones quique inde gignantur numeri, quotam autem partem poeticae Virgilianaeque potissimum numerositatis! Resera igitur arcas mercemque nobis selectiorem explica, quod te per Manes ipsos Virgilii optestatus oro perque locum in quo ille iacuit, quem ipse et invisis saepissime et reverentissime veneraris.

Act. Percalluisti,[127] Petre Summonti, qua me esses arte eam ad rem tracturus, quae fuerit ab hominibus nostris hactenus vel omnino despecta vel parum certe animadversa aut cognita, dum mercatorum mecum exemplo uteris atque consuetudine. Scis enim nobilitas haec nostra omnis ab mercaturae ipsius nomine quantopere abhorreat. Ne tu me igitur aut mercatorem existimes aut avarum, explicabo consilia tibi mea quaeque indagandis poeticis numeris a me fuere diligentius observata, non ut arbitrer me tamen assecutum quod et ipse voluissem et vos forte audire nunc expectatis. Prosequar itaque susceptam de numeris ipsis partem quodque per Virgilii tantum me es Manes optestatus, Virgilii fere unius exemplis agam, quando unus hic de nostris poeticarum virtutum instar est omnium, ac maxime numerorum.

35   Omnino poeticus numerus carminis ipsius structuram sequitur, structura vero ipsa constat e dictionibus, dictiones autem accentum constituunt, singulae singulos. Ipsi quoque accentus

we are sitting here—or even demands for its own sake.[149] Besides, as I can tell just from the laughter, our friend Summonte here is standing up with some outstanding utterance already in mind; and it is courteous of you to let him speak.

Summonte. In fact, Pardo, I think that our Sincero means to conceal many things from us so that afterward, as merchants like to do, he might sell what is set aside in his chest for a far greater price after his cheaper merchandise has been sold. You have discussed or rather laid out in detail for us, Azio, and indeed no less pleasingly than accurately, hiatus and elision and the rhythms generated from them, but what a small part of poetics, and especially of Vergilian rhythm! So unlock your chests and spread out your more select wares for us, I beseech you, calling on the very spirit of Vergil and the place in which he lies, which you yourself visit often and venerate with the greatest reverence.[150]

Azio. You know exactly, Pietro Summonte, how to bring me to the subject that up to now our people have either completely disdained or too little noticed or understood, when you use on me the example and practice of merchants. For you know how much this whole nobility of ours shrinks from the name of commerce. So, lest you think me a merchant or greedy for gain, I will explain my deliberations to you and the points that I have carefully observed in my investigation of poetic rhythm—not that I think that I have accomplished what I wished and what you perhaps now expect to hear. So I will proceed with the task I have undertaken concerning rhythm, and because you have called on me only by the spirit of Vergil, I will generally work with examples of Vergil alone since he alone of our Latin poets is the model of all poetic virtues and especially of rhythm.

In general poetic rhythm follows the structure of the meter, 35 but the structure consists of words; the words, moreover, establish the accent, with each word establishing an accent. The

dictionum ac syllabarum sequuntur tempora, quibus et lenitas adiuncta est et lenitati contraria asperitas, aliae item qualitates pro syllabarum natura litterarumque e quibus sunt dictiones constitutae. Unaquaeque autem dictio aut ex una tantum aut e duabus aut etiam e pluribus constituitur syllabis, singillatim tamen omnes unico dumtaxat a grammaticis suoque signandae dicuntur accentu. Sunt vero accentus ipsi duo, sibi e fronte adversi, alter acutus, gravis alter; quodque in hac controversia liceat medium quoque aliquod constituere, qui medius est accentus ex hisque conflatur duobus et dictus est et habitus moderatus, nomine alio circumflexus, quod nomen ductum est a propria eius peculiarique in scribendo nota. Tempora igitur syllabarum sint cum tantum duo, breve ac productum, ex hoc id existit atque efficitur, ut unaquaeque syllaba aut brevis sit aut producta, non nullae tamen communitate quasi quadam praeditae et produci possunt et spatio enuntiari breviori.[128]

36   His igitur in hunc modum explicatis, ad usum numerorum venio; qua in re nihil tam aut exigitur aut spectatur quam varietas; cum enim omni studio fugienda sit satietas, ea ne sequatur varietas ipsa praestabit. Complicationes autem sententiarum et nexus illi qui tum sententias ipsas tum sententiarum partes ac membra connectunt et insequentibus versibus per gradus quasi quosdam ductas eas claudunt, ut nunc alterum nunc tertium versum catena quasi quadam vinciant, assidua e continuatione vitium satietatis praecipue afferunt; quae ut rarae ac suis quibusdam in locis terminatae demulcent aures, sic e contrario continuatae ubi fuerint, satietate afficiunt. Ponam versus aliquot e Proserpina Claudiani, poetae tum summi quidem studii, tum magni etiam exercitatique ingenii, qui sunt:[129]

accents themselves also follow the quantities of words and syllables, to which are attached both smoothness and roughness,
its opposite, as well as other qualities depending on the nature
of the syllables and letters of which the words are composed.[151]
Moreover, each word consists of one syllable only or of two or
even more, yet the grammarians say that each must be marked
with its own single accent, and not more than one. In fact, there
are two accents, set in opposition to each other, the one acute,
the other grave; and what may also constitute a mean in this
opposition, a middle accent conflated of these two, both called
and considered moderate; it is also called circumflex, a name
derived from its own special sign in writing.[152] Although syllables have only two quantities, short and long, so that each and
every syllable must be either short or long, some are endowed
with a kind of common nature and can be either drawn out or
spoken in a shorter space of time.[153]

After having explained things in this fashion, I come to the 36
use of rhythm; and in this matter there is no greater require-
ment or concern than variety. Indeed, since every effort must be
made to avoid a surfeit, variety will guarantee that it does not
ensue. Interlockings of thoughts and links that tie together
thoughts and parts and pieces of thoughts, and bring them to a
close when they have been led along step by step by the subsequent verses, so that they bind now a second or third verse as if
in a sort of chain—these from constant succession especially
inflict the fault of surfeit. Just as they charm our ears when rare
and ending in their proper places, so on the contrary when they
have been continued without interruption they afflict them
with a surfeit. I will cite some verses from the *Proserpina* of
Claudian, a most painstaking poet of great and well-trained talent. Here they are.

Dux Herebi quondam tumidas exarsit in iras
proelia moturus superis quod solus egeret
connubio[130] sterilesque diu consumeret annos
impatiens nescire torum nullasque mariti
illecebras nec dulce patris cognoscere nomen.
Iam quaecunque latent ferali monstra baratro[131]
in turmas aciemque ruunt contraque Tonantem
coniurant Furiae, crinitaque sontibus hydris
Thisiphone[132] quatiens infausto lumine pinum
armatos ad castra movet pallentia Manes
pene reluctantis.[133] Iterum pugnantia rebus
rupissent elementa fidem penitusque revulso
carcere laxatis pubes Titania vinclis
vidisset coeleste iubar rursusque cruentus
Aegeon[134] positis arcto de corpore nodis
obvia centeno vibrasset[135] fulmina motu.
Sed Parcae vetuere minas orbique timentes
ante pedes soliumque ducis fudere severam
canitiem genibusque suas cum supplice fletu
admovere manus quarum sub iure tenentur
omnia, quae seriem fatorum pollice ducunt
longaque ferratis evolvunt secula pensis.[136]

Once upon a time the lord of Erebus burst into violent
    rage,
intending to war with the gods above because he alone
    lacked
a marriage and was long spending childless years,
not enduring to know not the marriage bed and to learn no
    delights
of a husband nor the sweet name of father.
Now all the monsters that lurk in the deadly pit
rush into squadrons and battle lines and the Furies conspire
against the Thunderer, and Tisiphone with dreadlocks of
poisonous snakes, shaking her pine torch with its unholy
    light,
marches into the ghastly camp the dead, armed for battle,
almost reluctant. Again in opposition to nature, the
    elements
would have broken faith, and with their prison torn open
deep within, the Titan brood, freed from chains,
would have seen the radiance of heaven, and bloody
    Aegaeon,
bonds cast aside from his tight-bound body, once more
brandished opposing thunderbolts, a hundred at a time.[154]
But the Parcae forbade the threats, and fearing for the
    world,
spread before the feet and throne of their lord their austere
white-haired old age, and to his knees with suppliant
    weeping
brought their hands under whose dispensation are held
all things — hands whose thumbs draw out the course of
    fate
and unwind long ages with iron threads. [Claudian, *De
    raptu Proserpinae* 1.32–53]

His autem versibus auspicatus est singularis poeta enarratio-
nem sui carminis. Delectat autem carmen ipsum; nam et spatia-
tur libere et constat sibi ipsi, quanquam in verbis praesefert
nimium fortasse studium eorum conquirendorum.

37   Exemplum tamen Virgilii si iusta ponatur, admonebit nimiae
nos continuationis nexuum ipsorum de quibus nunc loquimur:

> Vix e conspectu Siculae telluris in altum
> vela dabant leti et spumas salis aere ruebant,
> cum Iuno aeternum servans sub pectore vulnus
> haec secum: 'Me ne incepto desistere victam,
> nec posse Italia Teucrorum avertere regem?
> Quippe vetor fatis. Pallas ne exurere classem
> Argivum atque ipsos potuit submergere ponto
> unius ob noxam et furias Aiacis Oilei?
> Ipsa Iovis rapidum iaculata e nubibus ignem,
> disiecitque rates evertitque aequora ventis,
> illum expirantem transfixo pectore flammas
> turbine corripuit scopuloque infixit acuto;
> ast ego, quae divum incedo regina Iovisque
> et soror et coniunx, una cum gente tot annos
> bella gero. ecquisquam numen Iunonis adoret
> praeterea aut supplex aris imponat honorem?'
> Talia flammato secum dea corde volutans
> nimborum in patriam, loca foeta furentibus Austris,

With these verses the matchless poet has begun the exposition of his poem. Moreover, the poem itself is pleasing; for it ranges freely and is internally consistent, although in language it perhaps demonstrates too much effort in searching out words.

Yet if we juxtapose an example of Vergil, it will call our attention to the excessive succession of the links we are now discussing.   37

> They were just out of sight of Sicily into the deep water
> joyously stretching their sails and dashing salt spray with
>   their prows,
> when Juno, nursing an eternal grievance in her heart,
> thought to herself. "Shall I desist from my effort, beaten,
> nor be able to drive the Trojan king away from Italy?
> Of course, I am forbidden by the fates! Was Pallas able to
>   burn
> the fleet of the Argives and drown them under the sea
> because of the criminal frenzy of one man, Ajax, son of
>   Oileus?[155]
> She herself hurled Jupiter's raging fire from the clouds
> and scattered the ships and overturned waves with the
>   winds.
> As he breathed out flames from his pierced chest,
> she snatched him up in a whirlwind and impaled him on a
>   sharp crag.
> But I, who walk majestic, queen of the gods, and both
> sister and wife of Jupiter, have waged war with a single race
> for so many years. And who would worship Juno's divine
>   power
> after this, or as a suppliant put a gift on the altars?"
> Turning over such thoughts in burning wrath, the goddess
> came into the home of storm clouds, a place teeming with
>   raging winds,

Aeoliam venit. Hic vasto rex Aeolus antro
luctantis ventos tempestatesque sonoras
imperio premit ac vinclis et carcere frenat.[137]

Versus sunt fere totidem, locus ipse satis similis, hic praesefert
summum numerorum ac varietatis studium, ille unius connexi-
onis versuumque complicandorum, ut, praeterquam quod a dictione monosyllaba coepit, quae est *dux* ut Virgilii *vix*, nullum
eius sit exemplum secutus.

Ipsius autem complicationis qui sunt nimio plus studiosi
eorum quae admirationem praecipue pariunt ut obliviscantur
necesse est. Excurrit ille tanquam populabundus, nec sistens
aliquando pedem, nec ut regionem circumspectans sui ipsius
rationem habet. At Maro servandae gravitati intentus, secundum statim versum refersit vocibus duarum syllabarum, e quibus octo accentus extudit et ad quintum pedem e syllabis *re* et
ru invicem sibi alludentibus pene expressit remorum strepitum;
quae annominatio quasi quaedam mirifice blanditur auribus.
Adhaec singulis pene versibus sensus suos et graviter et magnifice claudit sistitque pro tempore, ut cum ait: '*Haec secum*' et
cum: '*Quippe vetor fatis.*' Ac ne varietatis appareret immemor,
post versus aliquot tam apposite structos, tam examussim qua-
dratos, insonuit versum longe illorum dissimilem:

unius ob noxam et furias Aiacis Oilei.

Quid quod ubi connexionibus utitur, stat, ut: *Aeoliam venit* et:
circum claustra fremunt.

Aeolia. Here king Aeolus in a vast cavern
controls the struggling winds and sounding tempests
with his power and bridles them with confinement and
    restraints. [*Aeneid* 1.34–54]

There are almost the same number of verses, the position in the
work is quite similar; this one demonstrates the greatest care
for rhythm and variety, the other for linkage alone and interlocking verses, so that beyond the fact that he begins with a
monosyllable (*dux*, like Vergil's *vix*), he follows Vergil's example
not at all.

Those who are excessively concerned with interlinkage alone,
however, inevitably lose sight of the qualities that especially create admiration. Claudian rushes out like a raider, and neither
checking his foot from time to time nor surveying the territory
does he pay attention to what he is doing. But Maro, intent on
preserving solemnity, at once filled his second verse with words
of two syllables, from which he has hammered out eight accents; and in the fifth foot from the syllables *re* and *ru* dashing
against each other in turn he has almost represented the sound
of oars — a certain kind of sound-play that marvelously pleases
the ear.[156] In addition, practically in individual verses he brings
the thought to a close in a dignified and lofty manner and
makes a pause appropriate to the situation, as when he says,
"[She] thought to herself," and "Of course, I am forbidden by
the fates!"[157] And lest he seem unmindful of variety, after several verses so suitably put together and so exactly squared up,
he uttered a verse with a very different sound from those that
preceded:

unius ob noxam et furias Aiacis Oilei. [*Aeneid* 1.41][158]

Notice too, that when he does use linkages, he comes to a stop,
as in "she came to Aeolia" and "(the winds) rage around their
barriers."[159]

Ille vero praetervolat suae tantum excursioni deditus, nullo hiatu vel ad efferendam vocem, vel ad sistendum tenorem usus. At Virgilius ad stabiliendum etiam numerum quaternos ad spondeos bis divertitur, in altero versu explosionem adhibens: *illum expirantem transfixo pectore flammas*, in altero nullo usus hiatu:[138] *luctantis ventos, tempestatesque*[139] *sonoras*. Quid cum summisit: *illi indignantes magno cum murmure*, et: *ni faciat maria ac terras?* Quantum utroque hiatu addidit numerorum gravitati! Quid quod dyssyllabarum dictionum memor illarumque numerositatis quater illas[140] arcessivit in auxilium: nunc senas, ut: *vela dabant leti et spumas salis aere ruebant*; nunc quinas: *circum claustra fremunt, celsa sedet Aeolus*; alibi quaternas, ut: *quippe vetor fatis. Pallas ne*; alibi ternas, *secum*[141] *dea corde*. In delectu autem verborum ac selectione Virgilius iudicari potest et studiosus et prudens, at ille rancidum nescio quid videtur sapere; verum de delectu ac structura dicere ocii est maioris operaeque magis elucubratae.

38   Varietas igitur affert suum numeris ornatum ac decorem eaque paratur multis ac diversis modis, de quibus in universum praecipi hoc a me potest, ne scilicet iisdem in numeris sit diutius consistendum, quo satietas prohibeatur, ne ve aures longa de continuatione fatigentur, quo vitio non pauci laborant. Particulatim autem attingam complura, nam omnia, infinitum pene id esset, nec necessarium iudico, quando via ipsa e paucis commonstratis[142] satis patefiet, vobis praesertim quibus studia haec sunt familiarissima.

Unisyllabae voces et inchoandis et finiendis versibus varietatem afferunt numerorum, valideque illos sistunt si a spondeis foveantur, auspicando praesertim versu; stabiliunt enim sonorem, qui unus est in unius syllabae voce; quod Virgilius

The other poet, however, flies ahead, absorbed only in his own digression, never running vowels together either to emphasize an auditory effect or to produce an accent.[160] But Vergil actually twice resorts to four spondees to stabilize the rhythm; in one verse adding an elision (*illum expirantem transfixo pectore flammas*), but in the other using no hiatus (*luctantes ventos, tempestatesque sonoras*).[161] And when he added below, *illi indignantes magno cum murmure*, and *ni faciat maria ac terras*, how much he added to the force of the rhythm with each hiatus![162] And consider this, that mindful of the rhythmical quality of disyllabic words, he invoked their aid in four verses, now six times in a line, as in *vela dabant laeti et spumas salis aere ruebant*, now five, *circum claustra fremunt, celsa sedet Aeolus*, in another place four, as in *quippe vetor fatis. Pallas ne*, in another three, *secum dea corde*.[163] Furthermore, in his choice and selection of words Vergil can be deemed both diligent and skillful, while the other seems to give off a kind of rancid smell. But to speak about selection and structure is a project that requires more time and hard work by candle light.

In short, variety imparts its own distinction and charm to rhythm, and it is achieved in many different ways, about which in general I can give this instruction, to wit: one must not stand still too long in the same rhythm, in order to avoid surfeit or lest ears be wearied from a long unbroken series — a not uncommon fault. But I will touch on several points separately, for it would be endless to mention everything, and I do not think it necessary since the path will be made quite clear from a few indications, especially to you to whom these studies are very familiar.

Words of one syllable impart rhythmical variety at the beginnings and ends of verses and give them a firm anchor if they are supported by spondees, especially at the opening of the verse; for they strengthen the sound, which is single in a word

38

frequentissime servavit in principiis enarrationum praecipue, ut:

urbs antiqua fuit;
est in conspectu[143] longo locus;
rex arva Latinus;
est specus ingens;
est curvo anfractu vallis;[144]
ut belli signum;
sic fatur lacrimans;
at regina gravi.

Non quod non et dactylus recte et commode iusta collocetur, ut:

tu quoque litoribus nostris,

et:

mos erat Hesperio in Latio,

et:

nox erat et somnus,[145]

verum aures si consulueris, stabilimentum illud soni ab ipso initio tanquam a fundamento firmiter iacto, nescio quid amplius plenitudine delectat sua.

In fine quoque eadem collocatio, dum tamen sit rara, delectat etiam varietate ipsa; praeponendus tamen est dactylus, qui eo in loco idem habet instar ad tarditatem temperandam quam ad moderandam in illo celeritatem spondeus; ibi tamen sequitur, hic praeit, ut

praeruptus aquae mons,

et:

fractae vires, aversa deae mens,

et:

of one syllable. Vergil very often observes this practice, especially at the beginning of a passage, as in:

there was an ancient city [*Aeneid* 1.12];
there is a place at the far range of sight [*Aeneid* 1.159];
king Latinus [ruled] the land [*Aeneid* 7.45];
there is a huge cave [*Georgics* 4.418];
there is a valley with winding recesses [*Aeneid* 11.522];
when the sign for war [*Aeneid* 8.1];
so he spoke weeping [*Aeneid* 6.1];
but the queen with a grievous [wound] [*Aeneid* 4.1].

It is true that a dactyl may also be put with it as properly and
suitably, for example:

you too to our shores [*Aeneid* 7.1]

and:

it was the custom in Hesperian Latium [*Aeneid* 7.601]

and:

night there was, and sleep. [*Aeneid* 3.147]

But if you consult your ears, somehow the support of sound
right from the beginning as if by a firmly laid foundation gives
a greater pleasure with its fullness.

The placement of a monosyllable at the end, too, provided
that it is rare, also gives pleasure just by its variety.[164] Yet the
foot must be preceded by a dactyl, which in this place has the
same effect of tempering slowness as a spondee at the beginning
has of moderating speed; there, however, it follows the monosyllable, but here it precedes, as in these examples:

of water a mountain sheer [*Aeneid* 1.105]

and:

strength broken, hostile the goddess' mind [*Aeneid* 2.170]

and:

ruit Oceano nox,

et:

divum pater atque hominum rex.

Sed nec Lucretius est veritus spondeum praemittere, cum dixit, *'et ingrati genitoribus inventi sunt.'*[146]

Eaedem quoque monosyllabae binae simul collocatae, maxime post dactylicam aliquam properationem, numerosae sunt in medio; sistunt enim tenorem, quem etiam varietate condiunt, ut in illo:

monstravit[147] caput acris equi, sic nam fore bello,

et:

praecipue cum iam hic trabibus contextus acernis,

et:

visa viri, nox cum terras obscura teneret,

item:

quae relligio[148] aut quae machina belli,

et:

Anna, refert,[149] quae me suspensam insomnia terrent.

In principio similem in modum, veluti ab ipso fundamento tenorem stabiliunt, ut:

quam tu urbem, soror, hanc cernes,

et:

nos te Dardania incensa,

from Ocean rushed up night [*Aeneid* 2.250]

and:

father of gods and of mortals king. [*Aeneid* 10.2]

But Lucretius was not even afraid to put a spondee in front of the monosyllable when he said, "and they were found ungrateful to their sires."[165]

The same monosyllables placed together as a pair, especially after a rush of dactyls, are also rhythmical in the middle of the verse; indeed, they steady the movement, and they even add pleasing variety, as in this case:

she revealed the head of a spirited horse; for thus would it
        be [eminent] in war [*Aeneid* 1.444][166]

and:

especially when now [it stood] here, fashioned of maple
        planks [*Aeneid* 2.112]

and:

she seemed [to hear the voice] of her husband when dark
        night gripped the earth, [*Aeneid* 4.461]

likewise:

what religious scruple or what machine of war [*Aeneid* 2.151]

and:

"Anna," she said, "what dreams make me anxious and
        frightened!" [*Aeneid* 4.9]

In a similar way, paired monosyllables at the beginning provide a firm foundation, so to speak, for the course of the line. For example:

what a city, sister, you will see here [*Aeneid* 4.47][167]

and:

we [followed] you when Troy burned [*Aeneid* 3.156]

et:

si nunc se nobis ille aureus arbore ramus.

In fine quoque id praestant, ut dactylicam aliquam properationem contineant ac maturent pausam, ut:

Dardaniumque ducem, Tyria Carthagine qui nunc,

et:

manibusque meis Mezentius hic est,

et:

quam pro me curam geris, hanc, pater[150] optime, pro me deponas.

Atque hic quidem versus et in principio et in fine atque in ipso medio monosyllabis instructus est magna cum dignitate. Illo vero[151] quid blandius? cumque sit versus maxime artificiosus, sponte tamen sua maxime etiam fusus apparet:

i decus, i, nostrum, melioribus utere fatis.

39   Duarum autem syllabarum vocibus suus ubique decor inest; quae ubi binatim fuerint aut ternatim collocatae aut forte quaternatim quinatimve, sive etiam senatim, sive inchoandis sive finiendis versibus sive intertexendis, mirum est quantopere delectent; repellunt enim satietatem illam auribus tam improbe inimicam, ut:

monstra deum refero,

et:

ture calent arae,

et:

proiice tela manu, sanguis meus,

and:

> if only the golden branch on the tree [might reveal] itself to
> us. [*Aeneid* 6.187][168]

In the end, too, they serve to stop a rush of dactyls and to bring
forward a stopping point.[169] For example:

> the Dardanian leader, who now in Tyrian Carthage [*Aeneid*
> 4.224]

and:

> and by my efforts here is Mezentius [*Aeneid* 11.16]

and:

> whatever anxiety you have for me, excellent father, for me
> put it away. [*Aeneid* 12.48–49]

And this last verse, indeed, is most excellently furnished in
both the beginning and the end as well as in the middle with
words of one syllable. But in fact, is anything more pleasing
than that other famous verse? And although it is especially artful, it still appears poured out quite spontaneously:

> go, our glorious one, go, enjoy better fates. [*Aeneid* 6.546][170]

In any position, however, words of two syllables have their   39
own elegance. When these are placed by twos or threes or perhaps by fours or fives, or even sixes, whether beginning or ending verses or being interspersed in them, they are wonderfully
pleasing; they banish that surfeit so excessively painful to the
ear. For example:

> I mention the portents of the gods [*Aeneid* 3.59]

and:

> the altars grow warm with incense [*Aeneid* 1.417]

and:

> throw the weapon from your hand, my son [*Aeneid* 6.835]

et:

    et campos[152] ubi Troia fuit, feror exul in altum,

et:

    ipsa canas oro. finem dedit ore loquendi,

et:

    constituam ante aras voti reus extaque salsos,

et:

    procubuit subito et coelum tonat omne fragore,

et:

    quid tum? sola fuga nautas comitabor?

Quid quod historici quoque voces huiuscemodi perlibenter videntur fuisse complexi, ut Sallustius: arma, tela, equi, viri, hostes atque cives permisti.[153]

Trium syllabarum verba ternatim collocata variant etiam numeros, quadam cum moderatione, ut *taciti ventura videbant*, et *croceo velamen acantho*. Qua in collocatione et textu si adhibeatur aut hiatus vocalium aut explosio, non parum sibi gravitatis numerus ipse adiunget, quadam etiam cum generositate, ut et:[154]

    omnis uno ordine habetis Achivos,

et:

    oculis Phrygia agmina circumspexit;

and:

> [I left] the plains where Troy once stood; I put to sea, an
> exile [*Aeneid* 3.11]

and:

> sing yourself, I pray; he made an end of speaking
> [*Aeneid* 6.76]

and:

> to pay my vow I will stand [a bull] before your altars and
> [cast] the entrails into the salt [sea] [*Aeneid* 5.237]

and:

> it suddenly fell, and the whole sky thundered with the crash
> [*Aeneid* 9.541]

and:

> what then? shall I accompany the sailors in flight by
> myself? [*Aeneid* 4.543]

Consider, too, that the historians also seem to have been happy
to embrace words of this kind, as Sallust does: "arms, spears,
horses, men, enemies and citizens mixed in confusion" [Sallust,
Bellum Iugurthinum 51.1].

Words of three syllables arranged in threes also vary the
rhythm, with some moderation, like: "in silence they saw
what was coming" and "a veil with yellow acanthus" [*Aeneid*
2.125, 1.649]. In this arrangement and combination if vowels
are either run together or ejected, the rhythm will acquire
great force with some degree of nobility besides. For example,
both:

> you place all Achaeans in the same category [*Aeneid* 2.102]

and:

> he surveyed the Phrygian lines with his gaze [*Aeneid* 2.68]

item et:

Troiae supremum audire laborem.

In primis quoque carminis partibus adiuvat textura haec nume-rositatem, ut: *mutemus clypeos Danaumque insignia*. Quod si colli-sio inciderit, tenorem utique versus efferet, ut: *undique collecti invadunt*, et: *gemini Atridae, Dolopumque exercitus*. Huiusmodi autem dictiones binae ubi collocabuntur, non est cur de his magna habeatur ratio, praesertim in principio, at ubi quaternae, numerum bene implent, ut:

lubrica convolvit sublato[155] pectore terga,

et:

Latonae tacitum pertentant gaudia pectus.

Magnam vero generositatem praesefert numerus quotiens pri-mas, medias et ultimas versus partes terna possederint trisyl-laba, ut

Romanos rerum dominos, gentemque togatam,

quem et contextum et numerum nunquam meo iudicio satis digne laudare quisquam poterit. Licet etiam cum dignitate et aurium gratia implere versum quinque etiam trisyllabis, ut:

talia narrabat relegens errata retrorsum
litora Achimenides.[156]

Tot vero trisyllaborum continuatio, ni magno fiat cum delectu, versum reddet ignobilem; Virgilius tamen ne parte ex aliqua varietati deesset, protulit hunc: *occurrit, veterem Anchisen agnovit amicum*, in quo praeter varietatis studium ac trium dictionum

likewise also:

to hear the last throes of Troy. [*Aeneid* 2.11][171]

In the first part of a verse this structure also supports the rhythmical quality, as in "we exchange shields and badges with the Greeks" [*Aeneid* 2.389].[172] But if collision of vowels occurs, it will certainly bring out the movement of the verse, as in "gathered together, they attack from all sides" and "the two sons of Atreus and the army of the Greeks" [*Aeneid* 2.414 and 415].[173] When words of this kind are arranged by twos, there is no reason to pay great attention to them, especially in the beginning of a line; but in groups of four they nicely fill out the rhythm, as in

chest erect, it rolls smooth coils [*Aeneid* 2.474]

and:

delight stirs the silent heart of Latona. [*Aeneid* 1.502]

The rhythm displays great nobility indeed whenever a group of three trisyllabic words occupies the first, middle and last parts of the verse, as in this example:

Romans, masters of the world, and the toga-clad people.
[*Aeneid* 1.282]

This is a structure and rhythm that no one, I think, can ever praise enough. Even with five trisyllables one may also fill out a fine verse that is pleasing to the ear, for example:

Achaemenides told this story as he retraced his steps
along the shore. [*Aeneid* 3.690–91][174]

Indeed, a succession of so many trisyllables, unless it is achieved with great discrimination, will make a verse undistinguished; yet Vergil, not to lack variety in any degree, produced this one: "he ran up and recognized his old friend Anchises" [*Aeneid* 3.82]. In this case I would not know anything praiseworthy

ab vocali *a* incipientium assonantiam,[157] nesciam quid insit quod iure laudetur. Inerit autem quod laudetur etiam vehementer si post duo trisyllaba tetrasyllabum collocabitur, ut:

currite ducentes subtegmina, currite, fusi.

40 Nec vero is sum[158] qui negare ausim huiusmodi multa faciendis versibus sponte sua ac pene fortuito occurrere, multo etiam plura ex habitu exercitationeque, verum tempus ipsum et artifex rerum harum est omnium et iudex. Itaque nec temere ab Horatio praecipitur nonum premi in annum opus debere. Quid enim numero hoc vel iucundius vel gravius:

an deus immensi venias maris et[159] tua nautae?

Qui cum sit constitutus primum e monosyllabo, inde e[160] dyssyllabo, deinde duobus e trisyllabis, post sequatur dyssyllabum ibique solvatur, deinceps exurgat rursus monosyllabum duobus cum dyssyllabis, fieri quidem potest uti similis eius versus sponte aliquando sua proveniat; plures tamen vix repentinus ille impetus effundet, quos longa quidem meditatio diuturniorque cogitatio et cura, quae habitus ipsius artisque comites atque ancillae sunt, et saepius et suo in loco construxerint. Quis enim domum omnem fortuito aedificatam aut navem dixerit? Num casus insequentem fecit versum an ars diuturniorque pensitatio:

numina sola colant, tibi serviat ultima Thyle,

qui constet e dactylico trisyllabo primum, tribus inde dyssyllabis, post duobus e trisyllabis, item dactylicis, ultimo e

except the concern for variety and the assonance of three words beginning with the vowel *a*.[175] On the other hand, the result will be extremely laudable if a four-syllable word is placed after two trisyllables, as in:

> run spindles, run, carrying the threads. [Catullus 64.327
> and repeated as a refrain]

I certainly would not venture to deny that in verse-making   40 many things of this sort occur spontaneously and almost by chance, and many more as a result of habit and training; but time itself is both the inventor and judge of all these matters. And so Horace did not lightly issue his dictum that a work should be suppressed until the ninth year.[176] Indeed, what is more pleasing or impressive than this rhythm?

> or may you come as the god of the vast sea and the sailors
>   [venerate] your [divinity]. [*Georgics* 1.29]

Although the line is constructed first of a monosyllable, then a disyllable, then two trisyllables, followed by a disyllable and diaeresis, and then a monosyllable rises again with two disyllables, it is certainly possible that once in a while a verse like it could come about by itself.[177] Nonetheless, that sudden impulse will hardly pour out more such verses, which long practice and still longer thought and care — qualities that are the companions and handmaidens of habit itself and of art — have constructed both fairly often and in the appropriate place. Would anyone claim that a whole house or ship was built by chance? What made the following verse — chance or art and long deliberation?

> Let them venerate your divinity alone, let ultima Thule
>   serve you. [*Georgics* 1.30]

It consists first of a dactyl of three syllables, then of three words of two syllables, then of two words of three syllables, also

dyssyllabo habeatque secum annominationem syllabarum, quae est ex primis, *tibi* et *Thyle*, et ex media dictionis quae dactylum quintum constituit?

41   Dictionum quae e quatuor constant syllabis ea ratio habenda est, ut neque ipsae mussent neque vastitatem faciant aliquam. Virgilius eas libenter in quarto et quinto pede collocat, et sistunt enim et implent numeros, temperantque celeritatem, siqua forte antecesserit, ut:

> tacitae per amica silentia lunae,

et:

> totoque ingens extenditur antro,[161]

et:

> Danaumque insignia nobis,

et:

> paribus curis vestigia figit,[162]

et:

> per tot ducta viros antiquae ab origine gentis.

Item:

> pocula siquando sevae infecere novercae,

et:

> aut hoc inclusi ligno occultantur Achivi,

et:

> Pergameamque voco, et[163] letam cognomine gentem,

et:

> manibusque meis Mezentius hic est.[164]

dactyls, and of a final disyllable; and it plays on the similar sound of the first syllables of *tibi* and *Thyle* and of the middle one in the word constituting the fifth dactyl [*ultima*].

In the case of four-syllable words one must take care that they neither drone on nor create a dreary expanse. Vergil likes to place them in the fourth and fifth foot, for they both support and fill out the rhythm, and they moderate whatever speed has preceded them. Thus:

41

silent, by the friendly silence of the moon [*Aeneid* 2.255][178]

and:

and huge, he is stretched out in the whole cave [*Aeneid* 6.423]

and:

and for us the badges of the Greeks [*Aeneid* 2.389]

and

he plants his steps with equal care [*Aeneid* 6.159]

and:

handed down through so many generations of men from the origin of their ancient race. [*Aeneid* 1.642]

Likewise:

if ever cruel stepmothers poisoned cups [*Georgics* 2.128]

and:

either Achaeans are hidden, enclosed by this wood [*Aeneid* 2.45]

and:

I call it Pergamea and [urge] the people rejoicing in the name [*Aeneid* 3.133]

and:

and by my efforts here is Mezentius. [*Aeneid* 11.16][179]

Collocat easdem libenter in primis etiam locis subiicitque saepenumero spondeum ubi dactylicae voces illae fuerint, ut:

interea Aeneas urbem designat,

et:

incipiam; fracti bello,

et:

insequitur clamorque virum,

et:

funereas inferre faces.

Non quod non et dactylum subnectat quandoque, adeo nihil in
iis perpetuum est quae ad varietatem pertinent, ut: *Myrmidonum
Dolopumve*, et: *Threiciamque*[165] *Samum*. Quin etiam spondeos
aliquando iungit, ut: *argumentum ingens*.

In quibus omnibus consulendae sunt aures videndumque ubi
aut celeritate maiore aut tarditate aliqua opus sit. Adhaec quotiens aliquot simul eodem in versu collocantur, interiiciendae
sunt dictiones aut duarum aut unius aut trium syllabarum, ut:

Misenum Aeoliden, quo non praestantior alter,

et:

Aeneadae in ferrum pro libertate ruebant,

et:

olli discurrere pares discrimine nullo,[166]

et:

virginei volucrum vultus, foedissima[167] ventris
proluvies,

He likes to place the same words in the first place too and often adds a spondee when they are dactylic, as in these examples:[180]

meanwhile, Aeneas marks out the city [*Aeneid* 5.755]

and:

I will begin; broken by war [*Aeneid* 2.13]

and:

and the shouting of men ensues [*Aeneid* 1.87]

and:

to bring destructive firebrands. [*Aeneid* 7.337]

But sometimes he also adds a dactyl, to such an extent is nothing set in stone in matters pertaining to variety. Thus: "of Myrmidons or Dolopes" and "Thracian Samos" [*Aeneid* 2.7, 7.208].[181] Occasionally he even joins spondees, as in "a mighty theme" [*Aeneid* 7.791].[182]

In all these matters one must consult the ear and see where greater speed or some slowing is needed. In addition, whenever several four-syllable words are placed at once in the same verse, words of two or one or three syllables must be mixed in. Here are some examples:

Aeolian Misenus, better than anyone [*Aeneid* 6.164]

and:

the Aeneadae rushed into battle for liberty [*Aeneid* 8.648]

and:

the pairs split off with no space between them [*Aeneid* 5.580]

and:

girlish the faces of the flying things, most foul the
        excrement
of their belly [*Aeneid* 3.216–17]

et:

> mittimus Eurypilum scitatum oracula Phoebi,

et:

> qualis populea moerens Philomela[168] sub umbra,

et:

> praecipitat suadentque cadentia sidera somnos.

Sed nec Lucretianus[169] ille praetereundus hoc loco est versus:

> squamigerum genus et volucres erumpere coelo.

Usus est Virgilius mirabili artificio cum vellet duas quatuor syllabarum voces easdemque dactylicas simul connectere; praemisit enim monosyllaba duo inter se copulata dixitque:

> hinc atque hinc glomerantur Oreades.

Quibus numeris quid excogitari potest vel hilarius vel quod auribus tam adulanter blandiatur? In quinto quoque et sexto mirifice huiusmodi dictiones implent aures, praesertim ubi fuerint spondaicae, ut:

> Pallantis[170] proavi de nomine Pallanteum,[171]

et:

> Pilumno quos ipsa decus dedit Orithia.[172]

Quid cum idem poeta tres simul collocavit quatuor syllabarum voces insonuitque:

> cornua velatarum obvertimus antennarum?

and:

> we sent Eurypylus to question the oracle of Phoebus
> [*Aeneid* 2.114]

and:

> like Philomela lamenting in the poplar's shade [*Georgics*
> 4.511]

and:

> [night] rushes down and the setting stars urge sleep.
> [*Aeneid* 2.9]

But in this place we also must not omit the well-known verse of Lucretius:

> scaly creatures and birds [could] burst forth from the sky.
> [Lucretius, *De rerum natura* 1.162]

Vergil employed wonderful artistry when he wanted to link two four-syllable dactylic words, for he placed ahead of them two interconnected monosyllables:

> on this side and that the Oreads gather. [*Aeneid* 1.500][183]

Can one possibly imagine anything more lively than these rhythms or that would be so pleasingly agreeable to the ear? In the fifth and sixth feet, too, words of this kind wonderfully fill the ears, especially when they are spondaic, like

> Pallanteum from the name of their ancestor Pallas [*Aeneid*
> 8.54]

and:

> which Orithyia herself gave as a gift to Pilumnus. [*Aeneid*
> 12.83]

And notice how it resounds when the same poet placed three words of four syllables together at once:

> we turn the ends of the sail-covered yards. [*Aeneid* 3.549][184]

Utque sonus esset vocalior, et explosionem adhibuit, cum etiam dicere posset *vertimus* et id praestitit, mediae ut syllabae assonarent ultimis. Hilarem profecto[173] ac maxime gratum numerum exhibuit Lucretius, duobus e tetrasyllabis iisque dactylicis, interiecto trisyllabo, post quoque collocato monosyllabo, inquiens:

omnigenis[174] perfusa coloribus in genere omni.

Lucretiano hoc si non hilariorem, pleniorem certe Maro effudit, cum dixit:

continuo ventis surgentibus aut freta ponti.

42   Sed agite, quaeso, quos subdam versus considerate, dictionumque e quibus constant collocationem ac pedum solutiones et loca in quibus solutiones ipsae fiunt:

Incipiunt agitata tumescere et horridus[175] altis
montibus audiri fragor ac[176] resonantia longe
litora misceri et nemorum increbrescere murmur.

Quibus considerandis neutique negligenda est litterarum syllabarumque assultatio illa et tanquam annominatio: *agitata tumescere* et *longe litora*.

Egregium quoque peperit etiam Virgilius numerum post dictionem tetrasyllabam in quarto collocatam, praepositis dyssyllabis tribus, cum subdidisset monosyllabum ac dyssyllabum, e quibus dactylum constituit cecinitque:

victor equus fontisque avertitur et pede terram.

And that the sound might be more euphonious he both added elision (although he could also have said *vertimus*) and made the middle syllables in assonance with the last.[185] Lively, to be sure, and very pleasing was the rhythm Lucretius produced from two four-syllable dactylic words with a trisyllable in between and then a monosyllable, when he said:

steeped with colors of every kind in every species.
[Lucretius, *De rerum natura* 2.821][186]

Vergil poured out a verse that was fuller at any rate, if not livelier, than the one of Lucretius when he said:

immediately as the winds rise, either the straits of the sea
[start to swell]. [*Georgics* 1.356]

But come now, please, consider the following verses and the placing of the words from which they are put together and the diaereses and the places in which those diaereses occur:

Stirred, [the straits of the sea] start to swell, and a terrible crash
is heard from the high mountains, and the shores ring with
a confused echo and the noise of the woods increases.
[*Georgics* 1.357–59]

In considering these verses one should by no means disregard the clashing of letters and syllables and the sound play in *agitata tumescere* and *longe litora*.[187]

And Vergil also produced a very fine rhythm after a four-syllable word in the fourth position following three disyllables, when he had added a monosyllable and disyllable making a dactyl. And so he sang:

the once victorious horse turns away from the spring and
with his hoof [paws] the ground. [*Georgics* 3.499][188]

42

Quam decenter igitur atque apposite, quanta etiam numerorum cura diversis in locis tetrasyllabas dictiones Virgilius disposuerit declarant qui sequuntur versus:

Interea medium Aeneas iam classe tenebat
certus iter fluctusque atros aquilone secabat,
moenia respiciens, quae iam infelicis Elisae
collucent flammis. Quae tantum accenderit ignem
causa latet; duri magno sed amore dolores
polluto, notumque furens quid foemina possit,
triste per augurium Teucrorum pectora ducunt.[177]

In illis quoque:

Arma diu senior desueta trementibus aevo
circumdat nequicquam humeris et inutile ferrum
cingitur ac densos fertur moriturus in hostes.
Aedibus in mediis nudoque sub aetheris axe
ingens ara fuit iustaque veterrima laurus
incumbens arae atque umbra complexa penates.
Hic Ecuba[178] et natae nequicquam altaria circum,
praecipites atra ceu tempestate columbae,
condensae et divum amplexae simulacra sedebant.
Ipsum autem sumptis Priamum iuvenilibus armis
ut vidit: 'Quae mens tam dira, miserrime coniunx,
impulit his cingi telis, aut quo ruis?' inquit.
'Non tali auxilio, nec defensoribus istis

The following verses demonstrate how fittingly and appropriately and with how much concern for rhythm Vergil has arranged four-syllable words in different positions:

> Meanwhile Aeneas was holding his course midway with the
>   fleet,
> resolute, and he was cleaving the waves made black by the
>   north wind,
> looking back at the ramparts, which were already glowing
>   red
> with the pyre of unhappy Elissa. The cause that fired such
>   a blaze
> was unknown; but the terrible sufferings when a great love
> is violated, and the knowledge of what a frenzied woman
>   can do,
> drew the hearts of the Trojans through sorrowful
>   speculation. [Aeneid 5.1–7][189]

Also in these:

> Arms long unused the old man placed in vain on shoulders
> trembling with age, and he girded on a useless sword
> and moved against the massed enemy to meet his death.
> In the heart of the building and under the open vault of the
>   sky
> there was a great altar and nearby an ancient laurel
> overhanging the altar, its shade embracing the penates.
> Here Hecuba and her daughters in vain around the altar,
> like doves driven headlong by a black tempest,
> huddled together and sat embracing the images of the gods.
> But when she saw Priam dressed in a young man's armor
> she said, "What terrible madness, my poor husband,
> drives you to gird on these weapons, or where are you
>   rushing?
> Not such assistance as this nor these defenses of yours

Tempus eget, non, si ipse meus nunc afforet Hector.
Huc tandem concede, haec ara tuebitur omnes,
Aut moriere simul.'

Est eiusdem poetae versus:

si periturus abis, et nos rape in omnia tecum,

quem ipse novem refersit accentibus, tot monosyllabas ac dyssyllabas voces in eum congessit, quod est rarissimum. Itaque
dum varietati consulit, nihil est quod non praestiterit, cui
condiendae summum adhibendum est a poeta studium[179] sin-
gularisque diligentia.

43   Earum dictionum quae pluribus quam e quatuor constant
syllabis magna quoque habenda est ratio. Prisci Latini Graecos
secuti auctores iis frequentissime ad ultimos usi sunt locos,
quibus scatet Lucretius, ut:

quae mare navigerum, quae terras frugiferentis,

et:

nata sit, an contra nascentibus insinuetur,

et:

ut puerorum aetas improvida ludificetur.[180]

Quin etiam locis ut his satisfacerent, solvebant dypthongos[181]
vocalesque[182] simul coactas, ut:

effice ut interea fera munera militiai;

quin etiam intermiscebant superfluentis syllabas, ut:

inter se nexu magis aut minus indupedita.

Does the time require, not if my Hector himself were here
now.
Please come here, this altar will protect us all,
or you will die with us." [*Aeneid* 2.509–24]

There is a verse of the same poet:

if you are leaving to meet your death, take us too into
everything with you. [*Aeneid* 2.675]

He has filled it up with nine accents, and — what is extremely
rare — he has heaped up in it so many monosyllables and disyllables.[190] And so while he was concerned with variety, to season
it he omitted nothing that demands the utmost zeal and a singular effort on the part of a poet.

Words of more than four syllables also require great atten-   43
tion. Archaic Latin writers, following Greek authors, used them
most often in the last feet. Lucretius is full of them. Thus:

who [fill] the ship-bearing sea, the crop-fruitful land
[Lucretius 1.3]

and:

whether it is born or rather into those being born finds its
way [Lucretius 1.113]

and:

that the innocent age of children might be deceived.
[Lucretius 1.939]

Indeed, to fill up those positions in the line, they even break up
diphthongs and vowels forced together, as in:

bring it about that the fierce deeds of warfare. [Lucretius
1.29][191]

Indeed, they even mix in extra syllables, as in:

in their joining to each other more or less intertwined.
[Lucretius 1.240][192]

Aliquando et Horatius auribus hunc suis numerum exhibuit, ut:

olim qui magnis legionibus imperitarint.[183]

Sed neque Virgilius numerum hunc omnino reiecit, ut:

quarum quae forma pulcherrima Deiopean,

et:

nec Thesea Pyrithoumque,

et:

his Laodomia,

et:

grave olentia centaurea.

Nihil est enim quod non raritas approbet, auribus tedium ac satietatem recusantibus, cum praesertim Graeca lingua numeris his mirifice letetur. Sed nec tamen debet raritas vacare diligentia. Enitet apud Virgilium nobilissimus hic dactylicus:

panditur interea domus omniparentis[184] Olympi;

quo in versu quod desiderare iure possis omnino nihil est; nam quod detrahitur accentibus, id vero suppletur multitudine syllabarum, ut etiam in hoc alio :

at Danaum proceres Agamemnoniaeque phalanges.

Et hunc quoque versum eadem multitudine syllabarum numerosum reddidit, trisyllabum statim pentasyllabo coniungens:

fortunatorum nemorum sedesque beatas.

Sometimes even Horace presents this rhythm to his ears, as in:

those who once commanded great legions. [Horace, *Satire* 1.6.4][193]

But Vergil did not completely reject this rhythm either, as in these examples:[194]

of these the one fairest of form, Deiopeia [*Aeneid* 1.72]

and:

nor Theseus and Pirithoos [*Aeneid* 6.393]

and:

to these Laodamia [*Aeneid* 6.447]

and:

strong-smelling centaury. [*Georgics* 4.270]

Indeed, since the ear objects to monotony and excess, rarity is always pleasing, especially since the Greek language takes wonderful pleasure in rhythms of this kind. But in any case rarity must not be devoid of care. This famous dactylic line in Vergil is stands out:

meanwhile the house of Olympus, parent of all, is opened. [*Aeneid* 10.1][195]

And certainly this verse has everything that you could rightly wish, for what it lacks in accents is supplied by its large number of syllables, as also in the following example:

but the Danaan chiefs and the phalanxes of Agamemnon. [*Aeneid* 6.489]

And this verse too he made rhythmical with the same number of syllables, joining a trisyllable directly to a five-syllable word:

and the blessed places of the blissful groves. [*Aeneid* 6.639]

Alium item, in quo simul illigat dyssyllaba etiam plura:

armentarius Afer agit, tectumque laremque.

Implentur etiam numeri, quotiens quartus et quintus locus occupantur ab huiusmodi dictionibus aut spondaicis aut dactylicis, ut: *immedicabile vulnus*,[185] et: *tempestatibus actus*,[186] et: *lychni laquearibus aureis* (cui numero multum est splendoris additum ab insequenti dyphthongo, quod facile intelliges si dixeris *laquearibus altis*), et: *Coribantiaque*[187] *aera*, et: *hinc, Drepani me portus et illetabilis ora*. Versus autem ille Petronianus, et si non abiiciendus, videri fortasse potest aliquanto vastior:

et periturorum deiecit tela Gigantum.

Prisci illi, ut fuere polysyllabarum studiosi dictionum, quo uti commodius illis possent, syllabam quandoque externam ac superfluentem interposuere, ut dixi; hinc manavit *induperator, indugredi, indupeditus.*

44　　Arte autem collocatae dictiones huiusmodi spondaicas post si trahant syllabas[188] sive dactylicas, venustatem profecto suam retinent. Atque ut[189] spondaicae implent sic dactylicae suapte natura exhilarant, ut:

O fortunatae gentes, Saturnia regna;

fortunatus et ille, deos qui novit agrestis,

et:

Likewise another, in which he even attaches several disyllables at once:

> the African herdsman brings [everything with him], both
> his house and its god. [*Georgics* 3.344]

The rhythm is also satisfied whenever the fourth and fifth feet are occupied by either spondaic or dactylic words of this kind, like "incurable wound," and "driven by tempests," and "lamps from paneled ceilings of gold" (to which great elegance is added by the diphthong at the end, which you may easily see if you say "high paneled ceilings" instead), and "and cymbals of the Corybants," and "then the port of Drepanum and the sorrowful shore [received] me."[196] But the following verse of Petronius, although not to be rejected, perhaps can seem somewhat harsh:

> and he scattered the weapons of the Giants, destined to die.
> [Petronius, *Satyricon* 123]

Archaic poets, in their fondness for polysyllabic words, sometimes introduced an extraneous or superfluous syllable in order to use them more conveniently, as I have said. This is the source of *induperator, indugredi, indupeditus*.[197]

Skilfully placed, words of this kind certainly retain a charm 44 of their own, whether they precede spondaic or dactylic syllables. And as spondaic syllables fill up the rhythm, so dactylic syllables by their nature brighten it, as in these examples:

> O fortunate races, realms of Saturn; [*Aeneid* 11.252]

> fortunate that one too, who knows the rustic gods [*Georgics*
> 2.493]

and:

Acrisioneis Danae fundasse colonis;

eruet ille Argos Agamemnoniasque Micenas.[190]

Quid ille?

degeneremque Neoptolemum narrare memento.

Quanto est temperamento conditus, dactylorum celeritate spondaica tarditate temperata! Item:

Ora modis Anchisiades pallentia miris.

Quid et hic?

et centumgeminus[191] Briareus ac belua Lernae.

Quam est generosus, nedum canorus et plenus,[192] quod praestat tum syllaba *eus* in dypthongum[193] coacta, tum particula *ac*, quae si inde eiiciatur, sonus ipse in medio pronuntiationis cursu concidet. Est etiam ille admodum plenus et gravis:

Amphitrioniadae magno divisque ferebat;

itemque:

Laomedontiadae, bellum ne inferre paratis?

Itaque ut primis in locis collocata et implent sonum et versum honestant, sic in fine faciunt illum quodammodo exilire nimiam ob celeritatem; sunt enim pene lubrica, ni polysyllabo-

[the city that] Danae [is said] to have founded with her
    Argive settlers; [*Aeneid* 7.410]

he will lay waste Argos and Agamemnon's Mycenae. [*Aeneid*
    6.838][198]

And this one:

and remember to tell of Neoptolemus worse than his father.
    [*Aeneid* 2.549]

With what perfect balance the line is composed, with the speed
of the dactyls tempered by spondaic slowness![199] Likewise:

the son of Anchises [saw] his face growing strangely pale.
    [*Aeneid* 10.822]

And this one:

and Briareus hundred-handed and the beast of Lerna.
    [*Aeneid* 6.287]

How superior it is, to say nothing of melodious and full, because of both the syllable *-eus*, compressed into a diphthong,
and the little word *ac*, whose removal would make the sound
drop in midcourse.[200] The next example is also very full and
impressive:

he was offering [a celebration] to Amphitryon's great son
    and the gods. [*Aeneid* 8.103]

Likewise:

sons of Laomedon, do you prepare to wage war? [*Aeneid*
    3.248]

And just as they fill out the sound and ennoble the verse
when placed in the first feet, so because of their excessive speed
they somehow make it thin at the end; for they are almost slip-
pery unless by the nature of the polysyllables themselves — that

rum ipsorum natura, hoc est litterae syllabaeque e quibus constant, tenorem sustentent, quale illud:

Hirtacidae[194] ante omnes exit locus Hippocoontis,

et:

. . . nec Thesea Pyrithoumque,[195]

et:

quales Threiciae cum flumina Termodoontis.[196]

Quocirca ars, adhibita industria, potest ubique numeris sub-
venire, ut:

ille pedem referens et inutilis inque ligatus.

Suffecit multitudine syllabarum quod aliter in pausa subtrac-
tum esset accentibus. Lucretius[197] quoque non indecenter ex-
coluit illum suum et dyssyllabis et monosyllabo et litterarum
syllabarumque annominationibus:

multa siti prostrata viam per proque voluta.

Non sine summa animi pensione collocavit Virgilius in
quarto et quinto loco polysyllabum, e cuius primis syllabis sta-
tueret spondeum:

                                                unus
qui fuit in Teucris et servantissimus aequi.

Horatius quoque prudenter artificioseque temperavit illum
suum:

disiecit[198] medium fortissima Tyndaridarum.

Versus hi Lucretiani declarare possunt quam sordescant huiusmodi numeri nisi dictiones ipsae sustentent eos:

is, the letters and syllables of which they consist — they rein in
the movement. For example:

> first was drawn the lot of Hippocoon, son of Hyrtacus
> [*Aeneid* 5.492]

and:

> . . . nor Theseus and Pirithoos [*Aeneid* 6.393]

and:

> like the Thracian women when [they strike] the streams of
> Thermodon. [*Aeneid* 11.659]

Therefore art, along with care, can come to the aid of rhythm
on every occasion, as in this case:

> he, stepping back, disabled and impeded. [*Aeneid* 10.794]

He supplies with the multitude of syllables what otherwise in
the junction would have been taken from the accents.[201] Lucretius, too, nicely polished this verse of his with disyllables and a
monosyllable and sound play of letters and syllables:

> many laid low by thirst and rolling forward through the
> street. [Lucretius 6.1264]

Not without the most careful consideration did Vergil place
in the fourth and fifth position a polysyllable whose first syllables formed a spondee:

> the one man
> who among the Trojans was also the most observant of
> justice. [*Aeneid* 2.426–27][202]

Horace also carefully and artfully regulated this verse of his:

> the bravest of Tydareus' daughters cut him in two. [Horace,
> *Satire* 1.100][203]

These Lucretian verses can demonstrate how poor rhythms like
this are if the language does not support them:

materies ut suppeditet rebus reparandis,

et:

sed[199] magis aeterna pollentia simplicitate,

et:

tandem deducunt[200] in tales disposituras.

Dat autem illi veniam vetustas numerorum rudis nec minus
etiam materia ipsa tam humilis quam certe est. Quid ille alius?

id facit exiguum clinamen principiorum.

Item alius:

et erunt et crescent inque[201] valebunt.

45   Multa possent iis subiici, sed neque poetam nunc institui-
mus et vos paucis his iure contenti esse potestis. Quocirca
attingamus etiam alia, cum praesertim e vitio comparetur aliquando laus, quae virtutis est propria.

Constat versus heroicus, quem non improprie agnominare
generosum possumus, sex e pedibus, unde Graeco nomine
hexameter, nostro *senarius* est vocatus; singuli pedes singula constituunt metra. Probantur versus illi maxime qui inter dimeti-
endum inveniuntur complicatis inter se pedibus invicemque
insertis, ut pes pedi sit tanquam catena vinctus. Nihilominus in
locis quibusdam qui[202] soluti inveniuntur reprehensione vacant,
ut cum post primum et quintum pedem solutio fit estque ipsa
dactylica; nimia tamen importunaque solutio vitiosa est. Ac nihilominus placet adeo varietas, ut interdum etiam solutione ab

so that matter might be at hand for remaking things
[Lucretius 1.547]

and:

but prevailing instead in eternal singleness [Lucretius 1.612]

and:

at last they bring [them] into such arrangements. [Lucretius
1.1027]

But he has an excuse in the fact that the archaic period was
unskilled in rhythm as well as in the subject itself, which is
certainly unexalted. And another example:

a tiny swerve of the first beginnings causes it. [Lucretius
2.292]

Likewise another:

they will both exist and grow and prevail. [Lucretius
2.301][204]

Much could be added to this, but I am not training a poet   45
now, and you can be quite contented with these few points.
Therefore let us touch on other matters, too, especially since
sometimes from a defect is attained the merit appropriate to
excellence.

Heroic verse, to which we can quite properly award the epithet "noble," consists of six feet, from which it is called by the
Greek name *hexameter*, in the Latin *senarius*; each foot consti-
tutes a metron. The verses are most highly regarded that are
found in scansion to have feet containing word breaks interlocking with each other, so that foot is linked to foot as in a
chain.[205] Nonetheless, those found to have diaeresis in certain
places are irreproachable, as when dactylic diaeresis occurs after
the first and fifth foot—but excessive and inappropriate diaeresis is a fault.[206] And yet variety is so pleasing that sometimes

ipsa quaeratur numerositas carminisque ipsius decorum; quod accuratior ars facile quidem praestat, id quod suis in locis iisque singulis conabor ostendere, ut in hoc:

iussi numina magna deum veneramur et inde.

Non eo inficias primum pedem saepissime solutum incedere ac sine ullis vinculis, praecipue cum voces illae aut trium fuerint[203] syllabarum ut: *unius ob noxam,* aut etiam unius syllabae,[204] ut: *haec sunt quae nostra liceat.* At cum sunt duarum et spondaicae, videtur sine aurium offensa vitium hoc fieri minime posse. Etenim Lucretianus[205] ille nescio quomodo tanquam deficiente hanelitu in pronuntiando concidit:

fulmen detulit in terram mortalibus ignem.

Nihilominus et hinc quoque numerum sibi egregium in versu quem dixi Virgilius comparavit, conferta post acie tot dactylis; quod idem servavit in aliis quibusdam versibus quos tamen dyssyllabis honestavit:

tantos illa suo rumpebat pectore questus;

item:

tanta mole viri turritis puppibus instant;

et si in his secundus sit pes complicatus, qui in illo est solutus, qua e re duplex illic facta est solutio; quam utramque fecit etiam in hoc:

the diaeresis itself is the source of rhythmical quality and metrical appropriateness. This is easily achieved by skillful art, a fact I will try to demonstrate in each of its separate positions, as in this example:[207]

> As bidden, we venerate the great powers of the gods, and
> then. [*Aeneid* 3.697]

I won't deny that the first foot often proceeds free and without any bonds, especially when the words are either of three syllables as in "because of the guilt of one man" [*Aeneid* 1.41] or even of only one syllable as in "these are the matters allowed (for you to be warned of) by our (voice)" [*Aeneid* 3.461]. But when the words are spondaic and of two syllables, this seems of necessity a fault offensive to the ear. Indeed, this Lucretian verse somehow falls as it is being pronounced as if it was running out of breath:

> Lightning brought fire down to earth for mortals.
> [*Lucretius* 5.1092][208]

Still, even in a case like this Vergil provided himself with an excellent rhythm in the verse I have mentioned, filling the line afterward with so many dactyls; and he maintained the same quality in certain other verses that he still made elegant with disyllables.[209] Thus:

> such laments she was pouring out from her heart. [*Aeneid*
> 4.553]

Likewise:

> men stand on towered ships of such great mass. [*Aeneid*
> 8.693]

But in these cases there is a caesura in the second foot, whereas in the former example the foot is free (in diaeresis) so that a double diaeresis is created.[210] He did both things in this example:

hic vir, hic est, tibi quem promitti saepius audis;

uterque tamen pes est dactylus, quam ob causam cum plures in hoc monosyllabae insint voces, solutiones ipsae minus apparent. Quod idem contingit etiam in hoc:

illi haec inter se dubiis de rebus agebant,

tum propter monosyllaba tum etiam propter hiatum; et in hoc quoque propter dactylum et monosyllabam vocem:

terres? haec via sola fuit, qua perdere posses.

At in hoc,[206] quia duo praecedunt monosyllaba sequiturque dactylus, apparet manifestius:

sed tu desine velle. deum praecepta secuti.

Quid ille in quo tres factae sunt solutiones eaeque dactylicae?

scilicet omnibus est labor impendendus, ⟨et omnes⟩.[207]

Temperavit tamen celeritatem illam iterati dactyli tertius utique dactylus e monosyllabo dyssyllaboque compactus, duos secum accentus afferens; tertiam vero solutionem moderatus est statim subdendo tetrasyllabum, e quo et struxit spondeum et inde adiecto monosyllabo quartum conflavit dactylum, duplicem quoque secum accentum trahentem.

46   Quae vero post secundum statim locum fiunt solutiones, eae quoque fiunt etiam cum dignitate quadamque aurium gratia, praesertim ubi insequuntur duo plura ve dyssyllaba numerique ipsi sunt dactylici, ut:

this is the man, this is the one you often hear promised to
you. [*Aeneid* 6.791]

Yet both feet are dactyls, so that although there are several
monosyllabic words in it, the diaereses themselves are less obvious. The same thing happens also in this one:

these things with each other they debated about their
perilous situation, [*Aeneid* 11.445]

because of both the monosyllables and also the elision. And in
this case too because of the dactyl and monosyllable:

Do you terrorize me? This was the only way that you could
destroy me. [*Aeneid* 10.879][211]

But in this example, because two monosyllables precede and a
dactyl follows, the diaeresis is more apparent:

Stop trying. Following the instructions of the gods. [*Georgics*
4.448]

And notice this verse, in which three dactylic diaereses have
been created:

to be sure, labor must be exerted on all of them, and all.
[*Georgics* 2.61]

Nonetheless, the speed of the repeated dactyl is regulated by
the third foot, a dactyl in fact, composed of a monosyllable and
disyllable, bringing two accents with it; but he moderated the
force of the third diaeresis by immediately appending a four-
syllable word, from which he both constructed a spondee and
then produced a fourth dactyl by adding a monosyllable that
also brought with it a double accent.[212]

The diaereses that occur immediately after the second foot   46
are also very well done and give a certain pleasure to the ear,
especially when two or more disyllables follow, and the rhythms
themselves are dactylic, as in:

aut aliquis latet error, equo ne credite, Teucri,

et:

nec iam se capit unda, volat vapor ater ad auras,

et:

extremi sinus orbis, ubi aera vincere summum,

aut etiam unum, videlicet cum alterum praecedit dyssyllabum, alterum subsequitur, ut:

apparet domus intus et atria longa patescunt,

quo in versu triplex etiam fit solutio. Magnam quoque praese-fert luculentiam ubi terna subsequuntur trisyllaba uno cum monosyllabo, ut:

artificis scelus et taciti ventura videbant.

Impletur mirum etiam in modum numerus ubi subsequuntur spondei, non sine monosyllabo, ut:

hoc Ithacus velit, et magno mercentur Atridae,

et:

visa viri, nox cum terras obscura teneret.

Denique non caret dignitate quacunque ratione solutio hac in parte fiat, ut:

nunc tantum sinus et statio male fida carinis,

et:

or else there is some hidden trickery. Do not trust the
   horse, Trojans. [*Aeneid* 2.48]

and:

the water is no longer contained, black steam rises up in the
   air [*Aeneid* 7.466]

and:

the nook at the edge of the world, where (no arrow can)
   rise above the upmost air. [*Georgics* 2.123]

This diaeresis works well followed even by a single disyllable — I
mean, when one disyllable precedes and another comes shortly
afterward. For example:

the house is visible within and the long halls lie open.
   [*Aeneid* 2.483]

In this verse there is triple diaeresis.[213] The second-foot diaeresis also displays great elegance when it is followed by three trisyllables with a single monosyllable, as in:

[they foretold] the crime of the schemer and in silence saw
   what was coming. [*Aeneid* 2.125][214]

The rhythm is also wonderfully satisfied when spondees follow,
not without a monosyllable, as in:

the Ithacan would like this, and the sons of Atreus pay a
   great price [*Aeneid* 2.104][215]

and:

she seemed [to hear the voice] of her husband when dark
   night gripped the earth. [*Aeneid* 4.461][216]

In short, diaeresis does not lack excellence no matter how it
occurs in this place. For example:

now only a bay and an unsafe harbor for ships [*Aeneid* 2.23]

and:

    classibus hic locus, hic acies certare solebant,

et:

    quo fremitus vocat et sullatus ad aethera clamor;

item:

    nunc, positis novus exuviis nitidusque iuventa,

et:

    impleri nemus et colles clamore relinqui,

et:

    coniugium vocat, hoc praetexit nomine culpam,

et:

    quo Phoebus vocat[208] errantis iubeatque reverti,

et:

    experiuntur et in medium quaesita reponunt;

quo in versu duo illa monosyllaba trium dactylorum praeprope-
ram festinationem magna cum aurium voluptate remorantur.
Persimilis[209] huius videtur Lucretianus hic:

    vociferantur et exponunt praeclara reperta.

Ut autem celeritatem in Virgiliano temperant bina monosyllaba
inter dactylos constituta sic in Lucretiano tarditatem condit
duos post dactylos monosyllabum duplici cum spondeo. Itaque

here was the place for their ships, here the armies used to
contend [*Aeneid* 2.30]

and:

where the battle din calls, and shouting raised up to the
heavens; [*Aeneid* 2.338]

likewise:

now new, his skin shed, and shining with youth
[*Aeneid* 2.473]

and:

the meadows were filled (with lowing) and the hills were
left with an uproar [*Aeneid* 8.216]

and:

she calls it marriage; with this name she cloaks her guilt
[*Aeneid* 4.172]

and:

where Phoebus calls and orders the wanderers to return
[*Aeneid* 3.101]

and:

they toil, and bring back their gains to the common store.
[*Georgics* 4.157]

In this verse the two monosyllables slow down the precipitate
speed of the three dactyls with great pleasure of the ear. This
verse of Lucretius seems very similar:

his songs speak out and set forth his glorious discoveries.
[Lucretius 1.732]

But just as in Vergil's verse the speed is slowed by two monosyllables placed within dactyls, so in Lucretius' slowness after two
dactyls is achieved by a monosyllable with a double spondee.[217]

solutiones hae ad secundum locum, dum sint artificiosae, sunt non solum gratae, verum etiam desiderabiles ob varietatem.

47   Tertio quoquo in loco solutio non fit sine dignitate, praecipue si tertius ipse locus fuerit dactylicus, et qui post sequuntur pedes fuerint et ipsi dactyli, ut:

horrescit strictis seges ensibus aeraque fulgent;

quo in versu quartus quoque solvitur. Implet aures nescio quid etiam amplius, si subsequatur statim monosyllabum aut[210] pes ipse tertius sistat in monosyllabo, ut:

una dolo divum si foemina victa duorum[211]

et:

externum tulit, aut cruor hic de stipite manat.

Habet et hic duplicem solutionem. Item:

interclusit hiems et terruit auster euntis;

intactamque[212] coli dedit et contemnere ventos;

demens,[213] et cantu vocat in certamina divos;

venturum Ausonios, en haec promissa fides est?

Hoc in versu et tertius desinit pes in monosyllabo[214] et cum alterum monosyllabum quartum ordiatur pedem, pausa ipsa conquiescit etiam tertio in monosyllabo, qui sextum claudit pedem.

And so these diaereses in the second position, as long as they are artistic, are not only pleasing but also desirable on account of their variety.

In the third position, too, diaeresis occurs very well, especially if the third foot is a dactyl and the following feet are also dactyls. Here is an example:

47

> a crop of drawn swords bristles and the bronze weapons gleam. [*Aeneid* 7.526]

In this verse the fourth foot is also free.[218] The ear is somehow even more satisfied if a monosyllable immediately follows or if the third foot itself ends in a monosyllable, as in:

> if one woman (has been) overcome by the trickery of two gods [*Aeneid* 4.95]

and:

> [Troy did not]
> bring forth a foreigner nor does this blood flow from wood. [*Aeneid* 3.43]

This has a double diaeresis. Likewise:

> a storm shut them in and the wind terrified them as they tried to go; [*Aeneid* 2.111]

> he allowed it to lie untouched and to pay no attention to the winds; [*Aeneid* 3.77]

> out of his mind, and he also challenged the gods to a contest in song; [*Aeneid* 6.172][219]

> [he said that you] would come to the Ausonian territory; is this what his promise is worth? [*Aeneid* 6.346]

In this verse the third foot ends in a monosyllable, and although the fourth foot begins with another, the stopping point comes to rest in yet a third monosyllable, which closes the sixth foot.[220]

Est etiam versus ille numerosus, atque, ut ita dixerim, affabrefactus:

Da deinde auxilium, pater, atque haec omina firma;

in quo quartus quoque pes liber incedit. Non caret etiam dignitate propter spondeos ac vocalium concursus versus ille:

Nereidum matri et Neptuno Aegaeo.

Sed raritas est quae Latina in lingua huiusmodi versus condiat.

Ad quartum locum facta solutio gignit magnitudinem,
quodam etiam cum supercilio, praecipue si accesserit etiam collisio aut monosyllabum subsequatur, ut:

vela cadunt, remis insurgimus; haud mora, nautae,

et:

mortalis hebetat visus tibi et humida circum,

et:

fixerit aeripedem cervam licet aut Erimanthi,

et:

incensae: moriamur et in media arma ruamus;

quo in versu tertius[215] quoque pes liber est. Habet pondus
quoque suum, ubi quartus ipse pes ab altero incipit dyssyllabo
desinitque in altero,[216] ut:

vela damus vastumque cava trabe currimus aequor.

This other well known verse is also rhythmical and, as I might say, artfully put together:[221]

> give aid hereafter, father, and strengthen these omens.
> [*Aeneid* 2.691]

In this verse, too, the fourth foot goes free.[222] The next example is excellent for its spondees and running together of vowels:

> to the mother of the Nereids and Aegean Neptune. [*Aeneid* 3.74]

But rarity is the seasoning of verses like this in Latin.[223]

A diaeresis produced at the fourth foot creates an elevated effect, together with a certain gravity, especially if either an elision or a monosyllable follows.[224] For example:

> the sails fall, we strain on our oars, the sailors without delay
> [*Aeneid* 3.207]

and:

> [the cloud that] dulls your mortal sight, and the dank
> [mist] around [*Aeneid* 2.605]

and:

> although he shot the bronze-footed deer or [pacified the groves] of Erymanthus [*Aeneid* 6.802]

and:

> burning; let us die and let us charge into the heart of the battle. [*Aeneid* 2.353]

In this last verse the third foot is also free.[225] A verse also has its own weight when the fourth foot takes its beginning from one disyllable and ends in another, as in:

> we set sail and run over the vast sea in our hollow bark.
> [*Aeneid* 3.191]

Hoc autem usuvenit propter accentus ipsos, qui numerum augent, quod manifesto cernitur in his qui subsequuntur versibus, neque enim eam retinent magnitudinem:

> regia portabat Tyriis duce letus Achate;

> insontem infando indicio, quia bella vetabat;

> praedixit, vobis Furiarum ego maxima pando;

> dant maria et lenis crepitans vocat auster in altum.

Contra quod inest subsequentibus pondus!

> insideat[217] quantus miserae deus, at memor ille;

> et campos ubi Troia fuit, feror exul in altum.

Item:

> olli somnum ingens rupit[218] pavor ossaque et artus;

> et Bellona manet te pronuba, nec face tantum.

Magna quoque inest et huic gravitas tum propter finale monosyllabum tum etiam propter explosionem:

> vertitur interea coelum et ruit Oceano nox.

This weight comes about because of the accents that augment the rhythm, as one can clearly see in the following verses, for they do not maintain the same intensity.[226]

he carried the royal [gifts] to the Tyrians, happy with
   Achates as his leader; [*Aeneid* 1.696]

[they condemned] the innocent man on an unspeakable
   charge because he opposed the war; [*Aeneid* 2.84]

[what . . .]
he predicted, I, greatest of the Furies, reveal to you;
   [*Aeneid* 3.252][227]

[the winds] give us the sea, and a gently rustling breeze calls
   us to the deep. [*Aeneid* 3.70]

On the other hand, what weight there is in the following examples!

how great a god clings to the poor woman; but he, mindful;
   [*Aeneid* 1.719]

and the plains where Troy once stood; I put to sea, an exile.
   [*Aeneid* 3.11][228]

Likewise:

great terror broke his sleep, and [sweat drenched] his bones
   and limbs; [*Aeneid* 7.458]

and as a bridesmaid Bellona awaits you; and with a torch
   not only. [*Aeneid* 7.319]

There is great force in the next example, too, both because of the final monosyllable and because of the elision:

meanwhile the heavens revolved and from Ocean hastened
   night. [*Aeneid* 2.250][229]

Longe huic alteri maior propter terna tetrasyllaba eaque dactylica, etiam ad solutionem ipsam adiecto monosyllabo, qui numerum ipsum profluentem sistat:

incipiunt agitata tumescere et aridus[219] altis,

cui numero ne syllabarum quidem annominatio defuit, ut ante diximus. Denique quid hoc ipso versu luculentius?

o patria, o divum domus, Ilium, et inclyta bello
moenia Dardanidum.

Praesefert[220] supercilium quasi quoddam et hic:

aspectans silvam immensam et, sic ore profatur;[221]

cum enim explosio tum monosyllaborum duplicitas spondaicis ipsis numeris pondus adiiciunt; quod idem praestant dactylicis in illo:

lapsa cadunt folia, aut ad terram gurgite ab alto,

quam ad rem non parum etiam confert prior solutio, quae fit ad tertium pedem.

48   Numerorum igitur varietas diversis modis quaerenda est, nec una tantum ratione complectenda, quam nunc pedum eorundem continuatio, nunc variatio illorum pariat. Spondei nanque continuati numeros stabiliunt redduntque illos subtristiores, neque enim fluere illos sinunt. Contra dactyli properare illos cogunt et hilaritatem quasi quandam afferunt. Eorum vero mistura illos temperat, quae tamen et ipsa fit non uno modo, sed nunc alternis, hoc est alterum post alterum collocando, nunc geminatim aut ternatim, alias hunc quam illum praeponendo selectius aut posterius statuendo.

The next verse has still greater force because of its three four-syllable words, all dactylic, with a monosyllable added at the diaeresis, to bring the overflowing rhythm to a halt:

> stirred, [the seas] begin to swell, and a dry [crash is heard]
> from the high [mountains]. [*Georgics* 1.357]

In this line sound play accompanies the number of syllables, as we noted earlier.[230] Finally, what is more brilliant than this verse?

> O homeland, O home of the gods, Ilium, and the walls of
> the Dardanians famous in war. [*Aeneid* 2.241–42]

This one, too, exhibits a kind of elevated effect:

> gazing at the great forest, and these words he utters.
> [*Aeneid* 6.186]

Both the elision and the double monosyllables add weight to the spondaic rhythm; they do the same thing for the dactylic rhythm in this verse:

> the leaves slip and fall, or to earth from the sea's depths.
> [*Aeneid* 6.310]

The first diaeresis, in the third foot, contributes no little to the effect.[231]

Well then, rhythmical variety is to be sought in different 48 ways, nor is it to be attained with one method alone since it is produced now by a succession of the same feet, now by mixing them up. A succession of spondees supports the rhythm and makes it more solemn, and does not allow it to run on. Dactyls, on the other hand, force the rhythm to hurry and impart what we could call a certain vivacity. But mixing them tempers the rhythm, and this is achieved in different ways, now by alternating, that is by placing one after the other, now by twos or threes, at other times more selectively, by putting the one before or setting it after the other.

Voces item ipsae aut unius aut duarum aut plurium syllabarum, nunc in hoc nunc alio atque alio in loco dispositae varietatem pariunt. Unius enim syllabae voces sistunt ac sustentant; duarum vero pro natura temporum aut remorantur aut festinant aut etiam moderantur; nam binatim, ternatim, quaternatim ve dispositae referciunt sonis versum atque illustrant numeros; e tribus vero aut e quatuor aut compluribus e syllabis constitutae voces similem in modum sequuntur naturam temporum, quae in ipsis sunt inconstantiora. Solutiones igitur et complicationes nexusque illi pedum, collisiones item atque explosiones hiatusque illi atque complosiones quantum conferant, loci etiam ipsi carminis, ex iis quae dicta sunt iudicari abunde potest.

49   Mirum est etiam quantum tum litterae tum syllabae aut adiungant numerositati aut demant ab ea, cum vocalium aliae sint plenae ac sonorae, aliae exiles, clarae aliae aut contra subobscurae, omnes denique pro natura coniunctarum consonantium aliam atque aliam qualitatem suscipiant, proque loco collocationis, ubi primae ultimae ve aut mediae fuerint in constituendis dictionibus. Adhaec consonantes quoque litterae causam afferunt lenitatis, asperitatis, optusionis, exibilationis, qualitatumque aliarum quae syllabis inhaerent et item vocibus. De quibus quoniam satis scio expectari a vobis aliquid, praestabo[222] et hoc perlibenter idque quanto fieri brevioribus poterit, in re[223] praesertim parum observata et tenui quaeque huberiorem videatur explicationem requirere.

Ea igitur sive figura sive ornatus condimentum quasi quoddam numeris affert. Placet autem nominare alliterationem,[224] quod e litterarum allusione constet. Fit itaque in versu quotiens dictiones continuatae, vel binae, vel ternae ab iisdem primis

Likewise, variety is provided by the words themselves, of one or two or more syllables, placed now in this place, now in another and another. Words of one syllable stop and support; but two-syllable words — depending on the the nature of their quantities — either slow down the rhythm or speed it up, or even moderate it.[232] Arranged by twos, threes, or fours they fill the verse with sounds and embellish the rhythm; but words made up of three or four or several syllables follow along with the nature of the quantities, which are more changeable in these words. As for diaereses, interlocking and intertwined feet, clashings and elisions and hiatus and the clapping sounds of unelided vowels, even the very feet of the meter — how much all these contribute — can be amply judged from what has been said of them.

It is remarkable how much both letters and syllables either   49
add to rhythm or detract from it, since some vowels are full and sonorous, others thin, some clear or, on the contrary, indistinct, and finally all, depending on the nature of the consonants joined to them, take on one quality or another, and depending on the place where they are put together, when they are first or last or in the middle in making up their words. Moreover, consonants also bring about smoothness, roughness, bluntness, sibilance, and other qualities inherent in syllables and likewise in words. Since I have a good idea that you expect something about these points, I will be happy to provide it, and this can be achieved the more briefly, especially in something subtle and little noticed that seems to demand a more copious exposition.

Well then, this figure or embellishment adds a certain seasoning to rhythm. It seems right to call it alliteration because it consists of a play on letters.[233] It comes about in a verse whenever successive words — two or three — begin with the same

consonantibus, mutatis aliquando vocalibus, aut ab iisdem incipiunt syllabis aut ab iisdem primis vocalibus. Delectat autem alliteratio haec mirifice in primis et ultimis locis facta, in mediis quoque, licet ibidem aures minus sint intentae, ut: *seva sedens super arma*, et: *tales casus Cassandra canebat*, et: *insontem infando indicio*, et: *longe*[225] *sale saxa sonabant*, et: *magno misceri murmure pontum*, et: *quaeque lacus late liquidos*. Fit[226] interdum per continuationem insequentis versus, ut in his Lucretianis: *adverso flabra, feruntur / flumine*.

Atqui alliteratio haec ne Ciceroni quidem displicuit in oratione soluta, ut cum dixit in *Bruto*: *Nulla res magis penetrat in animos eosque fingit, format, flectit*. Et in secundo *De oratore*: *quodque me solicitare summe solet*. Quid quod ne in iocis quidem illis tam lepidis neglecta est a Plauto? ut cum garrientem apud herum induxit Poenulum: *ne tu oratorem hunc pugnis plectas*[227] *postea*. Atque haec quidem alliteratio quem ad modum[228] tribus in iis fit vocibus, fit alibi etiam in duabus simili modo, ut: *taciti ventura videbant*, et: *Turno tempus erit*, et: *impulit impulsu*, et: *victu venatus alebat*, et: *duris*[229] *dolor ossibus ardet*, et:[230] *formae conscia coniunx*, et: *vasta se mole moventem*, et: *castra*[231] *fugae fidens*, et: *per loca senta situ*, et: *quo turbine*[232] *torqueat hastam*, et:[233] *quem metui moritura*. Cicero idem,[234] eloquentiae Romanae princeps, eadem hac in coagmentandis duabus una dictionibus alliteratione delectatur, ut cum dixit in *Bruto*: *sed dicere didicit a dicendi magistris* et: *Iovem, sicuti*[235] *aiunt, si Graece loquatur, loqui*.

Habet etiam suavissimum condimentum quotiens alliteratio ipsa eodem geminatur in versu, per diversas tamen dictiones ac syllabas, ut: *magna Manes ter voce vocavi*, et: *pharetramque fuga*

consonants, sometimes with changes of vowels, or with the same syllables, or with the same initial vowels. Moreover, alliteration is wonderfully pleasing when it has been produced in the first or last positions, but also in the middle, although there our ears are less attentive. For example: *saevae sedens super arma,* and *tales casus Cassandra canebat,* and *insontem infando indicio,* and *longe sale saxa sonabant,* and *magno misceri murmure pontum,* and *quaeque lacus late liquidos.*[234] Sometimes it is continued into the next verse, as in these words of Lucretius: *adverso flabra, feruntur / flumine.*[235]

What is more, not even Cicero objects to alliteration of this kind in prose, as when he says in *Brutus:* "Nothing penetrates more into their minds, and fashions, forms and flexes them" [*Brutus* 142]. And in the second book of *De oratore:* "What is wont to worry me worst" [*De oratore* 2.295]. And note that it is not even neglected by Plautus in his charming jests, as when he brought in Poenulus chattering in the presence of his master: "In future don't fight this speaker with your fists" [*Poenulus* 358].[236] And indeed just as this alliteration occurs in three words, elsewhere it occurs in similar fashion with two, as in these examples: *taciti ventura videbant; Turno tempus erit; impulit impulsu; victu venatus alebat; duris dolor ossibus ardet; formae conscia coniunx; vasta se mole moventem; castra fugae fidens; per loca senta situ; quo turbine torqueat hastam;* and *quem metui moritura.*[237] The same Cicero, prince of Roman eloquence, took pleasure in this same feature in joining two words with a single alliteration, as when he said in *Brutus,* "he gained skill in speech from teachers of speaking," and "so Jupiter would speak, they say, if he spoke Greek" [*Brutus* 119, 121].

It also has a most pleasant seasoning whenever alliteration is doubled in the same verse, but through different words and syllables, as in these examples: *magna Manes ter voce vocavi* and *pharetramque fuga sensere sonantem* [*Aeneid* 6.506, 9.660]. And in

sensere sonantem. Et apud Lucretium:[236] *multa munita virum vi.*
Fit geminatio interdum eiusdem alliterationis eodem in versu,
eaque nec vacua est iucunditate, ut in hoc: *nunc rapidus retro
atque aestu resoluta resorbens.* Quid cum fit per insequentis versus
allusionem, ut *verba vocantis / visa viri* atque ut apud Lucretium,[237] *et fera ferri / corpora constituunt?*

50   Virgiliana quoque alliteratio ea et rara est et aures non parum mulcet, quae constat partim ex continuatione, partim ex
intervallo annominantium syllabarum: *letum siliqua quassante legumen.* Neque insuavis est Lucretiana illa: *vesco sale saxa peresa.*
Neque item alia haec: *vera ratione repulsa,* aut: *clara loca candida
luce,* aut alia illa: *tenuia sputa minuta croci contacta colore.* Nam
Virgiliana illa ex continuatione est quam suavissima: *agitata
tumescere.* Sed nec inconcinna est illa, quae fit cum intervallo
dictionis unius, ut: *concessit moesta ad Manes,* et: *si nunc se nobis,*
et: *olli discurrere pares discrimine nullo*[238] et: *pleno se proluit auro.*
Quid autem annominatione illa iucundius: *ipsa canas oro. finem
dedit ore loquendi?* Quid etiam illa quae ex continuatione constat
atque interiecta dictione: *quam fessis finem rebus ferat,* et: *aut ulla
putatis / dona carere dolis Danaum?*

Non indecore, non insuaviter fit etiam alliteratio haec cum
allusione primarum litterarum syllabarum ve, ultimae ac primae
vocis, et desinentis qui antecedit versus et statim subsequentis,
ut: *tenuere coloni, / Carthago,* et: *luco tum forte parentis / Pilumni,*
et: *credere sensus; / sola viri,* et: *maxima*[239] *rerum / Roma colit.* Eadem haec alliteratio syllabarum affert quandam, ut ita dixerim,
auribus titillationem contextu in ipso, ubi desinente hinc, illinc
continuante dictione eadem hac sibi ratione utraque alludit, ut:

Lucretius: *multa munita virum vi* [Lucretius 1.728]. Sometimes doubling of the same alliteration occurs in the same verse, and it is pleasant as well. Thus: *nunc rapidus retro atque aestu resoluta resorbens* [Aeneid 11.627]. And consider when it occurs through a play with the following verse, as in *verba vocantis / visa viri*, and as in Lucretius: *et fera ferri / corpora constituunt* [Aeneid, 4.460–61; Lucretius, 2.103–4].[238]

Also both exquisite and quite delightful to the ear is the 50 Vergilian alliteration that consists partly of a succession, partly of a separation of the syllables in play: *letum siliqua quassante legumen* [Georgics 1.74]. And this Lucretian example is also rather pleasant: *vesco sale saxa peresa*; and likewise this one: *vera ratione repulsa*, and *clara loca candida luce*, and this other, *tenuia sputa minuta croci contacta colore* [Lucretius 1.326, 2.645, 5.779, 6.1188]. Indeed, this one of Vergil's from a succession of syllables is extremely agreeable: *agitata tumescere* [Georgics 1.357].[239] But the alliteration with a word in between is not inelegant either: *concessit moesta ad Manes* and *si nunc se nobis* and *olli discurrere pares discrimine nullo* and *pleno se proluit auro* [Aeneid 10.820, 6.187, 5.580, 1.739]. Moreover, what is more pleasing than this wordplay: *ipsa canas oro. finem dedit ore loquendi* [Aeneid 6.76]?[240] What more pleasing than this, which consists of a succession and a word in between: *quam fessis finem rebus ferat* and *aut ulla putatis / dona carere dolis Danaum* [Aeneid 3.145, 2.43–44]?

Also not unbecoming or unpleasant is the alliteration with play on the first letters or syllables, on the last or first word, and on the last word and the word immediately following in the next verse. For example: *tenuere coloni / Carthago* and *luco tum forte parentis / Pilumni* and *credere sensus; / sola viri* and *maxima rerum / Roma colit* [Aeneid 1.12–13, 9.3–4, 4.422–23, 7.602–3]. This same alliteration of syllables also tickles the ears a bit, so to speak, in the sequence where, with one word ending and the other continuing in the same way, each plays on the other.

aere ruebant, et: *lato te limite ducam*, et: *loricam ex aere rigentem*, et: *sidera retro*, et: *frustra moritura relinquat*, et: *coniunx iterum hospita Teucris*, et: *Ditis tamen ante.*

Non insuaviter etiam concursus earundem syllabarum mulcet aures; est enim genus quoddam complosionis: *ruit Oceano nox*, et: *Fama malum*, et: *date tela*, et: *cerno te tendere contra*, et: *stuppea flamma manu*, et: *glauca canentia fronde salicta.* Interdum ultima desinentis versus syllaba concurrit consonatque cum ultima vocis inchoantis insequentem, ut *diversa in parte furenti / turbantique viros.* Ut autem concursus ipse syllabarum delectat propter complosionem earundem litterarum, sic etiam ac multo magis earundem vocalium; quippe cum ex ipsa complosione magna fiat vocalitati accessio, ut: *si pereo hominum manibus, periisse iuvabit*, et *imponere Pelio Ossam*[240] et *nauticus*[241] *exoritur vario hortamine*[242] *clamor*, et *sub Ilio alto.* Verum complosio haec Graecorum est linguae quam nostrae familiarior, cui explosio magis est peculiaris, ut *dixerat et genua amplexus*, et *cum Troia*[243] *Achilles*, et *necdum fluctus latera ardua tinxit*, et *coelo capita alta ferentes*, et *porta adversa ingens.*[244]

51   Videtur res sane ridicula, rara tamen et affabrefacta; subblanditur enim auribus quaedam quasi strepens litterarum inter se sive concursatio sive conflictatio, ac nonnunquam etiam syllabarum; quae vis ipsis potius inest consonantibus quam vocalibus quae syllabas eas ineunt; exemplum est: *convulsum remis rostrisque ruentibus*[245] *aequor*, et *cristaque tegit galea aurea rubra*, et *fluitantia transtra*, et *ora puer prima*, et *quadrupedante putrem sonitu quatit ungula campum*, et *quod fieri ferro*, et *praefractaque*[246]

Thus: *aere ruebant; lato te limite ducam; loricam ex aere rigentem; sidera retro; frustra moritura relinquat; coniunx iterum hospita Teucris; Ditis tamen ante* [*Aeneid* 1.35, 9.323, 8.621, 4.489, 4.415, 6.93, 5.731].

A juxtaposition of the same syllables also delights the ear; indeed it is a certain kind of striking or clapping.[241] Thus: *ruit Oceano nox; Fama malum; date tela; cerno te tendere contra; stuppea flamma manu; glauca canentia fronde salicta* [*Aeneid* 2.250, 4.174, 9.37, 5.27, 8.694; *Georgics* 2.13]. Sometimes the last syllable at the end of a verse meets and chimes with the last syllable of the word beginning the next verse. Thus: *diversa in parte furenti / turbantique viros* [*Aeneid* 9.691.2]. Moreover, just as a juxtaposition of syllables is pleasing because of the clapping of the same letters, so too and much more pleasing is a juxtaposition of the same vowels, since from this clapping of unelided vowels arises a great addition to euphony. Thus: *si pereo, hominum manibus periise iuvabit* and *imponere Pelio Ossam* and *nauticus exoritur vario hortamine clamor* and *sub Ilio alto* [*Aeneid* 3.606; *Georgics* 1.281; *Aeneid* 3.128, 5.261].[242] But this kind of clapping belongs more to the Greek language than to ours, in which elision is more characteristic. Thus: *dixerat et genua amplexus* and *cum Troia Achilles* and *nec dum fluctus latera ardua tinxit* and *coelo capita alta ferentes* and *porta adversa ingens* [*Aeneid* 3.607, 5.804, 3.665, 3.678, 6.552].[243]

Of course, the thing seems almost laughable, but it is also 51 rare and ingeniously done; for a certain almost noisy clashing or striking of letters and sometimes even of syllables against each other charms the ear.[244] Consonants beginning a syllable have this effect more than vowels. For example: *convulsum remis rostrisque rudentibus aequor* and *cristaque tegit galea aurea rubra* and *fluitantia transtra* and *ora puer prima* and *quadrupedante putrem sonitu quatit ungula campum* and *quod fieri ferro* and *praefractaque*

quadrupedantum, et *infesta subit obvius hasta,* et *tribusque / transiit intextum tauris opus,* et *fugit illicet ocior Euro.*

Ac mihi quidem videtur[247] in pangendo carmine atque condiendis numeris illud idem usuvenire quod in puellari cultu atque munditiis, ut non modo gemmae cuiuspiam nitidioris, verum flosculi unius accessio permultum adiiciat cultui atque munditiis. Subiiciam itaque exempla quaedam Virgilianarum observationum in parte illa tum alliterationis, tum conflictationis; perexigua sane res, tamen nec pervulgate populariterque animadversa, sed quae et observata delectet, nec ulla sit ratione praetermittenda conanti quacunque possit arte audientium auribus subblandiri. Nunquid non etiam perquam suavis est allusio illa postremarum syllabarum, *sterneret aequor aquis?* Item illa mediae et ultimae: *animam abstulit hosti.* Alia item mediae ac primae: *qua semita monstrat; foliorum exhuberat umbra; vulnificusque Chalybs.* Nam de primis dictum est: *vellere vallum.* Quid cum primarum et ultimarum simul: *volat vapor ater?* Quid cum etiam primarum duarum et mediae dictionis inter utramque interiectae, ut *relegens errata retrorsum?*[248] Quid? etiam conflictationes ipsae quam sunt loco suo gratae, ut quidam quasi flosculi rariores inter prata niteant, ut *fulmineus Mnesteus,*[249] et *inter tela*[250] *rotasque viros,* et *stabula alta Latinus,* et *insertabam aptans,* et *nota intra tecta refugit,* et: *cristaque tegit galea aurea rubra.* Sed nec poenituerit subiunxisse Lucretianum illum: *nix acri concreta pruina.*

52   Neutique fortasse ad numeros quod subdam, sed magis ad poetae prudentiam spectabit: nihilominus numeros quoque ipsos illustriores reddit. Hoc autem tale est ut numeris ipsis fiat

quadrupedantum and *infesta subit obvius hasta* and *tribusque / transiit intextum tauris opus* and *fugit illicet ocior Euro* [*Aeneid* 5.143 = 8.690, 9.50, 10.306, 9.181, 8.596, 8.402, 11.614, 10.877, 10.784– 85, 12.733].[245]

Indeed, I think that the same thing is required in composing a poem and ornamenting rhythms as in the elegant dress of a young woman—that the addition of not only some gleaming jewel, but even a single little flower greatly enhances polish and elegance. And so I will add some examples of Vergil's practice in the area of both alliteration and clashing. It is a small thing, to be sure, yet not widely or generally noticed; but it gives pleasure when it is employed, and it is by no means to be neglected by someone trying in every possible way to please the ears of his audience. This play on adjacent syllables is certainly most agreeable: *sterneret aequor aquis* [*Aeneid* 8.89]. Likewise this one on the middle and final syllables: *animam abstulit hosti* [*Aeneid* 9.443]. Likewise these others on the middle and first: *qua semita monstrat; foliorum exhuberat umbra; vulnificusque Chalybs* [*Aeneid* 1.418; *Georgics* 1.191; *Aeneid* 8.446]. I have already talked about the first syllables: for example, *vellere vallum* [*Aeneid* 9.506]. Note also play on the first and last syllables at the same time: *volat vapor ater* [*Aeneid* 7.466].[246] Also play between two first syllables and the middle of the word put between them: *relegens errata retrorsum* [*Aeneid* 3.690]. But conflicts themselves are also pleasing in their place, so that they shine like rare little flowers in a meadow. For example: *fulmineus Mnesteus* and *inter tela rotasque viros* and *stabula alta Latinus* and *insertabam aptans* and *nota intra tecta refugit* and *cristaque tegit galea aurea rubra* [*Aeneid* 9.812, 9.318, 9.388, 2.672, 7.500, 9.50]. But I would also be pleased to add the Lucretian phrase, *nix acri concreta pruina* [Lucretius 3.20].

Perhaps what I am going to add pertains not at all to rhythm, but rather to the skill of the poet; nonetheless, it also makes rhythm itself more brilliant. Moreover, it is of a kind to make

52

satis etiam cum dignitate exprimendis affectibus, ut cum Virgilius Camillae vellet pedum celeritatem exprimere, pedum quoque ac syllabarum usus est celeritate:

ferret iter, celeres nec tingeret aequore plantas;

et, quod initio diximus, volucrem illum flammae strepitum his verbis ac numeris explicuit:

atque levem stipulam crepitantibus urere flammis.

Certum habeo senem nostrum aegre hoc laturum, referam tamen. Is cum vellet Lepidinae illius suae tardos ac defatigatos gressus innuere, versum ita statuit, ut verba ipsa pedesque videantur quodammodo aegre se trahere:

Nam defessa traho vix genua et ipsa[251] canistri
sarcina me gravat.

Quid enim his et verbis et numeris aut tardius aut defatigatius? Idem ipse Virgilius evaporantis aheni aestum ebullitionemque illam vix se se intra labrum continentis aquae cum explicaret, versum ita dilatavit, vix ut se ipsum capiat, quippe quem decem usque ad accentus extenderit nec habuerit quo amplius:

Nec iam se capit unda, volat vapor ater ad auras.

Quod idem servavit in Mezentio irato et seviente: praepeditur enim lingua iratorum ob excandescentiam, ut et[252] haereat et consistat et remoretur sonum ac verba interrumpatque sermonem ac concidat orationem ipsam:

rhythms alone sufficient to imitate particular qualities appropriately. Thus, when Vergil wanted to describe Camilla's fleetness of foot, he also employed fleetness of feet and syllables:

> she would go, and not get the quick soles of her feet wet on the sea's surface. [*Aeneid* 7.811]

And, as we said at the beginning, he showed the quick popping noises of fire with these words and rhythms:

> and to burn the light stubble with crackling flames. [*Georgics* 1.85][247]

I am sure that our old man will be displeased with this, but I will mention it anyway. When he wanted to indicate the slow and exhausted steps of that Lepidina of his, he so arranged the verse that the very words and feet seem somehow barely to plod along.

> Indeed I can hardly drag my legs along, and the very burden
> of the basket weighs me down. [Pontano, *Lepidina* 1.4.103]

For what is slower or tireder than these words and rhythms? Vergil himself, when he was describing the seething and bubbling of a steaming cauldron of water barely able to keep itself within the brim, extended the verse so that it scarcely contains itself, since he has stretched it out all the way to ten accents and could go no further:

> The water no longer contains itself, black steam flies to the sky. [*Aeneid* 7.466][248]

He follows the same method in the case of the enraged and violent Mezentius; for the tongue of angry people is tripped up because of their blazing rage, so that it both sticks and halts and holds back sound and words and interrupts utterance and dismembers speech itself.

'Nunc morere; ast de me divum pater atque hominum rex viderit.'

Quid enim est hoc ipso versu aut haesitantius, aut verbis interruptius, aut numeris etiam concisius? Quae quidem omnia praestantissimo cuique ingenio summa cura videnda esse censeo.

53 Quin etiam idem ipse Virgilius quacunque posset arte auribus ut satisfaceret, Graecos imitatus struxit quandoque tres simul voces in *e* desinentes, ut: *quatuor ex omni delectae classe carinae*, et *stant terrae*[253] *defixae hastae*. Alibi quatuor, ut:[254] *ite solutae / ite deae pelagi*. Quid cum dixit, *degere more ferae*? An est qui inficias eat numerum hunc summo fuisse studio conquisitum?

Aliquando tres item coniunxit voces eadem a vocali exordientes, ut: *insulae Ionio in magno*, et *ire iterum in lacrimas*. Aliquando etiam diversas diversa a vocali[255] incipientes, ut *regum aequabat opes animis*. Quid cum dixit: *omnes uno ordine habetis Achivos?* Illud vero omnino Homericum: *Glauco et Panopeae et Inoo Melicertae*.

Est et hoc tenerrimum in aures suavitatis infundibulum:

lacerum crudeliter ora,
ora manusque ambas;

et alibi:

ut[256] *vultum vidit morientis et ora,*
ora modis Anchisiades pallentia miris.

Neque parum etiam neque insuaviter mulcetur auditus numerique ipsi condiuntur ubi ultimae versuum dictiones itemque

Now die. But the father of gods and king of men
will see to me. [*Aeneid* 10.743–44][249]

Indeed, what is more hesitating than this verse, or more broken
off than its words, or even more cut up than its rhythms? In my
opinion every poet of outstanding talent must observe all these
points with the greatest care.

In fact, even the same Vergil himself, in order to satisfy the   53
ear in every possible way, sometimes imitated the Greeks and
piled up three words at a time ending in *e*.[250] For example:
quatuor ex omni delectae classe carinae and *stant terrae defixae hastae*
[*Aeneid* 5.115, 6.652]. Elsewhere, he put together four, as in *ite
solutae / ite deae pelagi* [*Aeneid* 9.116–17]. And what about *degere
more ferae* [*Aeneid* 4.551]? Who would deny that this rhythm
was sought out with the greatest care?

Furthermore, he has sometimes joined three words starting
with the same vowel, like *insulae Ionio in magno* and *ire iterum in
lacrimas* [*Aeneid* 3.211, 4.413]. Sometimes he has also joined
words beginning with a different vowel, like *regum aequabat opes
animis* [*Georgics* 4.132]. And what about *omnes uno ordine habetis
Achivos* [*Aeneid* 2.102]?[251] But this one is altogether Homeric:
Glauco et Panopeae et Inoo Melicertae [*Georgics* 1.437].[252]

And this is a most delicate means of pouring melodious
sound into the ear:

cruelly mutilated in the face,
his face and both hands, [*Aeneid* 6.495–96]

and in another place:

when the son of Anchises saw the dying man's expression
and face,
his face growing strangely pale. [*Aeneid* 10.821–22][253]

Neither too little nor unmelodiously does it caress the ear
and ornament the rhythm when the last words of verses and

primi, secundi, tertii et quarti loci invicem consonant in ultimis syllabis, ut:

stringentem ripas et pinguia culta secantem;

venerat extinctam ferroque extrema secutam;

vix adeo agnovit pavitantem et dira tegentem;

. . . longarum haec meta viarum;

ad terram misere aut ignibus aegra dedere;

vincla recusantum et sera sub nocte rudentum;

ad genitorem imas Herebi descendit ad umbras.

Nam qui statim sequuntur versus, quotiens vel recitari audio vel mecum eos ipse succino et aures et animum titillari mihi sentio:

Terribilem cristis galeam flammasque vomentem
fatiferumque ensem, loricamque ex aere rigentem,
sanguineam, ingentem.

Sed haec fortasse ad verborum collocationem spectant et ad structuram carminis potiusquam ad numeros; quamobrem ad ea quae reliqua sunt transeo.

54   Delectus ipse verborum poetae nobilitat supelectilem, verum satis non est delegisse, nisi etiam seligas; fit enim delectus plerumque e multis, selectio vero e paucis. Itaque et voces et syllabas, etiam litteras seligere oportet, quo versus ipse undique

likewise the first, second, third, and fourth places chime with each other in their final syllables. Here are some examples:[254]

skirting the banks and cleaving the rich fields; [*Aeneid* 8.63]

[the news] had come that you had died and ended your life
with the sword; [*Aeneid* 6.457]

he scarcely recognized him, trembling and hiding his
terrible [punishments]; [*Aeneid* 6.498]

this turning point of the long journey; [*Aeneid* 3.714]

they threw their weak [bodies] to the ground or gave them
up to the flames; [*Aeneid* 2.566]

[of lions] battling their bonds and roaring late in the night;
[*Aeneid* 7.16]

he went down to his father in the lowest shadows of
Erebus. [*Aeneid* 6.404]

Indeed, whenever I hear these next verses recited or else chant them over to myself, I feel that both my ears and my mind are stirred:

the helmet terrifying with plumes and spewing flames
and the fateful sword and the breastplate hard with bronze,
bloodred, huge. [*Aeneid* 8.620–22][255]

But perhaps these matters pertain to word arrangement and metrical structure rather than to rhythm, so I will go on to the points that remain.

Word choice ennobles a poet's resources, but it is not enough   54
to have chosen unless you also select, for one generally chooses from many, but selects from a few. So it is necessary to select both words and syllables, even letters, so that the verse hangs

sibi constet, ex eoque tanquam in quadram redacto numerum perficias, id quod versus hi paucis indicabunt:

illum expirantem transfixo pectore flammas.

An non poterat etiam sic, *traiecto pectore*, suo quidem ac proprio verbo? Sed cum ante collocasset vocem illam *expirantem*, post vero *flammas*, refertam utramque consonantibus litteris, voluit etiam in medio collocare vocem quae similibus quoque litteris consonaret, quippe cum in dictione *traiecto* ea non esset consonantium litterarum copia nec similitudo, quae utraque est in *transfixo*.

talia flammato secum dea corde volutans.

Cur non *talia succenso?* Nimirum quia vocalis *a* clarum e se edit sonum, at *u* vocalis subobscurum; itaque si *u* post duplex *a* subdidisset, claritatem quam affectabat eo in loco subobscurasset eamque ob rem summittendo alterum atque alterum *a*, adauxit litterae claritudinem; quid si dixisset *flammanti?* atqui claritas illa erat implenda auxilio vocalis sonorae et gravidae, non tenuanda exili, qualis est *i* vocalis.

. . . *loca foeta furentibus Austris.*

Cur non *plena?* Videlicet quod alliteratio delectet magis aures.

Aeoliam venit. Hic vasto rex Aeolus antro.

Potuit sic et cum praeterito tempore: *Aeoliam venit. Vasto hic rex Aeolus antro;* praeterquam autem quod praesens tempus repentinam vehementemque Iunonis commotionem indicat magis quam praeteritum, quando res ipsa geri iam videtur et hiatus ille et monosyllaborum duplicatio eo in loco tum versum tum

together everywhere, and when it has been squared up, so to speak, you may perfect the rhythm, as these verses will briefly demonstrate.[256]

illum expirantem transfixo pectore flammis. [*Aeneid* 1.44][257]

Could it not have been this way, too, and with a perfectly appropriate word: *traiecto pectore?* But since he had placed the word *expirantem* before it, and *flammas* after it, each filled with consonants, in the middle he wanted to place a word with similar letters to match the sound, since in *traiecto* there was neither the abundance of consonants nor the similarity, both of which are possessed by *transfixo.*

talia flammato secum dea corde volutans. [*Aeneid* 1.50][258]

Why not *talia succenso?* No doubt because the vowel *a* produces a clear sound, the vowel *u* one that is indistinct; and so if he had added *u* after the double *a,* he would have muffled the clear sound that he was trying to get in that place, and for that reason by adding another and yet another *a,* he increased the clear sound of the letter. What if he had said *flammanti?* But the clear sound I have been talking about needed to be completed with the aid of a resounding and full vowel, not attenuated with a thin one, like *i.*

loca foeta furentibus Austris. [*Aeneid* 1.51]

Why not *plena* for *foeta?* Evidently because alliteration is more pleasing to the ear.

Aeoliam venit. Hic vasto rex Aeolus antro. [*Aeneid* 1.52][259]

He could also have used the past tense: *Aeoliam venit. Vasto hic rex Aeolus antro;* but apart from the fact that the present tense indicates the sudden and violent movement of Juno better than the perfect does since the event seems to be happening now, both the elision and the double monosyllable in that place

numerum nimio plus stetissent, quod ipsum pronuntiando sentitur.

celsa sedet Aeolus arce
sceptra tenens mollitque animos et temperat iras.

In eo quod est *celsa sedet* et *sceptra tenens* simul insunt et allitera-tio et conflictatio, quae aures submulceant. Quod vero dixit *mollit* potiusquam *lenit*, hoc videtur fuisse causae, quod vocalis *e* cum sonorem demittat, si *lenit* dixisset, eam trigeminasset inde-que generosus ille canor, supra quam oportebat, demissus pene contabuisset; quem plenitudine sua vocalis *o* et sustentavit et illustrem reddidit, hac eum ratione moderatus.

Ex his igitur quanquam paucis licet cognoscere quanta matu-ritate et studio sit cum litteris cumque auribus habenda ratio. Qua de re dictum a me sit hactenus; nam progredi ulterius quidnam esset aliud quam structurae collocationisque campum ingredi? Quae materia haudquaquam est loci huius magnum-que volumen sola desiderat, ut de iis omnino taceam quae ad admirationem comparandam pertinent. Quocirca ad id quod reliquum videtur transeo.

55   Numerus ipse quoniam celeritate constat ac tarditate, qua-rum alteram dactylus, alteram spondeus secum habet (est au-tem sermo hic noster omnis heroicis, hoc est generosis de versi-bus), ex his opportune collocatis prudenterque simul mistis manat dignitas illa quae laudabile carmen reddit; quibus si ac-cesserit verborum delectus, selectio syllabarum, de quibus pauca quaedam dixi, prudentia item et verborum et syllabarum tem-perandarum, adhaec magnitudo sententiarum, explicatio rerum iucunda et gravis pro loco ac re, et haec ipsa numerorum artifi-ciosa varietas, decorumque illud quod in omni non modo vitae genere, verum etiam disciplinae ac facultatis a natura ipsa

would have checked both the verse and the rhythm far too much — an effect that is felt by saying it aloud.

celsa sedet Aeolus arce
sceptra tenens mollitque animos et temperat iras. [*Aeneid* 1.56–57]

The phrases *celsa sedet* and *sceptra tenens* contain alliteration and conflict at the same time, features that gently caress the ear.[260] He said *mollit* rather than *lenit*, and this seems to be the reason: the vowel *e* lowers the sound, and if he had said *lenit*, he would have used it three times; as a consequence the excellent melodic tone would have dropped too much, nearly wasting away. This tone the vowel *o* has sustained and made clear with its own fullness, and he has regulated it in this way.

From these examples, few as they are, one can understand with how much mature judgment and attention one must take both letters and sounds into account. About this matter let me stop here, for to go further would be nothing short of entering the field of structure and arrangement. This subject is not at all appropriate to this place and by itself requires a great volume — to say nothing about the matters concerned with winning admiration. And so I pass over to what seems to be left.

Since rhythm itself is composed of speed and slowness, one the quality of the dactyl, the other of the spondee (I am speaking here entirely about heroic — that is, noble — verse), from these when they are properly arranged and skilfully mingled arises the excellence that makes poetry praiseworthy. If to these is added word choice and selection of syllables, about which I have made a few comments, likewise skill in combining words and syllables, as well as greatness of thought, exposition of the subject that is agreeable or serious depending on the place and situation, and the artful variety of rhythm I have been talking about, as well as the decorum required by nature herself not only in every kind of life but also in every kind of discipline and

55

exigitur, ut de inventione, distributione iudicioque hac in parte taceam, nimirum admiratio illa plena laudis, quam poeticis senex noster proponit studiis, multa etiam cum commendatione ac fama comparabitur, quam sequendam ab illis duco qui in hac ipsa facultate excellere eminenter cupiunt.

Has autem res omnis et praestabit ars ingenio coniuncta et eas perficiet, ac pertinax illa et diligens cura, quae optimo cuique inesse debet artifici. Quodque pace omnium dixerim (quanquam, tecum,[257] Parde, hoc ad aurem dictum velim), et Cicero oratorum maximus et Ovidius poetarum maxime ingeniosus nolunt ipsi quidem artem apparere, ego vero non ibo inficias in iis hoc probandum artibus, quibus proposita est sola persuasio. At ipse nostris his in studiis laboro, contendo, enitor, meum ut carmen appareat etiam admirabile, ut industria innotescat mea, ut celebretur artificium, dici quoque de me ut possit: *Eris ab illo alter.* Dissimulat hic orator, alibi contra simulat quae sunt in causa, quo a iudice iure vel iniuria, dicendo tamen vel assequatur quod quaerit, vel extorqueat. At in hoc dicendi genere insidiae insunt nullae, nullum praeterquam famae compendium. Cupio igitur, et aventer quidem cupio, appareat industria mea in carmine, appareat diligentia, labores laudari pervelim meos. Incendor cupiditate gloriae, utque inter earundem rerum studiosos evadam etiam primus. An inficiatus est hoc Virgilius cum decantavit:

> Primus ego in patriam mecum, modo vita supersit,
> Aonio rediens deducam vertice Musas?

skill—to say nothing in this place of invention, arrangement, and taste—without a doubt the admiration full of praise that our old man holds out as the reward for poetic endeavors will be achieved with great commendation and fame. This I consider the necessary object of those who desire to be eminently superior in this field.

Moreover, all these things will be furnished and brought to fruition by art joined with talent and by that constant and devoted attention which must be present in all the best artists. And this I would say with all due respect to everyone (although in your presence, Pardo, I would prefer it said in a whisper), both Cicero, the greatest of orators, and Ovid, the most ingenious of poets, were unwilling for their art to be visible, and I will certainly not deny that this principle should be approved in arts whose only purpose is persuasion. But in these studies of ours I toil, I endeavor, I strive so that my poetry may appear worthy of admiration, that my industry may be noted, my artistry celebrated, and so that it can be said also of me, "You will be next after him."[261] At one point the orator may conceal, at another falsify the facts of the case, so that whether rightly or wrongly, but in any case by speaking, he may gain or wrest what he seeks from the judge. But in this kind of speaking there is no artifice, no profit beyond that of fame. So I desire, and indeed I earnestly desire that my industry appear in my poetry, that my attentiveness appear; I long for my labors to be praised. I am on fire with the desire for glory and that I may turn out to be first among those devoted to the same matters. Certainly Vergil did not fail to acknowledge this when he sang:

I will be first, provided that I live long enough, to return to
     my homeland
from the Aonian peak, leading the Muses with me in
     triumph. [*Georgics* 3.10–11]

Non inficiantur vel minores auctores, Ovidius atque Horatius, uterque tamen suo in genere abunde clarus:

Exegi monumentum aere perennius,

et:

Iamque opus exegi, quod nec Iovis ira, nec ignes,
nec ferrum poterit, nec edax abolere vetustas.

56   Nolim tamen intelligatur ars mea antequam lectorem mei carminis in admirationem eius traxerim; at postquam factus est illius admirator, vel introspiciat ipse consilia, laudet, commendet, extollat quaecunque etiam lineamenta. Quis statuarius, fusor, pictor vult se videri dum inumbrat, dum colores primos linit, dum primas illas quasi lituras effigiat? Post vero consumatum opus exponit illud et ambit publice laudari praeponique ob adhibitum studium coeteris artificibus omnibus. Etenim ab arte artifices sunt dicti finisque ipsius artificis, qua artem exercet, non qua lucrum inde quaerit, est bene consumateque in illa se se gerere opusque perficere a se susceptum. A poetis igitur non lucrum quaeritur, qua poetae sunt, sed admiratio cum commendatione operis suique ingenii; cuius quando comes est laus, laudari quoque se et palam et ore pleno tum cupient tum letabuntur; quanquam, etiamsi a nemine laudentur, possunt tamen sola ingenii artificiique sui conscientia esse contenti. Sed elucescat oportet ingenii et artis eorum magnitudo ac praestantia de quibus fama est proditura, quae ab illis omni studio affectatur. Sed cohibebo me ipsum, ne incensus studiorum meorum commendatione longius ab incepto sermone discessisse videar. Sit igitur satis me in vestram omnium, qui hic adestis, gratiam ea[258]

Nor did even Ovid and Horace deny it, lesser authors, yet each quite brilliant in his own genre:

> I have completed a monument more enduring than bronze
> [Horace, *Odes* 3.30.1]

and:

> Now I have completed my work, which neither Jove's wrath
> nor fire nor sword nor devouring time can destroy. [Ovid,
> *Metamorphoses* 15.871–72]

Nevertheless, I would not want my craftsmanship to be perceived before I drew the reader of my poetry into a state of wonder; but after he has been brought to marvel at it, let him look into my intentions, let him praise, commend, even extol every single feature. What sculptor, bronze founder, or painter wants to be watched while he sketches, while he lays on the first colors, while he gives those first smears a shape? But afterward he displays the finished work and campaigns to be praised and to be placed before all other artists for his efforts. In fact artists get their name from the word art, and the purpose of the artist, in so far as he practices his art and does not seek gain from it, is to act well and flawlessly in it and to perfect the work he has undertaken. Poets therefore, in so far as they are poets, do not seek profit, but rather admiration along with commendation of their work and talent; and since praise is the companion of wonder, they will also desire and rejoice to be praised openly and wholeheartedly, although even if no one praises them, they can still be content with the consciousness of their own talent and artistry alone. But it is necessary for the greatness and preeminence of their talent and art to shine forth, from which will proceed the fame they pursue with all their might. But I will restrain myself, lest on fire with the commendation of my studies I seem to have strayed too far from the original discussion. Let it be enough that I have related these things about rhythm

56

de numeris tradidisse. Quocirca cui sorte sua optigerit, loquendi possessionem ei trado, ne loci huius consuetudinem existimer aut neglexisse impudenter aut contempsisse superbe.

57   *Pud.* Vestrum qui adestis omnium officium arbitror non laudare solum quae a Sincero tam exacte dicta sunt de numeris, verum etiam admirari, dum qua via incedatur ad admirationem in poetica comparandam e numeris tam designanter et monstraverit nobis illam et expurgatis etiam scrupulis ac salebris complanaverit, id quod video a litteratoribus nostris praetermissum vel ignoratum potius. Recte itaque ab Antonio usurpatum memini poetam esse ipsum oportere poeticis qui de virtutibus loqui cum dignitate vellet.

Sum. Hoc nimirum fuit, Puderice, causae cur, qui ipse scirem grammaticis incomperta haec esse, Sincerum ad dicendum excitaverim, nec aut importunitatis poenitet me meae aut obsecrationis, per quam quid exanclatum fuerit ipse vides, ut neque iniuria neque praeter opinionem qui ea audivimus admiremur omnes. Utinam autem litteratores ipsi etiam in iis quae litteraturae sunt paulo essent diligentiores, cum praesertim videam senem nostrum vel minutissima quaeque pensitantem etiam in grammaticis!

Sed quid senem adhaec ipsa advocaverim, qui paucis ante diebus eadem hac in porticu audiverim Altilium hunc quaedam explanantem quae grammaticorum essent propria? Verum quis est eorum tanta solertia ut non alienis potiusquam suis rimetur oculis artis ipsius secreta? Venit in sermonem Ciceronis, qui *causam* duplici *s* scribere esset solitus, quod ipsum Romae adhuc quoque vetustissimo in monumento inscriptum legitur. Attendite, quaeso, quibus a principiis est exorsus; non enarraverim

to please all of you who are present. For this reason. I turn over the right to speak to the one to whom it has fallen by lot, lest I be thought either shameless in disregarding the custom of this place or arrogant in defying it.

Puderico. I think it is the duty of all of you who are present not   57 only to praise Sincero's precise discussion of rhythm but also to marvel at it since he has both pointed out to us so cogently what road to travel to win admiration in poetry through rhythm and smoothed the way by clearing away the stones and ruts. This is a subject that I see has been omitted by our literary men or rather has been unknown to them. And thus I remember that Antonio used to say quite rightly that it was necessary for anyone who wanted to speak with authority about poetic excellence to be a poet himself.[262]

Summonte. Truly, Puderico, this was why I called on Sincero to speak, since I was aware that these matters were unknown to grammarians; and I am not sorry that I kept after him and implored him because you yourself see what has been brought to light, so that, not without just cause or beyond expectation, all of us who have heard these things are in a state of admiration.[263] I wish that those engaged in literary studies were themselves in fact a little more diligent in matters pertaining to literature, especially since I see our old man weighing even the tiniest points in grammatical studies.

But why should I call upon the old man for these matters since just a few days ago in this very portico I heard Altilio here explaining certain matters that are the proper business of grammarians? But who of them is skillful enough to seek out the secrets of that art — not with other people's eyes, but with his own? He happened to be talking about Cicero, who had habitually written *causa* with a double *s*, the very spelling one also reads to this day inscribed on a very ancient monument in Rome. Please pay attention to his starting point; I would not

qua suavitate rem expresserit, ne videar in gratiam eius qui hic adest eloqui; nam mihi quidem grammatici ab omni videntur prorsus dicendi suavitate alieni, et si in cognoscenda vocum proprietate illisque contexendis omnis eorum fere versatur disciplina.

58   Prisci, inquit, illi qui Latium, a quo Latinam dictam esse linguam sunt qui velint, etiam ante Aborigines tenuere, plerique in *cavernis* habitabant, quae a *cavando* essent dictae; iis autem et aestus cavebant et frigora, pleraque etiam alia incommoda, in illisque se et sua *cautius* tutabantur. Qua e re verbum *caveo* ab iisdem esse deductum; quodque in *causa* ipsa *cavisse* oporteret, inde ab initio dictam esse *cavissam*; post vero, subtracta vocali, *caussam*, nomine ipso tris adhuc syllabas retinente; postremo prima et secunda syllaba duabusque illis vocalibus litteris in unum coactis, vocem ipsam factam esse dyssyllabam ac nihilominus duplex *s* mansisse; quod tandem leniendae vocis gratia simplex extitisset, quando duplex ipsum post *au* dypthongum sonaret horridius, praesertim *c* consonante dypthongum praecedente. Ab eodem illo verbo *cavo* factam esse primo *cavipam*, vas vinarium, ab eoque *caviponam* et *caviponem*, quod *cavis* in locis vel *cavis* doliis vinariam exercerent, e quibus posteriores vocalem *i* detraxissent, indeque esse hodie *cupas*, *au* in *u* productum verso, ut *claudo cludo*, et *cauponam cauponemque* et *cauponari*. Eosdem illos locos *fornices* dictos, a *foranda* olim vel terra vel saxo,

describe the charming way in which he expressed the idea, lest I seem to flatter anyone present. Indeed, in my view at least, grammarians seem completely alien to any charm in speaking, even though almost their whole discipline is concerned with understanding the proper use of words and putting them together.

Latium, he said, from which some think the Latin language takes its name, was inhabited by a primitive people even before the primeval Romans. For the most part they lived in caves [*cavernis*], so named from the word "excavating" [*cavando*]; there they took care [*cavebant*] against heat and cold and many other troubles as well, and in them they quite cautiously [*cautius*] safeguarded themselves and their possessions. Therefore, he said, the word *caveo* [be careful] was derived from the same words, and because in a legal case [*causa*] it was necessary to take care [*cavisse*], it was originally called *cavissa*, but later *caussa* with the vowel *i* removed and the word itself still keeping three syllables; finally, when the first and second syllables and the two vowels were contracted into one, the word itself became a disyllable and yet the double *s* remained; this in the end, to soften the sound, had become single, since the double *s* after the diphthong *au* sounded too harsh, especially with the consonant *c* preceding the diphthong. From the same word *cavo*, he said, first came *cavipa*, a vessel for wine, and from that *cavipona* [barmaid] and *cavipo* [barkeeper], because they practiced their wine trade in cavernous [*cavis*] places or with hollow [*cavis*] jars; from these words their descendants removed the vowel *i*, so that today we have *cupae* [casks] with the *au* turned into long *u* as in *claudo*, *cludo*, along with *caupona* and *caupo* as well as *cauponari* [to traffic in wine]. The same places were called *fornices* [vaults], formerly from the digging out [*forando*] of earth or rock—from

58

quam a Graeco verbo malebat, *fornicesque* ac *cavernas* idem in initio fuisse, pro varietate linguarum appellatione non una.

59   Venit etiam in sermonem verbi quod est *exanclo*. Videte, obsecro, rem unde vir Latinitatis amantissimus[259] repetierit; quod si, quae eius est verecundia, repeti a me forte non aequiore fert animo, avertat, quaeso, a dicente faciem aut alio paulisper inambulet. *Am*, inquit, vocula fuit apud priscos illos idem illud quod nunc est apud nos *circum*; inde *hamus*, et si post differentiae gratia praefixa ei fuit aspiratio; inde *annus*, quod in circulum rediret, mutata post *m* in semivocalem litteram concinnioris soni gratia. Eodem e fonte *amnis*, quod fluviorum cursus plerumque sint flexuosi, et *ambio* et *ambulo* et *ambedo*, *ambesusque*, inde etiam *anus*, oscena pars corporis, ab eius ambitu, et *anulus* et *anus*, vetula, quod propter annositatem senilis status corporis a capite proclinet in pedes efficiaturque incurva. Ex *anno* vero ductum esse *anniculum*, ut *bimum*, ut *trimum*, quasi *biamnum*, et *triamnum*, quae res indicat principio secundam *anni* litterarum fuisse *m*; ab *anniculo anniculare*, cumque tempestate ea hominum vita esset agrestior magnaeque daretur laudi fruges ipsas post annum asservasse, unde *perannare* factum esset, formatum primo verbum *exanniculo*, donec ex eo subductum fuit *exanclo*, quod verbum relatum esset ad labores, ad pericula, ad difficultates. Quid enim difficilius quam vina, triticum, poma in alium atque alium annum illesa[260] perducere aetatemque iis addere quibus a natura vix aliqua esset data?

a Greek verb, as he preferred — and *fornices* and *cavernae* had been the same thing in the beginning, but not with a single name because of the different language.

He also happened to talk about the verb *exanclo* [suffer or   59 endure]. Please pay attention to the thing from which this most devoted Latinist traced it. But if perchance — such is his modesty — he does not like having me retrace it, please let him turn his face away from me while I speak or go for a little walk somewhere else. The little word *am*, he said, meant the same thing among those primitive people that *circum* [around] does now with us; then it became *hamus* [hook], although later, to indicate the distinction, it had gained an initial aspirate; then *annus* [year], because it returns in a circle, with *m* later changed into a semivowel to make a pleasanter sound.[264] From the same source comes *amnis* [stream], because the courses of rivers are usually full of turns, and *ambio* [go around] and *ambulo* [walk around] and *ambedo* [eat around or consume] and *ambesus* [consumed], then also, from its circular shape *anus* [anus], an obscene part of the body, and *anulus* [ring] and *anus* [old woman], because on account of her years [*annositatem*] an old person's posture bends forward from the head to the feet and becomes curved. But from *annus* is derived *anniculus* [yearling], just like *bimus* [two years old] and *trimus* [three years old] as if equivalent to *biamnus* and *triamnus*, which indicates that originally the second letter of *annus* was *m*. From *anniculus* comes *anniculare* [to store for a year],[265] and since in those days people's way of life was more agricultural and it was very praiseworthy to have kept produce more than a year, from which was created *perannare* [live through the year], first the verb *exanniculo* was formed and at last *exanclo* [endure] was extracted from it — a verb related to toil, to danger, to hardship. Indeed what can be harder than to keep wine, grain, or fruit unharmed year after year and to add time to things scarcely given any at all by nature?

60   Addam et hoc: erat quaestio, qua ex origine deducta esset dictio haec *imbecillitas*. Animum advertite, quaeso, qua eam via deduxerit. *Via*, inquit, dicta principio est, quod ea *veherentur* et homines et res quae domum *devehebantur* initioque fuisse *veham*;[261] sic etiam *vehillam* et *vehicum*, quod illuc *veherentur* quae colligebantur ex agris; ea post mutata sunt in *villam* et *vicum*; factum est etiam nomen *vehiculum*, quo res ipsae *vehuntur*. A *via vietus, viator, viaticum*; a *villa villicus, villicatio*; a *vico vicinus, vicinitas, vicinia, vicatim*; quodque senes aetate iam confecti soli absque subsidio *vehi* pedibus suis nequirent, sumptus cum esset ab illis fustis *viae faciendae*, hoc est ambulandi gratia, *baculum* ex eo dictum, quasi *viaculum*, qui alio etiam nomine esset *scipio*, a *manus* scilicet *capione*; a *baculoque* factum esse nomen *imbecillum*, cui innixi incederent qui infirmis essent pedibus; quodque non absque labore ac difficultate etiam baculo *veherentur*, inde quoque manasse *vix*, quae vox est difficultatis ac laboris. Ab habitu igitur *imbecilli* hominis eiusque infirmitate deductum esse nomen *imbecillitatis* commutatione litterarum.

61   *Pud.* Et ex illis quae poeticis sunt de numeris a Sincero dicta et quae nunc a te, Summonti, referuntur grammaticis de rebus mirandum in modum incendor ardore audiendi aliquid de historia, quae nullos adhuc praeceptores habuerit, cum grammatica, rhetorica, philosophia institutores quidem plurimos eosque maximos ac praestantissimos viros promeruerit. Ac tametsi scio

I will also add this: a question arose about the origin of the   60
word *imbecillitas* [weakness]. Pay attention, please, to the road
[*via*] by which he derived it. *Via* [road], he said, was originally
so called because along it were carried [*veherentur*] both people
and things that were being conveyed [*devehebantur*] home, and
originially the word was *veha*, so also *vehilla* and *vehicus*, because
thither were carried [*veherentur*] the things they gathered from
the fields; later these words were changed to *villa* [farm] and
vicus [village]; also created was the name *vehiculum* [convey-
ance], by which the things were carried [*vehuntur*].[266] From *via*,
came *vietus* [shriveled], *viator* [traveler], *viaticum* [provisions for
a journey]; from *villa villicus* [overseer], *villicatio* [management of
a farm]; from *vicus vicinus* [neighbor], *vicinitas* [neighborhood],
vicinia [vicinity], *vicatim* [from town to town]. And because old
men exhausted by age cannot be carried [*vehi*] by their own feet
by themselves and without assistance, when they had taken up
a staff in order to make their way [*via*], that is, to walk, it was
called for that reason *baculum* [walking stick], almost *viaculum*
[way-maker], which by another name would be *scipio* [staff],
evidently from *manus capio* [a taking by the hand]; and from
baculum, on which those with bad feet lean as they go, was made
the word *imbecillus* [on a stick, weak]; and because they move
[*veherentur*] not without toil and difficulty even with a stick
[*baculum*], from that fact comes also *vix* [hardly], which is a
word of difficulty and toil. And so from the bearing of a man
leaning on his stick [*imbecillus*] and his weakness, by a change of
letters is derived the noun *imbecillitas*.[267]

Puderico. Both from what Sincero has said about poetic rhythm   61
and from your reports about matters of grammar, Summonte, I
am on fire with an astonishing desire to hear something about
history, since up to now it has had no instructors, although
grammar, rhetoric, and philosophy have won numerous teachers indeed, and very great and outstanding ones. And although

dictionem eam esse multiplicem, nec unius fortuitaeque consessionis, velim tamen non oratum modo, verum etiam exoratum Altilium, uti Actio succedens in dicendi possessione hac ipsa de re vel edisserat aliquid enucleatius, vel saltem, ut dici solet, de ea nobis innuat, dum accuratius quippiam de historia vel traditum ab eo accipiamus vel nutu ipso significatum. Quod tu, Altili, per Musas rogatus perque communem hunc consessum, cuius honestandi fuisti semper studiosissimus, nobis audiendi tui cupientissimis praestare ne recusaris.

62   *Alt.* Nec quid ipse mihi honeris, Puderice, imponas satis consideras, et ego inconsideratior fuerim, si tanto subire velim honeri humeris tam imbecillis. Quis enim ego sum aut rem ab eminentissimis viris reformidatam potiusquam intentatam quo aggrediar animo? aut eam aggressus quo e priscis vel consultore utar vel auctore?[262] Ne tamen aut vobis ipsis expetentibus aut loco deesse huic videar, innuens quidem, ut tu ipse, Puderice, exigis, potiusquam praecipiens, dicam de historia aliquid, quodque ipse quidem multa de lectione collegerim, magis quam quod auctore nitar aliquo, quem nullum, ut video, in hunc usque diem habuit historia.

Cuius mihi principium a natura ductum videtur, quando insitum est homini studium propagandi res suas ad posteros, nativa quadam cum cupiditate efficiendi memoriam sui quam maxime diuturnam; qua e re nomen id ei Graece fuit inditum. Romani vero, quod per annos singulos quae gesta essent mandare litteris consuessent, annales initio vocavere, post, accepto Graeco nomine, et ab illis quoque historia dicta est, prisco et Latino nomine pene obliterato. Eam maiores nostri quandam

I know that the discussion of it is complicated and not one for a single casual meeting, still I would like not only to ask Altilio, but to beseech him to succeed Azio in taking the floor and either to say something about the topic in minute detail or at least, as they say, to give us hints us about it, provided that we get something rather carefully thought out about history from him either as instructions or else as an indication with just a nod. Since you have been asked for this, Altilio, in the name of the Muses and in that of this assembly we share, which you have always been most eager to honor, do not refuse to provide it to us who are most desirous of hearing you.

Altilio. You do not give enough thought, Puderico, to what a bur-   62
den you are placing on me, and I would be too thoughtless myself if I were willing to take so great a burden on such weak shoulders. Indeed, who am I, or wouldn't it be arrogant of me to undertake a subject that the most distinguished men have not just left untried but actually dreaded? Or having once undertaken it, which of the ancients should I use as an advisor or authority? Nevertheless, lest I seem to fail in my duty either to you who are asking or to this place, I will say something about history, giving hints as you require, Puderico, rather than imparting instruction, and I will talk about what I have gathered from much reading rather than because I am relying on any authority — to this day history has not had one, as far as I can see.

I think it began naturally since man has an innate eagerness to hand down his affairs to posterity, along with a certain native desire of making his memory live as long as possible. And from this circumstance history got its name in Greek.[268] But the Romans, because they habitually recorded happenings by individual years, first used the term *annales;* later, accepting the Greek name, they called it history too, and the ancient Latin name was almost consigned to oblivion. Our ancestors considered it a

quasi solutam poeticam putavere, recteque ipsi quidem; plerumque enim habent inter se communia: ut rerum vetustarum ac remotarum repetitiones, ut locorum, populorum, nationum, gentium descriptiones, quin[263] etiam illorum situs, mores, leges, consuetudines, ut vitiorum insectationes, virtutum ac benefactorum laudes; utraque enim demonstrativo versatur in genere, nec minus etiam in deliberativo, quod ipsum conciones indicant ac consilia, quibus tum poetica tum historia maxime ornatur gloriaturque ex iis locupletiorem se se bonis ab auctoribus redditam. Adhaec repentini casus successusque, ipsi varii atque incerti, consilia item diversa quaeque praeter hominum ipsorum opinionem plurima contingunt in vita ac rebus gerendis. Nec vero, si poetica ipsa multa est in explicandis deorum tum consiliis tum rebus quae ab illis administrantur, non historia etiam deorum iras explicat, refert prodigia placatque illos votis, supplicationibus, ludis consulitque eorum oracula; utraque etiam gaudet amplificationibus, digressionibus item ac varietate, studetque movendis affectibus sequiturque decorum quaque in re ac materia suum. Itaque neutrius magis quam alterius aut propositum est aut studium ut doceat, delectet, moveat, ut etiam prosit, rem apparet eamque ante oculos ponat, ac nunc extollat aliud nunc aliud elevet.

Sed nec in deligendis tum rebus tum verbis iisdemque proprie ac decenter disponendis collocandisque altera cedit alteri; historia tamen est castior, illa vero lascivior; nec item in ornatu et cultu non eadem quoque utriusque sedulitas est et cura, tametsi historia cultu tantum contenta esse potest suo, eoque qui sit matrona dignus idoneusque continentiae, a fucoque abstineat ac purpurisso, quem quidem in altera illa theatra persaepe probant; idque ut in puella nequaquam aliquando

kind of prose poetry, and they were certainly correct.[269] Indeed, history and poetry have many points in common: like retelling of ancient and distant matters; like descriptions of places, peoples, nations, and tribes (what their geography was like, and their characters, laws, and customs); like censure of vices, praise of virtues and good deeds. In fact, both belong to the demonstrative genre and equally to the deliberative, as is shown by the orations and counsels with which both poetry and history are furnished to the highest degree and from which they boast of being enriched by good authors. In addition, they both contain sudden misfortunes and successes, themselves various and uncertain, as well as diverse intentions and events that happen in great numbers beyond human expectation in the activities of life. Moreover, if poetry is much concerned with laying out both the plans of the gods and the things accomplished by them, history for its part treats the wrath of the gods, reports portents, placates the gods with vows, supplications, and festivals and consults their oracles. Each delights in amplifications, digressions and variety as well; each strives to move the emotions and follows its own decorum in every subject and material. And the purpose or concern of the one is no more than that of the other: to teach, to please, to move, also to be useful, to prepare a subject and set it before one's eyes, and now to elevate one thing, now diminish another.

But also neither yields to the other in selecting both subjects and words and in arranging and placing them appropriately and becomingly; yet history is purer in style, poetry more extravagant. In adornment and attire they both take the same painstaking attention and care, although history can be content with her own garb alone and with the sort worthy of a matron and proper to her restraint. This style is free from the paint and rouge that audiences often approve in the other one — the sort that is sometimes permissible for a girl, provided that she

reprehenditur, dum tamen ipsa intelligat quid ingenuam inter et vulgarem intersit. In verbis item ac sententiis altera castigatior, altera ut etiam in numeris sic in verbis nunc liberalior est nunc etiam affectatior; nam parum contenta priscis atque usitatis vocibus exultat persaepe novandis illis aut peregre afferendis.

Proposito vero omnino pene aut maxime profecto differunt, cum altera veritati tantum explicandae, quamvis et exornandae quoque intenta esse debeat, poetica vero satis non habeat neque decorum suum servaverit nisi multa etiam aliunde comportaverit, nunc ex parte aut vera aut probabilia, nunc omnino ficta neque veri ullo modo similia, quo admirabiliora quae a se dicuntur appareant. Hoc tamen ipso mirifice conveniunt, quod utriusque propositum est quod susceperit dicendum illustrare et quoad possit sempiternum id efficere. Numeros quoque utraque suos habet itemque dicendi figuras, diversa tamen ratione. Ordine quoque enarrandarum rerum differunt inter se, cum historia rerum gestarum ordinem sequatur ac seriem, at illa altera persaepe a mediis, nonnunquam etiam pene ab ultimis narrandi principium capiat, assumens etiam extrinsecus personas pro rei ipsius natura, ut deorum, nympharum numinumque aliorum, ut vatum furentiumque. Quid quod vocem quoque dat et orationem rebus mutis, divinitatem tribuit insomniis, deos etiam ipsos mortalibus instruit affectionibus? Quae quidem omnia apud Graecos Homerus, apud nostros Virgilius passim ostendunt. Una vero re potissimum sibi ipsae conciliantur, quod utraque naturam sequitur, qua magistra et duce ambae quoque varietati student, cum ea ipsa natura cumprimis varietate

understands the difference between a young woman of quality and the common sort. In vocabulary and substance, too, the one is more restrained, the other in both rhythm and vocabulary now more abundant, now more artificial as well, for not content with old and familiar words, it often revels in coining or importing them.

Their purposes, however, are almost entirely different, or certainly very much so, since the one ought to be intent only on stating the truth, although also on expressing it elegantly as well, while poetry does not consider that sufficient and will not maintain its proper excellence if it does not bring in many details from elsewhere, now partly true or probable ones, now those altogether fictitious and unlike the truth in any way, in order that what it says may appear more deserving of admiration. Nevertheless, they agree marvelously in this respect: the purpose of each is to embellish what it has undertaken to say and (as far as possible) to make it live forever. Each also has its own rhythms and figures of speech, yet for a different reason. They also differ in the order in which they tell things, since history follows the order and sequence of events, but the other often begins its narration from the middle of the story, sometimes even almost from the end, also sometimes even adopting characters from outside depending on the nature of the situation, like gods, nymphs, and other divinities, like seers and those possessed. Furthermore, it also gives voice and speech to mute objects, ascribes divine power to dreams, even provides the gods themselves with human emotions. Homer among the Greeks and Vergil among our Latin authors exhibit these features everywhere. On one point especially, however, they are united: each follows the example of Nature, under whose tutelage and guidance they strive for variety, since Nature herself

letetur, et decorum illud quod ab eadem rei est cuique attribu-
tum cum venustate sequatur ac dignitate etiam summa.

63   Haec habui quae dicere in universum de re hac liceat et tanquam vobis innuens, qui una hic adestis, significare. Reliquum
est, quoniam historiam poeticam pene solutam esse quandam
de maiorum auctoritate dixi, ut, quoad vires meae tulerint et
locus hic patitur, talem esse eam exemplis quoque ipsis edo-
ceam. Licet autem in Livio Sallustioque, historiae Romanae
principibus, diversa tamen²⁶⁴ splendescant claritate quae historia digna sunt lumina, dicendique in altero maiestas heroica
pene quaedam emineat atque uterque fuerit poeticae admodum
studiosus (cum ille poeticis non solum numeris scripta sua,
verum etiam integris quandoque exornet versibus, hic Empedo-
clea in Latinum, ut Aratea Cicero, converterit neque poeticis
abhorreat a figuris),²⁶⁵ tamen Livius in plurimis oratori similior
est, Sallustius vero historicis tantum legibus ubique videtur ad-
dictus. Uterque tamen opus suum poeticis auspicatus a numeris, ille a semiversu dactylico, qui est: *Facturus ne operepretium*,
hic vero alter ab integro hexametro Iugurtina²⁶⁶ in historia,
quem tamen ita refersit spondeis, praeterquam quarto in loco,
ut vix agnoscatur esse hexameter, gravitatem tamen illam spon-
daicam retinuit inquiens: *Bellum scripturus sum, quod populus Romanus*, quae verba heroicum senarium, gravem quidem numeris
verbisque maxime accommodatis constituunt. Huius igitur
exemplis si utar familiarius, vestrum quidem mirari debuerit
nemo.²⁶⁷

Igitur cum in unaquaque ad dicendum suscepta materia primum sit poetae officium proponere qua sit de re explicaturus,
quod quidem docuit Virgilius, cum dicere est orsus: *Arma
virumque cano*, idem a Sallustio servatum intelligo, cum et ipse,

especially delights in variety and pursues the particular excellence variety has attributed to each thing with charm and the greatest authority.

These are the general remarks I can make about this matter 63 and what I can point out about it, giving hints so to speak, to you who are gathered here. It remains — since I have said on the authority of our ancestors that history is almost poetry in prose — to demonstrate that it is so with actual examples, as far as my strength will allow and this place permits. In Livy and Sallust, the princes of Roman history, the ornaments suitable to history gleam brightly (albeit not in the same way), and a certain almost heroic majesty of style is conspicuous in either one; each was also a great student of poetry (since Livy adorns his writings not only with poetic rhythms but sometimes even with whole verses, and Sallust translated Empedocles' works into Latin, as Cicero translated those of Aratus, and does not shrink from poetic figures).[270] Nevertheless, Livy in most things is more like an orator, but Sallust everywhere seems devoted to the laws of history alone. Even so, each begins his work with poetic rhythms. Livy begins with a dactylic half-verse, "Whether what I do will be worth the effort" [Livy, *Praefatio* 1.1.1].[271] Sallust in the history of Jugurtha begins with a complete hexameter, which he has filled so full of spondees except in the fourth foot that it is scarcely recognizable as a hexameter. He has held on to the majesty of the spondee when he says: "The war I will write, which the people of Rome" [*Bellum Iugurthinum* 5.1]. The words constitute a heroic senarius, solemn in rhythm, and with extremely appropriate words. Therefore, none of you should be surprised if I use examples from Sallust rather often.

Well then, since in every subject he has undertaken to treat, it is the poet's first duty to lay out the theme he will unfold, as Vergil of course demonstrated when he began, "I sing of arms and the man" [*Aeneid* 1.1], I feel that Sallust has followed the

quod paulo est ante dictum, coepit: *Bellum scripturus sum quod populus Romanus cum Iugurta*[268] *rege Numidarum gessit.* Atque, ut ille causam susceptae a se materiae statim asserit, difficillimos scilicet Aeneae errores bellumque summis viribus, maximis etiam periculis ab illo administratum, post quos eventus multiplicesque successus urbs Roma esset condita (hoc enim versus illi praeseferunt: *multum ille et terris iactatus et alto*), sic et hic ipse Sallustius suscepti causam reddit operis inquiens:

> primum quia magnum et atrox variaque victoria fuit, deinde quia tum primum potentiae nobilitatis obviam itum est. Quae contentio divina et humana cuncta permiscuit eoque vecordiae processit, ut studiis civilibus bellum atque vastitas Italiae finem fecerit.[269]

Quid? Livius ab exordio quamprimum secundi belli Punici non ne heroico quasi quodam cum supercilio ait:

> In parte operis mei licet mihi praefari, quod in principio summae totius professi plerique sunt rerum scriptores, bellum maxime omnium memorabile quae unquam gesta sunt me scripturum, quod Carthaginenses Annibale duce cum populo Romano gessere. Nam neque validiores opibus ullae inter se civitates gentesque contulerunt arma, neque iis ipsis tantum unquam virium ac roboris fuit, et haud ignotas belli artes inter se ⟨sed⟩ expertas primo Punico conserebant bello, et adeo varia belli fortuna ancepsque Mars fuit, ut propius periculo fuerint qui vicerunt.[270]

same rule since he too begins, as I said a moment ago: "The war I will write, which the people of Rome waged with Jugurtha, king of the Numidians." And just as Vergil at once declares the reason for undertaking his subject, that is, the difficult wanderings of Aeneas and the war he waged with all his might and the greatest perils, so that after these events and manifold successes Rome might be founded (for the verses proclaim it: "this man, much buffeted on land and sea" [*Aeneid* 1.3], so Sallust too announces the reason for undertaking his work. He says:

> first, because the war was great and terrible and victory went back and forth, then because for the first time resistance was made to the power of the nobility. The struggle threw into confusion everything both human and divine and proceeded to such a pitch of madness that only war and the devastation of Italy made an end to civil strife. [*Bellum Iugurthinum* 5.1–3]

Why, isn't it true that Livy right from the beginning of his account of the Second Punic War speaks with a certain almost heroic pride?

> In a part of my work I can say as a preface what most historians have claimed at the beginning of the whole, that I am going to write of the war most worthy to be remembered of all those that were ever fought, the one that the Carthaginians under Hannibal's leadership waged with the Roman people. For neither did any states and nations more powerful in resources ever join in battle with each other nor did they themselves ever have such great strength and manpower; and they employed not new arts of war against each other but those tested in the First Punic war; and so varied was the fortune of war and Mars so fickle that it was the victors who came closer to destruction. [Livy 21.1.1–2]

Altiores quoque repetitiones praesentique ab negocio longius remotarum rerum susceptae enarrationes et poeticae et historicae facultatis inter se necessitudinem quasi quandam arguunt. Declarant hoc et Virgilius et Sallustius, alter cum exorditur:

Rex arva Latinus et urbes
iam senior longa placidas in pace regebat.
Hunc Fauno et nympha genitum Laurente Marica
accipimus,

alter cum Iugurtino in bello, post redditas suscepti a se operis causas, repetendo incipit:

Bello Punico secundo, quo dux Carthaginensium Annibal, post magnitudinem Romani nominis, Italiae opes maxime attriverat, Masinisa, rex Numidarum, in amicitia receptus a Publio Scipione.[271]

Et in Catilinario :

Urbem Romam, sicuti ego accepi, condidere atque habuere initio Troiani, qui Aenea duce profugi sedibus incertis vagabantur.

64   Adhaec, quid cognatius quam quod uterque et poeta et historicus affert in medium causas edisseritque rationes antequam enarrare quam scribendam suscepit rem incipiat? In ipso Virgilius initio explicat errorum ac laborum Aeneae causas ac Iunonis irarum: *Urbs antiqua fuit, Tyrii tenuere coloni, / Carthago* usque ad eum versum: *Tantae molis erat Romanam condere gentem.* Et Livius:

The poetic and historical faculties also reveal a certain kinship with each other in that they trace events from remote antiquity and undertake the narration of matters far removed from the business at hand. Both Vergil and Sallust demonstrate this point, the one when he begins:

> King Latinus, now grown old,
> was ruling the land and tranquil towns in a long peace.
> We hear that he was the son of Faunus and the Laurentian
> nymph Marica. [*Aeneid* 7.45–48]

The other demonstrates it too, when in the *Jugurthine War*, after giving his reasons for undertaking the work, he begins by going back into the past:

> In the Second Punic War, when the Carthaginian leader Hannibal had dealt the greatest blow to Italian resources since the Roman nation had become great, Masinissa, king of the Numidians, was received in friendship by Publius Scipio. [*Bellum Iugurthinum* 5.4]

And in the *Catilinarian*:

> The city of Rome, as I understand, was first founded and settled by Trojans, who were wandering as exiles without a fixed home with Aeneas as their leader. [*Bellum Catilinae* 6.1]

In addition, what is a greater sign that the poet and the historian are closely related than the fact that both disclose their reasons and set forth their justifications before they begin to tell about what they have undertaken to write? In the very beginning Vergil states the reasons for the wanderings and labors of Aeneas and the wrath of Juno: "There was an ancient city (Tyrian settlers inhabited it), Carthage," all the way to this verse: "So great a task it was to found the Roman nation" [*Aeneid* 1.12–13, 1.33]. And Livy: 64

Odiis prope maioribus certatum est quam viribus, Romanis indignantibus quod victoribus victi ultro inferrent arma, Poenis quod superbe avareque crederent imperitatum victis esse.

Quaeque alia de Annibalis indignatione referuntur ob Siciliam Sardiniamque amissas. Idem quoque indicant descriptiones locorum, gentium, morum, legum, quod et ipsum Sallustius docuit, cum dixit:

Res postulare videtur Africae situm paucis exponere et eas gentes quibuscum nobis bellum aut amicitia fuit attingere.

Et Virgilius:

Est locus, Hesperiam Graii cognomine dicunt,
terra antiqua, potens armis atque hubere glebae.

Quid autem solutae poeticae tam simile quam Livianum illud?

Eaque uti rata scirent fore, agnum leva manu, dextra silicem retinens, si falleret, Iovem coeterosque precatus deos, ita se mactarent quemadmodum ipse agnum mactasset, et secundum precationem caput pecudis saxo elisit.

Quid tempestatis illa nimbique explicatio?

Dein cum iam spiritum includeret nec reciprocare animam sineret, aversi a vento parumper consedere. Tum vero ingenti sono coelum strepere et inter horrendos

The contest was waged with their hatred almost more than their might, the Romans outraged because the conquered were aggressively taking up arms against their conquerors, the Carthaginians because they believed that the rule over them in their defeat had been imperious and rapacious. [Livy 21.1.3]

(He relates other things as well about Hannibal's indignation because of the loss of Sicily and Sardinia.) The same authors also present descriptions of places, nations, customs, and laws, as Sallust shows when he says:

The subject seems to require a brief account of the geography of Africa and a mention of the nations with which we had war or alliance. [*Bellum Iugurthinum* 17.1]

And Vergil:

There is a place — the Greeks give it the name Hesperia — an ancient land, potent in arms and in the fertility of its soil. [*Aeneid* 1.530–31]

But what is more like poetry in prose than this passage of Livy?

And so that they might know that these things were binding, in his left hand holding a lamb, in his right a stone, he prayed to Jupiter and the other gods that if he was false they would slay him just as he had slain the lamb, and after the prayer he shattered the head of the animal with the stone. [Livy 21.45.8]

And what is so like poetry as this description of a rainstorm?

Then, since it obstructed their breathing and would not allow them to take a breath, they turned away from the wind for a while and sat down. Then the sky roared with a great

fragores micare ignes; capti auribus, oculis, metu omnes torpere.

Nam quid per Musas, o viri optimi, ex omni est parte magis illo poeticum?

Ex propinquo visa montium altitudo nivesque coelo prope immistae, tecta informia posita in rupibus, pecora iumentaque torrida frigore, homines intonsi, inculti, animalia inanimaliaque[272] omnia rigentia gelu, coetera visu quam dictu foediora.[273]

Utque poeticum omnino possis dicere, heroicis etiam numeris res ipsa clauditur:

ingentemque[274] fugam stragemque dedissent.

Fuit enim omnino poeticus Livius in toto transitu in Italiam Annibalis describendo, et cum ipse tum viros equosque transeuntes Rhodanum describit, ingenti sono fluminis, clamore vario nautarum ac militum, et qui nitebantur prorumpere impetum fluminis et qui ex altera parte ripae transeuntes suos hortabantur, tum etiam elephantes, quibus

primus erat pavor, cum soluta ab coeteris rate in altum raperentur. Ibi urgentes inter se, cedentibus extremis ab aqua, trepidationem aliquantum edebant, donec quietem ipse timor circumspicientibus[275] aquam fecisset.

sound and fires flashed between horrendous crashes; bereft of hearing and sight, they were all paralyzed with fear. [Livy 21.58.4]

By the Muses, gentlemen, what indeed is more poetic in every respect than this?

When seen up close, the height of the mountains and the snows almost intermingled with the sky, the ugly huts set on the cliffs, the flocks and pack animals pinched with cold, the people hairy and uncouth, animate and inanimate objects all stiff with frost, the rest more horrible to see than one can say. [Livy 21.32.7][272]

And so that you could say it is altogether poetic, the passage closes with heroic rhythms:

they might have caused both a great rout and a massacre. [Livy 21.32.8][273]

In fact, Livy was entirely poetic in describing Hannibal's whole crossing into Italy, both when at one point he describes the men and horses crossing the Rhone, with the great roar of the river, the varied shouting of sailors and soldiers — both those striving to rush across the current of the river and those on the other part of the bank encouraging them as they crossed, and when at another point he describes the elephants, for which:

the first fear arose when one raft was separated from the rest and they were swept into the deep water. There, huddling together, with the ones on the edges backing away from the water, they caused confusion for a while until terror produced quiet when they saw water all around them. [Livy 21.28.10–11]

Animadvertite adhuc, quaeso, quibus Annibal milites affatur verbis:

> mirari se quinam pectora semper impavida repens[276] terror invaserit; . . . nullas profecto terras coelum contingere, coli Alpes, gignere atque alere animantes; . . . eos ipsos quos cernant non pennis sublime elatos Alpes trangressos; ne maiores quidem eorum indigenas, sed advenas Italiae cultores ingentibus saepe agminibus cum liberis ac coniugibus migrantium modo tuto transmisisse. . . . Romam orbis terrarum caput petentibus quicquam adeo asperum atque arduum videri quod incoeptum moretur?

Quid cum ait:

> Equi maxime infestum agmen faciebant, qui et clamoribus dissonis, quos nemora repercussaeque valles augebant, territi trepidabant, et icti forte aut vulnerati adeo consternati sunt, ut stragem ingentem simul hominum ac sarcinarum omnis generis facerent.[277]

Quid etiam:

> Cum caedendum esset saxum illud, arboribus circa immanibus deiectis detruncatisque, struem ingentem lignorum faciunt, eamque, cum et vis venti apta faciundo igni coorta esset, succendunt ardentiaque saxa infuso aceto putrefaciunt; ita torridam incendio rupem ferro pandunt molliuntque anfractibus mollibus[278] clivos.

65   His haudquaquam grandiora plenioraque apud Virgilium leguntur, ubi Aeneam ab Antandro in Italiam devehit per tempestates, scopulos Harpiarumque[279] portenta ac Cyclopum, ne quidem cum ipse[280] ait:

In addition, please notice how Hannibal addresses his soldiers:

> He was surprised at what sudden terror had come over their ever fearless hearts and attacked them. . . . Surely no land touched the sky; the Alps were inhabited, bore and nourished living creatures. . . . The people they saw had not crossed the Alps carried aloft by wings; not even their ancestors were indigenous but as foreign inhabitants of Italy had often crossed safely in great multitudes with their children and wives in the way of migrating peoples. . . . To those seeking Rome, the capital of the world, could anything seem so difficult or arduous that it would delay their undertaking? [Livy 21.30.1–2, 7–8, 10, with some omissions]

What about when he says this?

> The horses especially endangered the column. Terrified by the dissonant shouting, which the glades and echoing valleys multiplied, they shied, and when they were struck or wounded they were so panicked that they caused a great loss of both men and every kind of baggage. [Livy 21.33.6]

And this?

> When they had to cut through rock, they felled great trees nearby and lopped off their branches and made a huge pile of wood. This pile, when the wind rose strongly enough to fan the flames, they set on fire, and they made the glowing rock crumble by pouring vinegar over it; with picks they laid open the cliff dried out by fire in this way and made the hills easier with gentle curving paths. [Livy 21.37.2]

One reads things not a bit grander and fuller than these passages of Livy in Vergil when he brings Aeneas from Antandros into Italy through tempests, cliffs, and the horrors of the Harpies and Cyclopes, and not even when he says: 65

vastumque cava trabe currimus aequor.
Postquam altum tenuere rates nec iam amplius ullae
apparent terrae, coelum undique et undique pontus,

aut cum:

Tristius haud illis monstrum, nec sevior ulla
pestis et ira deum Stygiis se se extulit undis.
Virginei volucrum vultus, foedissima ventris
proluvies uncaeque manus et pallida semper
ora fame.

Ne ve cum intonat:

Haec loca vi quondam et vasta convulsa ruina
(tantum aevi longinqua valet mutare vetustas)
dissiluisse ferunt, cum protinus utraque tellus
una foret: venit medio vi pontus et undis
Hesperium Siculo latus abscidit, arvaque et urbes
litore diductas angusto interluit aestu,

aut cum:

horrificis iusta tonat[281] Aetna ruinis,
interdumque atram prorumpit ad aethera nubem
turbine fumantem piceo et candente favilla,
attollitque globos flammarum et sidera lambit.
Interdum scopulos avulsaque viscera montis

We ran down the vast sea in our hollow bark.
After the ships held the deep, and no longer any land
was to be seen, sky everywhere and everywhere the sea.
    [*Aeneid* 3.191–93][274]

Or when he says:

No more ghastly monster than these or bane and wrath of
    the gods
more cruel ever raised itself from the waters of Styx.
Birds they are with faces of maidens, most vile the waste
of their bellies, and like claws their hands and their faces
ever pale with hunger. [*Aeneid* 3.214–18]

Nor when he thunders:

These places, they say, once violently torn by a terrible
    cataclysm
(long ages are able to make such a change),
burst asunder when the two lands were a single unbroken
whole: violently the sea rushed between and with its waves
cut the Hesperian from the Sicilian coast, and in a narrow
    strait
flowed between the fields and cities on separate shores.
    [*Aeneid* 3.414–19]

Or when he says:

    Etna thunders close by with horrific crashes;
and sometimes it throws out to the sky a black smoky cloud
with a pitch-black whirlwind and glowing ash
and sends up masses of flame and licks the stars.
Sometimes it belches and spews out boulders and the
    ripped-out entrails

erigit eructans liquefactaque saxa sub auras
cum gemitu glomerat fundoque exaestuat imo.

Quid quod hic idem Livius, quasi gemmis quibusdam, nunc verbis omnino poeticis, nunc figuris ac numeris insignit orationem atque illustrat historiam? ut cum ait: *anceps Mars* et: *agitare animo bellum,* et: *tela micare,* et: *dempto hoc fulgure nominis Romani,* et: *circumferebant ora oculosque,* et: *pandi agmen coepit,* et: *non Manes, non stirpem eius conquiescere viri,* et: *hunc iuvenem tanquam furiam facesque huius belli,* et: *inde equitum certamen erat,* et: *haec ubi dicta dedit,* et: *cum Poenis*[282] *bellum pro nobis suscipiatis.*

Ex his itaque perpaucis, quanquam videri haec ipsa multa quidem testimonio atque auctoritate possunt sua, satis tamen, ut arbitror, factum est ei parti quam probandam suscepi, haud male sensisse eos scilicet qui historiam censeant poeticam quasi quandam esse solutam. Quocirca, quod cum voluntate et gratia, Puderice, fiat tua horumque omnium qui dicentem me vel mussantem potius audiere tam attente et, ut video, tantum praeseferunt audiendi studium, ad ea iam transeamus quae a me potius observata quidem sunt quam quod ea praecepta quasi quaedam institutaque scribendae historiae existimari velim aut ex me ipso profecta et tradita.

66 *Pud.* Et me hoc, Altili, volente feceris et his ipsis qui tam intente atque aventer audiunt praecipue cupientibus. Coeterum Marcus Cicero locuples nobis auctor esse potest: *poetas alia*[283] *quadam lingua locutos.* Itaque videndum etiam atque etiam relinquitur, si poetae alia quam quae oratoris propria est locuti sunt lingua,

of the mountain, and with a roar rolls masses of molten
    rock
up to the sky and boils in its lowest depths. [*Aeneid*
    3.571–77][275]

What about the fact that this same Livy, as if with precious
gems, makes speech memorable and embellishes history now
with entirely poetic words, now with figures and rhythms? For
example: "fickle Mars," "to plot war in his heart," "spears flashed,"
"if the luster of the Roman name is taken away," "they turned
faces and eyes in every direction," "the column began to spread
out," "not the ghost, not the offspring of that man could rest,"
"this youth, like the fury and firebrand of this war," "then there
was a contest of the cavalry," "when he has given these utterances," and "you might undertake the war with the Carthaginians for us."[276]

From these few examples, numerous as they can appear in
the weight of their testimony, I think enough has been done for
the point I set out to prove, that those regarding history as a
kind of prose poetry have by no means been mistaken. Therefore, let it be with your permission and goodwill, Puderico, and
that of all those who have listened so attentively to my discourse, or rather mumbling, and, as I see, have demonstrated so
much interest in listening, that I now turn to things I would
like you to consider observations rather than precepts or instructions for writing history that I have developed and handed
down myself.

Puderico. I am glad to have you do this, Altilio, and those here   66
who are listening with such eager attention especially desire it,
too. But Marcus Cicero can be a sufficient authority for us with
his dictum: "Poets have spoken in some other language" [*De oratore* 2.61].[277] Accordingly, if poets have spoken in a language
different from that proper to the orator, it remains to be consid-

quonam modo historia poeticae erit quasi cuiusdam solutae similis. Locus igitur expurgandus hic tibi prius est scrupusque, Altili, excutiendus, nisi forte, posthabito Cicerone, Livius tibi unus satis futurus est ad haec et credenda et comprobanda.

Alt. Et Livii testimonio contenti esse unius possumus et Cicero minime est abiiciendus, vir ad omne genus eloquentiae genitus naturae ipsius munere atque ipsius Livii magister et doctor. Ac tute quidem ipse meminisse potes Ciceronem exigere maius quiddam in historia quam quod in annalibus pontificum aut in Fabii, Antiatis, Caelii ac Sisennae scriptis appareret. Nam de Sallustio omnino nihil, sive quod post Ciceronis obitum historias is scripserit, sive propter simultates, quodque ille ipse viveret, silentio eum praeteriit. Ipsum igitur illud maius quod a Cicerone desideratur praestitere postea eorum studia qui poeticae ornamenta et cultum sibi ante oculos posuerunt scriptitandae historiae, non verba quidem confragosa illa et perquam glutinata inter se, theatris apta, non senatui, ut *ferriclaves postes*, ut *hastas belliferratas*, ut *spumivomos fluctus*, ut *fluentisona litora*, ut talia haec gignendae permulta admirationi inventa, sed magnitudinem poetarum, sed varietatem descriptionesque locorum ac gentium, sed evagationes, amplificationes, digressiones, ornatum decorumque illud praecipue cui poetae imprimis videntur inservire. An, quaeso, tranandus erat Annibali Rhodanus sine strepitu, clamore, tumultu nautarum ac militum, sine pavore et consternatione elephantum, sine casu denique unius atque alterius in amnem e rate belluae?[284] Videlicet traiiciendae erant Alpes sine tempestate, sine nimbis frigoribusque, non

ered, and considered again, in what way history is like a kind of prose poetry. Therefore, first you must justify this position and get rid of doubt—unless by chance you consider Cicero less important and think that Livy alone will be enough for these things to be believed and confirmed.

Altilio. We can be content with the testimony of Livy alone, but Cicero is not to be rejected either, a man born for every kind of eloquence by the gift of nature herself and both the master and teacher of Livy. And indeed, you yourself can remember that Cicero demanded something greater in history than was found in the pontifical annals or in the writings of Fabius, Antias, Caelius, and Sisenna.[278] For about Sallust he says nothing at all, passing over him in silence whether because he wrote his histories after Cicero's death or out of animosity and because Sallust himself was still alive. Accordingly, that something greater Cicero was looking for was provided afterward by the efforts of those who kept before their eyes the ornaments and elegance of poetry as models for writing history. They did not look to rough words all glued together with each other (suitable for the stage, not the senate), like *ferriclaves postes* (iron-keyed doors), *hastae belliferratae* (spears steeled-for-war), *spumivomi fluctus* (foam-spewing waves), *fluentisona litora* (wave-sounding shores), and many of the same kind that have been invented to produce admiration.[279] Rather, they kept before them the inherent nobility of the poets, their variety and descriptions of places and nations, their wanderings, amplifications, digressions, elegance, and above all that decorum to which poets seem especially devoted. Was Hannibal to have crossed the Rhone, I ask you, without an uproar, the shouting, the agitation of sailors and soldiers, without the terror and confusion of the elephants, without one or two of the beasts, in fact, falling from the raft into the river? The Alps, I suppose, were to be passed over without a storm, without rain and cold; nor did that huge

frangendum erat incendio prius, insperso post aceto putrefa-
ciendum saxum illud immane, tantis copiis, tamque excellenti
duci obvium; non adeundum promontorium illud immane,
coelo proximum, omnis e quo despiceretur Italia, in cuius vertice constitutus Annibal suos cohortaretur Romamque orbis
caput illis ostentans diripiendam, magnifica etiam oratione,
obiiceret offerretque.

67   Hoc sibi vult igitur solutae poeticae similis historia, hoc de-
siderabatur a Cicerone, hac caruerunt laude et dignitate Caelius, Antias, Sisenna. Ac mihi quidem videtur Herodotus poetarum in scribendo instar habuisse, dum, contemptis qui ante
se scripserant historicis, magnitudinem assecutus[285] est illam et
varietatem et ornatum et cultum a Cicerone desideratum. Et
qui dicit poeticam picturae esse similem, num ideo dicit aut illud sentit, quod poeta usurus sit coloribus quibus pictores
utantur adumbrandis atque informandis rerum imaginibus?
Quin de varietate loquitur, de collocatione, de dignitate, vetustate, informatione, habitu, quibus in effingendis rebus poetae
pictorum more atque ad illorum exemplum uti debeant. Nec
verba quoque non sibi a poeta quandoque mutuabitur diligens
rerum scriptor, pudenter tamen ac tenerrimo cum delectu, ut
cum dixit Sallustius: *tuba hosticum cecinit*, et: *tela utrimque volare*,
et: *strepitus armorum ad coelum ferri*, et: *fors omnia regere*.

Non ne descriptio illa Africae mera est et soluta poetica?

Mare sevum, importuosum; ager frugum fertilis, bonus
pecori, arboribus[286] infoecundus; coelo terraque penuria
aquarum. Genus hominum salubri corpore, velox, patiens

boulder obstructing the march of so many troops and such an outstanding general first have to be broken up by fire, then made friable with lashings of vinegar; nor did they have to approach that great promontory next to the sky from which one could look down on all Italy, on whose peak Hannibal stood and encouraged his men and, showing them Rome, capital of the world, in a splendid speech offered and put it before them to sack.[280]

This, then, is the intent of history, to be like prose poetry; 67 this is what Cicero was looking for; this is the excellence and grandeur lacked by Caelius, Antias, and Sisenna. I think, too, that Herodotus had poets as his model in writing, since despising the historians who had written before him, he sought the greatness and variety and embellishment and elegance desired by Cicero. As for the one who said that a poem is like a picture, surely he did not say or think this, did he, because a poet will use the colors painters use in shading and shaping likenesses of things?[281] No, he was talking about the variety, arrangement, grandeur, antiquity, conception, and character that poets, like painters and following their example, should use in depicting things. Sometimes the careful writer of historical events will borrow his words, too, from the poet, but modestly and with very delicate selection, as when Sallust said: "the trumpet sounded a charge against the enemy," and "weapons flew in both directions," and "the clash of arms rose to the sky," and "chance ruled everything."[282]

Is not the following description of Africa pure prose poetry, too?

The sea is savage, without a harbor, the land fertile in grain, good for flocks, unsuitable for trees; there is a dearth of water from sky and land. The race of men is healthy in body,

laborum; plerosque senectus dissolvit, nisi qui ferro aut bestiis interiere.

An ne tibi Virgilianum illud videatur aliud, nisi quod solutum non est?

> Durum a stirpe genus, natos ad flumina primum
> deferimus sevoque gelu duramus et undis;
> venatu invigilant pueri silvasque fatigant,
> flectere ludus equos et spicula tendere cornu.
> At patiens operum parvoque assueta iuventus
> aut rastris terram domat aut quatit oppida bello.
> Omne aevum ferro teritur versaque iuvencum
> terga fatigamus hasta nec tarda senectus
> debilitat vires animi frangitque vigorem.
> Canitiem galea premimus semperque recentis
> convectare[287] iuvat praedas et vivere rapto.

Quid cum paulo post idem ait:

> Africam in initio habuere Getuli et Libyes, asperi incultique, quibus cibus erat caro ferina atque humi pabulum uti pecoribus. Hi neque moribus neque legibus aut imperio cuiusquam regebantur; vagi palantes, qua nox coegerat, sedes habebant.[288]

Quid magis poeticum dicas, nisi quod poeticis absque numeris? Age, quaeso, et aliud:

> Erat inter ingentis solitudines oppidum magnum atque valens nomine Capsa, cuius conditor Hercules Libys memorabatur. Eius cives apud Iugurtam immunes, leni

agile, enduring labor; old age breaks up most of them, except those who have perished by the sword or wild beasts. [*Bellum Iugurthinum* 17.5–6]

Does this passage from Vergil seem any different to you, except that it is not in prose?

A race of hardy stock, we first bring our sons
to the river and harden them up in bitter cold water;
As boys they live for the hunt and allow the forests no rest;
their sport is horse taming and aiming shafts from the bow.
But our youth, enduring toil and accustomed to little,
either conquer the soil with hoes or shake cities with war.
Our whole life is spent with iron, and with the butt end of
        the spear
we wear out the backs of bullocks, nor does slow old age
weaken our courage and break down our strength.
We put helmets on white hair and always it pleases us
to carry off fresh booty and live on our plunder. [*Aeneid* 9.603–13]

And what about this passage of Sallust a little later?

Originally Africa was inhabited by the Getuli and the Libyans, fierce and uncivilized peoples, whose food was the flesh of wild animals and vegetation as for cattle. They were not governed by custom, law, or anyone's authority; nomadic wanderers, they camped where night forced a halt. [*Bellum Iugurthinum* 18.1–2]

What would you call more poetic, except that it lacks poetic rhythms? Come, please; here is another example.

In the middle of great deserts was a large and powerful town called Capsa, whose founder was said to be Libyan Hercules. Its citizens were exempt from taxes with Jugurtha, under

imperio et ob ea fidelissimi habebantur, muniti adversum hostes non moenibus modo et armis atque viris, verum etiam multo magis locorum asperitate. Nam praeter oppido propinqua alia omnia vasta, inculta, egentia aquae, infesta serpentibus, quorum vis sicuti omnium ferarum inopia cibi acrior. Adhaec natura serpentium ipsa satis perniciosa, siti magis quam alia re accenditur.[289]

Descendit Crispus Romanae, ut putant, pater historiae, descendit, inquam, ad serpentes atque illorum naturam attingit, quae siti aestuque maxime incendatur. Ne[290] hoc mea quidem sententia minus poetice, perite, ornate quam a Virgilio illustre illud de asilo:

> Est lucos Silari circum[291] ilicibusque virentem
> plurimus Alburnum volitans, cui nomen asilo
> Romanum est, oestrum Graii vertere vocantes,
> asper, acerba sonans, quo tota exterrita silvis
> diffugiunt armenta.

68   Libentissime quoque ac peringenue Sallustius verba figurasque, numeros item a poeticis mutuatus est, ab illis praesertim qui annales scripsere, ut cum ait: *signum tuba dat*, et: *ignoto atque horribili sonitu repente exciti*, et: *iamque dies consumptus erat*; item: *et sane Marius illoque aliisque temporibus*; qui si *diebus* dixisset, senarium integrum heroum apte canoreque fudisset. Illa vero quantopere heroica:

> Spectaculum horribile in campis patentibus: sequi, fugere, occidi, capi, . . . postremo omnia, qua visus erat, constrata

mild control, and for that reason they were considered especially loyal. They were fortified against enemies not with walls alone and armed men, but far more by the difficult nature of the region. For apart from the area close to the town, everything else was wasteland, untilled, lacking water, infested with snakes, whose violence like that of all beasts is fiercer with lack of food. In addition, the very nature of snakes, deadly enough, is fired by thirst more than by anything else. [*Bellum Iugurthinum* 89.4–5]

Crispus [Sallust], considered the father of Roman history, stoops, stoops, I say, to snakes and touches on their nature, which is especially fired by thirst and heat. Not even this in my opinion is presented less poetically, skillfully, elegantly than that famous passage by Vergil on the gadfly:

> There is around the groves of Silarus and Alburnus green
> with oaks a swarming fly, whose Roman name
> is *asilus*, but the Greeks made a change, calling it *oestrus*;
> fierce, sharp sounding, from which whole herds in terror
> scatter in the forests. [*Georgics* 3.146–50]

Sallust also gladly and liberally borrowed words and figures   68
as well as rhythms from poets, especially from those who wrote annals, as when he says, "the trumpet gave the signal," and "suddenly wakened by an unknown and horrible sound," and "already the day was spent," as well as "and Marius on that and other occasions"—if he had said "days," he would have produced a full heroic senarius, neatly and harmoniously.[283] But these words are equally heroic:

> Horrible was the sight in the open plains: pursuit, flight,
> killing, capture . . . finally, all the ground as far as the eye

telis, armis, cadaveribus, et ea inter humus infecta sanguine.

Nesciam tamen quonam modo minus haec extant in Sallustio nec tam apparent atque exposita sunt quam in Livio, ut alter quodammodo praeseferre velit artem poeticaeque imitationem, alter celare eam, ut tanquam in nube[292] delitescat. Et vero oratoria ipsa, quamvis sit a poetis numerositatem illam generosam ac dignitatis plenam, ut a primis eloquentiae cultoribus mutuata antiquissimisque dicendi magistris, cumprimis tamen rerum gestarum scriptores ea seque resque suas fecere magnificas; ut interdum generositas illa eorum sermonis videatur solis pene e numeris constare in iisque tantum consistere, ut cum ait Livius:

> Nam neque validiores opibus ullae inter se civitates gentesque contulerunt arma, neque iis ipsis tantum unquam virium ac roboris fuit, et haud ignotas belli artes inter se, sed expertas primo Punico conserebant[293] bello.

Quid his numeris plenius, dignius, addo et generosius? Non minus tamen latine et haud minore cum ornatu dicentur et copia, siquis dixerit:

> Nam neque validiores opibus ullae inter se civitates gentesque arma contulerunt, neque in iis ipsis tantum unquam virium fuit ac roboris, neque ignotas belli artes inter se, sed expertas primo bello Punico conserebant.

Verum subtractis iis spondeis et numeris commutatis, omnis illa generositas nescio quomodo interit, deciditque orationis

could see was strewn with spears, arms, corpses, and the earth between them stained with blood. [*Bellum Iugurthinum* 101.11 with some omissions]

Yet somehow these features stand out less in Sallust and are less apparent and obvious than in Livy, so that the one somehow wants to display his art and poetic imitation, the other to conceal it, so that it lies hidden as if in a cloud. And in fact although oratory itself has borrowed its well-known noble and distinguished rhythmical quality from the poets, since they were the first devotees of eloquence and its most ancient teachers, nevertheless it was the writers of historical events especially who used it to make themselves and their subjects great, so that sometimes the nobility of their language seems to rest almost solely on rhythm and to consist only of it, as when Livy says:

For neither did any states and nations more powerful in resources ever join in battle with each other nor did they themselves ever have equal strength and manpower; and they employed not new arts of war against each other but those tested in the first Punic war. [Livy 21.1.2][284]

What could be fuller than these rhythms, more excellent, and, I would add, more noble? Yet they will be expressed no less correctly in Latin and with hardly less embellishment and abundance if someone should say:

For neither did any states and nations more powerful in resources with each other ever battle join, nor in themselves did ever exist equal strength and manpower, nor did they against each other employ new arts of war but those which in the first Punic war had been tested.

But when those spondees are taken away and the rhythm changed, all that former nobility somehow disappears, and the

supercilium. Atque his quidem numeris excellit in historia Livius et tanquam inter alios exultat. Ne te igitur animi dubium Cicero aut minus tibi te in hoc constantem faciat, quod poetas alia lingua usos dicat, scrupulum excute omnem atque ex animo eiice, deque forensibus illum actionibus, haud de historiis locutum tibi persuadeas velim. (Nam et a Roscio illo motum, gestumque discendum oratori ad imitandum in agendo, ubi causa ipsa exigat, non videatur esse Ciceroni alienum.) Nec inficiabimur[294] tamen Graecos poetas oratoriis a verbis ac dicendi figuris quam nostros multo abesse longius viderique *alia quadam lingua locutos.*

Pud. Et perpurgatus est hic a te, Altili, locus sentesque excisae sunt omnes et evagari iam tuto potes certis minimeque labentibus vestigiis, neque verendae offensiunculae, cum libera a scrupis ipsis sit via.

69   *Comp.* At ego passurus minime sum, Altili, evagari te ulterius, exultareque extra praescriptos fines, cumque sis ipse grammaticorum grammaticissimus, tui te oblitum non perferam, dum quae princeps est disciplinarum omnium, ut historiae satisfacias, e iure, auctoritate finibusque pene eiicis grammaticam suis. Habenda est igitur et tibi et nobis omnibus qui hic assumus illius ratio conservandusque ei debitus in disserendo locus, Antoniana lege hoc ipsum sanciente.

Etenim idem ipse Cicero *Axillam* ait factum esse *Ahalam,* fuga litterae vastioris. Quid (malum!) si vastior *x* est littera, si elementum minime simplex, in multis ea cur abutimur? Cur qui Graece[295] est Odisseus fuitque apud priscos Latinos *Ulysseus,* duplicata *s* littera factus est nunc *Ulixes?* Cur a *sessu,* hoc est *sessione* cum fiat *sexus,* quod sedendo occulatur pars ea

elevated effect of the language falls away.[285] And indeed it is
with rhythms like these that Livy excels in history and jumps
out, so to speak, among the rest. Therefore, lest Cicero raise
doubts in your mind or make you less sure of yourself on this
point because he says that poets use a different language, shake
off every bit of uneasiness and cast it out of your mind and let
me persuade you that he was talking about forensic proceedings
and not at all about histories. (On the other hand, Cicero
would not think it strange for the orator even to learn to imitate the movement and gesture of the famous Roscius in litigat-
ing when the case demands it.[286]) And yet we will not deny that
the Greek poets are much farther from the language and figures
of speech of oratory than ours and that they seem "to have spoken in some other language."

Puderico. You have cleared up this point, Altilio, and pruned away
all the brambles, and with these obstacles cleared from the path
you can range sure-footed with no fear of tripping.

Compatre. But I am certainly not going to allow you to range any
farther, Altilio, and waltz around outside the prescribed limits;
and since you are the most grammatical of grammarians I won't
let you forget yourself in order to do justice to history, while
you expel grammar, the foremost of all disciplines, from its
rights, authority and almost from its territory. You must take
account of it and so must all of us who are present, and when
speaking retain the place owed to it, as the law of Antonio or-
dains.

So then, Cicero himself said that *Axilla* had been made
Ahala, because of aversion to a harsh-sounding letter.[287] Why
the devil, if *x* is such a harsh letter, if it is not at all a single element—why do we misuse it in many cases?[288] Why has the
word that is *Odysseus* in Greek and was *Ulysseus* with a double *s*
among the ancient Latins now become *Ulixes*?[289] Why, since
sexus [sex] is made from *sessus*, that is, *sessio*, because the

69

corporis nostri quae est oscenior, litteras non retinuit suas? Neque enim *x* refert *s* duplicatum, sed tum *c s* tum etiam *g s*. Scimus omnes perantiquam[296] fuisse dictionem *pessum*, a qua dicti *pessuli*, quasi *pedessum* a calcandis *pedibus*, unde *pessundare* datumque verbum ipsum opprobrio atque ignaviae deque eo formatum nomen *pessimus*; cur sonum eius evastavimus *x* littera accepta? A *magno* deduxere primi illi *magnior* et *magnissimus*, quae voces postea contractis dictionibus ac subductis litteris fuere *maior* et *massimus*; cur passae sunt aures doctissimorum hominum audire tam diu *x* litterae vastitatem? Nam si a *massa* deductum sit nomen *maximus*, idem erit abusus, cum *massa* dicta sit a *magno*, eaque fuerit in initio *magnissa*, vel Graeco modo *maza*.[297] Cur *elixare*? Nam a *liquo, liquas*[298] principio fuit *liquasso*, ut a *levo, levas, levasso*,[299] post subtractis litteris *lisso* et *elisso*; cur, inquam, et in his vasta assumpta est atque asperius sonans littera? Cur in his[300] quoque, *palus, velum, paulum, talus, mala*, *l* mansuetioris litterae loco, accepta vastiore, abusu ex illo *paxillum, vexillum, pauxillum, taxillum* ac *maxillam* dicimus? Quando concentus ipsius suavitate capiantur aures mulceaturque audiendi sensus etiam concidendis quibusdam atque decurtandis vocibus?

Fuit primum a *sistendo sistlocus*, post *stlocus*, factus est postremo *locus*, repudiato confragoso sonitu. Eadem deductione et via a *sistendo sist[i]litis*,[301] quod sistendum esset in iudicio ad praetorem, inde fuit *stlitis*, post *litis*, ultimo *lis*, perconcinne quidem et commode. An non initio humani oris pars inferior, quod loquentibus atque edentibus aut etiam hiantibus nobis moveretur, dicta est *movimentum*, quae postmodum fuit *mentum*?

obscene part of our body is hidden by sitting [*sedendo*], did it not keep its letters? Nor in fact does *x* reflect double *s*, but both *c s* and *g s*. We all know that there was a very ancient word *pessum* [toward the feet, downward] from which *pessuli* [bolts] got their name, as if *pedessum*, from treading with the feet,[290] whence *pessundare* [to sink or ruin], and *pessimus*, a word formed from it for dishonor and worthlessness; why have we destroyed its sound, accepting the letter *x*?[291] From *magnus* [great] they first derived *magnior* and *magnissimus*, words that later became *maior* and *massimus* by contraction and the removal of letters; why have the ears of learned men so long endured hearing the harsh sound of the letter *x*? Indeed, if the word *maximus* be derived from *massa* [mass], the misuse will be the same, since *massa* comes from *magnus*, and it was originally *magnissa*, or in Greek *maza*. Why *elixare* [boil, seethe]? Well, in the beginning from *liquo, liquas* there was *liquasso*, like *levasso* from *levo, levas*; later, with letters removed, *lisso* and *elisso*. Why, I say, was the harsh and rough sounding letter received in these words as well? Why also in these, *palus, velum, paulum, talus, mala*, when the softer letter *l* has been replaced by the harsher sound, do we mistakenly say *paxillus, vexillum, pauxillum, taxillus*, and *maxilla*? Is it because our ears are taken by the sweetness of harmony and the sense of hearing is soothed both by dividing sounds and cutting them short?

From *sistere* [to cause to stand] first there was *sistlocus*, afterward *stlocus*, and finally the jarring sound was eliminated and *locus* was created. By the same process of subtraction, from *sistere* arose *sistlitis*, because one had to stand or present oneself [*sistendum esset*] in court before the praetor, and from that came *stlitis*, then *litis*, and finally *lis* [lawsuit], very harmoniously and conveniently.[292] Or in the beginning wasn't the lower part of the human face, which moves when we speak and eat and even yawn, called *movimentum*, afterward *mentum* [chin]? The de-

Quid autem mirum in sono et litteris factam esse ruinam, quando in significationibus quoque ipsis haud secus contigerit, neque recentioribus tantum seculis, verum etiam et priscis? Etenim dictionibus his: *amabilis, nabilis, flexibilis, vulnerabilis, reparabilis, flebilis, revocabilis* aptitudo quasi quaedam inest ad patiendum vel innata potius vis quaedam apud Latinos homines; non dubitavit tamen Virgilius, populo ut morem gereret etiam aberranti, dicere: *penetrabile frigus,* quod vim habeat penetrandi; non alii poetae: *telum exitiabile,* quod exitium afferat; non scriptores alii, quibus minus concessum est decedere e via. Itaque passim audias: *risibilem hominem, hinnibiles equos, sensibile animal,* deflexa ad agendum a patiendo significantia, quamvis postremum hoc Lucretiana auctoritate non careat.

At contra[302] miramur in Virgilio: *incana menta* et *incurvum aratrum,* quod in his insitam augeat *in* significationem; ac si non et Cicero dixerit *infractum,* ut qui vehementer esset *fractus.* Ac mihi credite, compangendis atque ineundis vocibus *in* frequentius auget quam imminuit, affirmatque potiusquam inficiatur. Idque licet videre enumeratis vocibus, quacunque a littera incipientibus: *inhabito, inambulo, imbibo, imbuo, incido, incutio, indo, induco, inhaereo, inest, influo, infero, ingero, ingluvies* (est enim *ingluvies* a verbo *inglubo*), *inhio, iniicio, illido, illudo, immitto, immuto, innatus, innato, inolesco, inhorreo, impello, impingo, inquino, inquiro, irruo, irretio, instillo, instruo, intego, intorqueo, inuro, invenio, invado.* Quid tu, Summonti, defesso mihi enumerandis his non affers suppetias? Non et ipse grammaticae locum tueris?

struction of sound and letters should not be surprising since it has also occurred in just the same way in meanings themselves, and not only in recent times but also in antiquity. For in the words *amabilis, nabilis, flexibilis, vulnerabilis, reparabilis, flebilis, revocabilis,* among the Latins there is a certain sort of fitness or rather inherent power to undergo some experience;[293] yet Vergil, to take into account the feelings of people shrinking from it, did not hesitate to say *penetrabile frigus* [penetrating cold], because it had the power to penetrate; nor did other poets: thus, *telum exitiabile* [deadly weapon], because it brings death; or other writers, who had less freedom in departing from the usual practice.[294] And so everywhere you might hear: *risibilis homo* [man characterized by laughter], *hinnibiles equi* [horses characterized by neighing], *sensibile animal* [living thing characterized by the faculty of sensation], with the meaning reversed to active from passive, although this last example has the authority of Lucretius.[295]

On the other hand, we are surprised at Vergil's expressions *incana menta* [hoary chins] and *incurvum aratrum* [bent plow], because the prefix *in* increases the meaning engrained in them — as if Cicero too did not say *infractus* of something very broken.[296] And believe me, in compounding and beginning words *in* increases more often than lessens, affirms rather than denies. One can see this from the following list of words, whatever letter they begin with: *inhabito, inambulo, imbibo, imbuo, incido, incutio, indo, induco, inhaereo, inest, influo, infero, ingero, ingluvies (ingluvies* comes from the verb *inglubo), inhio, iniicio, illido, illudo, immitto, immuto, innatus, innato, inolesco, inhorreo, impello, impingo, inquino, inquiro, irruo, irretio, instillo, instruo, intego, intorqueo, inuro, invenio, invado.* Why don't you help me, Summonte, when I am worn out by listing all these? Don't you yourself also defend the place of grammar?

70 *Sum.* Equidem ego illud ubique et sensi olim et hodie quoque sentio, litteratores nostros aberrasse non parum ab antiqua enuntiatione et sermone; concedendum tamen in plurimis esse populo usumque in multis sequendum, potiusquam rationem aut artem, quippe quae nata sit ab observatione. Atque de vasta ut littera dicam quod sentio, ea elementum minime simplex est, verum conglutinatio quaedam atque ad imminuendum in scribendo laborem inventa; nam initio cum fuisset in primo casu *calcis, lancis, arcis,* ut *plebes,* ut *scrobes,* ut *trabes,* quae nunc sunt *plebs, scrobs, trabs,* post subtracta littera *i* mansere *calcs, lancs, arcs;* inde inventa nova est figura, quae una duarum subiret et vicem litterarum et locum, scribique coeptum *calx, lanx, arx.*

Et quoniam in hunc sermonem incidimus, repetam hac in parte pauca quaedam, et si fortasse remotiora, neque iniucunda tamen, neque aliena ab umbratili hac aestivaque consessione nostra. Sermo coepit primum noster ab incultis et rusticanis, imo agrestibus ab hominibus; utque eorum erant res inopes, angustae, egenae, sic quoque sermo ipse inops minimeque affluens, verborumque perpaucorum ac sine ullo prorsus eorum excolendorum studio et cura. Crescentibus post artibus atque hominum rebus actionibusque, quod sermo esset ipse et componendus et maturandus, factae sunt praecisiones tum syllabarum, tum litterarum, non ab ipsis modo vocum principiis, verum etiam desinentibus a syllabis.

Principio enim constitutiones formaeque appellationum haudquaquam fuere quales nunc sunt, finalibus praesertim litteris. Nam quae sunt hodie *fex, grex, dux, rex, emax, vendax, fallax, minax* fuere primis illis seculis in casu nominante *fecis, gregis, ducis, regis, emacis, vendacis, fallacis, minacis;* amputatis contractisque post litteris, decurtatae terminationes sunt, utar autem Ciceroniano verbo. Qua e re id etiam secutum, ut figura haec,

Summonte. For my part, in all circumstances I thought once, and I 70
still think today, that our scholars have strayed not a little from
ancient enunciation and speech; yet for the most part one must
give in and follow popular usage on many points rather than
reason or art, since usage has arisen from observation. And to
say what I think about the rough letter *x*, it is by no means a
single element, but a joining together of some kind invented to
lessen the effort in writing. For although originally there were
in the nominative case *calcis, lancis, arcis* (compare *plebes, scrobes,
trabes,* which are now *plebs, scrobs, trabs*), afterward, when the
letter *i* was omitted, they were left as *calcs, lancs, arcs;* then a new
shape was invented, one letter to succeed to the function and
space of two, and they began to write *calx, lanx, arx.*

And since we happen to be on this topic, I will review a few
points in this place — although they are perhaps a little far
afield, they are still neither unpleasant nor unsuited to this
summer assembly we're holding in shaded seclusion. Our language first began with uncultivated and rustic people — peasants, in fact; and as their circumstances were poor, straitened,
and needy, so too their language was poor and by no means
copious, and of very few words and with no interest or concern
at all in improving them. Afterward, as human arts and circumstances and activities increased, because language itself also had
to be put in order and brought to maturity, both syllables and
letters were excised, not only from the beginnings of words, but
also from their final syllables.

In the beginning the structures and forms of nouns and adjectives were not at all as they are today, especially in their final
letters. The words that today are *faex, grex, dux, rex, emax,
vendax, fallax, minax* were in those first ages in the nominative
case *faecis, gregis, ducis, regis, emacis, vendacis, fallacis, minacis;* when
letters were later cut off and contracted the endings were cut
short, to use Cicero's term.[297] As a consequence, it also followed

quod dixi, duplex quidem ea sit inventa minuendi laboris gratia scriptumque *fex, grex, dux, rex, emax, vendax, fallax, minax,* quae voces prius habuerant *cs* aut *gs.* Excultioribus enim seculis contraxere *adeps,* quod nomen ante *adepis* fuerat, et *abs,* cuius postea locum subiit *ab,* et *ex,* cuius loco et vice *e* utimur, et *ast,* pro quo quibusdam magis placuit *at,* quod sonus ille esset vastior. Quid quod *donicum* fuit quod nunc est *donec, sedum* quod est *sed, sicce* quod est *sic, etiam* pro quo *et, sat* quoque quod fuerat *satis, lac* quod *lacte, tribunal* quod *tribunale, animal* quod *animale, sal* quod *salis, nil* quod *nilum, far* quod *farre?* Quid quod *forsit* pro *forsitan?* Quo non Horatius modo popularibus in sermonibus, sed Propertius in amatoriis est usus, cum dixit:

Iste quod est, ego saepe fui, sed forsit in hora
  hoc ipso eiecto carior alter erit.

71 Nec vero primarum tantum atque ultimarum sive litterarum sive syllabarum factae sunt amputationes, dum aut brevitati consulitur aut suavitati, verum a mediis quoque. Quidnam, quaeso, nunc est *taberna,* nisi quod olim *tabulerna,* facta litterarum subductione? Quid *venter* nisi *vehenter,* quod se implendo *evehat* vel quod *vehat* in cibum absumpta, unde ventrem exhonerare dicuntur qui excrementa eiiciunt? Quid *vultus* nisi *voluntus,* quod animi *voluntatem* indicet? Quid *lautus* nisi *lavatus,* a sorde scilicet liber atque extersus? Quid *coxae* nisi *coissae* a coeundo, vel in ipsa libidine, vel quod hinc illincque coeant ad oscenas partes vehendo corpori? Iam vero *fortuna* a *ferendo* dicta, et mutatis et subtractis litteris quasi *ferentuna;* terra *pulla,* quasi *pulvilla,* idest

that this double letter, as I have said, was invented to save effort, and they wrote the words that had previously had *cs* or *gs* as *faex, grex, dux, rex, emax, vendax, fallax, minax*. Indeed, in more cultivated ages they made the contraction *adeps*, a noun formerly *adepis*, and they shortened *abs*, which was later replaced by by *ab*, and *ex*, which we use alternately with *e*, and *ast*, for which some prefer *at* because *ast* sounds too harsh. In addition, what used to be *donicum* is now *donec*, *sedum* is now *sed*, *sicce* now *sic*, *et* is in place of *etiam*, *sat* also what used to be *satis*, *lac* is for *lacte*, *tribunal* for *tribunale*, *animal* for *animale*, *sal* for *salis*, *nil* for *nilum*, *far* for *farre*. And think of *forsit* for *forsitan* (perhaps), used not only by Horace in his colloquial *Satires* [*Satire* 1.6.49], but also by Propertius in his love poems when he said:

> That man of yours is what I often was, but perhaps in an
> hour
>   he will be thrown out and another will be more dear.
>   [Propertius 2.9.1–2]

In the interests of brevity and euphony amputations were   71
made not only of first and last letters or syllables but also of
those in the middle. What, I ask you, is the present *taberna* except what was once *tabulerna*, with letters subtracted? What is *venter* [belly] except *vehenter*, so called because in filling itself it carries away [*evehat*] or because it conveys [*vehat*] what has been consumed into nourishment, from which those who evacuate excrement are said to unload their belly [*ventrem*]? What is *vultus* [expression] except *voluntus*, because it indicates the disposition or desire [*voluntas*] of the mind?[298] What is *lautus* [washed] except *lavatus*, that is, scrubbed free of filth? What are *coxae* [hips] except *coissae* from *coeo* [come together], either in lust or because in carrying the body they come together from both directions at the obscene parts? Now one says *fortuna* from *fero*, essentially *ferentuna* with letters changed and subtracted; black

resolubilis et in pulverem versa, qualis est terra Campana, ut ait Columella, quae nequaquam nigra est, ut quidam perperam arbitrantur, sed resolubilis et putrida, quaeque saepius arata in pulverem abit. Est et *columna* a *columine*, quae fuit *columina*; et a *pascendo pabulum*, quod fuit *pascibulum*; et *panis pascinis*; et *pasta panista*; et *vinum* a *vite vitinum*; et *vinea vitinea*; et a *ferendo ferculum, fericulum*, quod in pompis ferantur fercula; *poculum* item *potaculum; flumen fluimen; tegmen tegimen; semen serimen; discrimen discernimen*; nam *prosa* quid est aliud quam *promissa oratio?* An, quaeso, *meditari* est aliud quam in *medio itinere* aliquid *itando* aut agere aut cogitare, quod est occupati animi aliudque quam iter agitantis?

Quid est etiam aliud *foenum* nisi *fovenum*, quo scilicet *foveantur* animalia hieme? Quid *foetus* nisi *fovetus*, quod a matribus *foveantur?* Retinentque propterea dypthongum *oe*; nam in primo verbo cum insit littera *o*, subtracta *v* littera. relinquitur *oe*. An non *postes* sunt a *positu* quasi *posites?* ac *testis, tecum sto* aut pro *te sisto?* nam et testes sistebant olim apud praetorem. *Tela* non ne *texula*, ut *tegula*, ut *regula? Cliens* non ne *coliens*, quod patronum utique coleret suum, e Romuli constitutione? *Castra* sunt qui putent a servanda *castitate* dicta, ambitiose sane, quippe quae

soil [*terra pulla*] is *pulvilla*, so to speak, or soil friable and turned
to dust [*pulvis*], like the soil of Campania, as Columella says,
which is not at all black, as some wrongly believe, but friable
and crumbly, which after frequent tilling has changed into
dust.[299] There is also *columna* [column] from *columen*, formerly
columina; and from *pasco* [feed] *pabulum* [food], originally *pascibulum*, as well as *panis* [bread], once *pascinis*, and *pasta* [dough]
from *panista*; and *vinum* [wine] from *vitis* [vine] from *vitinum*;
and *vinea* [vineyard] from *vitinea*; and from *fero* [carry] *ferculum*
[litter] from *fericulum*, because litters [(*fercula*] are carried [*feruntur*] in processions. Likewise *poculum* from *potaculum*, *flumen*
from *fluimen*, *tegmen* from *tegimen*, *semen* from *serimen*, *discrimen*
from *discernimen*. Indeed, what is *prosa* except extended [*promissa*] speech? Or, I ask, is *meditari* [meditate] anything except
doing or thinking something as one goes along [*itando*] in the
middle of a journey [*medio itinere*], which is the activity of a
busy mind and one thinking about something other than the
journey?

What is *foenum* [hay] except *fovenum*, by which animals are
kept warm [*foveantur*] in winter? What are *foetus* [offspring] except *fovetus*, because they are warmed [*foveantur*] by their mothers?[300] And for this reason the two words keep the diphthong
oe, for since the letter *o* was present in the original word, *oe* remained when the letter *v* was taken away. Or are not *postes*
[posts], essentially *posites*, from *positus* [situation]? And *testis*
[witness] from *tecum sto* [I stand with you] or for *te sisto* [I make
you stand]? (For formerly they made witnesses stand [*sistebant*]
before the praetor.) Is not *tela* [textile] *texula*, a word like *tegula*,
regula? And *cliens* [client] *coliens* because he cultivated [*coleret*]
his patron at all costs, from the time of the constitution of Ro-
mulus?[301] Some people think *castra* [camp] is so called from
preserving chastity [*castitas*], presumptuously indeed, since it is
from *claudo* [enclose], for an encampment was enclosed [*claude-*

sint a *claudendo,* claudebantur enim vallo et fossa. Sic et *casteria,* locus in triremi, sic etiam vallis illa *Caudina,* quod sit undique clausa montibus hodieque ex eo vocatur *Caudium.* Sic quoque et *castellum,* quod fossa claudatur et muris; erant etiam in aquarum ductibus *castella,* quod in iis aquae concluderentur, unde post largius effluerent. Atque ut a *dio dies,* sic a *gladio gladies,* pro qua est *clades;* fuitque *stratages,* pro qua est *strages;* et *stratagulum,* pro quo *stragulum;* et *stratamen,* pro quo *stramen;* quin etiam *sarriculum,* pro quo *sarculum* et *noviper* pro quo *nuper;* et *sequeculum* pro quo *seculum,* hoc est annorum multorum series ac sequela, qua in voce qui dypthongum *ae* scribunt male omnino sentiunt; neque enim prima eius producitur quod dypthongum habeat, sed quod veteres poetae geminaverunt in ea voce litteram *c,* quemadmodum in *religione* et *reliquiis l* et in *propagine p,* cum harum producunt primas syllabas, utque Lucretius *refficit* et *redducit.* An quia[303] quod imminutum fuit e litteris, cum *seculum* in initio fuerit, ut dixi, *sequeculum,* adiectum sit postea tempori hoc est quantitati? quod in multis aliis est servatum.[304] Sed dies me deficiat iis enumerandis.

72   Sermonem autem quo utimur ab agrestibus ac rudibus coepisse hominibus, illud declarat potissimum, quod pleraeque e primis illis impositionibus sunt rusticis incomptisque a rebus sumptae. Iam primum *palam, saepe, e vestigio* rusticorum quidem sunt inventa hominum; nam quod *saepes* spissa esset et densa, dixerunt *saepe* pro *frequenter* indeque et *saepissus spissus; e vestigio* pro *statim,* quasi non minus cito[305] quam *e vestigio* pes dimoveatur; *palam, aperte,* quod sit aperta quidem ac protenta *pala*

bantur] by a rampart and a ditch.[302] So too *casteria*, a place on a trireme, so too the famous *Caudine* valley, because it was enclosed [*clausa*] on all sides by mountains, and from that today it is called *Caudium*. So also *castellum* [castle], because it is enclosed by a moat and ramparts; there were also *castella* [reservoirs] in aquaducts because water was enclosed in them so that it could flow out more abundantly. And as *dies* [day] is from *dium* [sky], so from *gladius* [sword] *gladies*, for which now there is *clades* [massacre]; and there was *stratages*, for which there is *strages* [laying low, carnage], and *stratagulum*, for which *stragulum* [carpet], and *stratamen*, for which *stramen* [straw]; why even *sarriculum* for which *sarculum* [hoe] and *noviper* for which *nuper* [recently]; and *sequeculum* for which *seculum* [age], that is, a series and sequence of many years, and those who write a diphthong *ae* in this word are entirely mistaken, for its first syllable is not lengthened because it has a diphthong, but because the ancient poets doubled the *c* in this word just as they doubled the letter *l* in *religio* and *reliquiae* and the *p* in *propago* when they lengthened their first syllables, and as Lucretius wrote *refficit* and *redducit*. Or was it because it had lost letters (*seculum* being originally *sequeculum*, as I have noted), that this addition was later made to the length, that is, the quantity, of the syllable? This practice has been observed in many other cases. But I do not have time to list them.

Our language originated with uncultivated peasants, as is 72
evident from the fact that most of the first designations were taken from rough rustic matters. To begin with, *palam, saepe, e vestigio* were inventions of men who were clearly rustics. For because a *saepes* [hedge] was thick and dense, they said *saepe* for "frequently," and then *saepissus, spissus* [very thick]. They said *e vestigio* for *statim* [on the spot, at once], essentially meaning "no less swiftly than a foot moves out of its footprint." They said *palam* [openly], because a *pala* [spade] is certainly open and

nihilque cavum habeat aut complicatum, in quo latere quid collocatum possit. Nam *penes*, idest in manu atque in potestate, fuit olim, quod quidem ipse iuraverim, *penest*, accommodatum rudibus ab hominibus ex asinorum et iumentorum caudis, aut manu prehensis, unde fuit *manucapio*, aut capistro colligatis invicem; mos est enim alterum iumentum alterius caudae illigare, ne digrediendi illis sit potestas; post vero detracta littera *t*, mansit *penes*. Et *cernere*, unde *decernere* et *certare*, quae senatoria sunt atque imperatoria verba, indeque et *decreta* et *certamina*, manavit initio a *cernendis* leguminibus. Et *serere*, et *pangere* ruris sunt arborumque et seminum, e rure tamen in urbem atque a rusticis ad urbanos venere; et *series* rerum; et *sermo*; et *sermocinatio*; et *dissero*; et *disertus*; et *pangere* versum; et *pagina*; et *pagella*; quin etiam litterarum *exaratio*. Quodque pastores cogerent pecudes gregatim compascere, non sparsim, inde *compescere* est continere; quodque vehendis ex agro in oppida et vicos rebus instanter darent operam, factum est *vehestigo*, quod erat tunc eandem viam insistere eaque saepius itare; nam et *via* initio fuit *veha*;[306] factum item est *vehestigium*; quae nunc ademptis syllabis sunt *vestigo* et *vestigium* eaque ab iumentis atque a curribus in scolas profecta a philosophis etiam recepta sunt. Atque illis quidem seculis satis habebatur quali res cumque appellatione notare, nulla cum esset quantitatis ac temporum aut suavitatis cura formandis vocabulis. Quam post et curam et cogitationem

extended and has no hollow or fold for anything to be placed in and escape notice. Indeed, *penes*, that is, in hand or in one's power, was formerly, and I would swear to it, *penest* [it is by the tail], a term adapted by rough men from the tails of asses and pack animals, which they either grasped with their hands, whence the word *manucapio* [guarantee, provide security], or tied to each other by a halter, for it was the custom to tie one pack animal to the tail of another, so that they could not get separated; but later when the letter *t* was taken off, *penes* was left. Both *cernere* [decide], whence *decernere* [decree] and *certare* [contend], which are words of senators and generals, and then also *decreta* [decrees] and *certamina* [struggles], came originally from sorting [*cernendis*] beans. Both *serere* [put in a row] and *pangere* [make fast] are words of the country used of trees and seeds, yet they came from the country into the city and from rustics to city folk, to make *series* [series], used of things, and *sermo* [conversation], *sermocinatio* [discussion], *dissero* [discuss], *disertus* [eloquent]; and to compose [*pangere*] verse, and *pagina* and *pagella*, both meaning page; from the country too is *exaratio* [plowing], used for literary composition [*exaratio litterarum*]. And because shepherds herded their sheep to pasture [*compascere*] in flocks, not separately, *compescere* means to keep together. And because they worked hard in bringing [*veho*] things from the country into towns and villages, the word *vehestigo* was created, which was to set foot on the same road and to go that way often; for originally *via* [road] was *veha*; likewise *vehestigium* was created, which now by the removal of syllables has become *vestigo* [investigate] and *vestigium* [vestige] and these words that had their start with pack animals and carts have even been received into schools by philosophers.[303] And in those times indeed it was considered sufficient to designate things with any name at all, since in forming words there was no concern for the quantity and lengths of syllables or for euphony. Later the

primi poetae suscepere, dum urbanitatis suscipiunt patrocinium, donec senatus ac fori maiores agitationes atque actiones peperere eam quae post dicta est eloquentia. Qua quidem in explicatione, et si latissimus mihi se se offert campus, tamen quod et petenti subsidium Compatri videri potest satis pro virili factum esse; cum etiam brevis haec refrigeratio fuerit Altilio nostro non ingrata, et quod Puderici supercilium non est contemnendum, quem video grammaticis non satis aequum, loquendi possessionem tuumque ad continuandum de historia locum, Altili, et volens et libens tibi restituo.

73 *Alt.* Et refrigeratio ipsa fuit mihi pergrata et te interim vetustissimas repetentem res iucundissime audivi. Nam et ex iis quae explicasti principiis nata est historia, quae rudis in initio ipsa fuit, sine cultu, sine copia, nulla adhibita artis industria, perexigua etiam naturae; quippe cum ea cura pontificibus tantum esset demandata iique annis singulis quae gesta essent notabant populoque exponebant cognoscenda. Cui post et Piso et Fabius et Cato non ita multum addidere ornamenti, ut generis scribendi eorum magna fuerit a posterioribus ratio habita. Ne multo quidem quam horum maior habetur a Cicerone Caelii, nec Sisenna eius implet aures, quanquam vocaliorem is historiam fecit, cui, ut Ciceroni ipsi videtur, maiorem quendam Caelius sonum vocis addidisset. Adhaec Sisenna *parum libero ore locutus* Sallustio videtur, cum sit historiae e Ciceronis sententia prima illa lex,

nequid falsi dicere audeat, deinde nequid veri non audeat, nequa suspitio gratiae sit in scribendo, nequa simultas.[307]

poets first took on themselves this thoughtful care when they
became the patrons of refined speech, until at length the greater
activities and actions of the senate and the forum gave birth to
what was later called eloquence. Although a very wide field
presents itself to me in explicating this matter, nonetheless I
think I have done enough, as well as I could. to answer Compatre's plea for assistance. Since this rest, though brief, will have
been not unwelcome to our friend Altilio, and because one
must not defy the stern opinion of Puderico, who I see is a little
unfair to grammarians, willingly and gladly I return the floor to
you, Altilio, and your turn to go on talking about history.

Altilio. This rest was very welcome to me, and in the interim I   73
listened with the greatest pleasure to your review of ancient
matters. Indeed, history arose from those first beginnings you
described; it was rude itself in the beginning, without cultiva-
tion, without fullness, with no pains taken for art, very little
even for nature, since this task was entrusted only to the priests,
and they noted down the events of each year and published
them for the information of the populace.[304] Later Piso and
Fabius and Cato did not add enough embellishment to it for
later generations to take much account of their way of writing.
Cicero did not have a much higher opinion of Caelius than he
did of these, nor did Sisenna satisfy his ears although he made
history more sonorous, while Caelius, as Cicero himself
thought, had given it a more high-sounding style.[305] In addition, Sisenna, in Sallust's opinion, "did not speak frankly
enough" [*Bellum Iugurthinum* 95.2], since in Cicero's view the
first law of history is this:

> Let the historian not dare to say anything false, then let him
> be bold enough to speak the whole truth. Let there be no
> suspicion of partiality in his writing or any animosity. [*De
> oratore* 2.62]

Atque hi quidem progressus Romanae fuere historiae ad Ciceronis usque tempora. Nam de Graeca illi viderint qui Graece
praecipiunt; de qua tamen et Cicero ea attigit quae satis esse
Latinis nobis videri possint. Itaque, his sic dictis, me vobis
reddo, sive admonens sive innuens pauca quaedam,[308] ut dixi
utque sum pollicitus, potiusquam ut qui videri velim praecepta
tradidisse.

Principio, ut natura ipsa rerum generationi consulens suo
quodque in genere perficere ac consumare nititur, in aliis tamen
aliud eius atque aliud est propositum, sic dictio omnis et scriptio eo spectat, ut bene consumateque et dicatur et scribatur;
alibi tamen, hoc est forensibus in causis, ut consumate dicatur
etiam ad persuasionem, alibi ad laudationem approbationem-
que, ut in eo genere quod demonstrativum dicitur atque in
historia; cuius prima cum sit lex neque in gratiam loqui neque
opticere odio vera aut ea dissimulare, efficitur ut laudentur quae
sint commendatione digna, suo quidem et loco et tempore
utque improbentur turpiter atque imprudenter facta; alterum
sine spe, sine pretio, alterum sine simultate et metu; ita uti et
tuae pariter et illius de quo suscepta est laudatio famae hono-
rique pudenter ac modeste consulas. Nam qui pretio servit ac
malivolentiae veritati quonam pacto studeat? Ac mihi quidem
in laudando aut improbando videtur rerum gestarum scriptor
iudicis quasi cuiusdam personam debere induere, ne ab aequo
et iusto illo recedat, quod est inter praemium ac poenam medium.

74   Et quoniam res ab aliquo gestas historicus sibi scribendas
suscipit, primum videre illud debet, quod dicendi genus sequi
debeat; quod tale mihi quidem assumendum videtur quale est
genus fusum, lene, aequabiliter incedens, neque ita compressum

And these indeed were the advances in Roman history up to the time of Cicero. As to Greek history, that must be the business of those who teach Greek; in any case, Cicero's remarks on it could also seem sufficient for us Latins. And so, having said this, I turn back to you with a few reminders or suggestions, as I said and promised, rather than because I wish to seem to be giving instructions.

First, as Nature herself, who looks after the generation of things, strives to complete and perfect each thing in its kind, yet in different things has different purposes, so each utterance and composition aims at being spoken and written well and perfectly. Yet in one place, that is, in legal cases, it may be spoken perfectly for the sake of persuasion, in another for praise and approval, as in the genre called demonstrative, and in history. And since history's first law is neither to speak to win favor nor to refuse to speak the truth or hide it out of odium, it happens that things worthy of commendation are praised (at the proper time and place, to be sure), and that dishonorable and imprudent deeds are censured; the one without expectation, without reward, the other without animosity or fear, in such a way that discreetly and modestly you show equal concern both for your own reputation and dignity and for those of the person you have undertaken to praise. For how can the person who is in service to reward or spite pay attention to the truth? In my opinion, in meting out praise or blame, a person writing history ought to take on the character of a kind of judge, so as not to deviate from the equitable and just position that is midway between reward and punishment.

And since the historian undertakes to write about someone's 74 deeds, first he ought to see what style he should follow. In my opinion, at any rate, the style to be adopted is copious, moderate, proceeding uniformly, neither so compressed that it seems

ut inops videatur et languens, neque adeo amplum ut intumescat oratio et verba ipsa quodammodo exiliant, utque incedat oratio, non saliat aut titubet sitque incessus ipse non muliebris ac petulans, sed virilis et gravis.

Omnium autem iudicio laudatur potissimum in historia brevitas, cum ea sit maxime idonea ad docendum, ad delectandum, ad movendum. Nam nec docere bene potest qui loquaciter atque ambitiose explicat; parit enim loquacitas ac diffluentia ipsa tum contemptum tum etiam satietatem, quae docilitati adversantur ac delectationi. Nam quis omnino doceri velit molestia tedioque affectus? nec moveri et agi quo volumus animus eius potest, male qui libenter aut audit aut legit. Adhaec nimius verborum tractus effusiorque oratio memoriae quam officiat omnes videtis; de quo natum est Horatianum illud :

Quicquid praecipies, esto brevis.

Quo haec igitur aliaque vitentur in scribendo incommoda et vitia, danda erit opera ut brevitas ipsa sit aperta et clara quaeque apte colligat, non concise, lucide, non obscure. Nam et Cicero in Thucidide[309] ac Philisto, qui illum imitatus est, non probat eorum quasdam sententias, ut concisas, ut non satis lucidas, quaeque contractione sua officiant nimioque acumine. Equidem hac in parte pudore capior quodam, dicam tamen quod sentio ingenue, inter vos praesertim, dissertiones illustres illas quidem et puras et appositas, easdem etiam graves et suptiles, ita tamen nimio acumine ne officiant, non breves vocandas, sed accommodatas potius, sed et aequabiles et temperatas; arbitrorque nomen hoc brevitatis inde venisse in usum vel

meager and feeble nor so ample that the language is puffed up and the words themselves somehow stand out; the language should move in a measured fashion, not leap up or stagger, and its movement should not be effeminate or freakish but virile and impressive.[306]

In the judgment of all, however, it is brevity in history that wins the greatest praise, since it is best suited to teach, to delight, to move the emotions. A person who goes on loquaciously and ostentatiously cannot teach well; verbosity and rambling breed both disdain and satiety, which are incompatible with attention and pleasure.[307] For who would be willing to be taught if he was afflicted with annoyance and boredom? Nor can the mind of an unwilling listener or reader be moved and led where we wish. In addition, you all see how an excessive drawing out of words and too lavish a style get in the way of memory. From this arose Horace's famous words:

Whatever you teach, keep it short. [*Ars poetica* 335][308]

Well then, to avoid these and other troublesome mannerisms and faults in writing, one must take pains to make brevity itself straightforward and clear and of a kind that condenses things appropriately, not tersely; clearly, not unintelligibly. For example, in Thucydides and his imitator Philistus, Cicero also criticizes certain sentences as terse and insufficiently clear, and because they obstruct understanding with their compression and excessive cleverness.[309] On this point I am a little embarrassed, yet I will express my frank opinion, among you especially. I think that one should not use the designation "brief" for discourses — the brilliantly clear ones, that is — that are both unadorned and apposite, at the same time impressive and simple, in such a way that they do not get in the way with excessive cleverness. Rather, they should be called appropriate, but also moderate and restrained.[310] And I consider that this title of

potius in honorem, quod diffluentia illa et superfluens collectio
rerumque aggestio ac verborum tantopere improbaretur, ut eius
contraria brevitas favorem eo maiorem invenerit. Sed non sit
nobis de verbo ullo contentio, quod in Ciceronis sonet ore, dum
brevitas intelligatur esse apposita ipsa quidem et verbis ac sententiis accommodatis, collectione ipsa nec arcta nec pervagata,
in qua, perinde ut in agro bene culto, nullae insint sentes, quin
eniteant in ea ipsa omnia et virescant suo tempore, suo etiam et
florescant et maturescant. Hoc itaque sive breve et appositum,
sive aequabile atque accommodatum dicendi genus amplecten-
dum est historico; constetque appellatam brevitatem non quia
concisa et manca, verum quod multa complectatur verbis non
ita multis, quaeque pro rerum ac sententiarum complexu appareant etiam pauca.

Hoc est igitur illud genus quod paulo ante diximus assumendum: fusum, lene, aequabiliter defluens, neque ieiunum neque
intumescens atque corruptum. Etenim fusa oratio concisionem
longius a se repellit obscuritatis sociam sibique adversantem
atque contrariam. Lenis atque aequabilis aspernatur reiicitque
ab se se contortus illos ambitusque nimios ineptasque atque
asperas verborum collocationes strepitusque tum vocum ac syllabarum tum interruptos hiatus; ut quemadmodum sedatus
amnis feratur cursu tranquillo, nullis contortus gurgitibus aut
spumantibus obiectu saxorum aquis. Ieiuna vero atque inops
illa, quasi glareosus ager, quem afferre fructum potest, quando
quod laudandum suscepit reddit contemptibile illud ac ridiculum?

In brevi autem hoc et apposito dicendi genere, in repetendis
antiquitatibus, in revocandis memoriis, in describendis locis, in
referendis consiliis, in enarrandis casibus, in proeliis, victoriis,

brevity came into use, or rather into honor, because the rambling and excessive recapitulation and heaping up of things and words was so much condemned that its opposite, brevity, found correspondingly greater favor. But let us not quibble about any word that has sounded in the mouth of Cicero, provided that we understand that the term brevity is apposite when both words and thoughts are appropriate, when the argument itself is not too closely packed or all over the place — in which, just as in a well cultivated field, there are no brambles, but everything there shines forth and becomes verdant in its season, and in its season blossoms and ripens. And so this is the style — whether brief and apposite, or moderate and appropriate — that the historian should embrace; and let us agree to call it brevity, not because it is terse and weak, but because it covers many things in not so many words — words that also appear few in proportion to their grasp of matters and ideas.

This then, as we said a moment ago, is the style to be adopted: copious, moderate, flowing uniformly, and neither thin nor swollen and tasteless. A copious style stays away from dividing sentences into many short clauses, rejecting the practice as friendly to obscurity and hostile and contrary to itself. The moderate and even style spurns and avoids convolutions and excessive periphrases and awkward and rough arrangements of words, as well as both loud-clashing sounds and syllables and broken-off hiatuses — so that it flows in its tranquil course like a quiet stream, not roiled by whirlpools or with its waters turned to foam by rocks in its path.[311] But a style that is thin and meager is like a stony field: what fruit can it bear, since it makes contemptible and ridiculous what it undertakes to praise?

Furthermore, in this brief and apposite style, in recalling ancient times, reviving memories, describing places, reporting counsels, relating events, telling of battles, victories, defeats,

cladibus memorandis, extollendis praeclaris facinoribus, accusandis ac deprimendis ignavis et perditis, iudicio vetustatis magnus et clarus existit Sallustius, nam celeritate facile est princeps. In concionibus vero habendisque orationibus non idem video esse omnium iudicium, quasi parum habita ratione personarum, hoc est militum, populi, senatus, ad quos orationes ipsae habentur; adhaec et scabrosior in illis iudicatur et concisior in sententiis et contractus ac nimium acutus apud quos minime deceat. Quibus autem (quod de eloquente ait Cicero, quod mirabilius et magnificentius quam disertus augebit atque ornabit quae volet) quibus, inquam, mirabilior ac magnificentior magis placet oratio, iis vitandum est dicendi genus insolens, affectatum, tumidum (quibus scatet vitiis Marcellinus). Quo in genere scribendi Livius profecto regnat.

75   Quia vero exempla comparationesque declarant maxime virtutes ac dicendi figuras, afferam e Sallustio quos memoria teneo locos quosdam, tametsi quicquid dicit, simplex est et unum dumtaxat, ut Horatianis utar verbis. Loci erunt de ingenio Iugurtae et moribus :

> Qui ubi primum adolevit, pollens viribus, decora facie, sed multo maxime ingenio valido, non se luxui neque inertiae corrumpendum dedit, sed, uti mos gentis illius est, equitare, iaculari, cursu cum aequalibus certare et, cum omnis gloria anteiret, omnibus tamen carus esse. Adhaec pleraque tempora venando agere, leonem atque

extolling illustrious deeds, blaming and disparaging cowardly and profligate ones — it is Sallust who stands out as great and illustrious in the judgment of antiquity, for in speed he is easily the prince.[312] On his presentation of assemblies and the delivery of speeches, however, I see that the general view is not the same, as he takes too little account of the persons — that is, of the soldiers, people, senate — to whom the speeches are delivered; in addition, he is thought to be both too rough in these passages and too terse in thought, and compact and excessively pointed in a way that is by no means suited to his audience.[313] Moreover, those who are pleased by a more admirable and splendid style — the one that Cicero attributes to the eloquent man because he amplifies and adorns what he wants more admirably and splendidly than does the merely accomplished speaker — those, I say, must avoid a way of speaking that is excessive, affected, bombastic.[314] (Marcellinus overflows with these vices.)[315] In this style of writing, assuredly, Livy reigns supreme.

But because examples and comparisons best demonstrate 75 special properties and figures of speech, I will adduce a few passages I remember from Sallust, although whatever he says "is only of one kind and whole," as Horace says.[316] The passages will concern the abilities and character of Jugurtha.

> As soon as he grew up, strong in physique, with a handsome appearance, but most of all, with a very powerful intellect, he did not give himself up to be corrupted by luxury or sloth, but as is the custom of that nation, he rode, threw the javelin, competed in racing with his contemporaries, and although he surpassed them all in glory, he was still dear to all. In addition, he spent much of his time in hunting, was the

alias feras primus aut in primis ferire; plurimum facere, minimum ipse de se loqui.[310]

Et alibi:

Nam Iugurta, ut erat impigro atque acri ingenio, ubi naturam Publii Scipionis, qui tum Romanis imperator erat, et morem hostium cognovit, multo labore multaque cura, praeterea modestissime parendo et saepe obviam eundo periculis, in tantam claritudinem brevi pervenerat, uti nostris vehementer carus, Numantinis maximo terrori esset. Ac sane, quod difficillimum imprimis est, et proelio strenuus erat et bonus consilio, quorum alterum ex providentia timorem, alterum ex audacia temeritatem afferre plerunque solet. Igitur imperator omnes fere res asperas per Iugurtam agere et in amicis habere, magis magisque eum in dies amplecti, quippe cuius neque consilium neque inceptum ullum frustra erat. Huc accedebat munificentia animi et ingenii solertia.[311]

Singula verba res pene complectuntur singulas, ipsa quidem ita propria, ut nullo appareant modo conquisita, structura illaborata, cursus fluens ac sedatus, sonus lenis auribus maxime gratus, nihil denique quod artem praeseferat, cum tamen omnia sint ex arte: quodque de Amphionis cithara murisque Thebanis in fabulis dicitur, et verba et res sponte sua ac natura duce in unum confluunt.

Referam et Livianum de Annibale locum:

Nunquam ingenium idem ad res diversissimas, parendum atque imperandum, habilius fuit. Itaque haud facile

first or among the first to strike the lion and other beasts, accomplished a great deal, said very little about himself. [*Bellum Iugurthinum* 6.1]

And in another passage:

For Jugurtha, as he was energetic and astute by nature, when he recognized the ability of Publius Scipio, then commander of the Romans, and the character of the enemy, with great effort and care, especially by modest obedience and frequently exposing himself to dangers, soon had achieved such a great reputation that he was extremely dear to our side and a source of great terror to the Numantines. Indeed, he was also, a thing that is especially difficult, both energetic in battle and excellent in counsel — the one quality generally gives rise to fear out of prudence, the other to rashness from overconfidence. And so the commander managed almost all difficult matters through Jugurtha and counted him among his friends and valued him more and more as the days went on, since none of his counsels nor undertakings was in vain. He also possessed generosity of spirit and shrewdness of intellect. [*Bellum Iugurthinum* 7.4–7]

Almost individual words describe each point — these, indeed, so appropriate that they do not appear specially chosen at all; the structure is effortless, the progress flowing and dignified, the smooth sound most pleasing to the ear; in short, there is nothing that exhibits art, although each detail is the result of art. As they say in the fables of Amphion's cithara and the walls of Thebes, both words and things flow into a unified whole of their own accord under the direction of nature.[317]

I shall also report Livy's passage on Hannibal.

Never was the same nature more suited to the greatest opposites: obedience and command. And so you could not

discerneres, utrum imperatori aut exercitui carior esset; neque Asdrubal alium quenquam praeficere mallet, ubi quid fortiter ac strenue gerendum esset, neque milites alio duce plus confidere aut audere. Plurimum audaciae ad pericula capessenda, plurimum consilii inter ipsa pericula erat. Nullo labore aut corpus fatigari aut animus vinci poterat. Caloris ac frigoris patientia par; cibi potionisque desiderio naturali, non voluptate modus finitus; vigili-arumque somnique nec die nec nocte discriminata tem-pora. Id quod gerendis rebus superesset, quieti datum; ea neque molli strato neque silentio arcessita; multi saepe militari sagulo opertum humi iacentem intra custodias stationesque militum conspexerunt. Vestitus nihil intra aequales excellens; arma atque equi conspiciebantur. Equi-tum peditumque idem longe primus erat; princeps in proelium ibat, ultimus confecto proelio excedebat. Has tantas virtutes ingentia vitia aequabant: inhumana crude-litas, perfidia plusquam Punica, nihil veri, nihil sancti, nullus deum metus, nullum iusiurandum, nulla religio.[312]

Iudicare his praesertim e locis plane potestis in Sallustio maius esse brevitatis eius de qua loquimur studium, in hoc al-tero rerum adiectis verbis augendarum; illi curae est proprie simpliciterque expressa res, huic arcessitum atque extrinsecus allatum aliquid tanquam excolendae formae. Et lenis et fluxu tantum suo incitus placet Sallustio decursus, at Livio altior paulo, nec tam aliquando sedatus quam plenus ac personans. Ille in id intendit, ut natura videatur duce loqui, hic ut naturae bonis attulisse ex arte industriaque videri velit adminiculum.

easily have decided whether he was dearer to the commander or to the army; neither did Hasdrubal prefer to put anyone else in charge when some brave or strenuous activity was required, nor did the soldiers dare or venture more under another leader. He had the greatest daring in facing dangers, the most resourcefulness among the dangers themselves. By no labor could his body be exhausted or his spirit vanquished. He had equal endurance of heat and cold; the amount of his food and drink was bounded by natural desire, not by pleasure; his times of waking and sleeping were not apportioned by day or night. Only the time left over from action was given to rest; this was invited neither by a soft couch nor by silence; many men saw him covered by a soldier's cloak lying on the ground within the pickets and stations of the soldiers. He dressed no better than his peers; his arms and horses were conspicuous. He was foremost by far of both cavalry and infantry, he went first into battle; left last when the battle was done. His prodigious vices equaled such great virtues: inhuman cruelty, treachery more than Punic, nothing truthful, nothing sacred, no fear of the gods, no oath, no conscience. [Livy 21.4.3–9][318]

From these passages especially you can clearly decide that Sallust has a greater interest in the brevity we are talking about, the other a greater interest in enhancing things with added words; the one is concerned to express a matter properly and simply, the other to seek out and import something from outside as if to polish his style. Sallust likes a moderate course hastened along only by its own flow, but Livy likes one a little loftier, at times not so much tranquil as full and resonant. The one moves in the direction of seeming to speak under the prompting of nature, the other of wishing it to seem evident that he has systematically and deliberately brought assistance to

Utque alter ille virili et senatorio incessu graditur, ac pro loco et sistit interdum gradum et tanquam prospectat longius metiturque loca singula, sic alter hic et gestit quandoque et viribus suis letus exultat praefertque robur et artis et ingenii. Declarat hoc manifestius Lucii Catilinae de virtutibus et vitiis descriptio; locus tamen ille Liviano huic haudquaquam satis similis. Verum de iis sit suum cuique iudicium.

Quoniam igitur, ut Cicero maximus dicendi auctor sentit, pura et illustris esse debet brevitas atque, ut nos dicimus, aperta et clara, puritasque ipsa et claritas versentur tum in sententiis tum in verbis e quibus constat orationis contextio, nimirum omni studio fugienda est obscuritas loquendique perplexio ac dubietas. Evitabuntur autem vitia haec si verba ipsa bene fuerint collocata eaque non rancida, non obsoleta, non putida minimeque ancipitia; cursus non contortus, non verticosus, non lubricus; non concisa aut quasi in involvolum complicata, ut rustici loquuntur, textura; non spinosa sensa, verum series ipsa fusa et tracta. Quarum ubi rerum diligens habebitur cura, quasi fugatis nubibus, aperta apparebit ac serena brevitatis species.

76 Est brevitati coniuncta vel potius cognata celeritas, adeo in historia laudata, eaque existere absque brevitate omnino nequit. De qua innuendum est aliquid, ne partem hanc aut aegreferatis a me praeteritam aut parum omnino animadversam existimetis. Audite, quaeso, studiosissimi viri, quae a me dicentur, nequaquam tamen ut qui novi hausturi aliquid meo de fonte sitis, sed ut ab eo qui ea potius sit vobis in memoriam revocaturus de

the blessings of nature. And as the one proceeds with the vigorous stride of a senator[319] and, depending on the place, sometimes checks his steps and takes a long look ahead, as it were, and takes the measure of places one by one, so the other sometimes acts without restraint and runs riot, rejoicing in his own strength, and displays the power of his artistic talent. (The description of the virtues and vices of Lucius Catiline shows this more clearly; that passage, however is not similar enough to this one in Livy.)[320] But let everyone have his own opinion about these matters.

Therefore, since as Cicero, the greatest authority on eloquence, decrees, brevity must be unadorned and lucid, and as we say, straightforward and clear; and since plainness and clarity reside now in the thoughts and now in the words from which discourse is put together, it is evident that every effort must be made to avoid obscurity and ambiguity and uncertainty of speech.[321] Moreover, these vices will be avoided if the words themselves have been well placed and are not offensive, not hackneyed, not affected, and not equivocal in any way; if the course is not involved, not full of whirlpools, not unsteady; if the structure is not choppy or all rolled up like a caterpillar, as the rustics say;[322] if the thoughts are not crabbed, but the sequence itself is flowing and continuous. Whenever diligent care is taken of these matters, the face of brevity will appear, unobstructed and fair, as if the clouds had been put to flight.

Connected to brevity, or rather akin to it, is speed, so highly 76 praised in history; and this quality can by no means exist without brevity. A hint must be given about it so that you won't be annoyed that I have passed over this feature or think I have taken altogether too little notice of it. Listen, please, most learned gentlemen, to what I will say, yet not at all as if you were about to drink something new from my spring, but as if hearing from one who will remind you instead of matters that

quibus saepius eodem hoc in consessu non minus copiose quam diligenter est disputatum.

Differt itaque a brevitate celeritas, quod brevitas quocunque inesse in sermone et oratione potest, celeritas nec ubique nec semper potest. Etenim brevis est oratio haec: *Ubi quenque periculum ceperat, ibi stare.*[313] At si coniungas statim: *arma tela, viri equi, hostes atque cives permisti; nihil consilio neque imperio agi, fors omnia regere,* erit utique celeritas. Cuius etiam persimilis est illa:

> Deinde ipse pro re ac loco, sicuti e monte[314] descenderat, paulatim procedere, Marium post principia habere, ipse cum sinistrae alae equitibus esse.

Est igitur celeritas brevis et accurata sive complexio sive collectio conglutinatioque complurium simul rerum ac verborum, et quasi partium, quarum unaquaeque per se prolata sensum perficit; sive ea conglutinatio sit inconiuncta et absque copulatione aliqua, ut quas supra posui, sive copulatione constet, ut haec:

> Eodem tempore imperator et aciem instruere et hosti obviam ire et milites cohortari et quid facere quenque vellet imperare; neque voce neque manu usquam deesse.

Huius autem ipsius complexionis partes ac membra interdum singulis e verbis constant, ut: *arma, tela, viri, equi, hostes atque cives permisti;* interdum e pluribus qualis ea:

have often been the subject of both abundant and careful discussion in this same assembly.

Well, speed is different from brevity, because brevity can exist in any discourse or utterance, but speed cannot exist everywhere or on every occasion. For example, this statement is brief: "Wherever danger had overtaken anyone, there he took a stand." But if you immediately add, "arms, spears, men, horses, enemies and citizens were mixed up together; nothing was done by plan, nothing by command, chance determined everything" [*Bellum Iugurthinum* 51.1], there will undoubtedly be speed. This passage is like it:

> Then as the circumstances and the place required, he advanced little by little, just as he had come down from the mountain; he had Marius behind the front line, he himself was with the cavalry on the left wing. [*Bellum Iugurthinum* 50.2]

Speed, then, is a short and precise summing up or enumerating and combining of several things and words at the same time, and of parts, so to speak, each one of which makes sense if produced by itself—whether this combination be in asyndeton and without any link, like the previous examples, or be brought together by linking, like this:

> At the same time the commander both drew up the battle line and advanced against the enemy and exhorted the soldiers and said what he wanted each one to do; nor did he ever fail in voice or vigor.[323]

Moreover, the parts and limbs of this summing up consist sometimes of individual words, like "arms, spears, men, horses, enemies and citizens mixed up together," sometimes of several, like this one:

Nam, uti planities erat inter sinistros montes et inter dexteram rupem, octo cohortes in fronte constituit, reliquarum signa in subsidiis collocat. Ex his centuriones omnes
electos et evocatos, praeterea ex gregariis militibus optimum quenque armatum in primam aciem subducit. C.
Manlium in dextra, Fesulanum quendam in sinistra parte
curare iubet. Ipse cum libertis et colonis propter aquilam
assistit.[315]

Atque haec quidem ipsa celeritatis species minus apparet, nec
tam allicit lectorem, nihilominus varietas est quae eam condiat.
Contra mirifice trahit ad se legentem, ubi partes ipsae mistim
constituentur et e singulis et e pluribus verbis, ut:

Quibus rebus permota civitas atque immutata facies urbis
erat. Ex summa letitia atque lascivia, quae diuturna quies
pepererat, repente omnis tristitia invasit: festinare, trepi-
dare, neque loco neque homini cuiquam satis fidere, neque bellum gerere neque pacem habere, suo quisque metu
pericula metiri.[316]

Accedat et altera compago :

Adhaec mulieres, quibus rei publicae magnitudine belli
timor insolitus incesserat, afflictare se se, manus supplices
ad coelum tendere, miserari parvos liberos, rogitare deos,
omnia pavere, superbia atque delitiis omissis sibi patriaeque diffidere.[317]

For since there was level ground between mountains on the left and a crag on the right, he stationed eight cohorts in the front line, placed the standards of the rest among the reserves. From these he led into the first rank all the ablest centurions and veterans, as well as all the best armed men among the common soldiers. He ordered Gaius Manlius to take charge on the right and a man of Faesulae on the left. He himself stood beside the eagle with his freedmen and colonists. [Sallust, *Bellum Catilinae* 59.2–3]

And indeed, this kind of speed is less apparent and not so appealing to the reader; nonetheless there is variety to make it agreeable. On the other hand, it is wonderfully attractive to the reader when the constituent parts are placed in a mingled array consisting of both separate and multiple words. For example:

The community had been shaken by these events and the appearance of the city transformed. From the heights of gaiety and frivolity, the fruit of long peace, suddenly dejection took possession of everyone; they were restless, they were fearful, they had no trust in any place or person, they neither waged war nor maintained peace; each measured dangers by his own fear. [*Bellum Catilinae* 31.1–2]

A second section is added:

In addition, the women, unaccustomed to the fear of war because of the greatness of the state, were greatly distressed, raised their hands to heaven in supplication, grieved for their little children, called on the gods again and again, feared everything, with their pride and all their pleasures forgotten, despaired of themselves and their country. [*Bellum Catilinae* 31.3]

77   Ut autem naturae propria ac peculiaris est varietas, sic ea ipsa praecipue multum confert ad decorandam magnificandamque celeritatem. Quocirca videndum erit ne idem ubique sit eius tractus, sed mistus et varius filumque orationis non unum, verum aliae atque aliae partium texturae, qualis Sallustianus ille locus:

> Postquam eo ventum est, unde a ferentariis proelium committi posset, maximo clamore cum infestis signis concurritur; tela omittuntur, gladiis res geritur. Veterani pristinae virtutis memores cominus acriter instare, illi haud timide resistunt; maxima vi certatur. Interea Catilina cum expeditis in prima acie versari, laborantibus succurrere, integros pro sauciis arcessere, omnia providere, multum ipse pugnare, saepe hostem ferire; strenui militis et boni imperatoris officia simul exequebatur.[318]

Itaque neque omnia eodem aut semper filo contexenda sunt aut numerus variandus non est; cuique etiam rei adhibendus est modus, cunctorum enim sensuum satietas mala, aurium vero multo molestissima.

Fuit autem tantum virtutis huius in Sallustio studium uti divinam illam appellare non dubitaverit Marcus Fabius, aliis tamen multis et magnis virtutibus Livium assecutum, scilicet quod ad hanc ipsam aspirare minime potuerit. Neque tamen nos id aut sentimus aut dicimus, quod eam ipse Sallustiano sequi more contenderit. Sunt enim et dicendi sua fere cuique innata semina, sicuti et appetendi studiorumque coeterorum.

Est autem celeritas ipsa tum grandium magnificatrix rerum tum sullevatrix humilium; eadem effusa colligit, collecta nunc

Moreover, as variety is a particular property of nature, so it   77
also contributes greatly to embellishing and magnifying speed.
For that reason care must be taken that its movement is not the
same everywhere, but mixed and varied, and that there is not
just a single thread of the discourse but that the textures of the
parts differ from each other, as in this passage of Sallust.

> After they came to a place from which the skirmishers could
> join battle, with a great shout the hostile armies clashed;
> spears were thrown aside, they did their business with
> swords. The veterans, mindful of their ancient courage,
> fiercely went hand to hand; the others bravely stood their
> ground; a violent struggle ensued. Meanwhile, Catiline with
> the light-armed troops was engaged on the front line; he
> helped those who were struggling, called up rested troops to
> replace the wounded, anticipated everything, fought hard
> himself, often struck a foe; he carried out the duties of a
> valiant soldier and a good commander at the same time. [*Bellum Catilinae* 60.1–4]

And so neither should everything always be woven together
with the same thread, nor should the rhythm be invariable; a
limit must be placed on each thing, for satiety of all the senses
is an evil, but that of the ears is by far the most disagreeable.

Sallust cultivated this excellent quality to such a degree that
Marcus Fabius did not hesitate to call his use of it divine, saying that Livy nevertheless matched him in many other points of
great excellence, no doubt because he could not aspire to this
one.[324] Yet I do not feel or say this—that he strove to attain
speed in Sallust's way. In fact, in each person the seeds of
speaking are almost innate, just like those of appetite and other
pursuits.

Moreover, speed is both the magnifier of great events and
the exalter of humble ones.[325] It pulls together what is scat-

graviter nunc venuste pro materia digerit; quae multa sunt cogit in pauca, quae rursus pauca, ornat, insignit, auget. Ac perinde ut manus ad agendum, pedes ad inambulandum innitendumque multis pollent iuncturis, sic et ipsa celeritas suis arcticulis indefessa indefatigataque est. Atque ut pedes etiam ipsi ad ducendas quandoque serviunt choreas manusque ad decorandam formam, praeterquam quod pedes nati sunt ipsi ad incessuum labores atque ad ferendum honus corporis, manus vero ad robur viresque exercendas, sic ipsa quoque adiuvat confertque celeritas ad comptum, ad hilaritatem, ad venustatem, ad varietatem denique comparandam naturae profecto ipsius, narrantis appositissimum ministerium.

Quae Livius dum quaerit, alia etiam via ingressus atque profectus est. Cuius viri multae profecto magnaeque virtutes extitere, tum exornandis atque adaugendis rebus tum etiam complectendis ac variandis, ut nunquam illi aut res defuisse videantur aut ipse rebus defuerit. Denique ut nullus post Marcum Tullium extitit qui aures impleverit audientium in foro, in senatu, in populo orator actorque causarum, sic inventus necdum post Livium est ullus ex ore cuius in rebus bellicis terribilem dederit sonitum tuba, nec, ut vaticinor, ex alicuius ore datura est post multa etiam secula.

78 Qualis igitur et quae celeritas sit, iudicari ex iis quae dicta sunt potest, et si multa quoque a me praetermissa sunt quae quamvis minutiora, non exiguam tamen laudem afferunt scriptori. Comparatur autem et constituitur ea cum verborum tum rerum copia. Oportet enim perhuberem esse eam perque affluentem, cum necesse sit, multa, diversa, varia hinc atque illinc apportata et disquisita colligat collectaque quasi pleno e sinu

tered, puts in order what has been collected—sometimes impressively, sometimes delightfully, depending on the material. It condenses many things into a few; a few things, by contrast, it embellishes, makes distinguished, increases. And just as because of their many joints hands have the power to do things, feet to walk and support, so speed too because of its segments is tireless and indefatigable. And as feet also serve to lead dances and hands to adorn beauty, beyond the fact that feet have been created for the effort of forward movement and to bear the burden of the body, and the hands to exert strength and force, so speed also helps and contributes to ornament, to achieving the liveliness, the charm, and finally, the variety of nature herself, which is the most appropriate duty of the narrator.

While Livy was searching for these qualities, he embarked on and set out on another path. This man certainly had many great abilities, both in embellishing and expanding his material and in giving it scope and variety, so that his material seems never to have failed him and he never failed his material. Finally, just as no one came into existence after Marcus Tullius[326] to fill the ears of listeners in the forum, in the senate, before the people as an orator and advocate, so after Livy no one has yet been discovered from whose mouth the trumpet has sounded its terrifying blast in war, nor, as I predict, will that trumpet sound from the mouth of anyone even after many ages.

To sum up, you can judge from what has been said both 78 what speed is and what kind of thing it is, even if I have omitted many points that, although less important, nonetheless bring no little praise to the writer. It is provided and constituted, moreover, by an abundance of both words and material. Indeed it should be exceedingly copious[327] and rich, since it is necessary for it to bring together numerous diverse and various things imported and sought out from here and there and to

effundat, ut quae mirabiliter quoque inventa videantur: veluti cum Sallustius, ut paulo ante retulimus, dixisset *omnia pavere*, non ante subiunxit *sibi patriaeque diffidere*, quod abunde fuisset per se plenum, quam iniecisset *superbia ac delitiis omissis*, quadam cum admiratione et audientium et recitantium. Et Livius mira etiam celeritate usus cum esset, in virtutibus vitiisque Annibalis exponendis, cum dixisset *inhumana crudelitas, perfidia plus quam punica, nihil veri, nihil sancti, nullus deum metus, nullum iusiuran-dum*, quo maiora illa omnia faceret, tandem imo quasi e pectore erutum effudit: *nulla religio.*

Etenim celeritas quasi plenus et profundus amnis multa vehit et tanquam aquarum mole rotat versatque. Vitanda tamen confusa et inordinata permistio, eaque evitabitur si partes ipsae et quos dixi arcticuli separatim ipsi suis quique illustrentur atque impleantur verbis, si verba apte et plane explicent res, si loco et ordine subsequantur suo, si numerorum[319] quoque recta habeatur ratio, si incessus ac cursus ipse minime ut dici solet, pedem offendat. Quid vero hac ipsa Sallustiana copiosius, planius, tractius aut denique numerosius?

Ibi primum insuevit exercitus populi Romani amare, potare; signa, tabulas pictas, vasa caelata mirari, ea privatim et publice rapere, delubra spoliare, sacra profanaque omnia polluere. Igitur hi milites, postquam victoriam adepti sunt, nihil reliqui victis facere. Quippe secundae res sapientium fatigant animos, nedum illi corruptis moribus

pour out what has been collected as if from a full purse, so that the things may also seem miraculously discovered — for example, when Sallust, as I reported a little earlier, had said, "they feared everything," he did not add, "they despaired of themselves and their country," which would have been abundantly full by itself, before inserting, "with their pride and all their pleasures forgotten," to the wonder of both hearers and reciters.[328] And when Livy had employed wonderful speed in setting out the virtues and vices of Hannibal, when he had said, "inhuman cruelty, treachery more than Punic, nothing truthful, nothing sacred, no fear of the gods, no oath," to make everything greater, he finally poured out as if from the bottom of his heart, "no conscience."[329]

In fact, speed, like a full deep stream, carries many things and rolls and turns them as if in a mass of water. All the same, one should avoid a confused and disordered mixture, and it will be avoided if the parts and segments I have mentioned are each individually illuminated and filled out with their own words, if the words explain matters suitably and clearly, and if they follow in their own place and order, if correct attention is also paid to rhythm, if the progress and course is least likely to trip up the feet, as they say. Indeed, is there anything fuller, plainer, more flowing, and finally, more rhythmical than this passage of Sallust?

> There for the first time the army of the Roman people became accustomed to licentiousness, to drunkenness, to marvel at statues, paintings, and engraved vessels, to seize such things from private homes and public buildings, to desecrate shrines, to pollute all things sacred and profane. And so after these soldiers achieved victory, they left nothing for the vanquished. Indeed, success wears down the spirits of the wise; still less did these men, with their characters corrupted,

victoriae optemperarent. Postquam divitiae honori esse
coepere et eas gloria, imperium, potentia sequebatur,
hebescere imperium, paupertas probro haberi, innocentia
pro maleficentia duci coepit. Igitur ex divitiis iuventutem
ubi luxuria atque avaritia cum superbia invasere, rapere,
consumere, sua parvipendere, aliena cupere, pudorem, pu-
dicitiam, divina atque humana promiscua, nihil pensi, nihil moderati habere,

et quae post sequuntur.[320]

Erit igitur celeritas ut minime sordescens ac lutulenta, sic
undique sibi constans et conformata suoque loco adhibita; integra partibus, iucunda numeris, cursu lenis, rotunda, constituta,
magnifica, ac rerum plena, quemadmodum piscosus multarum-
que ac liquidarum aquarum fluvius. Locus autem virtuti est
huic maxime aptus cum multa se se offerunt quae breviter sint
pertractanda, aut cum prosequenda magnifice augendaque oratione, aut ubi res per se ipsa videtur exilior, estque et verbis tum
honestanda atque extollenda tum rebus locupletanda atque sententiis, iisque extrinsecus allatis.

Diximus de brevitate deque coniuncta ei celeritate, de illo
item dicendi genere quod historiae videatur accommodatum, et
si non exacte, plura fortasse quam consilium nostrum fuerat aut
quam ab eo qui innuere atque adumbrare tantum habeat promissum initio fuerit. Quocirca progrediamur ad reliqua.

79   Omnino historia, ut Cicero putat ac natura ipsa docet, partibus constat e duabus, hoc est rebus et verbis. Rebus autem ipsis
est ordo adiunctus; agendis enim negociis insunt et quae prius

comply with the requirements of victory. After riches began to be a source of honor, and glory, dominion, and power followed them, command began to grow weak, moderate circumstances began to be considered a disgrace, innocence to be regarded as wickedness. Therefore, when as a result of riches luxury and greed along with arrogance overmastered the youth, they seized, squandered, had little regard for their own goods, lusted after other people's, treated modesty, shame, divine and human things indiscriminately, had no scruple, no moderation. [*Bellum Catilinae* 11.6–12.2]

And so on.

Speed, then, will be not at all sloppy or murky, but everywhere consistent and skillfully shaped and applied in its own place; it will be complete in its parts, have a pleasing rhythm and a smooth course, and it will be polished, well arranged, distinguished, and full of material — like a deep stream of clear water abounding in fish. The most suitable occasion for this fine feature is when there are many details that require brief treatment or rich description or stylistic embellishment, or where the subject in itself seems too thin and must be dignified and elevated with language and enriched with material and ideas brought in from elsewhere.

I have spoken of brevity and the speed connected with it and also about the style that seems suited to history, even if not precisely, perhaps at greater length than I had intended or than would have been promised at the outset by someone who had only to present hints or an outline. Therefore, let us go on to the rest.

In general, as Cicero thinks and nature herself teaches us, 79 history consists of two elements, that is, events and words.[330] Moreover, order [*ordo*] is tied to the events, for in the conduct of affairs there are both things to be done earlier and those to

et quae posterius sint administranda. Rerum enim ac naturae ipsius ordine ut quaedam praecedunt, sic etiam sequuntur alia. Ac de rebus quidem ipsis existit enarratio; verbis autem series earum contexitur, quemadmodum e lapidum strue aedificiorum fabricatio. Ordo est qui materiam omnem prudenter ac recte disserit seriemque passim et universam informat et singulas eius partes moderatur ac digerit. Oportet igitur explicationem quidem ipsam esse ordinatam, quo veritas minime confusa incerta ve aut indistincta appareat. Parit igitur ex se se rerum ordo eam quae dispositio et totius et partium dicitur; cuius ea laus est, ut eius opera et cura, tanquam uno in corpore, omnia suo loco, suis partibus, apte, proprie, decore, prudenterque collocentur; terminataque suis finibus totum ipsum partesque ita simul vinciant inter se atque connectant, ut in unum coacta decenter consentiant existatque universi species tum honesta et gravis tum blanda et cum dignitate. Habebunt igitur ordo pariter ac[321] dispositio rationem non rerum modo distribuendarum suis in locis, verum suo quoque tempore, cuius spatio et ambitu cuncta comprehenduntur consistuntque quae sunt universa. Et quoniam actio omnis, geriturque atque administratur quodcunque, id aliquam ob causam susceptum est (causae nanque ubique antecedunt rerumque suscipiendarum fines), oportet rerum scriptorem causarum ipsarum ac finium cumprimis esse memorem certumque earum ac verum expositorem. Quibus exponendis summum est ab eo adhibendum studium maximeque diligens cura. Quodque causis iis quae propinquae quidem sunt aliquid tamen se se quandoque ostendit antiquius, huius quoque tanquam principii nobiliorisque originis facienda est repetitio, antiquitasque atque obliteratio ipsa in memoriam revocanda et tanquam exponenda in lucem; ut cum Sallustius,

be done later. Indeed, in the order of events and of nature herself, just as some things precede, so also others follow. And a narrative arises about the events; in fact, a continuous succession of them is woven together in words just as buildings are erected from a heap of stones. Order is what sets out all material skillfully and correctly and gives shape to the whole sequence everywhere and regulates and distributes its separate parts. And so the exposition itself must be well ordered for truth to be evident — in no way confused or uncertain or badly arranged. The order of events also gives birth to what is called arrangement [*dispositio*] of both the whole and its parts, whose merit is that by its effort and care, all things are put together, as if in a single body, in their own place, in their own parts of the work — tightly, appropriately, elegantly, skillfully; and all things, limited to their own territory, so bind and connect the whole and its parts to each other at the same time that, once brought into a unity, they work together in becoming harmony, and the shape of the whole assemblage emerges — handsome and serious on the one hand, agreeable and distinguished on the other. And so order and arrangement take account of distributing things not only in their proper places, but also in their own time, in whose space and circuit all things that exist — every single one — are contained and take their place. And since every action and whatever is carried out or accomplished is undertaken for some reason (for in all circumstances the causes and goals of undertakings are antecedent), the writer of history must be especially mindful of these causes and ends and be their sure and true interpreter. In explaining them he must exert the greatest effort and most diligent care. And because sometimes something more remote than these immediate causes manifests itself, it is necessary to go back to it too, as the beginning and more illustrious origin, and to call antiquity and forgetfulness back to memory and bring them into the light. So

quo Micipsae regis consilia magis magisque in aperto poneret, Numantino usque a bello repetit; utque ad Catilinae incepta progrederetur, suosque per tramites, coepit repetere ab urbe condita, et quibus primo artibus civitas creverit et quibus etiam moribus corrupta post iuventus fuerit, quae corruptio Catilinam ad ineundam coniurationem et traxit et perpulit.

Ipsis autem causis suscipiendi sive negocii sive belli coniuncta sunt consilia et hominum qui agendum quippiam decernunt sententiae ac voluntates; quae quod saepenumero sunt diversae, exponendae eae sunt a rerum scriptore in partem utranque; ut cum Livius Annonem alterius factionis principem inducit impugnantem Carthaginensis senatus sententiam de bello inferendo Romanis creandoque Annibale duce. Quo fit ut quandoque utriusque partis diversorumque consiliorum auctores ac principes inducendi sint altercatim disserentes in senatu, quo sententiae ipsae clariores appareant, illustreturque magis magisque historia et lectores ipsi apertius doceantur de altercationum causis consiliorumque ac sententiarum diversitate; quod servavit Sallustius, cum et Caesarem inducit et Catonem sentientes in senatu contraria.

80   Suscepto autem negocio aut bello explicando[322] (nam res gestae plerunque sunt bellicae) duo statim coniuncta sunt, et pene dixerim agnata, descriptione sua digna: belli dux ipsius atque imperator et vires atque opes rei publicae, si tum ea magistratibus regitur, aut regis ipsius, ubi sub unius moderatione urbs regnum ve temperatur. Itaque et Livius ingenium, institutionem moresque describit Annibalis et Iugurtae Sallustius ac Catilinae. Principum quoque senatus et civitatis mores qui sint

Sallust, in order to put the motives of King Micipsa into a clearer light, traces them all the way from the Numantine War.[331] And to proceed to the designs of Catiline, and by his own paths, he begins to trace his way back from the foundation of the city, and the arts by which the state first grew and also the habits by which the youth were later corrupted — the corruption that drew and propelled Catiline to enter upon his conspiracy.[332]

Moreover, to the causes of undertaking an activity or war are joined both the counsels and the opinions and wishes of the men who decide that something is to be done; because these are very often diverse, the historian must set them out on both sides, as when Livy introduces Hanno, leader of the opposing faction, opposing the decision of the Carthaginian senate to wage war with Rome and appoint Hannibal general.[333] So it happens that sometimes it is necessary to bring in the leaders and proponents of both sides and of opposing policies speaking in debate[334] in the senate so that their views may appear more clearly, and more and more light may be shed on the history, and the readers may be instructed more plainly about the reasons for the disputes and the diversity of counsels and opinions. Sallust follows this practice when he introduces Caesar and Cato expressing opposite views in the senate.[335]

Once the explication of politics or war has been undertaken 80 (for the actions are usually military), at once there are two connected (I would almost say kindred) matters worthy of description: the leader and commander of the war and the strength and resources of the state, if it is then led by magistrates, or of the king, when a city or kingdom is governed under the control of a single man.[336] And so Livy describes the ability, upbringing, and character of Hannibal, and Sallust describes those of Jugurtha and Catiline.[337] The characters and purposes of the foremost men of the senate and state must also be accurately set

quaeque instituta aperienda fideliter; opes item, amicitiae, societates. His accedit explicatio bellici apparatus, tum terrestris tum maritimi; quales et quantae utriusque partis copiae, armorum genera, equitum ac peditum numerus; quaeque alia his annexa sunt atque a scriptoribus minime omittenda, ut praesagia, auguria, vaticinia, oracula, visiones, sacrificia, transfugia denique atque explorationes; legationes item ac legatorum mandata, bellique ipsius indictio, atque indicendi modus ac ratio. Non praeteriit Annibalis insomnium illud Livius, quo vastitatem Italiae denuntiatam significat, non Catilinae epistolam Sallustius aut Scipionis ad Masinisam,[323] non uterque aut Marcii[324] vatis praedictionem, Cannensi de calamitate alter, alter de imperio Corneliorum familiae debendo in urbe Roma.

Post vero susceptas expeditiones ac bellum iam indictum motumque, quo aperta magis magisque sint quae narrantur omnia, describendae sunt regiones, loca, situs, qua ducendus exercitus, qua castra metanda, quibus aut campis aut collibus bellum administretur; ordo etiam ipse ductandi aperiendus, ut cum legitur triplici aut quadrato agmine incedere exercitum. Flumina quoque et montes siqui sunt et illorum naturae et siquid in his dignum memoratu ac rarum.

Erat, inquit Sallustius, in ea parte Numidiae, quam Adherbal in divisione possederat, flumen oriens a meridie, nomine Mutul, a quo aberat mons ferme millia passuum viginti tractu pari, vastus ab natura et humano cultu. Sed ex eo medio collis oriebatur in immensum pertingens, vestitus oleastro et myrtetis aliisque generibus arborum, quae in humo arida arenosaque gignuntur. Media autem

out, as well as their wealth, friendships, and alliances. In addition, one must explain the preparations for war on land and sea, the nature and size of forces on each side, the types of weapons, the number of cavalry and infantry. Other matters related to these points must certainly be included, like forebodings, auguries, prophecies, oracles, visions, sacrifices, desertions, and spying, as well as embassies and the commissions of ambassadors and the declaration of war itself and the method and grounds for declaring it. Livy did not leave out the famous dream of Hannibal in which he shows that the destruction of Italy was foretold; Sallust did not omit Catiline's letter or the letter of Scipio to Masinissa; nor did either leave out the prediction of the prophet Marcius, the one his prophecy about the disaster at Cannae, the other his prophecy about the supremacy destined to the family of the Cornelii in the city of Rome.[338]

After the campaigns have been undertaken and the war has already been declared and begun, in order to make the whole narrative clearer, the historian must describe the territories, places, sites where the army is to be led, where the camp is to be laid out, in what plains or hills the war is being conducted; he must also explain the order of march, as when one reads that the army is proceeding in triple columns or formed in a square.[339] He must also mention rivers and mountains, if there are any, and their natures and anything noteworthy and unusual in them. Thus Sallust says:

> In the part of Numidia that Adherbal had taken as his share there was a river rising from the south called Muthul, and about twenty miles away from it was a mountainous region, running parallel to the river, desolate by nature and uncultivated by man. But from the middle of it rose a hill extending a long way, covered with wild olive and myrtle and other kinds of trees that grow in dry and sandy soil. The interven-

planities deserta penuria aquae, praeter flumini propinqua loca; ea consita arbustis pecore atque cultoribus frequentabantur.[325]

Quo igitur et lectorem doceret et delectaret remque ante oculos quasi videndam exponeret, et situm omnem exequitur et qui situs esset ipsius habitus et quae soli natura. Et Livius:

Tumulus erat, inquit, inter castra Minutii et Poenorum; qui eum occupasset haud dubie iniquiorem erat hosti locum facturus. Eum non tam capere sine certamine volebat Annibal, quanquam id operepretium erat, quam causam certaminis cum Minutio, quem semper occursurum ad obsistendum satis sciebat, contrahere. Ager omnis medius erat prima specie inutilis insidiatori, quia non modo silvestre quicquam, sed ne vepribus quidem vestitum habebat, re ipsa natus detegendis insidiis, eo magis quod in nuda valle nulla talis fraus timeri poterat. Et erant in confractibus cavae rupes, ut quaedam earum ducenos armatos possent capere.[326]

Horum uterque loca describit insidiarum gratia aperitque et locorum aptitudinem et ducum consilia et quid uterque imperator designasset animo. Describit Africae situm Crispus, quo scilicet et situs ipse notus esset et qui amici qui ve inimici ex omni provincia. Cum obsidionem etiam castelli descripturus esset, licet ignobilis, tamen natura permuniti, situm ante eius exponit:

Haud longe a flumine Mulucca, quod Iugurtae Bocchique regnum disiungebat, erat inter planitiem mons saxeus,

ing plain was deserted through lack of water except for the places close to the river; these were covered with bushes and frequented by cattle and farmers. [*Bellum Iugurthinum* 48.3–4]

In order to instruct and entertain the reader and to set the thing before his eyes so that he might almost see it, he describes all the features of the landscape and the character of the place and the nature of the soil. And Livy says:

There was a hill between the camps of Minutius and the Carthaginians, and anyone seizing it would undoubtedly make the enemy's situation more difficult. Hannibal was less eager to take it without a struggle, although that was worth the effort, than to provoke a battle with Minutius who he well knew would always come up to oppose him. At first sight all the area between the armies was useless to anyone lying in ambush because it had not only no woodland, but not even the cover of bushes; in fact, it was born to reveal an ambush — all the more because in that bare valley no trick of that kind could be suspected. And there were hollow rocks in its ravines, some of them of a kind to hold two hundred armed men. [Livy 22.28.3–6]

Each of these writers describes places for ambushes and reveals the suitability of the places and the plans of the leaders and the scheme that each commander had in mind. Crispus describes the landscape of Africa, evidently so that it might be known, along with what friends or enemies there were in the whole province. And when he was preparing to describe the siege of a garrison that was insignificant yet well fortified by nature, he first explained its position.

Not far from the river Muluccha that separated the kingdoms of Jugurtha and Bocchus there was a rocky hill in the plain, wide enough in extent for a small fortification, and

mediocri castello satis patens, in immensum editus, uno
perangusto aditu relicto; nam per omnia natura velut
opera atque consulto praeceps erat. Quem locum Marius,
quod ibi regis thesauri erant, summa vi capere intendit.[327]

Urbium quoque origines gentiumque primordia procul repe-
tita, quae sint earum leges, qui mores studiaque, haud exiguam
historiae dignitatem afferunt, et propter varietatem ipsam et
quod pervetusta atque a memoria nostra longius remota vehementer delectant; ut cum Sallustius Maurorum gentis initia ad
Medos refert et Tacitus Iudaeorum nationis antiquitatem com-
memorat. Quibus referendis magna cura, non minore prudentia
opus est, cum eiusmodi pleraque aut incerta sint aut fabulosa.

81   Necubi vero plura quam bellicis in rebus accidunt improvisa,
insperata, non ante cogitata praeterque opinionem atque consilium eaque ipsa plena nunc terroris nunc spei, modo gaudii
modo tristitiae. Itaque casuum fortuitorumque in his eventuum
magna scriptori ratio habenda est. Tempestatum quoque, famis,
frigoris, aestus, pestilentiae, periculorum in faciendo itinere, in
conserendis manibus; item audaciae, metus, temeritatis, suspi-
tionis, insidiarum, falsorum rumorum, quaeque alia inter gerendum atque administrandum bellum sive consilio eveniunt
hominum sive casu. Ex his enim perspicitur potissimum qualis
fuerit scriptoris diligentia atque perpensio. Attingenda etiam
permulta, quae nihil tamen susceptam ad historiam, verum ut
extrinsecus allata novitate sua pariunt et admirationem et
voluptatem suntque condimentum quasi quoddam, atque ut

extremely high, with only a single very narrow approach, for it was naturally sheer in every direction as if by labor and intention. This place Marius intended to take by a supreme effort because the king's treasures were there. [*Bellum Iugurthinum* 92.5–6]

The origins of cities, too, and the tracing of the first beginnings of peoples far back in time and the nature of their laws, their customs, and their pursuits — all these add no small distinction to history, both on account of variety itself and because we take great pleasure in ancient matters far remote from our own time, as when Sallust traces the origins of the Moorish race back to the Medes and Tacitus recalls the antiquity of the Jewish nation. In recounting these matters there is need of great care and no less discretion since most details of this kind are either dubious or mythical.

Nor anywhere more than in war are there unexpected, unforeseen events — events not thought of before and beyond expectation and plan; and these things especially are sometimes full of terror, sometimes of hope, now of rejoicing, now of grief. Accordingly, the writer must pay great attention to calamities and chance events in warfare. He must take account also of storms, hunger, cold, heat, pestilence, dangers on the march and in joining battle, likewise of daring, fear, rashness, suspicion, treachery, false rumors, and the other things that happen whether by human intention or by chance in waging and conducting war. Indeed, it is from these things especially that the quality of the writer's care and judgment is demonstrated. Many matters must also be touched upon not pertaining to the history that has been undertaken, but producing both admiration and pleasure by their novelty, as details brought in from outside; these act as a kind of seasoning and by their foreign-

81

peregrina vehementer afficiunt; ut cum Sallustius Iugurtino in bello, quod solum susceperat scribendum, aliunde affert:

Per idem tempus adversum Gallos ab ducibus nostris Q. Cepione et M. Manlio male pugnatum. Quo metu Italia omnis contremuit. Illique et usque ad nostram memoriam Romani sic habuerunt, alia omnia virtuti suae prona esse, cum Gallis pro salute, non pro gloria certare.[328]

Et Livius,[329] cum belli Achaici adversus Mesenen particulam sibi referendam assumit. Eius autem verba sunt haec:

Cuius belli causam[330] et ordinem si expromere velim, immemor sim propositi quo statui non ultra attingere externa, nisi qua Romanis cohererent rebus. Eventus memorabilis est, quod cum bello superiores essent Achei,[331] Philopomenes, praetor eorum capitur, ad praeoccupandam Coroneam, quam hostes petebant, in valle iniqua cum equitibus paucis oppressus. Ipsum potuisse effugere Thracum Cretensiumque auxilio tradunt, sed pudor relinquendi equites, nobilissimos gentis ab ipso nuper lectos, tenuit. Quibus dum locum ad evadendas angustias cogendo ipse agmen praebet sustinens impetus hostium, prolapsus equo et suo ipse casu et honere equi super eum ruentis, haud multum abfuit quin exanimaretur, septuaginta annos iam natus et diutino morbo, ex quo tum primum reficiebatur, viribus admodum attenuatus. Iacentem hostes superfusi oppresserunt; cognitum primum

ness produce a powerful effect, as when Sallust in the Jugurthine war, the only subject of his work, brings in from elsewhere:

> At around the same time a battle against the Gauls was lost by our generals Quintus Caepio and Marcus Manlius. All Italy trembled with terror because of it. Both the Romans of that time and those down to our own day have considered that everything else is subject to their valor, but with the Gauls the struggle is not for glory but for survival. [*Bellum Iugurthinum* 114.1–2]

And here are Livy's words when he takes it on himself to report a small part of the Achaean war with Messene.

> If I wanted to explain the cause and progress of this war, I would be forgetful of my stated intention not to touch upon external matters except where they are connected with Roman affairs. This event is worth recording, because although the Achaeans had the upper hand in the war, Philopomenes, their praetor, was captured on his way to seize Coronea ahead of the approaching enemy, when he was surprised in a dangerous valley with a small force of cavalry. They say that he would have been able to escape with the help of the Thracians and Cretans, but shame of deserting the most noble knights of his nation, whom he had recently chosen himself, held him back. While he was providing a place for these to get through the narrow places by crowding together the line of march and holding out against the onslaught of the enemy, he fell from his horse, and with his fall and the weight of the horse crashing down on him, he was nearly killed — a man now seventy years old and with his strength weakened by a long illness from which he was just then beginning to recover. As he lay, the foe swept past and overtook him. As soon as they recognized him, out of respect and with the

verecundia memoriaque meritorum haud secus quam ducem suum attollunt reficiuntque, et ex valle devia in viam
portant.[332]

Quem quidem locum ita executus est Livius ut et funus referat
et honores pene divinos in eum collatos dicat et annum eum
celebrem morte trium clarissimorum ducum Annibalis, Philopomenis, Scipionis.

82 Iam vero cum sit homini data a natura oratio magna cum
excellentia animalium coeterorum ipsorumque hominum inter
ipsos, sitque orationis propria vis movere animos et quo velit
flectere, nuncque pro re ac loco, a metu trahat ad fiduciam, a
dolore ad letitiam, ab ocio ac mollicie ad laborem, eademque
fugientes retineat, irruentes impellat, dubitantes confirmet,
huius esse memor rerum gestarum scriptor cumprimis debet.
Itaque quotiens res tulerit, imperatores ipsos inducet nunc
confirmantes suos in periculis nunc excitantes illos ad ea ob-
eunda, alias exhortantes alias obiurgantes, et modo praemia
proponentes modo admonentes infamiae, turpitudinis, servitu-
tis, mortis. Videntur enim eiusmodi allocutiones, quae nunc ad
multos nunc ad singulos habentur, decorare historiam et quasi
animare eam. In quibus, quotiens res ipsa tulerit, nervos orationis atque ingenii sui ostendet rerum scriptor. Nec solum quae
dicta fuisse referuntur ab imperatoribus, verum etiam ea afferet
quae verisimilia quaeque dicenda tempus, periculum, reique ipsius natura postulare videatur; uteturque in increpando acrimo-
nia, in excitando vehementia, in sedando lenitate, in impellendo
contentione, in extollendis rebus propriis, adversarii deprimendis, magnitudine ac linguae suae acie, rerum ipsarum qualitates

memory of his merits, they picked him up and cared for him as if he had been their own general and then bore him from the remote valley onto the road. [Livy 39.48.6–49.5][340]

Livy continues the passage both by reporting his funeral rites and by saying that nearly divine honors were bestowed on him and that that year was notable for the death of three illustrious generals, Hannibal, Philopomenes, and Scipio.[341]

Now then, since nature has endowed men with speech, along with great superiority over other living things including their fellow human beings, and since it is the unique power of speech to move and turn minds where it will, and sometimes, depending on the circumstance and place, it brings them from fear to confidence, from grief to rejoicing, from idleness and irresolution to toil, and since it also holds back the fleeing, drives on those who attack, and encourages the hesitant, the writer of history must be especially mindful of it.[342] Whenever the situation requires, he will bring in the commanders themselves — now encouraging their men in danger, now rousing them to meet it, sometimes exhorting, sometimes castigating, and on occasion offering rewards or warning of disgrace, dishonor, slavery, death. Speeches of this kind, which are addressed sometimes to a multitude, sometimes to individuals, seem to adorn history and almost to bring it to life. In these speeches, whenever the situation requires, the writer of history will display the power both of the utterance and of his own talent. He will bring in not only the things reported to have been said by commanders but also what they might have said and what the time, danger, and nature of the situation itself seem to require, and he will use sharpness in rebuke, vehemence in arousing, mildness in calming, passion in urging, and the gravity and force of his language in exalting the deeds of his own side and disparaging those of the enemy — in conformity with the nature of the

82

ac ducum maxime personas secutus. Magnificant autem historiam conciones potissimum rectae illae quidem, ubi imperatores ipsi et loqui et agere introducuntur, ut quasi geri res videatur. Adhiberi tamen debent suo et loco et tempore suumque ubique decorum retinendum.

Illa vero trita sunt, ante pugnam instruere aciem, indicare animorum habitum, nunc victoriae nunc cladis praesagum; militum vel strenue in acie vel ignaviter facta referre; ducum solertiam, adhortationes, consilia et siquid strenue manu ediderint memorare; hic fortitudinis prudentiaeque, illic fortunae casusque mentionem facere; a quo primum cornu aut fuga coeperit[333] aut victoria declarare; post pugnam ac victoriam caedes, captivorum numerum, vexilla capta, praedam, spolia, direptiones recensere, praemia referre, commendare fortitudinem, accusare ignaviam, miserari humanos casus, varietatem ludumque fortunae mirari, aut deorum vel iras vel favorem, quaeque alia vel eventus natura vel ratio ipsa rerum laudanda aut vituperanda, iucunde aut aegre accipienda, miseranda aut accusanda docuerit, per ea evagari.

Audite, quaeso, Sallustium post Catilinae male decertatam pugnam:

> Strenuissimus quisque aut occiderat in proelio aut graviter vulneratus discesserat. Multi autem, qui e castris visendi aut spoliandi gratia processerant, volventes hostilia cadavera, amicum alii, pars hospitem atque[334] cognatum reperiebant; fuere item qui inimicos suos cognoscerent. Ita varie per omnem exercitum letitia, maeror, luctus atque gaudia agitabantur.

events and especially with the characters of the leaders. More-over, history is especially enhanced by those direct orations be-fore an assembly where the commanders themselves are brought in to speak and act, so that the event seems almost to be taking place before us. Nevertheless, these must be introduced in their own place and time and the decorum belonging to them must always be maintained.

But these things are commonplace: to draw up the battle ar-ray before the battle, to show the state of mind, anticipating now victory, now destruction; to report the soldiers' energetic or cowardly actions in the battle; to record the generals' skill, exhortations, counsels, and any energetic actions they per-formed by their own efforts; to mention fortitude and prudence in one place, fortune and mischance in another; to declare from what wing rout or victory first began; after the battle and vic-tory, to recount the slaughter, number of captives, captured standards, booty, spoils, pillaging; to report rewards, to com-mend bravery, to condemn cowardice, to pity human misfor-tune, to marvel at the variety and sport of fortune or the wrath or favor of the gods; and to range through whatever other things either the nature of the outcome or a consideration of the events has shown are to be praised or censured, received with joy or pain, pitied or reproached.

Listen, please to Sallust after the defeat of Catiline.

All the most active fighters had either perished in the battle or left with serious wounds. But many had come out of the camp to look or pillage; as they turned over the bodies of the enemy, some found a friend, some a guest and kinsman; there were also those who recognized personal enemies. So the various emotions of delight, grief, mourning, and joy moved rapidly through the whole army. [*Bellum Catilinae* 61.7–9]

Et post Metelli proelium cum Iugurta:

> Igitur pro metu repente gaudium exortum; milites alius alium appellant, acta edocent atque audiunt, sua quisque fortiter facta ad coelum fert. Quippe res humanae ita se habent: in victoria vel ignavis gloriari licet, adversae res etiam bonos detractant. Metellus in iisdem castris quatriduo moratus saucios cura reficit, meritos praemiis more militiae donat, universos in concione laudat atque agit gratias, hortatur ad coetera quae levia sunt parem animum uti gerant; pro victoria satis pugnatum, reliquos labores fore praedae.[335]

Nec pigeat referre quae a Livio dicuntur post stragem ad Thrasimenum[336] ab Annibale editam:

> Haec est illa nobilis ad Thrasimenum pugna atque inter paucas memorata populi Romani clades; quindecim millia Romanorum in acie caesa sunt; decem millia sparsa fuga per omnem Etruriam diversis itineribus urbem petiere; mille quingenti hostium in acie, multi postea utrinque ex vulneribus periere.[337]

Et post pugnam ad Trebiam factam primo quid Annibal fecerit refert:

> Finis insequendi hostis Poenis flumen Trebia fuit; ita torpentes gelu in castra rediere, ut vix letitiam victoria senserint.[338]

Deinde transit ad ea quae Romae agitabantur post cladis nuntium:

And after Metellus' battle with Jugurtha:

> Then joy suddenly arose in place of fear; the soldiers called out to each other; they related and listened to accounts of exploits; each one praised his own brave deeds to the sky. And so it is in human affairs; in victory even cowards may boast; defeat discredits even the brave. Metellus, staying in the same camp for four days, cared for the wounded, presented the deserving with prizes according to military custom, gave general praise and thanks in the assembly, encouraged them to approach other, easy tasks with the same courage; they had fought enough for victory; their remaining labors would be for booty. [*Bellum Iugurthinum* 53.8–54.1]

Nor should it be displeasing to report Livy's words after the destruction inflicted at Trasimenus by Hannibal:

> This is the famous battle at Trasimenus and recorded among the few disasters of the Roman people. Fifteen thousand Romans were killed in the battle; ten thousand were scattered in flight through all Etruria and sought the city by different routes; fifteen hundred of the enemy perished in the battle; many on both sides afterward died of their wounds. [Livy 22.7.1–3]

And after the battle fought at the Trebia he first reports what Hannibal did.

> The river Trebia was the end of the Carthaginian pursuit of the enemy. They returned to camp so numb with cold that they scarcely felt joy in their victory. [Livy 21.56.7]

Then he passes on to the alarm in Rome after the news of the disaster.

Romam tantus terror ex hac clade perlatus est, ut iam
ad urbem crederent infestis signis hostem venturum, nec
quicquam spei aut auxilii esse qua portis moenibusque
vim arcerent; uno consule ad Ticinum victo, altero e Sicilia revocato, duobus consulibus, duobus consularibus
exercitibus victis, quos alios duces, quas alias legiones esse
quae arcesserentur?[339]

Quanta vero[340] hac in parte scriptores varietate sint usi, magis
ut appareat, subdam tertium quoque e Livio locum. Post supe-
ratum enim Beneventanorum in campis a Sempronio Gracco[341]
Annonem Poenum, postque donatos libertate volones donisque
militaribus veteranos atque ignominiae nota quos par erat affec-
tos,

> Signum deinde Graccus colligendi vasa dedit. Milites
> praedam portantes agentesque per lasciviam ac iocum
> ita ludibundi Beneventum rediere, ut ab epulis celebrem
> festumque diem actis, non ex acie reverti viderentur.
> Beneventani omnes turba effusa, cum obviam ad portas
> exissent, conspectis militibus gratulari, vocare in hospi-
> tium. Apparata convivia omnibus in propatulo aedium
> fuerant; ad ea invitabant, Graccum orabant epulari per-
> mitteret militibus. Et Graccus ita permisit, in publico
> epularentur omnes. Ante suas cuiusque fores prolata om-
> nia. Pileatis aut lana alba velatis capitibus volones epulati
> sunt, alii accubantes, alii stantes, qui simul ministrabant
> vescebantur.[342]

So great was the terror brought to Rome from this disaster that they believed that the enemy would soon march on the city and that there was no hope or aid by which they might keep violence from the gates and walls. One consul had been defeated at the Ticinus; the other had been recalled from Sicily. With two consuls and two consular armies defeated, what other commanders, what other legions did they have to call to aid? [Livy 21.57.1–2]

Indeed, in order to make it clearer how much variety writers have used on this point, I will also add a third passage from Livy. After the Carthaginian Hanno had been conquered by Sempronius Gracchus in the plains of the Beneventans and after the slave volunteers had been given their liberty and the veterans their military prizes and those who deserved it had been afflicted with the brand of disgrace,

next Gracchus gave the signal to gather up the baggage. Soldiers carrying and driving their plunder returned rejoicing and jesting to Beneventum in such high spirits that they seemed to be coming back from a banquet held on a solemn feast day, not from a battle. The people of Beneventum all poured out in a crowd and when they had come out to meet them at the gates, congratulated the soldiers when they caught sight of them and offered them hospitality. Banquets had been set out for everyone in the courtyards of the houses; they invited them to these, and begged Gracchus to allow the soldiers to feast. And Gracchus permitted them on the condition that they all feast in public. Everything was put out before the house of each one. The slave volunteers feasted, their heads covered with freedom caps or white wool, some reclining, others standing, who were serving and eating at the same time. [Livy 24.16.14–18]

Placuit locos hos duorum ex eloquentissimorum scriptorum historiis referre, ut intelligeretis qua varietate sint usi rerum explicatores[343] post eiusmodi strages enarratas, quae varietas perlectis etiam proeliis aliis longe maior apparebit.

83   Eadem habenda est ratio in obsidionibus expugnationibusque. Oportet enim aperire prius naturam et loci et civium, genus obsidionis ac machinarum; quid intra urbem paretur, quid geratur in castris edocere; dolos, artes, insidias, diurnos nocturnosque labores, ruinas, instaurationes referre, quaeque permulta et obsidentibus et obsessis aut virtus contulit, aut fortuna ipsa diligentiave, aut negligentia partis alterius repente optulit obiecitque, vel abstulit eripuitque consulto. Livius cum[344] Thaumatorum[345] situm describeret, quam urbem Philippus obsidebat rex, dum nomen ipsum interpretari vult, locum illum historiae mirifice illustravit, inquiens:

> Ubi ventum ad hanc urbem est, repente velut maris vasti, sic immensa[346] panditur planities, ut subiectos campos terminare oculis haud facile queas; ab eo miraculo Thaumati appellati, nec altitudine solum tuta urbs, sed quod saxo undique abscisso rupibus imposita est.

Audiamus, quaeso, et Sallustium, fortuitam rem quanta cum dignitate sit executus:

> At Marius, multis diebus et laboribus consumptis, anxius trahere animo omitteret ne inceptum, quoniam frustra erat, an fortunam opperiretur, qua saepe prospera usus fuerat. Quae cum multos dies noctesque aestuans agitaret,

I decided to quote these passages from the histories of two most eloquent writers so that you might understand what variety commentators on events have employed after telling of disasters of this kind;[343] when you have also read about other battles, this variety will appear far greater.

The same method should be followed in sieges and assaults. 83 First it is necessary to reveal the nature of both the place and its citizens, the type of siege and siege machines; to explain the preparations inside the city, the activities in the camp; to report treachery, stratagems, ambushes, toil by night and day, failures and repeated efforts, the great assistance that courage or fortune or care brought to besiegers and besieged alike, or that the carelessness of the other side suddenly offered or held out or intentionally took or snatched away. When Livy was describing the site of Thaumaci, the city that king Philip had under siege, he wanted to explain the name and wonderfully embellished that passage of his history, saying:

> When you come to this city, suddenly, like an immense sea, a plain so vast opens up that your eyes cannot easily determine the boundaries of the fields below. From this marvel Thaumaci takes its name, and the city is not protected by its height alone, but also because it is set on a mass of rock with sheer cliffs all around. [Livy 32.4.4][344]

Let us also listen to Sallust, please, and note how excellently he describes a chance event.

> But Marius, having wasted much time and effort, anxiously tried to decide whether to abandon his attempt since it was fruitless, or wait for a stroke of good luck, which he had often enjoyed. When he was turning over this question for many days and nights without being able to make a decision,

forte quidam Ligus, e cohortibus auxiliariis miles grega-
rius, castris aquatum egressus, haud procul ab latere castelli, quod aversum proeliantibus erat, animadvertit inter
saxa reptantes cocleas; quarum cum unam atque alteram,
dein plures peteret, studio legendi paulatim prope ad
summum montis egressus est. Ubi postquam solitudinem
intellexit, more ingenii humani cupido difficilia faciendi
animum vertit ut forte eo in loco grandis ilex coaluerat
inter saxa, paulum modo prona, deinde flexa atque aucta
in altitudinem, quo cuncta gignentium natura fert; cuius
ramis modo, modo eminentibus saxis nixus Ligus castelli
planitiem describit, quod cuncti Numidae intenti proeliantibus aderant. Exploratis omnibus, quae mox usui fore
ducebat, eadem regreditur, non temere uti ascenderat, sed
tentans omnia et circumspiciens. Itaque Marium propere
adit, acta edocet, hortatur,[347]

et quae sequuntur. Videtis quae sit loci huius explicatio quan-
taque cum tenuitate ac verborum gratia.

Non exornavit[348] modo orationem, verum etiam magnificavit
res ipsas Livius, cum quasi repente oblatam causam ab ipso libri
illius initio exorsus est, his quidem verbis atque his etiam verborum numeris:

Inter bellorum magnorum aut vixdum finitorum aut im-
minentium curas intercessit res parva dictu, sed quae studiis in magnum certamen excesserit. M. Fundanius et L.
Valerius, tr. pl. ad plebem tulerunt de Oppia lege abro-
ganda. Tulerant eam M. Oppius et T. Romulius, tr. pl.,

by chance a Ligurian, a common soldier of the auxiliary co-horts, left the camp to fetch water and noticed snails crawl-ing between the rocks not far from the side of the fortress turned away from the fighting. When he went after one or two of these, then several, eager to collect them, little by lit-tle he got almost to the top of the mountain. After he saw that it was deserted, human nature being what it is, the de-sire of doing difficult things directed his attention to a place where a great oak had happened to take root among the rocks, now bent down a little, then turning and growing up-ward as the entire nature of plants requires. Putting his weight now on its branches, now on the projecting rocks, the Ligurian observed the level area of the fortress, because all the Numidians were intent on the fighting. Investigating ev-erything he thought likely to be useful, he went back the same way — not rashly, the way he had gone up, but testing and observing everything. And so he quickly approached Marius, told him what he had done, and encouraged him . . . [Bellum Iugurthinum 93.1–5]

And the passage continues. You see how this passage unfolds, how precise it is, and how pleasing the language.

Livy not only embellished speech but also made the events themselves important when at the very beginning of a book he embarked on a matter as if it had suddenly arisen, in these words and even in these rhythms.[345]

Amid the cares of great wars either barely brought to an end or on the horizon there arose a matter trivial to mention, but which because of passions grew into a heated conflict. Mar-cus Fundanius and Lucius Valerius, tribunes of the plebs, proposed the repeal of the Oppian Law to the plebs. This law had been passed at the height of the Punic War by Mar-cus Oppius and Titus Romulius, tribunes of the plebs, in the

Q. Fabio, T. Sempronio consulibus, in medio ardore Punici belli: ne qua mulier plus semuntiam auri haberet, neu vestimento versicolori uteretur, neu iuncto vehiculo in urbe oppido ve aut propius inde mille passus, nisi sacrorum publicorum causa veheretur. M. et T. Iunius tr. pl. legem Oppiam tuebantur, nec eam se abrogari passuros aiebant. Ad suadendum dissuadendumque multi nobiles prodibant; Capitolium turba hominum faventium adversantiumque legi complebatur. Matronae nulla nec auctoritate nec verecundia nec imperio virorum contineri limine poterant, omnis vias urbis aditusque in forum obsidebant, viros descendentes ad forum orantes ut florente re publica, crescente in dies privata omnium fortuna, matronis quoque pristinum ornatum reddi paterentur. Augebatur haec frequentia mulierum in dies, nam etiam ex oppidis conciliabulisque convenerant. Iam et consules praetoresque et alios magistratus adire et rogare audebant.[349]

84   Tam multa autem animadvertenda sunt ab historicis, ut non reliquerit inexpressum Livius inenarratumque Numidarum equitum equorumque habitum ac fedam[350] speciem:

At Numidae equos conscendunt et obequitare stationibus, neminem lacessentes coeperunt. Nihil primo aspectu contemptius: equi hominesque paululi et graciles, discinctus et inermis eques, praeterquam quod iacula secum portat, equi sine frenis, deformes, ipse cursus rigida cervice et extento capite currentium; hunc contemptum de industria augentes labi ex equis ac per ludibrium spectaculo esse.[351]

consulship of Quintus Fabius and Titus Sempronius, that no woman might have more than half an ounce of gold or wear multicolored garments or ride in a carriage in the city or town or within a mile therefrom, except for the purpose of religious ceremonies. The tribunes of the plebs Marcus and Titus Iunius defended the Oppian Law and said that they would not allow it to be repealed. Many nobles came forward to urge or dissuade; the Capitol was filled with a crowd of people favoring or opposing the law. The women could not be kept at home by any authority or modesty or the control of their husbands; they besieged all the streets of the city and approaches to the forum, importuning the men going down to the forum, saying that with the state flourishing and everyone's private wealth increasing day by day, they should let their original adornment also be returned to the women. This crowd of women was increasing every day, for they had also gathered from the towns and marketplaces. Now they were venturing to approach and appeal to consuls and praetors and other magistrates. [Livy 34.1.1–7]

Moreover, so many things must be noted by historians that Livy did not leave out a description of the bearing and repulsive appearance of the Numidian cavalry and horses. 84

But the Numidians mounted their horses and began to ride up to the outposts, attacking no one. At first sight nothing was more contemptible. Horses and men were puny and thin, the cavalry without equipment or arms except that they carried javelins with them, the horses ugly, without reins, their very progress stiff-necked and with head extended as they ran. Deliberately increasing contempt, they slipped off their horses and were a spectacle for mockery. [Livy 35.11.6–8][346]

Nec Sallustius non et ipse faciem quoque ac nidorem Tulliani carceris explicuit:

> circiter quatuordecim pedes humi depressus; eum muniunt undique parietes atque insuper camera lapideis fornicibus vincta, sed inculta tenebris, foeda odore atque terribilis facies eius.[352]

Hos locos ab eminentissimis viris sumptos afferre placuit, non ut auctoritatem ab iis dictis comparemus nostris, verum ut praeceptorum locum apud vos quique haec e vobis audierint optineant utque diligentiores etiam multo quam estis efficiamini explorandis locis aliis iisque considerandis, quibus tum Livius Sallustiusque praecipue tum alii rerum scriptores historias suas et locupletarunt abunde et insigniter etiam decorarunt.

Iam vero post expugnationes direptio et caedes ipsa campum praebet quam latissimum edisserendi quae libido, ira, superbia, crudelitas, dolor, avaritia suadet victoribus quaeque perpetienda victis atque expugnatis. Quae quidem ipsa clariora sunt quam ut exemplis sint illustranda. Hi tamen loci praecipue et scriptoris ingenium quantum valeat ad movendos indicant animos et quae sit in eo augendi atque magnificandi virtus ac dicendi copia.

85   Illud vero rerum scriptori servandum maxime atque in tota rerum serie, ut pro locis, rebus, occasionibus, iudicis ipse personam induat, ut laudet, condemnet, admiretur, deprimat, misereatur; nunc rideat humanos casus, nunc deploret, demum meminerit demonstrativo in dicendi genere se versari, ac tum laudandi tum vituperandi honus a se esse susceptum. Sallustius in explicandis Catilinae perversis consiliis atque coniurationis apparatibus quasi dolore victus prorupit in haec verba:

Nor did Sallust fail to describe the appearance and stench of the Tullianum dungeon:

> It is about fourteen feet underground; walls enclose it on every side and the chamber above is encircled by stone arches, but its aspect is squalid in the darkness, foul smelling, and terrifying. [*Bellum Catilinae* 55.3–5]

I decided to present these passages taken from the most eminent men not to get authority from them for my words, but that they might take the place of teachers with you and with those who will hear these things from you, and that you might become even more diligent than you are at seeking out and considering other passages with which not only Livy and Sallust in particular but other historians as well have both greatly enriched and notably embellished their works.

Moreover, the pillaging and slaughter after assaults certainly provide a wide field for analyzing the effect of lust, anger, arrogance, cruelty, hatred, and greed on the victors and what the vanquished and captured must endure. These matters are too obvious to require illustration by examples. Nevertheless, these passages especially show the power of the writer's talent to move our minds and his ability and command of language to enhance and make things great.

But the historian must take care above all in the whole sequence of events — in accordance with the places, events, circumstances — to assume the role of a judge, to praise, condemn, admire, disparage, pity. Now let him laugh at human events, now lament; finally, let him remember that he is engaged in the demonstrative genre of speaking and that he has undertaken the task of both praising and censuring. Sallust, in laying out the evil plans of Catiline and the preparations of his conspiracy, bursts out in these words, as if overcome by grief: 85

Ea tempestate mihi imperium populi Romani multo maxime miserabile visum est. Cui cum ad occasum ab ortu solis omnia domita armis parerent, domi ocium atque divitiae, quae prima mortales putant, affluerent, fuere tamen cives qui seque et rem publicam obstinatis animis perditum irent. Nanque duobus senatus decretis ex tanta multitudine neque praemio inductus coniurationem patefecerat neque ex castris Catilinae quisquam omnium discesserat: tanta vis morbi uti tabes plerosque civium animos invaserat.[353]

Et post captum a Mario oppidum, de quo paulo est ante sermo habitus, sententiam quasi iudicialem protulit:

Sic forte correcta Marii temeritas gloriam ex virtute[354] invenit.

Et Livius in explicando ad Capuam militum Annibalis langore ac desidia:

Maius, inquit, id peccatum ducis apud peritos artium militarium haberetur quam quod non ex Cannensi acie protinus ad urbem Romam duxisset exercitum. Illa enim cunctatio distulisse modo victoriam videri potuit, hic error vires ademisse ad vincendum.[355]

Item post eruptionem ad Nolam a Marcello factam:

Ingens eo die res ac nescio an maxima illo bello gesta sit; non vinci enim ab Annibale[356] difficilius fuit quam postea vincere.

At that time the empire of the Roman people seemed to me to be in a most pitiable condition. Although the whole world to the setting from the rising sun had been conquered and was subject to its arms, and at home peace and wealth abounded, blessings mortals prize the most, nonetheless there were citizens obstinately bent on destroying both themselves and the state. For even after two decrees of the senate no one from such a great multitude had either been induced by reward to reveal the conspiracy nor had a single man deserted the camp of Catiline. So violent a disease, like a plague, had attacked the minds of most citizens. [*Bellum Catilinae* 36.4–5]

And after Marius took the town I mentioned a little while ago, Sallust pronounced sentence like a judge:[347]

Thus Marius' rashness, corrected by a lucky chance, won glory after an act of courage. [*Bellum Iugurthinum* 94.7]

And Livy in describing the lassitude and idleness of Hannibal's soldiers at Capua, says:

This was considered a greater fault on the general's part among military experts than his failure to lead his army directly from the battle of Cannae to the city of Rome. That delay could have been regarded as having only delayed victory, this blunder as having taken away the power to win. [Livy 23.18.12–13][348]

Likewise after Marcellus' sally at Nola:

On that day was accomplished a great deed, perhaps the greatest in that war. For it was harder not to be conquered by Hannibal than it was to conquer him afterward. [Livy 23.16.16]

Et alibi:[357]

> Eludant nunc antiqua mirantes. Non equidem, siqua sit
> sapientium civitas, quam docti fingunt magis quam no-
> runt, ⟨a⟩ut ⟨principes⟩ graviores temperatioresque a cupi-
> dine imperii aut multitudinem melius moratam censeam
> fieri posse.[358]

Eiusmodi autem exempla affatim multa extant, quae sequenda
sunt rerum gestarum scriptori sua cum maxima laude et historiae dignitate. His itaque servandis non laudatorem modo se
nobilium nunc facinorum praeclarissimarumque actionum nunc
reprehensorem turpium abiectorumque ostendet egregius rerum gestarum expositor, verum etiam virtutis ipsius patronum
admonitoremque sapientiae praeseferet et quasi magistrum,
quando historia ipsa vitae est hominum ac rerum humanarum
magistra.

Idem Livius[359] de Annibale Italia excedente sic loquitur:

> Raro quenquam hominem patriam exilii causa relinquen-
> tem tam moestum abiisse ferunt quam Annibalem hos-
> tium terra excedentem: respexisse saepe Italiae litora, et
> deos hominesque accusantem, se quoque ac suum ipsius
> caput execratum, quod non cruentum ab Cannensi victo-
> ria militem Romam duxisset. Scipionem ire ad Cartagi-
> nem ausum, qui consul hostem Poenum in Italia non vi-
> disset; se, centum millibus armatorum ad Thrasimennum
> aut Cannas caesis, circa Casilinum Cumasque et Nolam
> consenuisse. Haec accusans querensque ex diutina posses-
> sione Italiae est detractus.[360]

And in another place:

> Now let them make fun of those who admire antiquity. I do not think, if there should be any state of the wise (a place existing in scholars' imagination rather than in their experience), that either ⟨its leaders⟩ could be more worthy or more restrained in their political ambition or its populace be of better character. [Livy 26.22.14]

There are plenty of examples like this for a historian to follow to his own great praise and to the esteem of history. By paying attention to them the excellent interpreter of events not only will show himself now as a eulogist of noble and illustrious deeds, now as a harsh critic of infamous and unprincipled ones, but he will also present himself as a defender of moral excellence and a monitor of wisdom, indeed almost as a teacher, since history itself is the guide of life and human affairs.[349]

The same Livy we have been speaking of describes Hannibal on his departure from Italy in this way:

> Rarely, so they say, had any man leaving his homeland into exile departed as sorrowfully as Hannibal as he withdrew from the land of the enemy. They say he often looked back at the shores of Italy, blaming both gods and men, cursing himself and his life, because he had not led his army on to Rome while they were bloodstained from their victory at Cannae. Scipio had dared to go to Carthage although as consul he had not seen the Carthaginian enemy in Italy; but he himself had wasted away around Casilinum and Cumae and Nola after slaying a hundred thousand armed men at Trasimene and Cannae. Uttering these recriminations and complaints, he was torn away from his long possession of Italy. [Livy 30.20.7–9]

Hic igitur praecipue locus admonere rerum scriptores potest, qua animi pensione uti debeant quodque adhibere iudicium ac curam, non in enarrandis modo rebus ipsis quae gestae sint, sed illis etiam innuendis effingendisque quae concipi cogitatione et colligi coniectura possunt, pro rebus, negociis, temporibus, personis. Quae singula velle complecti, nec consessus est huius et videtur esse satis admonuisse, cum praesertim sit ostensum historiam poeticae maxime esse similem, ipsa vero poetica naturam potissimum imitetur.

86   Diximus hactenus de rebus, quibus disserendis fuimus fortasse longiores, reliquum est de verbis ut dicamus, cum iis e duobus historia, ut dictum est, constet. Illud igitur videndum est primum, ut ea sint propria, accommodata, delecta, usitata bonis ab auctoribus, pro loco ac re sumpta, quanquam interdum, pro rei magnitudine, a poetis quoque mutuanda ea sunt, quod frequentissime omnium servavit Livius, et Cicero ait poetam oratori esse finitimum; deinde ut ea bene sint opportuneque collocata ipsaque ut collocatio sit artificiosa, varia, multiplex, numerosa habeatque rationem non aequabilis solum sibique consentientis texturae, verum etiam decursus ac soni, qua quidem de re aures sunt potissimum consulendae. Adhaec summa ea cura expolienda exornandaque, ut nec forma ornatu careat extrinseco nec ornatus appareat aut negligenter adhibitus aut alienus a forma, retineatque tum venustatem dignitatemque pro re ac loco, tum etiam gravitatem ac supercilium. Quarum rerum omnium Cicero optimum se nobis magistrum exhibebit.

This passage especially can remind historians of the careful attention they must employ and the discernment and thought they must exercise not only in telling about the things that have been done, but also in suggesting and portraying what can be thought and conjectured in accordance with the events, circumstances, times, and persons. Trying to describe these things individually is not a matter for this present gathering, and it seems enough to have mentioned them, especially since history has been shown to be very like poetry, and poetry certainly imitates nature above all.

Up to this point we have spoken about events, perhaps discoursing about them too long; it remains to discuss words, since history, as it has been said, consists of these two elements.[350] Well then, first one must take care that the words be suitable and apposite, well chosen, used by good authors, and employed in accordance with the place and situation, although sometimes, depending on the magnitude of the event, they must also be borrowed from the poets. Livy follows this practice most frequently of all, and Cicero says that the poet is a close kinsman of the orator.[351] Next one must see to it that they are well and suitably placed and that the placement is artful, varied, multilayered, and rhythmical, and that it pays attention not only to a uniform and internally consistent texture, but also to movement and sound. On this point the ears are by far the best guide. In addition, the words must be polished and embellished with the greatest care so that the design does not lack external ornament nor does the ornament appear carelessly applied or alien to the design, and so that it preserves not only charm and distinction appropriate to the circumstance and place but also seriousness and formality. Cicero will show himself the best teacher of all these matters.

86

Usuvenit autem in componenda historia quod in aedificandis tum domibus tum navibus, multas subinde fieri rerum commissuras et quasi membrorum inter se coniunctiones, quas prudentia ordinisque solers ac circumspecta ratio moderetur oportet quaeque et ipsa locorum quoque ac temporum rationem habeat, ut post narratas explicate diligenterque res alias transgrediatur ad alias; indeque postquam parti huic satisfecerit, ad continuandam regrediatur priorem materiam; rursus, ea quantum satis erit explanata, reditum ad alteram illam faciat, aut, si rei ratio tulerit, ad aliam moxque ad aliam; ut cum Livius post descensum ex Alpibus Annibalis postque proelium cum Scipione factum proditumque Clastidium subiungit rem navalem, inquiens:

> Interim circa Siciliam insulasque Italiae imminentes . . . viginti[361] quinqueremes cum mille armatis ad depopulandam oram Italiae a Carthaginensibus missae; novem Liparas, octo ad insulam Vulcani tenuerunt, tres in fretum avertit aestus maris.

Deinde revertitur ad res ab Annibale gestas postque Placentinam pugnam transit in Hispaniam: *Dum haec in Italia geruntur, Cn. Scipio in Hispaniam cum classe missus.*[362] Hae igitur, sive commissurae sive diversarum in historia rerum inter se connexiones, eiusmodi esse debent ut partes quae hinc atque illinc explicandae subiunguntur, sint per se integrae, clarae, minime perplexae atque ab ipso quamprimum initio appareant esse aliae; quod praestabunt verba primo loco et ipsis quasi in foribus posita, qualia sunt *interim* et *dum haec geruntur* et *per id tempus* quaeque et Sallustius et Livius et coeteri omnes usurpant. Itaque committendis atque subnectendis his primum omnium id

Moreover, in composing history as in building houses or ships one finds from time to time that many seams are created where things come together, like the joints that connect limbs to each other. These must be handled with skill and an adroit and well considered concern for order, and one that takes account of places and times so that after clearly and carefully relating some events it may pass on to others, and then after it has paid enough attention to this part, it may return to a continuation of the earlier material; again, with this sufficiently explained, it may make a return to the other, or if the plan of the thing allows, to another and then to another. In this way, after Hannibal's descent from the Alps and the battle fought with Scipio and the betrayal of Clastidium, Livy adds a naval matter, saying:

> Meanwhile, around Sicily and the islands close to Italy . . . twenty quinqueremes with a thousand armed men were sent by the Carthaginians to lay waste the shore of Italy. Nine made for Lipari, eight for the island of Vulcano; the rough sea drove three into the straits. [Livy 21.49.1–2 with some omissions][352]

Then he returns to Hannibal's activities and after the battle of Piacenza moves into Spain: "While this was going on in Italy, Gnaeus Scipio was sent to Spain with the fleet" [Livy 21.60.1]. These intersections then, or interconnections of different events in a history, must be of a kind that the parts to be treated, that are added from one place or another, are complete in themselves, clear, not at all convoluted; and they must appear different right from the beginning. This difference will be indicated by words placed in the first position and at the entrance, so to speak—expressions like "meanwhile," "while this was going on," and "around this time," which both Sallust and Livy and all the rest employ. Accordingly, in connecting and adding parts, first

videndum, uti diversitas materiae confestim elucescat intelliga-
turque quasi membrum quoddam corporis ab alio membro diversum ac nihilominus ut membra nostri corporis nervis com-
plicantur, sic partes hae verbis quam maxime aptis nervorumque
praestantibus officium apte inter se prudenterque iungantur.
Quocirca ad ingenium atque a natura tributa dicendi dona
adiungenda est lectio optimi cuiusque ex Graecorum ac Latinorum auctoribus; quaeque in illis cernuntur apparentque eminen-
tissima, ad ea tanquam ad metam dirigenda est omnis scriptorum opera et cura, ut similes, ut pares, si superare illos minus
valuerint, aut imitatores saltem boni ut evadant, laudemque, si
non primi aut secundi loci, aliquam quoque et ipsi certam pro-
priamque ac studiis suis dignam consequantur.

87   Ac mihi quidem res gestas memoriae qui mandant officioque
funguntur tradendi ad posteros res praeteritas non minore fortasse laude digni videantur quam qui leges tradidere vivendi. Illi
enim praecepta, exempla hi nobis tradidere; quippe cum proprium eorum officium ac munus sit sustentare ingenio suo vitae
nostrae imbecillitatem atque mortalitati ire obviam, ne, quantum in ipsis est, dicta factaque memoratu digna resque prae-
clare atque excellenter gestas tempus obscuret ne ve eae omnino
e memoria excidant; quaeque imitatione atque cognitione digna
sunt, aevo ea ne intercidant, quibus mortale genus ad virtutem
excitetur et gloriam; ut qui legunt, qui de iis loquuntur intelli-
gant omnes quo ore quoque animo laudentur honesta, vitupe-
rentur turpia et improba; ut fortunam, ut varietatem inconstan-
tiamque rerum humanarum animadvertentes discant in adversis
esse patientes ac firmi, in prosperis continentes et lenes, in

of all one must see to it that the diversity of the material clearly emerges at once and is recognized as if it were a particular limb of the body, separate from another limb, and yet that just as the limbs of our body are connected by sinews, these parts are joined to each other closely and skillfully by the most suitable possible words, performing the function of sinews. Therefore, to talent and the gifts of speech bestowed by nature must be added the reading of all the best Greek and Latin authors. The whole effort and attention of writers must be directed, as if to a goal post, to what is perceived and appears most outstanding in them, so that they may turn out to match or resemble if they cannot surpass them, or at least to be good imitators, and so that they themselves may also attain a reputation, which if not of the first or second rank, is something secure and their own and worthy of their exertions.

In my view, at any rate, those who record what has happened 87 and perform the service of handing down events from the past to posterity are perhaps no less praiseworthy than those who have bequeathed the rules for living. Those have left us precepts; these have left examples.[353] In fact, it is their particular obligation and duty to support the weakness of our life with their talent and to resist mortality, so that—to the extent of their ability—they may prevent time from blotting out words and deeds that deserve to be told and outstanding acts of brilliant achievement, and keep these things from falling altogether out of memory; so that things worthy of being known and imitated that rouse the race of mortals to virtue and glory might not perish with time; so that those who read and speak about them may all understand with what eloquence and what feeling honorable deeds are praised, shameless and disgraceful ones condemned; so that, becoming aware of fortune, of the variety and inconstancy of human affairs, they may learn to be patient and resolute in adversity, continent and mild in prosperity, in

deiectionibus ac ruinis fortes robustique ac spirante fortuna mansueti, faciles, placidi, in opulentia liberales ac benefici,[363] in inopia sorte sua si non[364] contenti, saltem non abiecti non squalidi;[365] ut nihil quod accidat homini novum existiment, nihil repentinum mirentur, nihil non aliquando reantur aut posse accidere aut putent non quandoque etiam accidisse.

Macti igitur diuturnitate estote ac laude, rerum scriptores, quorum opera et studio effectum est ut sciamus qui primi deum cognoverint intelligamusque quibus eum sacrificiis, votis, suppliciisque veneremur, colamus, placemus; quorum item beneficium ac munus fuit ut cognosceremus qui leges tulerint, naturae secreta aperuerint, artes invenerint, vivendi praecepta tradiderint. Quae dum sequitur genus hominum, e silvis atque a fero victu cultuque liberum in urbes se contulit atque in libertatem; in quibus pietatem, fidem, aequitatem, amicitiam, humanitatem, iustitiam, urbanitatem denique omnem exerceat seque homo ipse diis non modo gratum ipsis, verum etiam persimilem invicem gratuitoque benefaciendo reddat.

Constat igitur historia et rebus et verbis; verba vero esse debent, ut ultimo dictum est loco, elegantia et propria et bene decenterque collocata et sparsa. Res ipsae constant ordine et dispositione, quibus coniunctae sunt descriptiones causarum, temporum, rerum praeteritarum antecessionumque, ingenii morumque eorum qui bellum administrant, virium, societatum, apparatuum; item descriptiones regionum, locorum, urbium, fluminum, montium, et siqua in illis memoratu digna; itinerum quoque, casuum, eventuum, pugnarum, quaeque pugnam sequuntur; adhaec, obsidionum, oppugnationum expugnationumque, quaeque expugnationem comitari consueverunt. Accedunt

humiliation and catastrophe brave and strong, and when fortune smiles, gentle, courteous, and calm, in wealth liberal and beneficent, in poverty, if not content with their lot, at least not dispirited or squalid; so that they may consider nothing that happens to man a novelty, marvel at nothing as unexpected, nor think that there is nothing that can never happen, or suppose that there is nothing that has not happened from time to time.

Therefore, be honored with lasting fame and praise, writers of history, by whose effort and study it has been brought to pass that we know what men first recognized god and we understand by what sacrifices, vows, and supplications to adore, worship, and please him; whose kindness and gift it was that we learned who passed the laws, uncovered the secrets of nature, discovered arts, handed down precepts for living. While the human race was observing these things, it took itself out of the forests and, free from a wild state of life and culture, took itself into cities and freedom, into circumstances where it might practice religious observance and faith, equity, friendship, philanthropy, justice — in short, every virtue of civilized life — and where man might make himself not only pleasing to the gods themselves, but also very like them by freely conferring benefits in turn.

In sum then, history consists of events and words; the words, in fact, as we have just said, must be elegant and appropriate and well and tastefully arranged and distributed. The events are hang together in order and arrangement, to which are connected the descriptions of causes, times, past events and antecedent causes, the nature and character of those directing the war, of forces, alliances, preparations; likewise descriptions of regions, places, cities, rivers, mountains and anything noteworthy in them, also of marches, mishaps, successes, battles, and what follows the battle; in addition, descriptions of sieges, assaults, sacks, and the things that generally accompany a sack.

his personae, laudantis scilicet aut improbantis, pro re ac tempore. Lectio item atque imitatio.

De genere autem ipso dicendi, quale scilicet conveniat historiae dictum est, de brevitate similiter ac celeritate, quarum altera est historiae commendatrix, altera locupletat eam atque magnificat. Itaque plura de re hac loqui praecipientis est velle personam assumere. Quocirca ne mihi sit cum grammaticae patrocinatoribus contentio posthac ulla, finem dicendi facio meque a promisso absolvo, quando factum est a me, ut arbitror, satis promisso et fortasse amplius quam iudicari possit esse promissum.

88 *Pud.*[366] Et promissis a te satisfactum, Altili, confitemur omnes et disserendis iis incredibili voluptate nos affecisti, dum rem sparsam ac passim iactatam colligis collectamque ordine suo suaque regula ac lege sic componis, ut siqui posthac redacturi ea sint in praecepta, facile quidem praestituri id videantur. Nec his contentus laudes quoque historiae addidisti et quam ea sit utilis mortalium generi multa cum gravitate docuisti et copia. Coeterum nesciam volensne an negligens praeterieris ea quae ad scribendas magnorum virorum vitas spectant, quo in genere historiae Graece Latineque versati sunt permulti.

Alt. Atqui, Puderice,[367] de toto et integro nos historiae corpore locuti, non de parte sumus, quae et ipsa ad totius imaginem componi pro natura sua potest. Itaque ut pauca quaedam in hoc quoque genere scribendi tradamus, quod ipsum[368] demonstrativum est genus et[369] qui vitam alicuius scribit in locos nunc laudis nunc vituperationis incidit, cuius rei monitum fecisse eum satis est, tria cumprimis servanda censemus: ut scriptio ipsa sit

Added to these are the characters assumed by the historian as he praises or blames according to the situation. So too, selection and imitation.

We have talked about the style of speaking appropriate to history, likewise about brevity and speed, of which the one makes history agreeable, the other enriches and enhances it. Accordingly, to say more about the matter is to try to assume the role of instructor. Therefore, to avoid any future dispute with the defenders of grammar, I will stop speaking and absolve myself of my promise, since, as I believe, I have done enough to fulfill my promise, and perhaps more than I could be thought to have promised.

Puderico. We all acknowledge that you have fulfilled your promise, 88 Altilio, and in discussing these matters you have given us exceptional pleasure. You pull together a subject scattered and discussed here and there, and when you have pulled it together in its proper order with its own standard and rule, you lay it out in such a way that people turning these things into precepts hereafter will seem to do so with ease. Not content with this, you have also added the praises of history and have shown with great force and fullness of expression how useful it is to mankind. For the rest, I do not know whether or not you meant to leave out what pertains to writing the lives of great men, a type of history in which many writers in Greek and Latin have been engaged.

Altilio. Of course, Puderico, we have been speaking about the full body of history in its entirety, not a part that in accordance with its nature can be constructed along the lines of the whole. So to pass on a few suggestions on this type of writing, too, because it is of the demonstrative type, and anyone who writes someone's life comes across subjects now of praise, now of censure (for him to be forewarned of this fact is sufficient), I consider that three points especially must be observed: that the

brevis, sit diligens atque etiam gravis; adde, si placet, et quartum, ut sit ea quam maxime quoque elegans. Brevitas autem erit talis, ut rerum summas paucis complectatur; diligentia tanta, ut nihil omittat quod iudicetur memoratu dignum; gravitas item ea quae addat explicationi ac dictis pondus quaeque et auctorem rerum et scriptorem commendet. Nam praeter veritatem nihil potest esse commendabile. Quid, obsecro, tam est adversum quam vanitas historiae, quae vitae magistra esse dicitur? Elegantiam iccirco dicendi maximam hac praesertim in parte exigimus, quod haec ipsa scribendi pars permultis sit aliis laudibus ac virtutibus caritura.

Itaque compensetur utique elegantia quod deerit de cultu coeteroque splendore; cuius rei Caesar gravissimus esse potest et testis et monitor; de cuius commentariis et si multa in exemplum adduci a nobis poterant, tamen scribendi genus historicum ex omni parte minime complexus est Caesar, quippe qui materiam et praebere et relinquere maluerit aliis de se scribendi. Et qui pictor aut statuarius imaginem facturus est, quae totius referat corporis pulchritudinem, nimirum pulcherrimi cuiusque viri speciem sibi in exemplum assumit; non eius qui parte tantum praecellat aliqua, sed qui omnibus. Nam quanquam et Tacitus et Curtius abunde sunt laudibus ac virtutibus ornati suis, laus tamen omnis Latinae historiae penes duos putatur existere diverso(s)que[370] in dicendi genere, Livium ac Sallustium. Adhaec iniquitas temporum Trogum nobis omnino abstulit, et Curtium ac Tacitum quasi mutilatas videmus statuas, licetque suspicari potius ac coniicere quam omnino de iis iudicium aliquod absolutum ac certum tradere. Quid quod noster paulo ante Actius uno fuit ubique fere contentus Virgilio? Videlicet

work itself be brief, that it be thorough, and also authoritative; add a fourth, too, if you like: that it also be as elegant as possible. Moreover, the brevity will be of a kind to cover the chief points in few words, the thoroughness so great that it omits nothing that would be judged worth mentioning, likewise the authority of a sort to add weight to the words and exposition and make the author and writer of history deserving of praise. Indeed, nothing except truth can be praiseworthy. What, I ask you, can be so contrary to history as falsehood, since history is said to be the guide of human life?[354] We require the greatest elegance of language in this biographical branch of history especially, because this branch of writing is apt to lack many other merits and virtues.

And so let elegance, at least, compensate for any lack of ornament or other excellence. In this matter Caesar can be the greatest witness and guide. Although we could have introduced many things by way of example from his *Commentaries*, nevertheless Caesar did not embrace a type of writing that was historical in every respect, since he preferred to provide the material and to leave it to others to write about him.[355] And the painter or sculptor who intends to make a likeness that reflects the beauty of the whole body certainly takes as his model the form of the most beautiful man — the man who excels in every respect, not just in one. For, although Tacitus and Curtius are abundantly provided with their own merits and virtues, nevertheless all the renown of history in Latin is considered to be in the possession of two men, Livy and Sallust, different in style.[356] In addition, time has unfairly deprived us altogether of Trogus, and we look at Curtius and Tacitus as if they were mutilated statues, and one may admire and make guesses about them rather than deliver an opinion fully developed and definite in every respect.[357] Why is it that our Actius just now was content almost everywhere with Vergil alone? Clearly because authority

quod ab optimo quoque suo in genere quaerenda est semper
auctoritas. Quod autem, sicuti ex oculis ac vultu coniicio, Prassicius[371] hic noster dicere paratus est aliquid officiumque absolutum est meum, dicat pro arbitrio vir et in poetica et in oratoria maxime exercitatus depromatque de pectore apprime
foecundo dignum aliquid seque et hoc ipso consessu, ut munus
et ipse quoque suum adimpleat.

Pud. Atqui et ordo lexque ipsa sessionis huius id ipsum exigit et
nos omnes non istud ipsum modo petimus, verum etiam ro-
gamus atque exposcimus.

89 Paul.[372] Equidem ex iis quae acute, graviter eruditeque ab Altilio
sunt de lege historiae dicta quaeque ante Sincerus poeticis de
numeris, ipse vero Altilius de verbis nuper atque ornamentis
disseruit magis magisque incendor ad pervestigandum poeticae
finem, quem ex ore senis nostri esse Sincerus initio retulit bene
atque apposite dicere ad admirationem comparandam. Conver-
tor autem ad te, Parde, potissimum, quem dicendi labor non
adeo ut hos ipsos delassavit, audientiam primo abs te expos-
cens, deinde sententiam in his quoque requirens tuam.

Pard. Et audientem me perque intentum in dicendo habebis, et
paratum etiam respondere ad ea quae ex me intelligere ipse
voles aut quid ipse sentiam aperire, si opinionem fortasse meam
tentando sciscitaberis.

Paul.[373] Principio quod Cicero aiat finitimum esse oratori poetam,
duo, ut mihi videtur, cur in eam sententiam venerit omnino illum movere: et quod uterque versatur in dicendo et quod
utriusque communes sunt laudationes, quod demonstrativum
genus dicitur, tametsi et deliberationes quoque; apud poetas
enim tot deorum concilia consultationesque non ne hoc nobis
palam faciunt? Habent igitur tum laudationes tum deliberationes inter se communes, bene item et consumate dicere, suo

is always to be sought from what is best of its kind. But because, as I surmise from his look and expression, our friend Prassicio here is ready to say something, and my task is done, let a man especially well versed in both poetry and oratory express his opinion, and bring forth from his fertile breast something worthy of himself and this gathering so that he too may fulfill his obligation.

Puderico. By all means, and the rule of succession of this meeting requires the very thing you mention; we all not only request, but even urge and demand it.

Paolo. Indeed, from Altilio's perceptive, authoritative, and learned discussion on the law of history. and Sincero's comments earlier about poetic rhythms, and Altilio's just now about words and rhetorical embellishments, I am more and more on fire to seek out the end of poetry, which at the beginning Sincero reported our old man as saying is to speak well and in a way suited to win admiration.[358] But I turn to you, Pardo, in particular, whom the toil of speaking has not worn out so much as it has these, first asking you for a hearing, then seeking your view on these matters, too.

89

Pardo. You will have me as a very attentive listener while you speak; and I am also ready either to respond to what you want to learn from me or to explain my own views if by chance you are trying to find out my opinion with your inquiries.

Paolo. To begin with — as to Cicero's saying that the poet is closely akin to the orator[359] — it seems to me that two points in general prompted him to take that opinion: that each is engaged in speaking, and that encomia are common to both because the style is called demonstrative, although there are also deliberations as well — indeed, does the presence in the poets of so many councils and consultations of the gods not make that clear to us? So then, they have encomia and deliberations in common, likewise excellent and consummate speech, each in

uterque in genere dicendi, cum alter solutus incedat atque pro-
missus, alter astrictus numeris ac pedibus certa lege coercitis.
Quin verba quoque et ipsa sunt inter eos communia; verum alterius digna foro ac senatu quaeque gravitatem satis est uti se-
quantur retineantque dignitatem, alterius quae magnificentiam,
altitudinem excellentiamque quasi quandam ostentent.

Neque enim gravitas comparandae admirationi satis est sola,
ni magnificentia accesserit excellentiaque et verborum et rerum,
utque ego arbitror, hoc illud est quod ait Horatius:

> mediocribus esse poetis
> non homines, non dii, non concessere columnae,

cum oporteat eos suo in genere excellere neque aliter digni eo
nomine videantur. Hoc etiam est et illud quod a Cicerone dicitur singulis vix seculis bonum poetam inventum. Perrara
nanque omnis est excellentia, quodque oratori satis est bene
dicere atque apposite, id oportet in poeta sit ut excellenter. Ac
tametsi oratoris quoque est aliquando et magnifice et excellenter, tamen id non ubique neque semper, cum poetae hoc ipsum
ubique suum sit ac peculiare, etiam cum in minutissimis atque
humilibus versatur rebus, siquidem necesse est et minutissimis
et humilibus describendis rebus appareat etiam eius excellentia.
Nam et quae fuit naturae excellentia creando in homine, eadem
nec minor pro specie illarum ac forma in apibus atque formicis
fuit.

90   Utriusque etiam, oratoris ac poetae officium est movere et
flectere auditorem; verum quo nam, quo, inquam, haec et com-
motio et flexio et maximum utriusque in hoc ipso studium?
Oratoris scilicet ut persuadeat iudici, poetae ut admirationem
sibi ex audiente ac legente comparet, cum ille pro victoria

his own style of speaking, since the one proceeds unfettered and at length, the other confined by rhythms and feet held together by a fixed rule. They even have language itself in common between them, but the words of the one are suitable to forum and senate, and it is sufficient for these to achieve seriousness and hold on to excellence; the words of the other must display grandeur, nobility, and almost a certain perfection.

Indeed, seriousness alone is not enough to win admiration without the addition of grandeur and superiority of language and subject. I think this is what Horace means when he says:

for poets to be mediocre
not men, not gods, not bookshops have allowed. [Horace,
Ars poetica 372–73]

They must be outstanding in their style or appear unworthy of the title of poet. There is also the comment by Cicero that a good poet is found hardly once in a generation.[360] Indeed, all excellence is extremely rare; although it is sufficient for an orator to speak well and appropriately, the utterance of a poet must be brilliant. And even if it is sometimes the duty of the orator to speak superbly and brilliantly, yet that is not always the case on every occasion or at all times, whereas this very thing is the particular responsibility of the poet, even when he is treating very insignificant and humble matters, since indeed it is necessary for his brilliance to be evident even in describing very insignificant and humble things. Indeed, the brilliance that was nature's in creating man was no less in proportion to their kind and form in the case of bees and ants.

It is also the duty of both orator and poet to move and sway   90
the hearer, but for what purpose, I say, for what purpose is this moving and swaying and very great effort of each in this matter? Obviously for the orator to persuade the judge, for the poet to win himself admiration from hearer and reader, since the

nitatur, hic pro fama et gloria, quae videtur sola ac maxime ab hoc scriptorum genere quaeri. Et orator quidem ubi minime persuaserit, potest fine suo contentus esse, quod bene, quod apposite, quod consumate dixerit in causa: at poeta fine omnino defraudabitur suo nisi in audientis ac legentis animo pepererit infixeritque admirationem, per quam sit famam venerationemque assecuturus. Nec vero audientem aut legentem eum nos intelligi volumus cui sit admirationi Bavius aut Maximianus, sed cui magnam quoque mentem Delius inspiraverit vates; vix enim de bono poeta, nisi et ipse auditor bonus poeta fuerit, iudicare recte potest. Tametsi nescio quomodo, a natura ipsa instituti non nulli, alii in musicis, alii in pictura, in poeticis alii, neque poetae tamen ipsi neque pictores aut musicam professi, bonum quid in ea sit arte sentiunt; optimum vero sentire haud poterit nisi quem ars quoque cum natura ipsa ingeniosum pariter atque solertem fecerint. Quocirca mediocritas illa quae in rebus plerisque omnibus conceditur, poetae omnino adversatur eique minime est concessa; nisi forte dicendi excellentia et magnificentia illa sit vocanda mediocritas in genere dicendi poetico, quando excellentia dicendi in poeta ut vacua esse debet inflatione atque intumescentia, sic nullo debet modo de gradu suo deiici. Quid quod oratorem, multitudinis praesertim impleturum aures aut unius iudicis aut paucorum admodum, multae illum adiuvare res possunt; at poeta solis excellentibus ingenioque excellenti praeditis sola et una cum excellentia potest satisfacere. Quocirca coniunctus et ipse ratione hac historico est, quod lectoribus iisque litteratissimis viris, non iudici scribit aut multitudini. His itaque permotus senis nostri sententiae

former strives for victory, but the latter for reputation and glory, which seems the only goal and the one most sought by this type of writer. And indeed the orator when he has failed to persuade can still be content with his purpose because he has spoken well, appropriately, perfectly in his case; but the poet will be cheated entirely of his purpose if he has not created and fixed in the mind of his hearer and reader the admiration whereby he will achieve fame and the highest respect. And by hearer or reader I do not mean someone who would admire Bavius or Maximianus, but someone whom the Delian prophet has inspired with great understanding; for the hearer will scarcely be able to make a correct judgment about a good poet unless he himself is also a good poet.[361] And yet, somehow, not a few, instructed by nature herself—some in music, others in painting, others in poetry, but not poets themselves or painters or musicians—recognize what is good in that field. But to recognize the best—that can be done only by someone whom art also, together with nature herself, has made gifted and skilled at the same time. Therefore, the middling achievement allowed to everyone in most things is altogether incompatible with the poet and by no means allowed to him, unless perhaps brilliance and grandeur of language is to be called a middle state in the poetic style of speaking, since just as brilliance of language in a poet should be devoid of puffery and bombast, so it must in no way be lowered from its proper level. And consider the fact that many factors can assist the orator, whether his chief aim is to satisfy the ears of a multitude, or of a single judge, or of just a few people; but with brilliance and brilliance alone can the poet satisfy only brilliant people and those endowed with brilliant intellect. Therefore he is related to the historian in this respect, because he writes for readers and the best educated men at that, not for a judge or a multitude. And so, moved by these considerations, I agree with the view of our old man that the purpose

accedo poetae sive finem sive officium esse bene atque excellenter loqui ad admirationem. Quod si, Parde, probaveris (nam
Sincerum id probaturum testificari ea possunt quae in initio
dissertionis suae attigit), Altilium sat scio, qua est observantia
in senem et cultu, minime dissensurum.

91 *Pard.* Visus es mihi, Prassici,[374] probandis poeticis his non minus
quam ex Aristotelica disciplina, ex ipsa etiam rei natura esse
locutus, et quod multa sunt oratori et poetae communia et
quod in non paucis etiam differant inter se. De fine vero officioque poetae siquis aliter sentiat, meo iudicio invide magis
quam vere sentire videbitur, dum quod poetae ipsi gloriantur se
tantum quaerere, nomen scilicet ac famam, invidere illis et pretium et laborum tantorum summam volunt. Et quod in oratore
exigitur bene et consumate, id in poeta esse debere excellenter,
id profecto mihi et verissime et appositissime a te dictum videtur. Nam, te obsecro per Musas ipsas perque tantopere a nostro
cultam sene Uraniam, quid nisi admiratio, quid, inquam, nisi
una et sola admiratio quaeritur ex magnificis illis et maxime
numerosis verbis dictisque?

> Dicam horrida bella,
> dicam acies actosque animis in funera reges
> Tyrrhenamque manum totamque sub arma coactam
> Hesperiam. Maior rerum mihi nascitur ordo,
> Maius opus moveo.

Quid cum?

or duty of the poet is to speak well and brilliantly to win admiration. If you approve this, Pardo (for Sincero's approval can be guaranteed by what he touched on in the beginning of his discourse), I am sure that Altilio — such is his regard and veneration for the old man — will not disagree in the slightest.

Pardo. In these recommendations of poetry, Prassicio, I think you 91 have spoken as much in accordance with the very nature of the subject as with Aristotelian teaching, saying both that the orator and poet have many points in common and that they also differ from each other in several ways. If fact, if anyone should disagree about the purpose and duty of the poet, in my view he will appear to speak more enviously than truthfully since people of this kind want to begrudge to the poets what they boast is their sole object — to wit, reputation and fame, and the reward and crowning glory of such great efforts. And your statement, that what is required to be done well and flawlessly in the case of the orator must be done brilliantly in that of the poet, certainly seems most true and apposite to me. Indeed — by the very Muses I ask you and by Urania so greatly venerated by our old man — what except admiration — what, I say, except admiration and admiration alone — is sought in the following splendid and most rhythmical words and utterances?[362]

> I will tell of terrible wars,
> I will tell of battles and kings driven to death by their
> courage
> and the Etruscan force and all Hesperia mustered under
> arms.
> A greater succession of events opens before me.
> I begin a greater task. [*Aeneid* 7.41–45]

And what about this?

> stabuli de culmine summo
> pastorale canit signum cornuque recurvo
> Tartaream intendit vocem, qua protinus omne
> contremuit nemus et silvae intonuere profundae;
> Audiit et Triviae longe lacus, audiit amnis
> sulfurea Nar albus aqua fontesque Velini.[375]

Quid amplius?

> et trepidae matres pressere ad pectora natos.

Quo, quaeso, et res et verba tanta cum industria et arte inventa et posita nisi ad movendam spectant admirationem? Quo, inquam, et illa?

> assum dirarum a sede sororum,
> bella manu letumque gero.

et:

> Olli somnum ingens rupit[376] pavor.

Itaque non verbis modo magnificis, sed rebus quoque et inventis excellenter et expressis admiratio a poetis quaeritur, ut, cum poetica sicut historia constet rebus ac verbis, his utrisque poeta ad admirationem conciliandam non utatur modo, verum etiam innitatur. Quamobrem, quod veritas praestare hoc sola minus posset, veritatem nunc inumbrant fictis fabulosisque commentis, nunc ea comminiscuntur quae omnino abhorreant a vero atque a rerum natura, ut cum:

> fit tortile collo
> aurum ingens coluber,

et:

> virginei volucrum vultus,

           From the high roof peak of the cottage
she sounded the shepherds' alarm, and with her curved
    horn
sent out a hellish blast, at which at once the whole
glade trembled and the deep woods roared.
Trivia's lake heard it afar, the stream Nar heard,
white with its sulfur waters, and Velinus' springs. [*Aeneid*
    7.512–17][363]

And the next verse:

and frightened mothers clasped babes to their breasts.
    [*Aeneid* 7.518][364]

For what purpose, I ask, have both words and substance been
found and placed with such care and skill if not with the aim of
inspiring admiration? What is the aim of this, I say?

    I have come from the place of the dread sisters;
war and death I bring in my hand [*Aeneid* 7.454–55][365]

and:

A great terror broke off his sleep. [*Aeneid* 7.458]

    And so poets win admiration not only with lofty words but
also by the brilliant invention and expression of events; as a result, since poetry, like history, consists of events and words, the
poet not only uses but also depends on both elements to gain
admiration. For this reason, because truth alone cannot provide
it, they sometimes obscure truth with invented and incredible
fictions, sometimes devise things entirely foreign to reality and
the natural order of things. Thus:

    the great serpent turned into
a golden chain on her neck [*Aeneid* 7.351–52]

and:

the girl-like faces of the winged things [*Aeneid* 3.216]

et:

Tertia sed postquam maiore hastilia nisu
aggredior.

Itaque quae a te, Prassici,[377] in tota hac quaestione dicta et dis-
putata sunt, omni e parte a me, ac summopere etiam probantur,
et, cum de admiratione loquamur, ne discedamus a cognatis
verbis, mirifice etiam probantur. Quocirca perge ad reliqua.

92 *Paul.*[378] Quaeri autem ab illis admirationem, hoc est approbatio-
nem et plausum quasi quendam eorum quae dicantur, cum
animorum admiratione illorum qui audiunt et qui legunt, quae
a te delibata sunt, Parde, duo illa potissimum docent, et res et
verba: siquidem neque res ipsae quales gestae sunt perinde
atque ab historicis narrantur neque poetae ipsi verbis semper
agunt usitatis ac simplicibus; nam et rebus gestis ornatum
aliunde et magnitudinem et decorem ubique fere arcessunt a
figmentis videlicet; ut cum scripturus esset Virgilius navium
Aeneae concremationem, finxit ea quae leguntur de Cybele, de
Iove, de navium conversione in nymphas:

cum[379] virgineae, mirabile monstrum,
reddunt se totidem facies pontoque feruntur.

Quo enim maiora atque admirabiliora quae ab ipsis dicuntur
appareant, humana ad deos transferunt, fingunt monstra, mit-
tunt insomnia, deos denique in homines vertunt. Compara-
tiones quoque, quibus frequentissime utuntur, non magis ad
docendum atque illustrandum pertinent quam ad movendam
admirationem. Quid, obsecro, sibi vult aliud Cupido in Ascanium?[380] quid Mercurius totiens e coelo in terras missus, nisi ut
qui legunt admiratione impleantur? Parum profecto, parum
erat utique Maroni tempestatem describere, quae per se ipsa

and:

> But after I attacked the third branches
> with a greater effort. [*Aeneid* 3.37–38]

And so, Prassicio, I entirely and to the highest degree approve of the case you have made on this whole question, and since we are speaking of admiration or wonder — not to get away from cognate words — I approve of it wonderfully, too. So go on to the rest.

Paolo. To be sure, poets seek admiration, that is, approval and a   92 certain applause for what is said, to the admiration of the minds of their hearers and readers. The point is demonstrated above all, Pardo, by the two elements you have touched upon, events and words, since neither are the events themselves of the kind that historians relate nor do the poets always deal with common or simple words. Indeed, in almost every case they summon the embellishment and greatness and elegance for actions from elsewhere, namely from fiction. For example, when Vergil was going to write about the burning of Aeneas' ships, he invented what we read about Cybele, about Jupiter, about the transformation of the ships into nymphs:

> when in the form of the same number of maidens —
> an amazing wonder — they come back in sight and course
> over the sea. [*Aeneid* 9.120, 122]

So that the things they say might appear greater and more wonderful, they transfer human qualities to the gods, invent marvels, send dreams, even change gods into men. The similes, too, which they use very often, are designed as much to excite admiration as to explain and illustrate. What else, I ask you, is meant by Cupid turned into Ascanius, what by Mercury so often sent to earth from the sky, unless to fill readers with admiration? It was not enough indeed, not enough for Maro in any case, to describe the tempest, which by itself was certainly great

magna quidem erat atque horribilis, sed Iunonis ad Aeolum,
sed Aeoli ad Iunonem allocutiones admirabilem multo maxime
eam faciunt, ventorum ipsorum deo illam exciente. Itaque into-
nantur magis quam dicuntur illa:

> cavum conversa cuspide montem
> impulit in latus, ac venti, velut agmine facto,
> qua data porta, ruunt et terras turbine perflant.

Quid excogitatius ad conciliandam admirationem? Re autem
vera Aeneas a Lacinio, Calabriae promontorio, sacris Iunoni rite
prius persolutis, solvens, quo praeterita Sicilia ad oras Latinorum classem appelleret, fuit a tempestatibus Drepanum perlatus; videte, obsecro, quibus veritatem commentis concinnaverit,
quo admirabiliora cuncta redderet. Verba autem ipsa poetae
quique vere dicuntur poetae non solum simul compangunt aut
ea novant, ut *mare velivolum*, ut *silvas comantes*, horum ipsorum
quae nunc a me dicuntur gratia, verum ea transferunt, nec verba
tantum, sed orationem persaepe omnem. Quin etiam et exces-
sum et superlationem iis persaepe adiiciunt a natura penitus
recedentes, ut:

> praeruptus aquae mons,

et:

> vastos tollunt ad sidera[381] fluctus,

et:

> Tollimur in coelum sullato gurgite et iidem
> subducta ad Manes imos descendimus unda.[382]

Nec vero tenorem hunc comparandae admirationis in gravio-
ribus ac seriis tantum servant rebus, verum in iis quoque in

and terrible; but the speeches of Juno to Aeolus, of Aeolus to Juno, make it most admirable by far, with the god of the winds himself producing the storm. And so these words are thundered rather than spoken:

> turning his spear, he struck the side
> of the hollow mountain; and the winds, as in a battle line,
> rush through the open gate and blow over the lands in a
> whirling tempest. [*Aeneid* 1.81–83]

What could be more designed to win admiration? But in fact Aeneas, his offerings to Juno first duly made, and setting sail from Lacinium, the promontory of Calabria, to skirt Sicily and land his fleet on the shores of the Latins, was borne by storms to Drepanum.[366] See, if you please, with what inventions he has touched up the truth in order to make everything more worthy of admiration. Moreover, poets deserving of the name not only make compound words or use them in new ways, like "sail-winged sea" or "shaggy forests" to achieve the effects I am talking about, but also use them in a figurative sense — and not just words but very often a whole passage.[367] Indeed, they very often even add digression and hyperbole to them, departing entirely from nature. Thus:

> a sheer mountain of water [*Aeneid* 1.105]

and:

> they raise great waves to the stars [*Aeneid* 1.86]

and:

> we are raised to the sky by the whirlpool beneath and
> descend to the lowest shades when the wave is carried away.
> [*Aeneid* 3.564–65]

And indeed they observe this process of winning admiration not only in matters that are important and serious, but also in

quibus lectorum atque auditorum delectatio voluptasque sola quaeritur, ut:

Ambrosiaeque comae divinum vertice odorem
spiravere,

et:

fotum gremio dea tollit in altos
Idaliae lucos, ubi mollis amaracus illum
floribus et dulci aspirans complectitur umbra.

Singulis pene e verbis Venerisque e gestibus gignitur virtus haec de qua nobis est nunc quaestio, quam et in docendo et in movendo nec minus in delectando assequi poetae omni arte studioque contendunt. Tu vero quid adhaec, Parde? Nam et gravitatem hic tuam et iudicandi pondus requirimus.

93 *Pard.* Ego quidem, Paule Prassici,[383] censeo te assecutum quod disputatione hac quaeris, ipsis et rationibus et exemplis, quae duo non in disciplinis modo, verum etiam in vita agenda moribusque probandis et laudis et testificationis secum vim auctoritatemque omnem ferunt. Coeterum, quoniam a Sincero de poetis sermo coepit,[384] ut ab eo quoque desinat, reliqua siqua sunt, ab illo potius sciscitare. Quin, ut video surrexisse eum iam, interrogandi te labore liberabit.

Act. Equidem, Parde, dicenti Paulo[385] sic assentior, ut semper existimaverim in quacunque ad dicendum suscepta materia atque in dicendi quoque genere magnitudinem sullimitatemque ipsam poetae esse propriam, nunquam mediocritate contentam, quod Virgilii agricultura docere plane potest; utque implere generosos illos spiritus quacunque ratione poetae valeant, coelestes etiam res mortalium rebus inseruisse eos refersisseque

those where the sole object is the delight and pleasure of readers and hearers. Thus:

> The immortal locks on her head breathed out a fragrance
> divine [*Aeneid* 1.403–4]

and:

> the goddess carries him close in her bosom
> to the high groves of Idalia, where the soft marjoram
>   breathes
> fragrance and surrounds him with flowers and sweet shade.
>   [*Aeneid* 1.692–94]

Almost every single word and almost every movement of Venus
creates the special excellence we are talking about, which poets
strive to attain through description and stirring emotions as
well as through giving pleasure, doing so with all their art and
zeal. What do you say to this, Pardo? We require your authority and weighty judgment on this point.

Pardo. For my part, Paolo Prassicio, I believe that you have   93
achieved your goal in this discussion with both reasoning and
examples, two elements that bring with them the full force and
authority of praise and testimony not only in the disciplines but
also in leading one's life and judging character. But the conversation about poets began with Sincero; so that it should end
with him, too, if there are any remaining points, you should ask
him instead. In fact, since I see that he has already stood up, he
will save you the trouble of asking.

Azio. Indeed, Pardo, I agree with what Paolo says, just as I have
always thought that, regardless of the material chosen for expression and the style of expressing it, the special quality of the
poet is a greatness and sublimity never content with a middle
course — a point that Vergil's poem on farming can clearly demonstrate. And that poets might attain those noble qualities in
every possible way, they have even inserted divine matters into

carmen suum commentis atque fabulis, quibus ipsa sullimitas ad summum usque, hoc est ad admirationem incresceret; hocque illud esse quod paulo ante dicebatur, alia quadam lingua locutos. Nam cum oratoriae sit mediocritas aequabilitasque illa quidem dicendi, siquando magnitudinem assumptura est aliquam, per poeticae vagatur atque exultat campos, ut cognatae facultatis sibique finitimae; qua in re Cicero e nostris eminuit. Nam historia, ubi magnifica esse vult, ubi heroica videri ac grandis, et figuras et verba de poetis mutuatur. Qua de re multa et erudite et graviter disseruisse mihi visi estis. Coeterum tanta rerum arcessitarum copia, tantus etiam verborum ornatus, tanta et rerum et verborum sullimitas ut desit necesse est, implendae tubae cantuque Maeonio, ni fabulosa commenta affatim ea suppeditent verbaque fabulosis apta rebus illisque explicandis idonea. Hinc:

Aeris in campis latis.

Hinc:

cavum conversa cuspide montem;

Ac:[386]

Tuba terribilem sonitum procul aere canoro intonuit.[387]

An non audientibus nobis illa capillus ipse surrigitur animusque concutitur et pene horrescit?

At iuveni oranti subito tremor occupat artus,
diriguere oculi: tot Erinnis[388] sibilat hydris,
tantaque se facies aperit; tum flammea torquens
lumina cunctantem et quaerentem dicere plura

the affairs of mortals and stuffed their poetry with inventions and fables, whereby that sublimity might advance to the highest point—to admiration. This is the idea that was stated a little earlier: that they have spoken almost in another language.[368] Indeed, since moderation and uniformity of style are characteristic of oratory, whenever it means to take on some greatness, it roams and gambols through the fields of poetry as a kindred and neighboring faculty; and among our writers Cicero is preeminent in this. Indeed, history, when it wants to be great, when it wants to seem heroic and lofty, borrows both figures and words from the poets. Concerning this matter I think you have treated many points with both learning and authority. Still, such an abundance of added material, such great embellishment of language, such sublimity of both matter and language is necessarily lacking, as are the trumpets to be filled with Maeonian song, unless these things are sufficiently provided by fictitious inventions and words suited to fabulous matters and capable of treating them.[369] Hence:

in the broad fields of air. [*Aeneid* 6.887]

Hence:

the hollow mountain with his reversed spear [*Aeneid* 1.81]

and:

the trumpet with ringing bronze thundered
its terrible call afar. [*Aeneid* 9.503–4]

Or when we hear the following lines does our hair not stand on end, and our heart beat fast and almost quake with fear?

But a sudden trembling seized the young man's limbs as he
spoke;
his eyes grew fixed: the Fury hissed with so many snakes,
and her shape grew so large; then rolling her flaming eyes,
she drove him back, as he hesitated and tried to say more,

reppulit et geminos erexit crinibus angues
verberaque insonuit.

94   Itaque dum poetae haec ipsa et fingunt et ficta suaviter,
magnifice admirabiliterque loquuntur, alios ipsi eloqui docuere.
Nam imitati eos postea qui causas egere, qui in senatu de ca-
piendis consiliis disseruere, qui res gestas memoriae mandavere,
eloquentiam perfecerunt solutam illam ac vagantem. Quo fit ut
omne dicendi genus a poetica manaverit. Nam et primi docto-
rum omnium cum extiterint poetae, omnia quoque carmine ac
numeris sunt complexi; testisque horum omnium est Homerus,
qui quantum ubique dicendo valeat et suspiciunt docti et admi-
rantur indocti. Ab hoc philosophi, ab hoc physici, ab hoc et
rhetores facultatis suae praecepta et aucupati sunt et auspicati.
Solon quas Atheniensibus[389] tradebat leges carmine auspicatus
legitur; cumque ipse stultitiam simulasset, legendis ac recitan-
dis in publico versibus quos de Salamine bello revendicanda
scripserat, Pisistrato optimatibusque omnibus collaudantibus,
cives traxit ad abdicandam legem quae populi totius suffragio
constituta fuerat, ne cui unquam de ea re mentionem facere li-
ceret ne ve ad populum ferre idque capitale esse. Itaque et de-
cretum factum est et Solon ipse belli dux delectus; tantum carmine illo suo valuit. Romanorum rex Numa, versibus a se de
diis deque deorum rebus compositis iisque in sacris publicis ac
ludis rite decantatis, ferocissimam gentem, dum id assiduus
agit, ad mores humaniores transtulit cultumque dei maiorem.

Aperuit rerum naturam generi hominum carmine suo Empedocles, sideralis disciplinae Dorotheus Sidonius, quos Latine

and she raised up two snakes from her hair
and cracked her whip. [*Aeneid* 7.446–51]

And so while poets invented these things and uttered their   94
inventions pleasingly, splendidly, and admirably, they taught
others to speak eloquently. Afterward, in imitating them, those
who pled cases, those who argued in the senate about making
resolutions, and those who committed great deeds to the historical record perfected discursive eloquence in prose. So it
happens that every style had its origin in poetry. Indeed, since
of all learned men it was the poets who appeared first, they also
expressed everything in verse and rhythm, and the proof of all
this is Homer. Both the learned esteem him and the ignorant
marvel at him because in all circumstances he is so powerful in
his utterance. From him the philosophers, the natural philosophers, and the rhetoricians have sought out and inaugurated the
rules of their discipline. One reads that it was with poetry that
Solon began the laws he handed down to the Athenians.[370]
When he had feigned madness, by reading and reciting in public the verses he had written about laying claim to Salamis by
war, winning the praise of Pisistratus and the whole aristocratic
party, he persuaded the citizens to reject the law that had been
established by the vote of the entire populace that no one
should be allowed to mention the matter or bring it to the
people on pain of death.[371] Accordingly, the decree was passed
and Solon himself was chosen to lead the war; so much did he
accomplish with that poem of his. The Roman king Numa,
composing verses about the gods and religious matters and duly
chanting them in public sacrifices and games, by constant repetition brought a fierce people to more civilized conduct and
greater worship of the god.

Empedocles revealed the nature of the universe to mankind
in his poetry, Dorotheus of Sidon the nature of astrology in

imitati Lucretius ac Manilius. Christe optime, quid copiae, quid ornatus, quantus e clarissimis luminibus eius emicat in altero splendor! Rapit quo vult lectorem, probat ad quod intendit, summa cum subtilitate et artificio, hortatur, deterret, incitat, retrahit, demum omnia cum magnitudine, ubi opus est, atque decoro, et hac de qua disputatum est admiratione, ut expurgatis rudioribus illis vetustatis numeris, quibus postea Virgilius Romanam illustravit poeticam nihil omnino defuisse videatur. Alteri vero in Astronomicis, siquid ornatus[390] poeticoque defuit decori, additum nuper ac suffectum a nostro est sene, de cuius Urania, ut arbitror, iudicabunt posteri fortasse liberius, quod, certo scio, de ea sentient minus invidenter.

Quibus igitur verbis aut quo nam ore gestuque assurgemus poeticae? Quae princeps de deo et disseruit et eius laudes cecinit, instituitque sacra, unde primi poetae sacerdotes vocati, verbisque eum placavit et cantibus, docuitque habere rerum humanarum curam, benigneque cum probis agere, excandescenter[391] cum improbis. Haec prima excitavit ad virtutem homines, dum animae immortalitatem profitetur, haec e terris piorum animos in coelum devexit,[392] impiorum detrusit in Tartara; haec bonis tandem praemia retribuit, malos poenis postremisque insecuta est cruciatibus. Salve igitur, doctrinarum omnium mater foecundissima; salve iterum! Tu enim mortalitati occurristi inventorum ac scriptorum tuorum perpetuitate; tu e silvis homines eruisti atque e speluncis. Per te noscimus, per te praeterita ante oculos cernimus, per te deum sapimus religionemque retinemus ac pietatem deoque ipsi accepti supernam etiam in sedem ab eo evocamur arasque cum ipso meremur et templa.

his; and Lucretius and Manilius imitated them in Latin.[372] Good Christ! What abundance, what embellishment, what great brilliance flashes from his most striking figures in the case of the former! He sweeps the reader along where he wishes, he proves the case he wants to make; with the greatest subtlety and art he urges, terrifies, rouses, calls back—everything, finally, with greatness and propriety where required, and inspiring the admiration we have been talking about, so that once they were cleansed of rough archaic qualities, nothing at all seems lacking to the rhythms with which Vergil later gave glory to Roman poetry. But for the latter poet, any defects of ornament and poetic decorum in the *Astronomica* have recently been supplied and corrected by our old man, whose *Urania*, I think, posterity will perhaps judge more frankly because, I am sure, they will think of it with less envy.[373]

With what words or expression and gesture shall we honor poetry? It first discoursed on god and sang his praises, and established his sacred rites, from which the first poets were called priests, and it placated him with words and song, and taught that he cares for human affairs, deals kindly with the righteous, wrathfully with the wicked. Poetry first roused men to virtue since it proclaims the immortality of the soul; it has carried the souls of the pious from earth to the sky, thrust those of the wicked into Tartarus; in short, it has repaid the good with rewards, pursued the wicked with punishment and the most terrible torments. So hail, most fertile mother of every kind of learning, again hail![374] You have counteracted mortality with the permanence of your inventions and writings; you have brought mankind out of the forests and caves. Through you we gain knowledge, through you we perceive the past before our eyes, through you we know god, hold on to reverence and piety, and if we are acceptable to god we are called by him to the celestial seat and with him we deserve altars and temples.

Pud. Peregregie quidem, Acti, et pie et sancte, imo et recte admodum, ut, sicuti a religione sermo coepit tuus, in religione quoque idem desinat, quodque fervor perfractus est iam canicularis vocamurque familiaribus a negociis, solventes conventum hunc, et feliciter abeamus et recte valeamus omnes.

Puderico. Excellently you have spoken, to be sure, Azio, and piously and reverently, and indeed very correctly, so that just as your discussion began with religion, it also ends in religion; and because now the heat of the dog days is broken and we are called by our domestic affairs, dissolving this gathering, let us depart auspiciously and all fare well.

P. Summontius Francisco Puderico patritio Neapolitano S. D.

1 Persuasit mihi auctoritas tua, Francisce Puderice, ut Pontani *Actium* secunda hac excusione potissimum ederem, rarum sane de numeris poeticis et lege historiae dialogum. Nam cum illius opera tam multa sint et ea aeque egregia omnia, hinc mihi hoc, hinc illud edendum prius occurrebat, fiebatque ut difficilis redderetur electio propter pulchritudinis paritatem. Sed cum postea tecum sentire Suardinum Suardum Pontani nostri familiarissimum audirem, currentem quasi me doctus vir et gravis incitavit. Quam quidem sententiam eo libentius secutus sum quod, cum superiori foetura carmina praecesserint, exornandi postea et carminis ratio quae hoc volumine traditur subsequi debebat;[1] digna profecto investigatio, quae ad communem hominum utilitatem quam primum omnibus nota esset. Non enim ab aliquo fortasse grammatico de re poetica deque historica disputatur, sed ab illo praecipitur Ioviano Pontano, cuius quidem in utroque genere post tot annorum depravationem nova quaedam admirandaque apparet felicitas, ut non iniuria saepe a te illud usurpatum sit, coepisse eum, ut de Christo Optimo Maximo dicitur, et facere pariter et docere.

2 Nec vero mihi dubium est quin iucundum tibi futurum sit officium meum. Nam praeterquam quod Actii Synceri[2] loquens persona, a quo opus hoc denominatur, non parum te pro veteri amicitia delectabit, tuae quoque hic tibi sunt partes, nec res ipsa tota

APPENDIX I

Summonte's Dedication to the Actius

Pietro Summonte to the noble Neapolitan Francesco Puderico[1]

Your encouragement, Francesco Puderico, has convinced me in 1
this second publication to publish Pontano's *Actius* most of all—a
truly remarkable dialogue on poetic rhythms and the law of history.[2] Indeed, since his works are so numerous and every one of
them is equally outstanding, formerly one or another would occur
to me to be published for this reason or that, and it was hard to
make a choice because they were equally fine. But when I heard
afterward that Suardo Suardino, our Pontano's trusted close
friend, agreed with you, the eminent and learned man spurred me
on like a willing horse.[3] I have been the more pleased to follow
this advice because, with the poetry coming first in the earlier publication, it was appropriate for the account of poetic embellishment related in this volume to follow close behind. The inquiry is
undoubtedly worthy of being known as soon as possible to everyone for the general advantage of mankind. Indeed, it is not a discussion of poetics and history by some grammarian or other but
instruction by the famous Gioviano Pontano whose particular
new and wonderful felicity in both genres makes its appearance,
after the corruption of so many years, so that you have often
rightly used of him what is said of Christ, greatest and best, that
he began to act and to teach at the same time.[4]

I have every confidence that my undertaking will be pleasing to 2
you. In addition to the fact that the speaking role of Azio Sincero,[5] for whom the work is named, will delight you because of
your longstanding friendship, you have a role here too, and the
whole subject is especially pertinent to you since you have always

de qua agitur non in primis ad te pertinet, cum poeticae concinnitatis, cuius maxime ferax est Pontaniana[3] Academia, semper ipse et studiosus observator fueris et censor acerrimus vixque summis, ut ita dixerim, naribus, adeo omni de carmine exacte iudices, ut merito te omnes emunctae naris hominem, ut ait Horatius, appellent. Par in historiis censura est tua, quarum tenacissimam in te videmus memoriam et gravitatem simul in te tantam, modo refellendis fabulosis, modo veris comprobandis comparandisque scriptoribus ipsis, nemo est nostrum qui non admiretur. Quo fit ut omni e parte iucunda tibique maxime propria haec sit prorsus lectio futura.

3   Tuum igitur tibi *Actium* habe, libroque hoc et Synceri ipsius optato e Galliis reditu, quod facis, magis magisque laetare. Nam ut omittam summam eius in Pontani scripta pietatem, quae post illius obitum sopita ac neglecta e tenebris primus in lucem tum Francisci Aelii consilio tum opera usus mea revocavit, advexit nuper ex Heduorum usque finibus atque e Turonibus dona quaedam mirum in modum placitura literatis viris, Martialis, Ausonii et Solini codices, novae atque incognitae emendationis tamque a nostris diversos, ut hos certo ac legitimo partu natos, reliquos vero liceat spurios existimare. Praetereo epigrammata, quae tam multa hic leguntur, alibi hactenus non visa. Imo Solini liber hic auctore ab ipso, quod iam titulus indicat, nec eius negat vetustas, et recognitus est et editus. Is etiam ad nos attulit Ovidii fragmentum *De piscibus*, Grattii poetae *Cynegeticon*, cuius meminit Ovidius ultima *De Ponto* elegia, *Cynegeticon* item Aurelii Nemesiani, qui floruit sub Numeriano imperatore, et Rutilii Namatiani *Elegos*, quorum tenuitatem et elegantiam e seculo illo agnoscas Claudiani. Atque haec quidem omnia statim post Pontani libros emittentur.

been a studious observer and keen judge of elegant poetic style in which the Academia Pontaniana is especially fruitful, and you form your opinion of each poem so precisely (not with the tip of your nose so to speak) that everyone rightly calls you a man "of clear nostrils," as Horace says.[6] You have equal discrimination in history, in which we see in you both the most retentive memory and at the same time such great authority, now in refuting fables, now in confirming facts and comparing the writers themselves, that every one of us regards you with admiration. Accordingly, this will certainly be a text pleasing and particularly appropriate for you in every respect.

So take your *Actius*, and in this book and in the longed-for re- 3 turn of Sincero himself from France rejoice more and more, as you do.[7] For to say nothing of his extreme piety with regard to the works of Pontano, which lay dormant and neglected after his death and which he was the first to call back from the darkness into the light, relying both on the counsel of Francesco Elio and on my own efforts,[8] recently he has brought back all the way from the territory of the Aedui and from the Turones gifts that will bring wonderful pleasure to learned men: manuscripts of Martial, Ausonius, and Solinus of a new and unparalleled state of correction, and so different from ours that one may regard them as of certain and legitimate descent, and the rest as spurious.[9] I pass over the epigrams, which are read in such numbers here, but have not been seen elsewhere up to now.[10] But the text of Solinus, as its title indicates (nor does its antiquity deny it), was both corrected and promulgated by the author himself.[11] He has also brought us a fragment of Ovid's *De piscibus*, the *Cynegeticon* of the poet Grattius mentioned by Ovid in the last elegy of *De ponto*, also the *Cynegeticon* of Aurelius Nemesianus, who flourished under the emperor Numerianus, and the *Elegies* of Rutilius Namatianus, whose delicacy and elegance you would identify with the age of Claudian.[12] And all these, indeed, will be published at once after the

Non ne applaudendum iure fuit redeunti Actio nostro, veluti novo rei literariae Camillo? Non ne gestanda et illi ob cives servatos merito querna? Adde exquisitissima Actii ipsius, quibus iunior lusit, partim lyrica, partim elegiaca nostro etiam charactere propediem excudenda cumque his novas illas piscatorio genere *Eclogas*, denique divinum de Christo opus, cui summam nunc imponere decrevit manum; ut post nescio quos Sedulios et Prudentios, in quibus pene nihil praeter nudam religionem invenias, Marones tandem Christianos habeamus. Quocirca triste Pontani desiderium Actii nostri vita pensemus, ac laetemur potius benigno agi fato cum patria nostra, cui nunquam fere Pontanus aliquis videatur defuturus.

4   Illius itaque nomine illustrati tantoque instituti magistro congratulemur nobis, cuius praeter aeterna librorum monumenta ea quoque fuerint in literis, dum vixit, exempla, ea consilia, ea doctrinae communicatio, ut perfacilem aliis eo perveniendi viam ostenderit, quo sine aliquo duce felix ipse pervenit. O praestantis ingenii et doctrinae virum! O de temporibus nostris optime meritum et per quem non invidemus antiquitati! Clamantem te non temere toties audivi, Puderice, ut qui ab Errico patre ad eum puer deductus eoque semper familiarissime usus probe hominem nosses: 'Aspicite vivum hunc, amici, dum licet; huius, dum licet, aspectu exaturate oculos; non multos dabitur intueri Pontanos.' Quam verum tuum illud iudicium fuit! Etenim eius ingenium penitus qui perspicit iure illum optimo alteram quasi naturam appellabit, quippe, ut alia taceam, in describendis informandisque rebus ita illum vides quodcumque proponit absolvere, ita perficere undique,

books of Pontano.[13] Does our Azio not deserve to be applauded on his return, like a new Camillus of literature?[14] Has he not earned the right to wear an oak-leaf crown for saving his fellow citizens?[15] Add the most exquisite poetry of Azio himself: the playful youthful efforts, some lyric, some elegiac, soon to be printed also with our type, and along with them the new eclogues of the kind concerned with fishing, and finally, the divine work on Christ, on which he has now resolved to put the final touches, so that after all the Seduliuses and Prudentiuses, in which you find nothing but naked piety, at last we have Christian Vergils.[16] Thus let us compensate for the grievous loss of Pontano with the life of our Azio and let us rejoice the more gladly that fate has dealt kindly with our homeland, which seems destined almost never to lack a Pontano.

And so, given luster by his renown and instructed by so great a   4
teacher, let us congratulate ourselves, since in addition to the eternal monuments of his books, there were also in his letters as long as he lived such examples, such counsel, such imparting of learning that he showed others an easy way to reach the place where he himself had successfully arrived without a guide. How outstanding the man was in intellect and learning! How fine a benefactor to our time, and one on account of whom we do not envy antiquity! How often, Puderico, have I heard you exclaim with good reason, because you knew the man well (you had been brought to him as a boy by your father Enrico[17] and were always on the most familiar terms with him): "Look at this man alive, friends, while you may; while you may, sate your eyes with the sight of him; you won't have many Pontanos to gaze upon."[18] How well founded was your opinion! Indeed, anyone who thoroughly examines his genius will rightly call him almost a second Nature, since, to pass over the rest, you see that in representing and shaping things, he so accomplishes, so brings to perfection from every point of view, whatever he proposes that you would say that nothing is missing from ei-

ut nihil tanquam integro corpori singulisve membris deesse dicas. Quod si comparatio sit de eo facienda, multos, qui opponendi tanto viro fortasse videantur, cultos illos quidem et elegantes, aridos tandem invenias ac steriles. Hunc vero in summo cultu splendoreque huberrimum, foecundissimum, nulla in re non profluentem suspicias, hunc Natura ab ipsa raro exemplo creatum existimes, quique ingenii magnitudine nulli omnino cesserit antiquorum. Hinc tentandi omnia Pontani illa felix audacia. Genus autem dicendi, in quo maxime aetas nostra decipitur, ita ad antiquorum imitationem effinxit, ut nihil te in eo peregrinum offendat, nihil conquisitum, utque ipse dicere solebat, violatum, sed unum quodque plane Romanum videatur. Quo magis ridenda censeo quorundam iudicia de tanto viro parum pie loquentium, qui hoc ipso nullius se omnino iudicii arguunt, quod Iovianam sublimitatem non cognoverunt.

5   Verum ut ad editionis huius rationem redeam (illius enim laudes quis enumeret?), non omiserim hoc loco id quod in eiusdem quoque carminibus feci quodque tu mecum saepius egisti, omnes qui haec legent admonere prius, et per Ioviani manes obtestari, ut, habita praemortui ratione, aequos se in his iudices praebeant, quae cum non nullis aliis nostra posthac opera edendis non dum ab illo fuerint emendata. Sed quid ego nunc exorare quemquam hac in parte studiosius laborem, cum Pontanus, ut spero, ipse per se satis omnino sit unicuique superque facturus? Quod vero ad me attinet, qui huius rei curam tam libenter suscipiam, non verebor, quod gravissimus vir Actius Syncerus iam pridem de me scripsit, epistolae huic carmen subnectere. An placere mihi dissimulaverim pietatis erga amicos nomine probari? Liceat itaque

ther the body as a whole or its individual members. But if a comparison should be made in regard to him, many people — indeed cultivated and elegant ones — who could conceivably be weighed against such a great man, you would find to be dry and uninspired in the end. But you would look up to this man, most copious in style and brilliance, of most fertile invention, fluent in every detail; you would think that this man had been created by Nature herself on a rare pattern and as one who in greatness of talent would come in second to none of the ancients. Hence Pontano's fortunate boldness in attempting everything. Oratorical style especially frustrates our age; he so fashioned it in imitation of the ancients that nothing in it strikes you as foreign, nothing strained, and, as he used to say, "spoiled"; but every single detail seems completely Roman. For this reason I consider more laughable the opinions of certain people who speak of such a great man with too little respect — people who convict themselves of a complete lack of taste precisely because they fail to recognize the sublimity of Gioviano.

But to get back to the matter of this edition (for who could list 5 the praises of that man?), in this place I should not omit what I have done also in the case of his poetry and what you have very often talked about with me: to urge all future readers in advance and to beseech them by the spirit of Gioviano to take his premature death into account and to show themselves fair-minded judges in dealing with these works, since, along with some others to be published later by our efforts, they had not yet been corrected by him. But why should I now work too hard to persuade anyone on this point, since Pontano himself, as I expect, will have attended to every detail by himself enough and to spare? As for myself, since I so willingly undertake the care of this matter, I will not be afraid to attach to this letter the poem that the eminent Azio Sincero wrote about me some time ago. Or should I hide my pleasure in being approved for my piety to my friends? I hope that I may

mihi non immeritam fortasse mercedem hanc exigere laboris mei.
Vale.

6   EX LIBRO EPIGRAMMATUM ACTII SYNCERI:

Excitat obstrictas tumulis Summontius umbras,
    Impleat ut sanctae munus amicitiae,
Utque prius vivos sic et post fata sodales
    Observat, tristes et sedet ante rogos.
5 Nec tantum violas cineri ac bene olentia ponit
    Serta, sed et lacrimis irrigat ossa piis.
Parva loquor, cultis reparat monumenta libellis,
    Cum possint longam saxa timere diem.
At tu, vivaci quae fulcis nomina fama,
10   Poscenti gratas, Musa, repende vices,
Ut quoniam dulces optat sic vivere amicos,
    Vivat et in libris sit sacer ille meis.

be allowed to ask this as a not undeserved reward for my toil. Farewell.

From the book of *Epigrams* of Azio Sincero:[19]   6

Summonte raises shades confined in their tombs
to fulfill the sacred duty of friendship,
and cares for his friends after death as before
while they lived, and lingers beside their sad pyres.
On their ashes he sets violets and sweet-smelling   5
garlands; with pious tears he moistens their bones.
Not only this. He refashions their monuments
with learned books since stones can dread the passage of time.
But you, Muse, who support renown with long-living fame,
repay one who requires a grateful return,   10
so that, since he wants his dear friends to live in this way,
he too may live on and be blessed in my books.

APPENDIX II

Interlocutors in Actius

ALTILIO, GABRIELE (Gabriel Altilius, ca. 1440–1501), interlocutor in *Actius* and *Asinus*. Altilio, bishop of Policastro, was a distinguished poet as well as the tutor and later political secretary of Ferrandino. Pontano used his name for one of the warriors in the epic in *Antonius* (metrum xi.8). He is a dedicatee of *De magnificentia*, the addressee of *Baiae* 1.25, and mentioned in *Baiae* 1.10. Pontano laments his death in *Tumuli* 1.18 and *Aegidius*. Galateo dedicated *De podagra* to him in honor of his gout. See F. Nicolini, "Altilio, Gabriele," *DBI* 2 (1960): 565–67; Minieri Riccio, *Biografie*, 43–56; Altamura, *L'Umanesimo*, 51–53.

AZIO (Azio Sincero, Actius Sincerus, Jacopo Sannazaro, 1456–1530), interlocutor in *Actius* and *Asinus*. His absence is regretted in *Aegidius*, and he is mentioned in Summonte's dedication of *Actius*, 2–3 and 6. Sannazaro, a Neapolitan aristocrat, was one of the most important poets of his age in both Latin and Italian. Along with Pontano, he took part in the negotiations between King Ferrante and Innocent VIII during the Second Barons' Revolt; after the French conquest of Naples, he accompanied King Federico into his exile in France. Together with Caracciolo, Marchese, and Tomacelli (q.v.), he oversaw the transfer of many of Pontano's books to the library of San Domenico Maggiore in Naples in 1505 (Pèrcopo, *Vita di Giovanni Pontano*, 313–14); and he took part in the sodality's project of printing Pontano's works. Pontano used his name for one of the warriors in the epic in *Antonius* (metrum xi.20–45). He is the dedicatee of *De liberalitate* and the addressee of *Baiae* 1.11; his name is given to a shepherd in *Eclogue* 3, and he is quoted in *De sermone* 6.2.7–8 and 6.4.16. See Minieri Riccio, *Biografie*, 490–516; L. Gualdo Rosa in Arnaldi et al., *Poeti latini del Quattrocento*, 1101–2.

COMPATRE, PIETRO (Petrus Compater, Pietro Golino, 1431–1501), interlocutor in *Antonius* and *Actius*. Compatre held various offices under the

Aragonese dynasty. Like Tomacelli (q.v.), he was one of Pontano's oldest friends. Pontano used his name for one of the warriors in the epic in *Antonius* (metrum xi.46–54). He is the dedicatee of *Tumuli* 1 and 2 and of *Commentationes super centum sententiis Ptolemaei*. He is mentioned in *Parthenopeus* 1.26, addressed in *Baiae* 1.9 and 1.10, and addressed jointly with Tomacelli in *Baiae* 1.1 and 2.28. He is mentioned with Tomacelli in the dedication and conclusion of *De aspiratione*, and he appears in a vignette in *De sermone* 4.3.36 that also features Tomacelli and Summonte (q.v.). Pontano mourns his death in *Tumuli* 2.19 and *Aegidius*. See Liliana Monti Sabia in Arnaldi et al., *Poeti latini del Quattrocento*, 528–29; Altamura, *L'Umanesimo*, 56–57.

GOLINO. See Compatre.

MARCHESE, FRANCESCO ELIO (also Aelius, Haelius, 1430/35–1517), interlocutor in *Aegidius*; mentioned in Summonte's dedication of *Actius*, 3. Marchese, Neapolitan by birth, moved between Naples and Rome and was a member of the academies of both Pomponio and Pontano. (He was awarded the academy name Haelius, or Aelius, in Pomponio's academy.) Together with Caracciolo, Sannazaro, and Tomacelli (q.v.), he oversaw the transfer of many of Pontano's books to the library of San Domenico Maggiore in Naples in 1505 (Pèrcopo, *Vita di Giovanni Pontano*, 313–14); and he took part in the sodality's project of printing Pontano's works. He is the addressee of *Hendecasyllabi* 1.10 and *Eridanus* 2.1, his tomb is described in *Tumuli* 2.12, and he is quoted in *De sermone* 6.2.1–3. See C. Bianca, "Marchese, Francesco Elio," *DBI* 69 (2007): 564–66; Monti Sabia, "La mano del Pontano in due Livii," 103 n. 1.

PAOLO. See Prassicio.

PARDO, GIOVANNI (Ioannes Pardus, d. 1512?), interlocutor in *Actius*, *Aegidius*, and *Asinus*. Pardo, a Spanish priest, was a scholar and a poet as well as a secretary in the royal chancellery. He is praised as a Peripatetic philosopher in *De fortuna* 2.19.1. His name is used for one of the warriors in the epic in *Antonius* (metrum ix.135). He is the dedicatee of *De rebus coelestibus* 3 and *De conviventia* and the addressee of *Eridanus* 1.31 and *Baiae* 2.6 and 2.23; he is quoted in *De sermone* 1.30.3 and 5.2.49. He was a great

friend of Cariteo (Benet Gareth), who refers to his poetry; see *Le rime di Benedetto Gareth detto il Chariteo*, ed. E. Pèrcopo (Naples, 1892), ccxiv, referring to canzone 10.53–60. See Minieri Riccio, *Biografie*, 12–16; Altamura, *L'Umanesimo*, 58–59; Tateo, ed., *De fortuna*, 124, n. 60.

PETO, FRANCESCO (Franciscus Poetus, ca. 1475/80–after 1531), interlocutor in *Aegidius* and tentatively added by Summonte in Vat. lat. 2843 as a mute character in *Actius* (see Note on the Text). Peto, from Fondi, was a latecomer to the Neapolitan sodality, like Suardino Suardo (q.v.). Together with Suardino, he is the dedicatee of Summonte's edition of *Asinus* (Pontano 1507). Pontano quotes him in *De sermone* 6.2.9. See L. Miletti, "Peto, Francesco," *DBI* 82 (2015): 665–67; Minieri Riccio, *Biografie*, 16–18.

PIETRO. See Summonte.

PRASSICIO, PAOLO (Paulus Prassitius, d. around 1511), interlocutor in *Actius*. Prassicio, descended from a patrician family, was a canon of the cathedral of Aversa and enjoyed a reputation as a philosopher. See Minieri Riccio, *Biografie*, 162–63.

PUCCI, FRANCESCO (Franciscus Puccius, 1463–1512), interlocutor in *Aegidius* and originally included by Pontano in Vat. lat. 5984 as a mute character in *Actius* (see Note on the Text). Pucci, an early pupil of Angelo Poliziano, arrived in Naples in 1485 or 1486, becoming a professor in the university and a librarian of the royal library. His name is used for one of the warriors in the epic in *Antonius* (metrum xi.129–34). He is the dedicatee of *Baiae* 2.9, and he is mentioned in *Baiae* 2.25; he is quoted in *De sermone* 4.3.38 and 6.2.4–5. See Monti Sabia in Arnaldi et al., *Poeti latini del Quattrocento*, 646–47; Monti Sabia, "La mano del Summonte," 248; Mario Santoro, *Uno scolaro del Poliziano a Napoli: Francesco Pucci* (Naples, 1948).

PUDERICO, FRANCESCO (Franciscus Pudericus, d. 1528), interlocutor in *Actius* and *Aegidius*. Puderico, a Neapolitan aristocrat, was a devoted admirer of Pontano, having been brought to him as a boy for instruction by his father, Enrico (an interlocutor in *Antonius*). He is the dedicatee of Summonte's edition of *Actius* (Pontano 1507), appropriately, since he was

a highly respected student of poetry as well as a friend of Sannazaro, who had him read *De partu virginis*. He is the dedicatee of *De rebus coelestibus* 4 and *De prudentia* and the addressee of *Eridanus* 2.30, *Baiae* 2.15, and *Tumuli* 1.13. See Minieri Riccio, *Biografie*, 156–61; Altamura, *L'Umanesimo*, 58; Monti Sabia, "Manipolazioni," 276 n. 2.

SANNAZARO. See Azio.

SINCERO. See Azio.

SUARDINO SUARDO (Giovanni Battista Suardo, d. ca. 1536), interlocutor in *Aegidius* and tentatively added by Summonte in Vat. lat. 2843 as a mute character in *Actius* (see Note on the Text). Suardino, from Bergamo, was a latecomer to the Neapolitan sodality, like Francesco Peto (q.v.). In 1502 Pontano sent him to Aldo Manuzio in Venice with some of his poetry and a dialogue for publication. The dialogue is usually identified as *Aegidius*, although Monti argues that it was the *Actius* ("Ricerche," 306–11; "Per la storia," 281–92). Suardino is mentioned in the dedication of Summonte's edition of *Actius* (Pontano 1507); together with Peto, he is a dedicatee of Summonte's edition of *Asinus* (Pontano 1507). He is the dedicatee of *De rebus coelestibus* 6 and the addressee of *Baiae* 2.37, and he is quoted in *De sermone* 6.2.12. See Minieri Riccio, *Biografie*, 170–73; Monti Sabia, "Manipolazioni," 281–82; "La mano del Summonte," 251–52.

SUMMONTE, PIETRO (1463–1526), interlocutor in *Actius* and *Aegidius*. Summonte is best known as the devoted disciple of Pontano. He copied many manuscripts for him, and after Pontano's death he became a leader of the sodality, along with Girolamo Carbone. He worked assiduously to preserve and edit Pontano's works, sometimes making changes for the sake of religious or grammatical orthodoxy or altering names of speakers (especially in *De sermone*). See the Introduction and the Note on the Text and Translation in Pontano, *The Virtues and Vices of Speech*, ed. G. W. Pigman III, I Tatti Renaissance Library 87 (Cambridge, MA, 2019). He is addressed in *Eridanus* 2.15; *Baiae* 1.24, 2.18, 2.19; and *Tumuli* 2.33. He is quoted in *De sermone* 4.3.36, a vignette that also features Tomacelli and Compatre (q.v.). See Minieri Riccio, *Biografie*, 418–36; Monti Sabia, "Pietro Summonte e l'*editio princeps*"; "La mano del Summonte"; "Manipolazioni."

APPENDIX III

Passages Deleted from Actius

For these passages, see the Note on the Text.

1. *Passage Deleted from the End of Section 17*
(V, fols. 14v–15r)

Non patitur alius e grammaticis dici *paulisper* diminutivum quendam in modum indicandi temporis, cum dicat Sallustius:

> sin captus pravis cupidinibus ad inertiam et voluptates corporis est pessumdatus,[1] perniciosa libidine paulisper usus, ubi per secordiam vires tempus ingenium diffluxere, naturae infirmitas accusatur.

Item alibi: Metellus postquam de rebus Vaccae actis comperit, paulisper moestus e conspectu abiit. Alio etiam in loco: Sed milites Iugurtini, paulisper ab rege substentati sunt.[2] Alio item in loco: Qui in proximo locati sunt, paulisper territi turbantur,[3] reliqui cito subveniunt. Et Cicero ad Atticum: Sed in ipsa decessione significavit sperasse se aliquid et id quod animum induxerat paulisper non tenuit. Item ad eundem: Recordor enim quam bella paulisper nobis gubernantibus civitas fuerit, quae mihi gratia relata sit. In alia quoque ad eundem epistula: Propius accedere, ut suades quomodo sine lictoribus, quos ego non[4] paulisper cum baculis in turbam conieci ad oppidum accedens nequis militum impetus fieret. Et in primo de legibus; Ab omni societate rei publicae cuius partem nec norunt ullam, neque unquam nosse voluerunt, paulisper facessant rogemus.

In English

Another grammarian will not allow the use of the diminutive *pau-lisper* ["for a little while"] in any way to indicate time, although Sallust says:

> But if ⟨the mind⟩, captured by base desires, has sunk into sloth and bodily pleasures, yielding for a little while to destructive passion, when strength, time, and talent have vanished through idleness, blame is placed on the weakness of human nature.[5]

Similarly elsewhere: "After Metellus discovered what had happened at Vaga, for a time he was dejected and went into isolation."[6] Also in another place: "But Jugurtha's men were supported for a while by the king."[7] Also in another place: "Those stationed in the nearest position were terrified and in disarray for a little while; the others swiftly came to their aid."[8] And Cicero to Atticus: "But in the very moment of departure he indicated that he had hoped for something and for a time did not hold on to his resolve."[9] And the same to the same: "Indeed, I remember how fine the state was for a little while when I was at the helm, and what thanks I got for it."[10] And in another letter to the same man: "How to approach, as you advise, without lictors? . . . Not a little while ago I sent them into a mob with staves when I was approaching the town lest there should be some attack of the soldiery."[11] And in Book One of *De legibus:* "Let us ask them to retire for a time from every association with the state, of which they neither understand nor ever wished to understand a single part."[12]

2. *Passage Deleted at the End of Section 35*
(V, fols. 37r–39r)

Quae brevis est syllaba ubique acuitur. Quae producta nunc gravi signatur nota, nunc moderata, quanquam et breves ipsae gravem aliquando notam accipiunt. Sunt autem latina in lingua dictiones rarissimae quae gravem sustineant; haec autem ipsa gravitas in ultimis tantum syllabis manifesta appareat. Voces igitur una tantum e syllaba constitutae, quas grammatici appellant monosyllabas, suapte quidem natura productae, moderatum reddunt accentum, ut *dôs*, *rôs*, *môs*, *vêr*; breves vero acutum, ut *ób*, *néc*, *pér*, *fér*. Idem autem hoc usuvenit cum non sponte sua sed consonantium litterarum illas ineuntium duplicatione producuntur, ut *móx*, *póst*, *déns*, *gláns*, *núnc*.

Quae duarum sunt syllabarum dicunturque dyssyllabae,[13] quamvis[14] etiam ratione breves ipsae fuerint,[15] acuuntur ad primam syllabam, ut *méus*, *déus*, *féra*, *léa*, *béne*, *mále*. Illae item quae prima e brevi constant, ultima vero producta, ut *népos*, *ámant*, *férunt*. Adde et illas quae producunt primam ob duplices quae insequuntur vocalem consonantes, ut *férte*, *véstis*, *múltus*, *ánnus*. At circumflectuntur quae sponte sua producunt primam, corripiunt tamen ultimam, ut *sûdor*, *nîdor*, *vîsus*, *tôtus*. Trium etiam quatuorque syllabarum, quaeque plurium etiam sunt, unde trisyllabae, tetrasyllabae, polysyllabae sunt vocatae, acuuntur ad eam quidem syllabam, quae tertia est ab ultima, sive omnes fuerint simul breves, ut *áquila*, sive ultima ac tertia. Illa producantur, dum quae media inter eas est, vocaturque penultima, sit correpta, ut *vénerant*, *continuáverant*. Sin ultima quaeque ultimae proxima est, producentur ambae, acuetur quae est penultima (sic enim grammatici eam vocant, et quam tertiam diximus antepenultimam) ut *contentiónes*, *deploratiónes*. At ubi ultima brevis ipsa quidem fuerit, illi vero

proxima sponte sua producta, haec ipsa penultima moderatum ac-
cinet, ut *amavêre, conticuêre, Aventînus, Perusînus,* ast acutum, ubi
consonantium aggestione producetur, ut *proeliántur, aetérnus, vetérnus.* Gravis ut dixi accentus apud nos est perquam rarus, isque ad
ultimam statuitur syllabam, ut in adverbiis his, *penè, ponè, aliàs,
aliò;* particulae autem illae *ne, ve, que,* inclinant, idest trahunt
ubique accentum ad[16] precedentes syllabas, sive breves sive produc-
tas, ut *arma virúmque* et *tantaéne animis caelestibus irae.* Qua e re
dictae sunt a recentioribus tum[17] inclinativae tum encliticae graeco
nomine. Sunt aliquot etiam dictiones quae priscis illis temporibus
vel moderatum habebant in penultima, ut *Maecenâtis, nostrâtis,* vel
acutum, ut *hícce illícce istícce,* et huiusmodi quaedam alia, e quibus
post detruncatae sunt ultimae syllabae, mansitque *Maecenás, nostrás, illíc, istíc;* mansit suo item in loco accentus sive moderatus, sive
acutus; malunt tamen in gravem conversum. Aliquot etiam in
dictionibus iisque compositis, quo videatur una e duabus vox ef-
fecta, accentus ipse non sequitur syllabarum tempora, ut *dúmtaxat,
enímvero, ápprime;* acuitur enim in prima, nam si penultima notetur
accentu, apparebunt voces ipsae inter pronuntiandum disiunctae.

Sunt etiam[18] non nulli qui hodie in his etiam dictionibus, *Mercúrius, Virgílius, Quintílius,* cum acuatur iure suo in iis ea quae tertia
est ab ultima, neque unquam accentus e loco dimoveatur suo hoc
idem servent, ubi ventum est ad casus vocandi, qui sunt *Mercúri,
Virgíli, Quintíli,* ac enim accentus ipse perstat suo in loco; hinc penultima eorum ita personat ac si esset syllaba ipsa producta. Itaque
dum verentur ipsi ne putentur ignorare quanti eae sint temporis,
secus quam natura accentus exigit, transferunt illum ad eam quae
est ante ipsam penultimam idest dictionis ipsius primam in casu
vocandi.[19] Simile in modum *satisfácio, convénio.* Quaedam quoque
alia acuuntur ad tertiam ab ultima quibus inflectendis cum fiat syllabae unius diminutio. (*Satisfacis* enim et *satisfacit* una vincuntur
syllaba a prima verbi persona.) Acutus ille accentus qui erat in
prima persona ad tertiam adhuc quoque permanet; sua in illa syl-

laba quae facta est ex inflexione penultima, quaeque licet sit brevis, ob accentum tamen, pronuntiatur non aliter quam si esset producta. Quocirca acuenda ipsa est similiter et in his *convénis* et *convénit*; vincit tamen in plurimis ignorantia atque ab ignorantia profectus abusus. Differt autem *convenit* praesentis temporis ab illo quod est praeteriti, nam cum est praeteriti media ipsa hoc est penultima circumflectitur ut producta cum vero praesentis acuitur utrumque autem ob eam ipsam rationem evenit de qua supra est dictum quod accentus ob casuum aut temporum inflexionem decurtationemque syllabarum nunquam mutatur. Graecis familiarissimus mos est, notare accentu syllabas etiam breves ac pronuntiare eas perinde atque essent productae, quod apud nostros ita rarus est, ut si qui naturam ignorent accentus, vitio vertant quotiens aliter pronuntiari senserint.

In English

A short syllable has an acute accent in every position. A long one is marked now with a grave accent, now with a circumflex, although even the shorts too sometimes are marked with a grave. Moreover, Latin has very few words that take a grave; this heaviness manifests itself only in final syllables. And so words consisting of only a single syllable, which grammarians call monosyllables, that is, the naturally long ones, produce a circumflex accent, like *dôs, rôs, môs, vêr*; but the shorts produce an acute, like *ób, néc, pér, fér*. Moreover, the same thing happens when they are long not by themselves but because of the presence of two consonants, like *móx, póst, déns, gláns, núnc.*

The words that are of two syllables and are called disyllables, although they may be short by rule, have an acute accent on the first syllable, like *méus, déus, féra, léa, béne, mále*. Likewise those that have a short first syllable, but a long final one, like *népos, ámant, férunt*. Also those that lengthen the first syllable because of two

consonants following the vowel, like *férte, véstis, múltus, ánnus*. But those that lengthen the first syllable by themselves, but shorten the final one are circumflex, like *sûdor, nîdor, vîsus, tôtus*. Also those of three and four syllables and even more, from which they are called trisyllables, tetrasyllables, polysyllables, have an acute accent on the third from last syllable, whether all are short at the same time, like *áquila*, or whether only the third and final syllables. These are lengthened provided that the syllable between them (called the penult) is short, like *vénerant, continuáverant*. But if the final syllable and the one next to it are both long, the penult is acute (for that is what the grammarians call it and they call antepenult what we call the third from the end), like *contentiónes, deploratiónes*. But when the last one itself is in fact short, but the next one is long by itself, the penult has an in-between sound [has the circumflex accent], like *amavêre, conticuêre, Aventînus, Perusînus*, but an acute when it is lengthened by a piling up of consonants, like *proeliántur, aetérnus, vetérnus*. The grave accent, as I have said, is extremely rare with us, and it stands at the final syllable, as in these adverbs, *penè, ponè, aliàs, aliò*; but the particles *ne, ve, que* are enclitics, that is, in every position they draw the accent to the preceding syllables whether short or long, like *arma virúmque et tantaéne animis caelestibus irae*.[20] For this reason recent scholars have called them both *inclinativae* and by the Greek name *encliticae*. There are also some words that in early times had either a circumflex in the penult, like *Maecenâtis, nostrâtis*, or an acute, like *hícce illícce istícce*, and certain others of this kind, and from which the final syllables were later lopped off, leaving *Maecenás, nostrás, illíc, istíc*; the accent likewise stayed in its place, whether circumflex or acute, but they prefer changing into a grave. In some words and those compounded with them, where one word seems to have been made out of two, the accent itself does not follow the quantity of the syllables, like *dúmtaxat, enímvero. ápprime*; indeed there is an acute on the first syllable, for if the

penult should be accented, the words will seem separate in pronunciation.

There are also some people who today in these words, *Mercúrius*, *Virgílius*, *Quintílius* — on the grounds that the third from last syllable is acute in its own right and an accent is never moved from its own place — keep it the same when it comes to the vocative cases, which are *Mercúri*, *Virgíli*, *Quintíli*, and indeed the accent itself stays in its place; hence the penult of these sounds as if the syllable itself were lengthened.[21] And so, while they are afraid of being thought ignorant of the syllables' quantity, contrary to what the nature of the accent requires, they transfer the accent to the syllable before the penult, that is, to the first syllable in the vocative case. In similar fashion, *satisfácio*, *convénio*. Certain others also have an acute accent on the third from last syllable although a syllable is lost in inflecting them. (Indeed, both *satisfacis* and *satisfacit* are diminished by a syllable from the first person of the verb.) The acute accent that was present in the first person also still remains in the third; the syllable in it that became its penult by inflection, although it is short, because of the accent, is pronounced as though it were long. For this reason that syllable must be given an acute accent in the same way also in these words, *convénis* and *convénit*; nonetheless, ignorance prevails in most people and from ignorance stems misusage. Moreover, *convenit* of the present tense differs from that of the past, for when it is the past, the middle syllable, that is, the penult, is made circumflex since it is long, although it is acute in the present, and each comes about for the very reason spoken of earlier, that the accent is never changed because of the inflecting of tenses and cutting off of syllables. The habit is very familiar to the Greeks of marking even short syllables with an accent and pronouncing them just as if they were long; this is so rare with us that those ignorant of the nature of accent count it a fault whenever they hear a different pronunciation.

NOTES

1. pessumdatus est *V*; est pessum datus *modern eds.*

2. sunt *V*; *not printed in modern eds.*

3. sunt *V*; fuerant *modern eds.* turbantur *V*; perturbantur *modern eds.*

4. non *V*; *the traditional reading, obelized by modern eds.*

5. *Bellum Iugurthinum* 1.4.

6. *Bellum Iugurthinum* 68.1.

7. *Bellum Iugurthinum* 56.6.

8. *Bellum Iugurthinum* 59.2.

9. *Epistulae ad Atticum* 7.3.8.

10. *Epistulae ad Atticum* 4.18.2.

11. *Epistulae ad Atticum* 11.6.2 with omissions.

12. Cicero, *De legibus* 1.39.

13. dyssyllabae *A*; disyllabae *V manu Summontis*

14. quamvis *V, corrected from* quavis *manu Pontani*; quavis *A*

15. ipsae fuerint *V, added manu Pontani*

16. ad *A; deleted in V, perhaps wrongly*

17. tum *V, added manu Pontani*

18. sunt etiam . . . in casu *V, fol. 38v, crossed out with diagonal slashes, with* vacat *in both right and left margins. This is roughly the bottom half of the page.*

19. vocandi *V, first word on fol. 39r, unintentionally deleted when the rest of the line was crossed out*

20. Vergil, *Aeneid* 1.1, 1.11.

21. Pontano's explanation is confusing. His point is that the accent in the vocative in these words does not move from its syllable in the nominative (*Mercúrius*, nominative, *Mercúri*, vocative). Those whom he criticizes think the accent must always be on the antepenult and move it from its proper position to what is the antepenult in the vocative, creating, for example, *Mércuri*.

Note on the Text

のうへん

The *Actius* exists in three versions produced within about a decade of each other: the manuscripts Vat. lat. 5984 (A) and Vat. lat. 2843 (V) and the first edition printed in Naples in 1507 (see sigla, below). A is in Pontano's own hand; it is incomplete, ending in section 63 and covering only two-thirds of the dialogue. V was transcribed by Pietro Summonte, revised by Pontano, and revised again by Summonte. Its source was Vat. lat. 5984. Ed. 1507 was edited by Summonte, almost certainly from V; it shows both Pontano's and Summonte's revisions (the latter probably added in preparation for the edition), as well as some differences from the manuscript, probably the result of further revisions by Summonte. Most of these changes are small ones, but there are also two major differences to be discussed below: the manuscript and the edition present different names of witnesses in section 4 and interlocutors in sections 88 to 93, and the edition presents an abbreviated version of Abbot Ferrante's reply to Actius about the afterlife in section 8. The question of Summonte's revisions is also raised by a point of agreement between the manuscript and the edition: two substantial passages are deleted in V and omitted from the edition, a defense of the word *paulisper* (§17) and a discussion of word accent (§35). These deletions will be discussed below. Two shorter deletions, undoubtedly by Pontano himself (at the ends of §§17 and 35), are treated in the textual notes.

The principal source used for the present edition is V, corrected and supplemented as necessary by A and ed. 1507. In the absence of evidence to the contrary, I have worked on the assumption that A is the immediate source of V and that V is the immediate source of ed. 1507. Summonte was a careful scribe, but not a perfect one. He sometimes misunderstood his source, he often followed his own spelling preferences instead of Pontano's, and he also occasionally made changes to Pontano's additions and revisions in V. The texts in Pontano's own hand (in both A

and V) are essential in distinguishing between Summonte's practice and the intent and usage of Pontano himself.

PREVIOUS SCHOLARSHIP ON THE TEXT

An important edition of *Actius* was published by Francesco Tateo in 2018 (*Giovanni Pontano, Actius de numeris poeticis, de lege historiae*), unfortunately too late to be consulted for this edition, which was already in press. Before Tateo, the only modern critical edition of *Actius* was that of Carmelo Previtera, printed in *Giovanni Pontano: I Dialoghi* (Florence, 1943). Previtera based his text on ed. 1507 and V, somewhat indiscriminately and without trying to assess their relative importance. He was unaware of A, which was first described by Salvatore Monti in 1969 ("Per la storia del testo dell'*Actius* di G. Pontano"). Previtera's edition was harshly criticized for misprints, for omissions and misreadings of ed. 1507, for not giving priority to V, and for its apparatus, cluttered with readings from sixteenth-century editions. But it had the obvious virtue of making *Actius* and the other dialogues conveniently available to modern readers. It also inspired its critics to closer scrutiny of the text and its sources.

In 1947 both Scevola Mariotti and Nicola Terzaghi published critiques of Previtera. Terzaghi ("Attorno al Pontano") pointed out some errors and drew attention to Previtera's failure to give priority to V. Mariotti's more substantial article ("Per lo studio dei *Dialoghi* del Pontano"), which preceded Terzaghi's review by a few months, presented both general appreciation of the dialogues and specific criticisms of Previtera's edition, especially of *Actius*. Mariotti emphasized the importance of V, identifying it as the immediate source of ed. 1507, gave a detailed list of corrections to Previtera, and pointed out the differences between V and ed. 1507 in the names of witnesses (§4) and of interlocutors (§§88–93). He also noted Summonte's changes in ed. 1507 to the speech of Ferrante (§8), suggesting that Summonte had omitted parts of the speech for reasons of religious orthodoxy.

In 1964 Francesco Tateo published a long and detailed analysis of the text of *Actius* ("Per l'edizione critica dell'*Actius* di G. Pontano"). In this invaluable article, which also took V as the immediate source of ed. 1507,

Tateo presented a long (but still not complete) list of Previtera's errors in transcription from ed. 1507, treated differences between V and ed. 1507, including those in the names of witnesses (§4) and interlocutors (§§88–93) and the text of Ferrante's speech (§8), identified problems in Summonte's transcription in V and proposed solutions for them, pointed out the importance of distinguishing between the hands of Summonte and Pontano in V, and treated Pontano's orthography.

In "Per la storia del testo dell'*Actius* di G. Pontano", Salvatore Monti presented a detailed description of A, which he dated to around 1495 and identified as the immediate source of V. Monti's discovery and description of Pontano's autograph are of great importance to the history of the text; together with V, the manuscript allows us to follow Pontano's successive additions and revisions as he refined the style and enhanced the content of his work. It also provides valuable clues about the text, confirming Pontano's spelling preferences and sometimes both revealing mistakes in Summonte's transcription in V and vindicating him against charges of error leveled by Tateo. In the same article Monti questioned the primacy of V vis à vis ed. 1507, suggesting that the immediate source of the edition was not V and postulating an intermediate manuscript now lost that would have incorporated not only Pontano's revisions to V but also his subsequent and final decisions about the text. Monti's suggestion, if correct, would have important implications. It would make ed. 1507 the authoritative source, validating both its presentation of the names of witnesses and interlocutors in sections 4 and 88–93 and its abbreviated version of Ferrante's speech in section 8, now to be seen as reflecting not Summonte's orthodoxy but that of Pontano himself, a view that Monti favored. In the present state of our knowledge, however, Monti's proposal remains only a hypothesis, as he himself acknowledged. It has been neither criticized nor supported by other scholars. Indeed, in two articles published long after Monti's proposal (which she did not mention), Liliana Monti Sabia, citing Mariotti, treated the revision in ed. 1507 of Ferrante's speech as the work of Summonte, thus implicitly supporting the authority of V; see "Pietro Summonte e l'*editio princeps* delle opere pontaniane," 218–20; "La mano del Summonte nelle edizioni pontaniane postume," 243–44 n. 1. Nonetheless, she quietly left room for

Monti's hypothetical manuscript in a footnote, saying of V not that it is the immediate source of ed. 1507, but that it could be ("potrebbe essere l'originale di stampa"; "La mano," 245 n. 3).

THE SPEECH OF ABBOT FERRANTE (§8)

The present edition prints Ferrante's words on the afterlife as they appear in both A and V. The speech appears only in an abbreviated form in ed. 1507. I follow Mariotti and Tateo, who see Summonte as responsible for the abbreviation. It can be attributed to Pontano himself only if one regards ed. 1507 as the authoritative source of the text, based on a hypothetical manuscript incorporating Pontano's final corrections and superseding V. For the abbreviated version, see the textual note *ad loc*.

THE NAMES OF WITNESSES (§4) AND INTERLOCUTORS (§§88–93)

At the close of the comic opening scene, the notary calls on several humanists to witness the transfer of the cottage and pigsty to its new owner. The list of names (§4) has been revised in A, copied and subsequently revised again in V, and finally presented in still a different form in ed. 1507.

In A (fol. 320r) Pontano's first version of the list appears as follows: Actius Sincerus, Franciscus Pudericus, Ioannes Pardus, Gabriel Altilius, Franciscus Putius, Petrus Summontanus, Paulus Pressitius. His revision adds two names and changes the order of a third: after Gabriel Altilius he has added Petrus Compater in the right margin and moved Paulus Pressicius from the end of the list to the left margin (changing the spelling of his name from Pressitius); he has added Ioannes Musephilus above the line after Franciscus Putius.

In V (fol. 3r) Summonte originally transcribed Pontano's revised list from A, making two spelling changes: Prassicius for Pressicius and Summontius for Summontanus. Later the names of Putius and Musephilus were both erased and crossed out; traces of their names can still be discerned, as Monti observed ("Per la storia," 938–39). Two names have been added in the right margin: Suardinus Suardus and Franciscus Poe-

tus. The hand is probably that of Summonte, the ink is much darker than elsewhere on the page, and the letters are substantially thicker. Another hand, perhaps not that of Summonte, has added "Sannazarius" after the name Actius Sincerus.

In ed. 1507 the list is as follows: Actius Syncerus Sannazarius, Franciscus Pudericus, Ioannes Pardus, Gabriel Altilius, Petrus Compater, Paulus Prassicius, Petrus Summontius. It is important to note that the name of Actius Sincerus appears in the form Actius Syncerus Sannazarius, and that Suardinus Suardus and Franciscus Poetus have been omitted.

It seems clear that the list of witnesses was intended to identify the cast of the dialogue — its interlocutors, of course, but originally perhaps also nonspeaking characters presented as part of the gathering. It is also clear that Pontano changed his mind about the list at least once, and that Summonte, with or without Pontano's instructions, made further changes. Monti ("Per la storia," 934–45) argued that the changes in both V and ed. 1507 were Pontano's: that he had Summonte alter the names in V, and that the further alterations in ed. 1507 derive from those made by Pontano in the hypothetical intermediate manuscript that was the immediate source of the edition. Tateo cautiously attributed the added names in V to Summonte ("Per l'edizione critica," 148 n. 9) but did not go further into the matter. Monti Sabia saw the alternations in V as one example among many of Summonte's habit of changing the names assigned by Pontano for his own purposes ("La mano," 251–52).

Related to the question of the list of witnesses in the first scene is that of the names of interlocutors in the last (§§88–93). This scene is missing in A, which breaks off in section 63. In V, names of two of the interlocutors have been replaced; the substitution can be seen as provisional, since the new names are not written on the manuscript itself but on small pieces of paper pasted in the margin or over the names of the original speakers. The new names are precisely those added to the list of witnesses above: Suardinus Suardus and Franciscus Poetus. Suardus is substituted for Pudericus twice on fol. 96v, and Poetus replaces Prassicius eight times in fols. 97v–102v (Monti, "Per la storia," 939 n. 2). Ed. 1507 reverts to the original names.

Pontano's final intentions about the names in sections 4 and 88–93 cannot be conclusively demonstrated, but the treatment in our three sources suggests a probable history and solution of the problem. In his revision of A Pontano named as witnesses the seven humanists who appear as interlocutors both in the existing portions of that manuscript and in V up to the pasted additions in sections 88–93 (Actius, Pudericus, Pardus, Altilius, Compater, Prassicius, and Summontius); he also names two humanists who have no speaking role (Putius and Musephilus). In V the names of Putius and Musephilus have been erased, very likely on the instructions of Pontano himself, probably because he had decided to omit mute characters; the obliteration of their names might have been motivated by a tactful reluctance to leave evidence that he had not awarded them roles as interlocutors. At some later point, however, Summonte without Pontano's instructions added the names of Suardus and Poetus to the list and provisionally substituted them for Pudericus and Prassicius in the final scene. He subsequently repented, returning in ed. 1507 to Pontano's original witnesses and interlocutors, and making a small change in Actius' name in the list of witnesses. The present edition, then, follows ed. 1507, but prints Pontano's "Actius Sincerus" rather than Summonte's "Actius Syncerus Sannazarius."

THE DELETIONS IN SECTIONS 17 AND 35

The two passages both appear in Pontano's autograph (A, fol. 332r–v and fols. 352v–354v), and both were transcribed essentially unchanged into V (fols. 14v–15r and fols. 37r–39r), although the second and longer passage (on accents in §35) has frequent corrections and additions in Pontano's hand. Both passages were subsequently deleted, but in slightly different ways. The defense of *paulisper* in section 17 begins with a few lines on fol. 14v. These are bracketed and crossed out with diagonal slashes, and the word *vacat* is written in the right margin. The continuation on fol. 15r is encircled by a line and crossed out with a large X-shaped slash; *vacat* is written midpage in the right margin. The discussion of accents in section 35 shows two types of deletion. Most of the passage (fols. 37r through the first half of fol. 38v, and all of fol. 39v) is encircled by a line, and the dele-

tion is further indicated by an additional vertical line running through the center of the text. The lines on the second half of fol. 38v are bracketed and crossed out with diagonal slashes; *vacat* is written midpage in both margins and level with the beginning of that deletion.

It is not clear whether it was Pontano or Summonte who made the deletions in sections 17 and 35, but two clues may allow us to hazard a guess: the word *vacat* and the style of the deletions. *Vacat* seems to be in Pontano's own hand (although we should note that sometimes Summonte made corrections in a hand rather like Pontano's), and the word also appears in deletions marked by brackets and made with slashing diagonals, but not with those marked by rough circles or ovals and made with centered vertical lines. Provisionally, then, one may identify the *vacat* deletions as Pontano's, the others as Summonte's. Accordingly, we may suggest that Pontano deleted the passage in section 17 on *paulisper* and a small portion of the discussion of accents in section 35, and that the major deletion in section 35 is the work of Summonte.

Support for this idea is provided by the context in section 17 and by the state of both manuscripts in section 35. The discussion of *paulisper* falls at the end of section 17, immediately after an elegant paragraph rounding off the preceding discussion. It is followed by an unrelated new discussion beginning in section 18. Essentially a list of passages using *paulisper* and without any real argument, the passage would be both anticlimactic after what precedes and unconnected with what follows. It is easily dispensed with, and Pontano deleted it.

The discussion of word accent in section 35 follows a short introductory paragraph on the relation of rhythm to quantity and accent. The deleted portion is detailed and technical, although not more so than the discussions of elision and alliteration elsewhere in the dialogue. It is followed by words appropriate to follow a detailed explanation: "After having explained these things in this fashion" (§36). The whole discussion has been corrected by Pontano in both manuscripts, but with increasing frequency near the end, precisely in the lines we have provisionally identified as deleted by Pontano himself (V, fol. 38v, second half). The two styles of deletion in the passage suggest that the deletions were made by two hands at different times, first by Pontano, indicating the omission we

have attributed to him, with *vacat*, brackets, and diagonal slashes, and at a later point by Summonte, either on Pontano's instructions or as he was readying the work for the press.

For the texts of the deleted passages see Appendix III.

ORTHOGRAPHY: SOME GENERAL POINTS

I give priority to the spelling in A and in the autograph sections of V. Often all three sources use the same spelling, but sometimes Summonte deviates from Pontano's practice, particularly in the edition, where he often uses classical spelling instead. In most cases I use Pontano's spelling without discussion, including his spelling of proper names (e.g., Ecuba for Hecuba). His spelling preferences have been much studied, and many examples have been well documented by others (e.g., de Nichilo, Tateo, and Mariotti).

Some cases, however, do merit notice.

SPACING

Pontano treats as compounds many phrases written separately in modern editions, for example, those listed below:

aegrefero
animipendo (§§15 and 30). See Ramminger, s.v.; Tateo 192 n. 32. *animi pensionis*, by contrast, appears as either one word or two, but Pontano probably preferred the latter; *animi pensionis* appears in both manuscripts in section 44, and in V in his own hand in section 85.
praesefero throughout both manuscripts and ed. 1507.
usuvenit is seemingly Pontano's preferred spelling, but he is not consistent, even in his autograph. It appears as a single word in section 51 in V in his own hand.

Pontano also habitually but not always writes *et si* for *etsi* and separates the enclitic particles *-ve* and *-ne*. The separated forms are printed in ed. 1507. They are also printed in this edition of *Actius*, as in Tateo's editions of *Aegidius* and *Asinus*.

PONTANO'S PREFERRED SPELLINGS

alliteratio but *littera*/etc. See also Tateo 188–90.

Annibal. Pontano's preferred spelling, as he states in *De aspiratione* (*Opera Omnia* 1518–19, 15r–v). It appears in his own hand on fol. 93v. See also Tateo 191 n. 28.

Anno. Pontano's preferred spelling, as he states in *De aspiratione,* op. cit., 15v. Also see Tateo 191 n. 28.

arctus/*articulus.* See Tateo 192.

Bocchus. In section 28 *Bocchus* appears in A as well as in V. In section 80, on the other hand, Summonte in V corrects *Bocchique* to *Bochique.* See de Nichilo 86 n. 19.

cepi (seized) and *coepi* (began). The spellings are used in this edition in order to avoid confusion. Pontano's preferred spellings are signaled in the notes. Pontano prefers *coepi* for *cepi* (three times in §8 and again in §76, as well as in the Naples 1491 edition of *Charon and Antonius*) and *cepi* for *coepi* (although *coepit* appears once in A). Summonte in V has a clear preference for *coepi* (but uses *cepi,* etc. several times).

dypthongus. ("dipthongus" appears once, in §43). Pontano probably found the spelling with unaspirated *p* in manuscripts of the grammarians, where it is the usual form; see Schad 132.

dyssyllabus. Early in the text Pontano sometimes used *dyssyllabicus,* but later he omitted the *–ic* in A and often deleted it in V. See also Tateo 169, 189, and the textual note 88 (on §24) in this edition.

foedus. The spelling oscillates between *foedus* and *fedus* in both manuscripts. In V, fol. 93r (§84) both *foedus* and *fedus* appear in Pontano's hand in the same addition to the text.

Graccus. Pontano oscillates between *Graccus* and *Gracchus.* He certainly means to prefer *Graccus;* he undoubtedly knew the reference to *Graccus* as the very ancient spelling in Quintilian 1.5.20, and in *De asperatione* 39r he described *Gracchus* as now out of favor. In section 82, however, where the name appears four times, he still writes it once as *Gracchus.*

Iugurta and *Iugurtinus.* See Tateo 190.

lenis, lenio, leniter, etc. Pontano's spelling of the root in A varies between *len-* and *laen-,* but his final choice seems to have been *len-,* which ap-

pears in *lenitati* added in his hand in V, fol. 36v. Summonte always writes *laen-* in V, but changes to *len-* in ed. 1507. See Tateo 186–87.

letus, letitia, letor. The predominant spelling in A and in Pontano's additions to V. Summonte prefers *laetus*, etc. in both V and in ed. 1507.

seculum. The predominant spelling in A, and specifically vouched for in section 71.

sevus. Pontano's spelling, always in A and in his additions to V. Summonte almost always uses *saevus.*

SIGLA

A	Vatican City, Biblioteca Apostolica Vaticana, MS Vat. lat. 5984. Pontano's autograph of *Actius*. Breaks off in section 63 (fol. 372v).
V	Vatican City, Biblioteca Apostolica Vaticana, MS Vat. lat. 2843. Manuscript of *Actius* transcribed by Summonte with corrections by Pontano and Summonte.
de Nichilo	Mauro de Nichilo, ed., *I Poemi astrologici di Giovanni Pontano. Storia del testo* (Bari, 1975).
ed. 1507	Giovanni Gioviano Pontano, *Actius de numeris poeticis & lege historiæ. Aegidius multiplicis argumenti. Tertius dialogus de ingratitudine qui Asinus inscribitur* (Naples: ex officina Sigismundi Mayr, 1507).
Mariotti	Scevola Mariotti, "Per lo studio dei *Dialoghi* del Pontano," *Scritti medievali e umanistici*, ed. Silvia Rizzo (Rome, 1994), reprinted from *Belfagor* 2 (1947): 332–44.
modern eds.	Readings printed in modern editions of classical authors
Pont.	The consensus of V, A, and ed. 1507 for the texts of classical authors (in *Actius* §§1–62) and of V and ed. 1507 (in *Actius* §§63–94).
Prev.	Giovanni Pontano, *I Dialogi*, ed. Carmelo Previtera (Florence, 1943).
Tateo	Francesco Tateo, "Per l'edizione critica dell'*Actius* di G. Pontano," *Studi mediolatini e volgari* 12 (1964): 145–94.

Notes to the Text

ACTIUS

Tit. IOANNIS IOVIANI PONTANI DIALOGUS INCIPIT QUI ACTIUS INSCRI-
BITUR *V*: De poeticis numeris deque historiae lege dialogus *Pontano in a
letter of 1499; see Monti Sabbia and Monte, Studi, 2:257*: Actius de Numeris
Poeticis: & lege Historiae *ed. 1507*

1. Caeparius notarius, Pascutius et Segnitius *A; heading omitted V;*
Caeparius et Segnitius colloquuntur *ed. 1507*

2. sarcularius *V corrected manu Summontis from* spatularius *as in A;* sarcularius *ed. 1507. For* spatularius *as a neologism or coinage of Pontano's, see
Tateo 159.*

3. vetuverbio *A;* vetuverbio *V corrected to* proverbio *manu Summontis. And
see F. Tateo, "Sul genere e l'ordinamento dei dialoghi di Pontano: Note marginali
a una nuova edizione," in* Filologia e linguistica. Studi in onore di A. Cor-
nagliotti, *ed. L. Bellone and G. Curacurà et al. (Alessandria, 2012), 616.*

4. crumeram *ed. 1507;* tuam in crumeram *V, corrected from* tuum in granarium *manu Pontani;* tuum in granarium *A*

5. asserculatumque *a coinage from* asserculus *(beam). But Pontano seems to
have been undecided about the spelling, writing* asserculatumque *in A, but cor-
recting to* asserulatumque. *Summonte wrote* asserculatumque *in V, which either he or Pontano corrected to* asserulatumque. *See also Tateo 159 n. 5; Tateo,
"Giovanni Pontano e la nuova frontiera," 59–60.*

6. bacem *V; ed. 1507;* bacem grabulatum *(with* grabulatum *deleted) A*

7. Actius Sincerus *V, A*: Sannazarius *V added manu Summontis (?)*: Actius
Syncerus Sannazarius *ed. 1507*

8. *For composition of the list of names, see Note on the Text.*

9. Actius *A;* Actius Sincerus *V, with* Sincerus *added manu Summontis (?)
and* Sannazarius *added in a third hand*: Actius Syncerus *ed. 1507*

10. tedet *A, V*; taedet *ed. 1507.* Tedet *is Pontano's preferred spelling. Cf.* te-dium, *section 18 and passim.*

11. et Robertus Bonifatius . . . nomino *A; crossed out in V; omitted in ed. 1507. For Summonte's suppression of the name, see Monti Sabia, "La mano del Summonte,"* 252.

12. abbas *A*; abas *V, ed. 1507*

13. qui aderamus *A, inserted after* nostrorum *manu Pontani; wrongly placed before* nostrorum *V manu Summontis*

14. desiderio *V, A*; voluntati *ed. 1507. See Tateo 155.*

15. tuoque *V, A*; tuaeque *ed. 1507. See Tateo 155.*

16. letitiae *A*; laetitiae *V, ed. 1507. See Note on the Text.*

17. cepit *(three times in this sentence) Prev.*; coepit *V, A, ed. 1507. See Note on the Text.*

18. sospitem *V corrected manu Pontani from* reducem *as in A;* sospitem *ed. 1507*

19. coepi *V, ed. 1507*; cepi *A. See Note on the Text.*

20. Dicam . . . discessit *V, A. The passage is revised as follows in ed. 1507:* 'Dicam,' inquit, 'Syncere Acti, dicam vere, fatebor ingenue, asseverabo constanter, nos qui e vita iam migravimus, eo desiderio teneri, in vitam illam remigrandi quae animae cum corpore est communis.' Atque his dictis, demissis iisdemque conniventibus oculis ac superciliis, quasi abiens salutaret, discessit. *See Note on the Text; also see Tateo 155–56; Mariotti 277–78; Monti, "Per la storia," 913 n.3.*

21. pene *V added manu Pontani. For the force and probable intention of this and Pontano's next four additions, see Tateo 156.*

22. non immemores *V added manu Pontani*

23. hospitium et *V added manu Pontani*

24. vita in hac *V added manu Pontani*

25. et tanquam *V added manu Pontani*

26. apud me futura est *A, corrected from* futura est apud me *V*; futura est apud me *ed. 1507*

27. tanto incenduntur ardore *V, A*; eo tenentur desiderio *ed. 1507. See Tateo 156.*

28. his *V*; iis *A*

29. COMPATER *ed. 1507*; PETRUS Compater *V*; P. Compater *A*

30. ut *Pont.*; aut *modern eds.*

31. paratum *Pont.*; paratiorem *modern eds.*

32. item in libro . . . Africa *V added manu Pontani*

33. plenum *V, ed. 1507*; opimum *either printed or obelized in modern eds.*

34. plenus officio *Pont.*; plenus officii *modern eds.* / plenum . . . diligentia *Pont.*; hoc τέρας horribili vigiliantia, celeritate, diligentia *modern eds.*

35. Lepidi . . . estis *V manu Pontani over an erasure*; Q. Catuli: Ne placabilitas *followed by a line and a half left blank in A*

36. vestri *V, ed. 1507*; vostra *modern eds.*

37. ⟨sestertiorum⟩ *Mariotti 279*; sestertium numum, numorum *V, A, ed. 1507*

38. animipendit *V, A, ed. 1507. See Note on the Text.*

39. Graecos est ipsos *V, with est added, sit deleted manu Pontani*; Graecos ipsos *A*; Graecos sit ipsos *ed. 1507. Tateo 152–53 defends Pontano's ungrammatical* est, *suggesting that he made the change to avoid two occurrences of* sit *so close together.*

40. Et sedem . . . himber *V added manu Pontani*; *A added manu Pontani. The addition was missed by Summonte in the transcription of V.*

41. *Modern eds. have a period after* signi *and read* Aegocero, *not* Aegoceri.

42. lenirentur *A, ed. 1507*; laenirentur *V. See Note on the Text.*

43. Palemon *V, A*; Palaemon *ed. 1507*

44. Odisseus *V, A*; Odysseus *ed. 1507*

45. Ulisses *V, A*; Ulysses *ed. 1507*

46. Polydeuces *ed. 1507*; Polidectes *V added manu Pontani, corrected to* Πολυδεύκης *manu Summontis. See Tateo 158–60.*

47. ita *A; omitted in V*

48. reflaverint *Pont.*; reflant *modern eds. Added after* reflaverint *manu Pontani* A: ad M. Caelium. Qua re etsi, cum tu haec leges, ego iam annuum munus confecero, tamen obviae mihi velim sint tuae litterae [*Cicero, Ep. fam. 2.12.1*]; *omitted from* V, *perhaps on Pontano's instructions, since here* etsi *is used with the indicative.*

49. Dolabellam *A*: Dolobellam *V, ed. 1507*

50. Dolabella *A*: Dolobella *V, ed. 1507*

51. transtulerim *Pont.*; transfuderim *modern eds.*

52. amico *Pont.*; Caninio *modern eds.*

53. In primo Academicorum . . . delectari *V added manu Pontani. The quotations from the 'Academica' (*In primo Academicorum . . . iudicem), *present in A, were omitted in V. Pontano restored them, along with the quotations from 'De oratore.'*

54. negaret *Pont.*; negat *modern eds.*

55. se *Pont.*; sese *modern eds.*

56. se se *Pont.*; eumque *modern eds.*

57. Livio *V added manu Pontani*

58. Et Livii libro xxvi° . . . satis auderet *V added manu Pontani*

59. aliquanto minore spe multitudinis nec unquam *V, ed. 1507*; aliquanto minor spe multitudo nec cum qua *modern eds.*

60. particulas *JHG*; particulam *A* V. *Pontano apparently neglected to change* particulam *to* particulas *when he added* ac ne modo *to* V.

61. ac ne modo *V added manu Pontani*

62. nedum *Pont.*; novum *modern eds.*

63. Livius quoque . . . augeret *V added manu Pontani*

64. Anno *V (see Note on the Text)*; Hanno *ed. 1507, modern eds.* ne modo *V, ed. 1507*; non modo *modern eds.* inquisitionem *V, ed. 1507*; conquisitionem *modern eds. Pontano perhaps found both* ne modo *and* inquisitionem *in his manuscript of Livy (Biblioteca Nazionale, MS ex-Vind. Lat. 33), on which see Monti Sabia, "La mano del Pontano."*

65. Nec alienum . . . opertam *V added manu Pontani. The passage perhaps should be bracketed since it does not contain* ne modo.

66. flagella *ed. 1507, Prev.;* fragella *A, V*

67. *Here a page is deleted in V manu Pontani. The omitted page is printed in Appendix III, with a discussion in Note on the Text.*

68. epistularum *A, modern eds.;* literarum *V, ed. 1507.* Tiro *ed. 1507, modern eds.;* Tyro *A, V (both manuscripts, however, have* Tironem *in §13).*

69. illa quidem *A, modern eds.;* quidem illa *V, ed. 1507*

70. *Here the example of 'Heroides' 7.19 is deleted manu Pontani (V). This part of the paragraph otherwise treats examples of* instar *from Vergil and Cicero. The 'Heroides' example disrupts the pattern.*

71. omnium *Pont.;* centum milium *(Orelli's emendation for* omnium *of the archetype) modern eds.*

72. praeseferunt *V, A, ed. 1507. See Note on the Text.*

73. quod ipse alibi . . . iussit *V added manu Pontani*

74. Tusculanos *Pont.;* Tusculanensis *modern eds.*

75. quod et Virgilius . . . orbitatis *(at the end of the paragraph) V added manu Pontani*

76. illo *V, ed. 1507;* ipso *modern eds.*

77. *Here added in V manu Summonte and printed in ed. 1507 and Prev.:* Nam et apud Ciceronem legitur 'instar mortis' itemque. *The insertion interrupts the quotations from Pliny and should be omitted. See Tateo 155, 165–66.*

78. sapor *A;* sopor *modern eds.;* liquor *V, ed. 1507*

79. accipere *A in a correction manu Pontani;* accidere *V, ed. 1507 (Summonte's misreading of Pontano's correction). Many years before the discovery of A, Mariotti 280 proposed the correct* accipere, *taking it in the sense of Greek* παθεῖν.

80. sine *A; V added manu Summontis*

81. vir neque doctissimi . . . demonstrata *V added manu Pontani*

82. a te *post* igitur *A; post* suasus *V, manu Pontani*

83. Panhormita *V, ed. 1507;* Panormita *A*

84. animi pensionis *JHG*; animipensionis *V, A, ed. 1507. See Note on the Text.*

85. tutemet *A*; tu met *V, ed. 1507*

86. languor *A*; langor *V, ed. 1507*

87. particulae *JHG*; particula *V, A, ed. 1507*

88. dyssyllabis *Pontano's final preferred spelling*; dyssyllabicis *A*; disyllabicis *V, corrected from* dyssyllabicis *manu Summontis*; disyllabicis *ed. 1507. See Note on the Text.*

89. Sic cum dixit . . . legunt *V, added manu Pontani*

90. coepit *V, ed. 1507*; cepit *A*

91. inclinativa *A*; inclinante *V corrected manu Summontis from* inclinativa; inclinante **ed. 1507**

92. lacrimans *Pont.*; memorans *modern eds.*

93. eia *V corrected manu Pontani or manu Summontis from* illi; illi *A*

94. Alibi . . . videtis *(at the end of §27) V added manu Pontani*

95. Orodem *V, ed. 1507*; Oroden *modern eds.* viris *V, ed. 1507*; viri *modern eds.* quae *V, ed. 1507*; quem *modern eds.*

96. deserta siti *V corrected manu Pontani from* vastata feris; vastata feris *A*

97. fame *V corrected manu Pontani from* iubis; iubis *A*

98. Tingitanam *ed. 1507*; Tyngitanam *V, A*

99. Cynips *V, A*; Cyniphs *ed. 1507*; Cinyps *Prev.* Cynips *is confirmed as Pontano's spelling by the autograph of Urania; see Mariotti 279.*

100. latebras *V corrected manu Pontani from* saltus *as in A*

101. Masinisa *V, A, ed. 1507*

102. ostentans *V corrected manu Summontis (?) from* ostentare *as in A*

103. qui nam *V, corrected manu Pontani (?) from* quid nam; qui nam *ed. 1507*; quid nam *A*; quianam *modern eds. Pontano explicitly rejects* quia *as well as* quid. *See Notes to the Translation ad loc.*

104. Nec me quorundam . . . haec est opinio *V, added manu Pontani. The addition defends his reading* qui, *no doubt added at the same time.*

105. monstrarat *(here and in the same verse quoted below)* V, *corrected manu Summontis (?) from* monstravit *as in* A. *In section 38 Pontano's* monstravit *is left uncorrected; see textual note ad loc.*

106. umbra *Pont.;* umbrae *most modern eds.*

107. Aeacidae V; Eacidae A

108. ⟨et⟩ *Prev., supported by Mariotti 279.* et magnos membrorum . . . exuit V *added manu Pontani.*

109. ora *V, ed. 1507;* ossa *modern eds.*

110. item V *corrected manu Pontani from* itemque; itemque A

111. iamque iter . . . cernebant V *added manu Pontani*

112. nucis e foetu *Pont.;* et fetu nucis *modern eds.*

113. classemque . . . Idae et V *added manu Pontani*

114. tritimemeris, heptimemeris, enneamemeris V, A, *ed. 1507.* tritimimeris, heptemimeris, enneamimeris *Prev. The omission of* pentimemeris *before* heptimemeris *may be a lapse on Pontano's part; Mariotti 280 thought that it was omitted by Summonte from V through homoioteleuton, but it is also lacking in* A.

115. Ossan *Pont.;* Ossam *modern eds. In section 50 both manuscripts read* Ossam.

116. (nam priscis . . . octo) *For the position of the parentheses, see Mariotti 279. That the words in the parentheses are a unit is also confirmed by the fact that they were an addition in V.*

117. et *V, ed. 1507;* tum *modern eds.*

118. syllabae A; *lacking in V, ed. 1507, Prev.*

119. *Verses 3–6 and 11 are omitted, but perhaps Pontano hoped to include them later. A fol. 349v has a marginal note "relinquatur [?] spatium pro V versibus"; V fol. 33r leaves about five lines blank; there is no blank space in ed. 1507.*

120. imponet *modern eds.,* A *(here and in the same verse below);* imponat V, *ed. 1507. But see textual note on section 36.*

121. *After this verse the following passage in V is deleted manu Pontani with a bracket, diagonal slashes, and the marginal note* vacat: Erramus vento huc et

379

vastis fluctibus acti. Magnam dignitatis partem amiserit si commutaveris: erramus vento et vastis huc fluctibus acti. Qua ratione erit collisio ipsa copulandi tantum causa, idest ex necessitate. At illo modo implendi atque sistendi soni gratia ab arte profecta, nam et hiatus implet et dua illa monosyllaba sistunt numerum. *The lines nearly repeat the paragraph in section 31, beginning:* Erramus vento huc et vastis fluctibus acti. Magnam dignitatis *etc. Pontano had originally deleted the whole discussion from* erramus vento *through the verse beginning* sevus ubi Aeacidae. *He subsequently changed his mind and restored the rest, crossing out the bracket and* vacat *and writing* non vacat *and* continuantur *in the margin. But the whole passage repeats the discussion in section 31 almost verbatim, and only the first quoted verse (*haec ait, *etc.) is new. Given Pontano's own indecision, the restored passage should not be deleted, but bracketing it seems appropriate.*

122. haec *Pont.*; sic *modern eds.*

123. ut dictum est *V added manu Pontani*

124. Phaethontis *A*; Phaetontis *V, ed. 1507*

125. portus *A, V*; muros *ed. 1507, modern eds.*

126. Summontius *V, ed. 1507*; Summontanus *A*

127. Percalluisti . . . numerorum *V manu Pontani; lacking in A, where fol. 351v is left blank for an addition with a note* relique hoc (hic?) spatium

128. *Here two-and-a-half folios are deleted in V manu Pontani. The omitted passages are printed in Appendix III, with a discussion in Note on the Text.*

129. *Pontano clearly consulted a text of Claudian and revised 'De raptu Proserpinae' 1.32–53 after the transcription of V. A fol. 355r contains a marginal note manu Pontani beside l. 39:* vide in codice quia puto hic deesse versus. *A lacks both the end of l. 43 and lines 44–45, and the phrase* vidisset caeleste iubar *from l. 45 follows l. 46. V shows the following changes manu Pontani. For other textual questions, see next note.*

  (l. 38) turmas aciemque *V*; furias bellumque *A*
  (l. 41) movet *V*; vocat *A, modern eds.*
  (l. 43) penitusque revulso *V*; rursusque *A*
  (ll. 44–45) carcere . . . / . . . cruentus *V added; lacking in A*
  (l. 46) arcto *V*; atro *A*; aucto *modern eds.*

(after l. 46) *deleted*: vidisset caeleste iubar *V*
(l. 50) suas *V*; flexis *A*

130. connubio *Pont.*; conubiis *modern eds.*

131. baratro *Pont.*; barathro *modern eds.*

132. Thisiphone *Pont.*; Tesiphone *modern eds.*

133. reluctantis *Pont.*; reluctatis *modern eds.*

134. Aegeon *A*; Aegaeon *V manu Summontis*

135. vibrasset *Pont.*; vexasset *modern eds.*

136. pensis *Pont.*; fusis *modern eds.*

137. ecquisquam *Pont.*; et quisquam *modern eds.* adoret *Pont.*; adorat *modern eds.* imponat *Pont.*; imponet *modern eds. Pontano is inconsistent here; in section 33 A he writes* imponet. *See Note on the Text.*

138. nullo usus hiatu *V, where* nullo usus *is a marginal addition by Pontano with a mark of insertion before* hiatu; hiatu nullo usus *ed. 1507*

139. tempestatesque *ed. 1507, modern eds.*; tempestatisque *V, A. But in quoting the phrase earlier, both MSS have* tempestatesque.

140. illas . . . senas . . . quinas . . . quaternas . . . ternas *suggested by Prev. in his Appendix, 319 (the antecedent is* dictionum), *accepted by Mariotti 279;* illos . . . senos . . . quinos ... quaternos . . . ternos *V, A, ed. 1507*

141. ternas <ternos> secum *V, A*; ternas <ternos> ut secum *ed. 1507. Pontano intentionally omitted* ut *as he did just above between* quinos *and* circum; *see Mariotti 276; Tateo 151.*

142. commonstratis *V*; commostratis *A, ed. 1507*

143. conspectu *Pont.*; secessu *modern eds.*

144. vallis *Pont.*; valles *modern eds.*

145. somnus *Pont.*; terris *modern eds. Pontano has inadvertently replaced* terris *with* somnus, *which appears later in the verse.*

146. Sed nec Lucretius . . . inventi sunt *V added manu Pontani*

147. monstravit *V, A*; monstrarat *ed. 1507, modern eds. Cf.* monstrarat *twice in section 30, corrected by Summonte from* monstravit, *and see textual note ad loc.*

148. relligio *Pont.*; religio *modern eds. Since the spelling elsewhere in both A and V is always* religio, *perhaps Pontano found* relligio *in his text of Vergil.*

149. refert *V, A*; soror *ed. 1507, modern eds.*

150. pater *Pont.*; precor *modern eds.*

151. magna cum dignitate. Illo vero . . . utere fatis *V added manu Pontani*

152. et et campos *ed. 1507, Prev.*; et campos *V, A*

153. Quid quod . . . permisti *V added manu Pontani*

154. et *V, A*; si *ed. 1507. For a defense of* et *see Tateo 152.*

155. sublato *Pont. Elsewhere Pontano writes* sullatus. *Perhaps he saw* sublato *in his text of Vergil, as Tateo 189 n. 18 suggests.*

156. Achimenides *V, A*; Achaemenides *ed. 1507*

157. ac trium . . . assonantiam *V added manu Pontani*

158. Nec vero is sum . . . quintum constituit (*i.e., all of* §40) *V added manu Pontani*

159. et *V, ed. 1507*; ac *modern eds.*

160. e *V; lacking in ed. 1507*

161. toto . . . antro *V added manu Pontani*

162. paribus . . . figit *V added manu Pontani*

163. et *A; lacking in V, ed. 1507*

164. manibus . . . hic est *V added manu Pontani*

165. Threiciamque *A*; Treiciamque *V, ed. 1507*

166. discrimine nullo *Pont.*; atque agmina terni *modern eds.*

167. foedissima. *For the spelling see Note on the Text.*

168. Philomela *A, ed. 1507*; Philomena *V manu Summontis*

169. Sed nec Lucretianus . . . coelo *V added manu Pontani*

170. Pallantis *A, V, corrected from* Palantis; Palantis *ed. 1507*

171. Pallanteum *A*; Palanteum *V, ed. 1507*

172. Orithia *V, A*; Orithyia *ed. 1507, modern eds.*

173. Hilarem profecto . . . longe litora (*in* §42) *V added manu Pontani*

174. omnigenis *V manu Pontani, ed. 1507*; omne genus *(Lachmann) modern eds.*

175. horridus *V manu Pontani*; aridus *ed. 1507, modern eds. In section 47 Summonte has corrected to* aridus; *see textual note ad loc.* ac *V, ed. 1507*; aut *modern eds.*

176. ac *V*; aut *modern eds.*

177. Elisae *Pont.*; Elissae *modern eds.* magno sed *V corrected manu Summontis from* magnoque in *as in A.* polluto *V corrected manu Summontis from* occurrunt *as in A. (Perhaps Pontano was quoting from memory in A.)*

178. Ecuba *V, A*; Hecuba *ed. 1507, modern eds.*

179. adhibendum est a poeta studium *V*; adhibendum a poeta est studium *ed. 1507.* a poeta *was added manu Pontano to V, and Summonte misread his insertion point, putting the addition in the wrong place. Cf. Tateo 150–51.*

180. ut puerum . . . ludificetur *V added manu Pontani*

181. dypthongos *JHG*; dipthongos *A, V*; diphthongos *ed. 1507. For* dypthongus *as Pontano's preferred spelling, see Note on the Text.*

182. vocalesque *V corrected manu Summontis (?) from* idest vocales *as in A. The correction was probably made because properly speaking the last two letters in* militiai *do not qualify as a diphthong. See Notes to the Translation n. 191.*

183. imperitarint *Pont.*; imperitarent *modern eds.*

184. omniparentis *Pont.*; omnipotentis *modern eds.*

185. vulnus *Pont.*; corpus *modern eds.*

186. actus *A, modern eds.*; actas *V, ed. 1507*

187. Coribantiaque *V, A*; Corybantiaque *ed. 1507, modern eds.*

188. spondaicas post si trahant syllabas *The interpretation of a correction manu Pontani in V printed in ed. 1507 and supported by Tateo 148 n. 7*; sive trahunt post se spondaicas syllabas *A*; sive spondaicas post si trahant syllabas *Prev.*

189. ut *V corrected manu Pontani from* utque *as in A*; uti *ed. 1507*

190. Micenas *V, A*; Mycenas *ed. 1507, modern eds.*

191. centumgeminus *A, ed. 1507, modern eds.*; centum geminus *V*

192. canorus et plenus *V corrected manu Summontis from* plenus et sonans *as in A. See Tateo 183, who thinks Summonte changed to achieve a rhythmical effect.*

193. dypthongum *V manu Pontani;* diphthongum *ed. 1507;* accentum *A*

194. Hirtacidae *Pont.;* Hyrtacidae *modern eds.*

195. Pyrithoumque *V, A;* Pirithoumque *ed. 1507, modern eds.*

196. Threiciae *A, ed. 1507, modern eds.;* Treiiciae *V. cum V corrected manu Summontis from* prope *as in A, modern eds.* Termodoontis *A, V;* Thermo-doontis *ed. 1507;* Thermodontis *modern eds.*

197. Lucretius quoque . . . voluta *V added manu Pontani*

198. disiecit *V, A;* divisit *ed. 1507, modern eds.*

199. et Sed magis . . . disposituras *V added manu Pontani*

200. deducunt *V, ed. 1507;* deveniunt *modern eds.*

201. inque *Pont.;* vique, *modern eds. (crediting Pontano)*

202. nihilominus in locis quibusdam qui *V corrected manu Pontani from* qui tamen aliquibus in locis; nihilominus quibusdam qui in locis *ed. 1507. Summonte misread Pontano's corrections, not seeing that his addition* quibusdam qui *was to follow* in locis, *not the separate addition* nihilominus.

203. fuerint . . . ob noxam *V added manu Pontani*

204. syllabae . . . liceat *V added manu Pontani*

205. Etenim Lucretianus . . . ignem *V added manu Pontani*

206. at in hoc . . . secuti *V added manu Pontani*

207. et omnes *supplied by Prev., approved by Mariotti 279*

208. vocat *Pont.;* vocet *modern eds.*

209. persimilis . . . spondeo *V added manu Pontani*

210. aut pes ipse . . . duorum. et: *V added manu Pontani*

211. duorum *V, ed. 1507;* duorum est *modern eds.*

212. intactamque *Pont.;* immotamque *modern eds.*

213. demens . . . affabrefactus *V added manu Pontani*

214. monosyllabo *V manu Pontani;* monosyllabum *ed. 1507. See Tateo 152–53.*

215. tertius *V, A, ed. 1507. But see Notes to the Translation ad loc.*

216. altero *A*, alterum *V corrected manu Summontis (?) from* altero, *ed. 1507.* See *Tateo 153, 162–63.*

217. insideat *Pont.*; insidat *modern eds.*

218. rupit *Pont.*; rumpit *modern eds.*

219. aridus *A*; aridus *V corrected manu Summontis from* horridus. *Compare the verse in section 42, and see textual note 175.*

220. Praesefert . . . tertium pedem *V added manu Pontani*

221. ore profatur *V, ed. 1507*; forte precatur *modern eds.*

222. praestabo et hoc perlibenter *V manu Pontani, corrected from* etiam a me ut explicetur quod *as in A*

223. in re . . . sive ornatus *V added manu Pontani*

224. alliterationem. Alliteratio *is Pontano's preferred spelling. See Note on the Text.*

225. longe sale . . . sonabant et *V added manu Pontani*

226. fit interdum . . . postea *V added manu Pontani*

227. plectas *V manu Pontani, ed. 1507*; pectas *modern eds.*

228. quem ad modum *V added manu Pontani*; quemadmodum *ed. 1507*

229. duris . . . ardet *V added manu Pontani*

230. et *ed. 1507*; *lacking in V*

231. castra . . . fidens et *V added manu Pontani*

232. quo turbine . . . hastam *V added manu Pontani*

233. et *ed. 1507*; *lacking in V*

234. Cicero idem . . . loquatur, loqui *V added manu Pontani*

235. sicuti *V manu Pontani, ed. 1507*; sic *modern eds.*

236. Et apud Lucretium . . . resorbens *V added manu Pontani*

237. atque ut apud Lucretium . . . dolis Danaum *(in §50) V added manu Pontani*

238. discrimine nullo *V manu Pontani, ed. 1507*; atque agmina terni *modern eds.*

239. maxima . . . colit *V added manu Pontani*

240. Ossam *A, V, modern eds.*; Ossan *ed.* 1507. *But Pontano wrote* Ossan *in section* 32; *see textual note ad loc.*

241. et nauticus . . . alto *V added manu Pontani*

242. hortamine *V manu Pontani*; certamine *modern eds.*

243. cum Troia . . . et *V added manu Pontani*

244. et porta . . . ingens *V added manu Pontani*

245. ruentibus *V corrected manu Summontis from* stridentibus, *as in A, ed.* 1507; tridentibus *modern eds.*

246. praefractaque *Pont.*; perfractaque *modern eds.*

247. Ac mihi quidem videtur . . . Quin etiam idem ipse Virgilius (*beginning of* §53) *V added manu Pontani*

248. retrorsum *V manu Pontani, ed.* 1507; retrorsus *modern eds.*

249. Mnesteus *V, ed.* 1507; Mnestheus *modern eds.*

250. tela *V manu Pontani, ed.* 1507; lora *modern eds.*

251. ipsa *V manu Pontani, corrected to* inepta *manu Summontis*; inepta *ed.* 1507. *See Tateo* 167–68.

252. et *V manu Pontani; lacking in ed.* 1507

253. terrae *Pont.*; terra *modern eds.*

254. Alibi quatuor ut . . . conquisitum *V added manu Pontani*

255. diversa a vocali incipientes *V manu Pontani*

256. ut *included in quotation A*; ut *separated from it V, ed.* 1507

257. tecum *A*; tibi *V corrected manu Summontis from* tecum. *For a defense of* tecum *see Tateo* 162–63.

258. satis me in vestram omnium qui hic adestis gratiam ea *Tateo* 170–71; satis haec me in vestram omnium qui hic adestis gratiam ea *V corrected manu Pontani from* satis haec me in gratiam vestram omnium qui hic adestis *as in A. Tateo suggests that when Pontano added* ea *in the revision he forgot to delete* haec, *which was now redundant.*

259. vir Latinitatis amantissimus *V added manu Summontis, probably to be bracketed. For the phrase as a late addition, see Tateo* 159, *but he takes it to refer to Pontano rather than to the obvious Altilio.*

260. illesa *V, A*; illaesa *ed. 1507*

261. veham *V corrected manu Summontis from* veam *as in A*. veham *appears below in section 72. See Notes to the Translation n. 266. Also see Tateo 166 n. 12.*

262. vel auctore *A*; vel auctore Tullio et Quintiliano *V, with* Tullio et Quntiliano, *a marginal addition manu Pontani. The addition seems out of place since Altilio just below insists that up to his day there has been no authority on history. See also Tateo 154–55, who says that the addition is not "molto opportuno." The addition is lacking in ed. 1507.*

263. quin *Prev., approved by Mariotti 279*; qui *V, A, ed. 1507*

264. tamen *A and V (where it is deleted manu Summontis); lacking in ed. 1507*

265. neque poeticis abhorreat a figuris *V added manu Pontani*

266. Iugurtina *Pont., Pontano's preferred spelling. See Note on the Text.*

267. *A ends here, fol. 375v. midpage.*

268. Iugurta *V, ed. 1507. Pontano's preferred spelling. See Note on the Text.*

269. potentiae *Pont.*; superbiae *modern eds.*; fecerit *V, Pont.*; faceret *modern eds.*

270. Carthaginenses *Pont. (apparently Pontano's preferred spelling, perhaps from his manuscript of Livy)*; Carthaginienses *modern eds*. Annibale *V*; Hannibale *ed. 1507. See Note on the Text*. validiores *V corrected manu Summontis from* validioribus. *See Tateo 167*. iis *Pont.*; his *modern eds.* se *Pont.*; sese *modern eds.* sed *added JHG (included in later quotations of the passage and perhaps omitted here by haplography).* conserebant *Pont.*; conferebant *modern eds. But the spelling, whether of Pontano or Summonte (Pontano's autograph breaks off before this point), is not consistent. See textual note on section 68. See also Tateo 167.*

271. Romani nominis *Pont.*; nominis Romani *modern eds*. Masinisa *V corrected from* Masinissa; Masinisa *ed. 1507.* amicitia *Pont.*; amicitiam *modern eds.*

272. inanimaliaque *Pont.*; inanimaque *modern eds. Pontano perhaps found* inanimaliaque *in his manuscript of Livy; see Monti Sabia, "La mano del Pontano," 123.*

273. *Pontano does not include the end of Livy's sentence:* terrorem renovarunt.

274. ingentemque *Pont.*; ingentem *modern eds.*

275. circumspicientibus *Pont.*; circumspectantibus *modern eds.*

276. repens *V*; recens *modern eds.*

277. Nemora *Pont.*; nemora etiam *modern eds.* consternati sunt *Pont.*; consternabantur *modern eds.*

278. mollibus *Pont.*; modicis *modern eds.*

279. Harpiarumque *V*; Harpyiarumque *ed. 1507*

280. ne quidem cum ipse *V*; ne cum ipse quidem *ed. 1507, Prev. For defense of* ne quidem *see Mariotti 276, Tateo 153.* ne quidem *also appears in Antonius 23 and 59.*

281. tonat *V corrected manu Summontis from* sonat; tonat *modern eds. In Antonius 38 and 45 the text has* tonat. *See also Tateo 166 n. 13.*

282. cum Poenis *Pont.*; sed paene *modern eds.*

283. alia *Pont.*; quasi alia *modern eds.*

284. belluae *V*; beluae *ed. 1507. Tateo 191 n. 26 says that* bellua *is Pontano's preferred spelling. Contrast* belua *(A and V) in a quotation of Vergil in section 44.*

285. assecutus *V corrected manu Summontis (?) from* secutus

286. arboribus *Pont.*; arbori *modern eds.*

287. convectare *Pont.*; comportare *modern eds.*

288. Libyes *V corrected manu Summontis from* Libies, *which was perhaps Pontano's spelling; see de Nichilo 85.* Quibus *Pont.*; quis *modern eds.* hi *Pont.*; ii *modern eds.* legibus *Pont.*; lege *modern eds.* qua *Pont.*; quas *modern eds.*

289. Libys *V corrected manu Summontis from* Libis. leni *Pont.*; levi *modern eds.* adhaec *Pont.*; ad hoc *modern eds.*

290. Ne *V, defended by Tateo 173–74;* nec *suggested by Mariotti 281*

291. circum *Pont.*; circa *modern eds.*

292. nube *V, corrected manu Summontis to* nubecula; nubecula *ed. 1507. Tateo 160 defends* nube.

293. conserebant *(here and immediately below) V (corrected manu Summontis from* conferebant), *ed. 1507;* conferebant *modern eds. (both readings are found*

in the manuscripts). In section 63 the text reads conserebant *(see textual note ad loc.). Since Pontano's original breaks off before both passages, it is not clear which he preferred. See also Tateo 167.*

294. Nec inficiabimur . . . alia quadam lingua locutos *V added manu Pontani. Summonte added* quasi *after* alia *to conform with the text in Cicero (where the order, however, is* quasi alia*). But Pontano also omitted* quasi *and wrote* alia quadam *above, in section 66.* quasi *should be omitted. See also Tateo 162, 164.*

295. Cur qui Graece . . . littera accepta *V first version, to which Summonte later made several changes (shown in boldface):* Cur qui Graece est **Odysseus** . . . factus est nunc a **quibusdam Ulyxes**? Cur a sessu, hoc est sessione **si** fiat sexus, quod sedendo **ut quidam volunt** occulatur . . . cur sonum eius **evastant** x littera accepta? *See also Tateo 160–61.*

296. perantiquam *V corrected manu Pontani or Summontis from* antiquam

297. vel Graeco modo maza *V added manu Pontani*

298. liquas *V, corrected from* seu liqueo *manu Summontis*

299. ut a levo, levas, levasso *V added manu Pontano*

300. Cur . . . dicimus *V added manu Pontani*

301. Sist[i]litis *Mariotti 281 suggests bracketing the "i";* sistilitis *V*

302. Ac contra . . . inficiatur *V, first version, to which Summonte later made substantial changes (shown in boldface):* At contra miramur in Virgilio: *incana menta* et *incurvum aratrum,* quod in his **in sitam** [*or* **in suam**] augeat [**in**] significationem; ac si non et Cicero dixerit *infractum,* ut qui vehementer esset *fractus.* **Quae quidem vox, ut nomin**a **omittam,** compangendis atque ineundis **verbis augere solet, non imminuere, affirmare, non inficiari.** *See also Tateo 161.*

303. An quia . . . est servatum *V added manu Pontani*

304. est servatum *V manu Pontani, ed. 1507*

305. non minus cito *V corrected manu Pontani from* celerius

306. veha *V. See textual note 261 on section 60.*

307. simultas *Pont.;* simultatis *modern eds.*

308. pauca quaedam *V added manu Pontani*

309. Thucidide *V, corrected to* Thucydide *manu Summontis. See Tateo 193.*

310. valido *Pont.*; validus *modern eds.* luxui *Pont.*; lusu *modern eds.* adhaec *Pont.*; ad hoc *modern eds.* venando *Pont.*; in venando *modern eds.*

311. uti nostris *Pont.*; ut nostris *modern eds.* agere et in *Pont.*; agere in *modern eds.*

312. mallet *Pont.*; malle *modern eds.* gerendum *Pont.*; agendum *modern eds.* confecto *Pont.*; conserto *modern eds.* virtutes *Pont.*; viri virtutes *modern eds.*

313. ceperat *Prev.*; coeperat *Pont.* stare *Pont.*; resistere *modern eds.*

314. e monte *Pont.*; monte *modern eds.*

315. inter dexteram rupem *Pont.*; ab dextra rupe aspera *modern eds.* in subsidiis *Pont.*; in subsidio artius *modern eds.*; ex his *Pont.*; ab eis *modern eds.* electos *Pont.*; lectos *modern eds.*

316. facies urbis *Pont.*; urbis facies *modern eds.* fidere *Pont.*; credere *modern eds.*

317. adhaec *Pont.*; ad hoc *modern eds.* rogitare deos omnia *Pont.*; rogitare omnia ⟨omni rumore⟩ *modern eds.*

318. concurritur tela omittuntur *Pont.*; concurrunt pila omittunt *modern eds.* timide *Pont.*; timidi *modern eds.*

319. numerorum *V corrected manu Summontis from* numerum. *But perhaps* numerum *should be read.*

320. hi *Pont.*; ei *modern eds.* facere *Pont.*; fecere *modern eds.* fatigant animos *Pont.*; animos fatigant *modern eds.* nedum *Pont.*; ne *modern eds.* optemperarent *V*; obtemperarent *ed. 1507*; temperarent *modern eds.* coepere *ed. 1507*; cepere *V.* hebescere imperium *Pont.*; hebescere virtus *modern eds.* maleficentia *Pont.*; malivolentia *modern eds.* ubi luxuria *Pont.*; luxuria *modern eds.* parvipendere *Pont.*; parvi pendere *modern eds.* nihil moderati *Pont.*; neque moderati *modern eds.*

321. ac *V corrected manu Summontis from* et

322. explicando *V added manu Pontani*

323. Masinisa *Pontano's preferred spelling (see §§28 and 63)*; Masinissa *V*

324. Martii *Pont.*; Marcii *modern eds. Pontano perhaps saw* Martii *in his manuscript of Livy.*

325. Mutul *Pont.*; Muthul *modern eds.* collis *Pont.*; quasi collis *modern eds.* in humo arida arenosaque *Pont.*; humi arido atque harenoso *modern eds.*

326. qui eum *Pont.*; quem qui *modern eds.* occursurum *Pont.*; procursurum *modern eds.* detegendis *Pont. and the MSS, contradicted by the sense of the passage*; tegendis *modern eds.* (*a sixteenth-century correction*). confractibus *Pont.*; anfractibus *modern eds.*

327. Mulucca *Pont.*; Muluccha *modern eds.* Bocchique *V, corrected to* Bochique *manu Summontis. See Note on the Text.* planitiem *Pont.*; ceteram planitiem *modern eds.* per omnia *Pont.*; omnis *modern eds.* opera *Pont.*; opere *modern eds.* praeceps erat *Pont.*; praeceps *modern eds.*

328. M *Pont.*; Cn. *modern eds.* usque *Pont.*; inde usque *modern eds.* habuerunt *Pont.*; habuere *modern eds.*

329. Et Livius . . . Philopomenis, Scipionis (*at the end of* §81) *V added manu Pontani*

330. causam *Pont.*; et causas *modern eds.* cohererent *V manu Pontani*; cohaererent *ed. 1507*

331. Achei *V manu Pontani, ed. 1507*; Achaei *modern eds.*

332. Philopomenes *Pont.*; Philopoemen *modern eds.* Coroneam *Pont.*; Coronen *modern eds.* in valle *Pont.*; in⟨ita⟩ valle *OCT (but variously emended in modern eds.).* prolapsus *Pont.*; prolapso *modern eds.* attenuatus *Pont.*; attenuatis *modern eds.* cognitum primum *Pont.*; cognitumque praetorem *modern eds.* verecundia *Pont.*; a verecundia *modern eds.* viam *ed. 1507, modern eds.*

333. coeperit *ed. 1507*; ceperit *V*

334. atque *Pont.*; aut *modern eds.*

335. exortum *Pont.*; mutatur *Priscian and some modern eds.* appellant *Pont.*; laeti appellant *modern eds.* detractant *V, Prev.*; detrectant *ed. 1507, modern eds.* praemiis *Pont.*; in proeliis *modern eds.* uti gerant *Pont.*; gerant *modern eds.* fore praedae *Pont.*; pro praeda fore *modern eds.*

336. Thrasimenum *Pont. This is Pontano's preferred spelling; see Tateo 186 n. 7.*

337. illa *Pont.*; *omitted in modern eds.* mille *Pont.*; duo milia *modern eds.* utrinque *Pont.*; *bracketed or omitted in modern eds.*

338. ita *Pont.*; et ita *modern eds.* victoria *Pont.*; victoriae *modern eds.* senserint *Pont.*; sentirent *modern eds.*

339. urbem *Pont.*; urbem Romanam *modern eds.* qua *Pont.*; quo *or* quo a *modern eds.* altero . . . revocato *Pont.*; alterum . . . revocatum *modern eds.* arcesserentur *Pont.*; arcessantur *modern eds.*

340. Quanta vero . . . vescebantur *V added manu Pontani*

341. Gracco *V manu Pontani, ed. 1507*; Graccho *modern eds. Graccus is Pontano's preferred spelling, but he is inconsistent; see following note and Note on the Text.*

342. Graccus *ed. 1507*; Gracchus *V manu Pontani; omitted in modern eds.* celebrem *Pont.*; per celebrem *modern eds.* conspectis militibus *Pont.*; complecti milites *modern eds.* Graccum *Pont.*; Gracchumque *modern eds.* Graccus *Pont.*; Gracchus *modern eds.* cuiusque *V corrected manu Pontani from* quisque; quisque *modern eds.* pileatis *Pont.*; pilleati *modern eds.* vescebantur *Pont.*; vescebanturque *modern eds.*

343. explicatores *V corrected manu Pontani from* scriptores

344. Livius cum . . . verborum gratia *(at the end of the paragraph) V added manu Pontani*

345. Thaumatorum *Pont.*; Thaumacorum *Prev., with a reference to 'De aspiratione' 41v. But Pontano saw the spelling* Thaumati *in his manuscript of Livy; see Notes to the Translation 344.*

346. immensa *Pont.*; universa immensa *modern eds.*

347. animo *Pont.*; cum animo suo *modern eds.* prospera *Pont.*; prospere *modern eds.* animadvertit *Pont.*; animum advortit *modern eds.* reptantes *Pont.*; repentis *modern eds.* animum vertit *Pont.*; animum ⟨alio⟩ vortit *or* animum adorta *modern eds.* ut *Pont.*; et *modern eds.* flexa *Pont.*; inflexa *modern eds.* castelli planitiem describit *Pont.*; in castelli planitiem pervenit *modern eds.*

348. Non exornavit . . . etiam decorarunt *(end of penultimate paragraph of §84) V added manu Pontani*

349. tulerant eam M. Oppius et T. Romulius *Pont.*; tulerat eam C. Oppius *modern eds.* T. *Pont.*; Ti. *modern eds.* T. Iunius *Pont.*; P. Iunii Bruti *modern eds.* convenerant *Pont.*; conveniebant *modern eds.*

350. fedam *V manu Pontani; contrast* foedam *manu Pontani in quotation from Sallust below*

351. At *Pont.; omitted in modern eds.* stationibus *Pont.;* stationibus hostium *modern eds.* deformes *Pont.;* deformis *modern eds.*

352. quatuordecim *Pont.;* duodecim *modern eds.* vincta/iuncta *Pont.;* vincta *modern eds.* inculta *Pont.;* incultu *modern eds.* foeda odore *Pont.;* odore foeda *modern eds.* facies eius *Pont.;* eius facies est *modern eds.*

353. et rem *Pont.;* remque *modern eds.* uti *Pont.;* atque uti *or* aeque uti *modern eds.*

354. virtute *Pont.;* culpa *modern eds.;* virtute *is perhaps a slip caused by association with* gloriam

355. Romam *Pont.;* Romanam *modern eds.* exercitum *Pont.; not in modern eds.*

356. Annibale *V;* Hannibale *ed. 1507;* Hannibale tunc *modern eds.*

357. Et alibi . . . fieri posse *V added manu Pontani. Pontano apparently copied Livy's text in a hurry, writing* ut *for* aut *and omitting* principes, *after which either he or Summonte made some mistaken corrections. I print Pontano's original version, adding in Roman type in angle brackets what I believe he omitted from his exemplar.*

358. aut *modern eds.;* ut *V, deleted manu Summontis or Pontani; lacking in ed. 1507.* principes *supplied JHG from modern eds.; omitted in Pont.;* graviores *modern eds., V corrected manu Summontis or Pontani to* graviorem; graviorem *ed. 1507.* temperatioresque *modern eds., V corrected manu Summontis or Pontani to* temperatioremque; temperatioremque *ed. 1507.* multitudinem *modern eds., V corrected manu Summontis or Pontani to* multitudine; multitudine *ed. 1507*

359. Idem Livius . . . potissimum imitetur *(end of §86) V added manu Pontani*

360. hominem *Pont.;* alium *modern eds.* se *Pont.;* in se *modern eds.* Cartaginem *Pont. (elsewhere always* Carthago, Carthaginis; *Pontano probably took this spelling from his text of Livy);* Carthaginem *ed. 1507, modern eds.* Thrasimennum *V corrected manu Pontani from* Trasimennum; Thrasimenum *ed. 1507;* Trasumennum *modern eds.* aut *Pont.;* ad *modern eds.*

361. imminentes viginti *V. Pontano has omitted the passage between these words*: et a Sempronio consule et ante adventum eius terra marique res gestae.

362. Cn. Scipio *Pont.*; Cn. Cornelius Scipio *modern eds.* classe *Pont.*; classe et exercitu *modern eds.*

363. ac benefici *V added manu Pontani*

364. si non *V added manu Pontani*

365. saltem non abiecti non squalidi *V added manu Pontani*

366. Pu⟨dericus⟩ *V, ed. 1507*; Suardus *V added manu Summontis but crossed out, on a slip of paper pasted in the margin. See Note on the Text.*

367. Puderice *V, ed. 1507*; Suarde *V added manu Summontis on a slip of paper pasted in the margin. See Note on the Text.*

368. quod ipsum . . . satis est *V added manu Pontani*

369. et *V manu Pontani, corrected to* nam *manu Summontis, who also put parentheses around* nam qui vitam . . . satis est

370. diverso⟨s⟩que *Mariotti 282*; diversoque *V, defended by Tateo 175–76*

371. Prassicius *ed. 1507*; Poetus *V added manu Summontis on a slip of paper pasted over* Prassicius. *See Note on the Text.*

372. Pau⟨lus⟩ *ed. 1507.* Poetus *V added manu Summontis on a slip of paper pasted over* Paulus. *See Note on the Text.*

373. Pau⟨lus⟩ *ed. 1507*; Poe⟨tus⟩ *V added manu Summontis on a slip of paper pasted over* Paulus. *See Note on the Text.*

374. Prassici *ed. 1507*; Poete *V added manu Summontis on a slip of paper pasted over* Prassici. *See See Note on the Text.*

375. de *Pont.*; et de *modern eds.* intonuere *Pont.*; insonuere *modern eds.*

376. rupit *Pont.*; rumpit *modern eds.*

377. Prassici *ed. 1507*; Poete *V added manu Summontis on a slip of paper pasted over* Prassici. *See Note on the Text.*

378. Pau⟨lus⟩ *ed. 1507*; Poe⟨tus⟩ *V added manu Summontis on a slip of paper pasted over* Paulus. *See Note on the Text.*

379. cum *Pont.*; hinc *modern eds.*

380. Ascanium *Mariotti p. 282 would supply a participle (e.g.,* versus) *after* Ascanium. *Tateo p. 174 suggests that an appropriate participle can be understood from the parallel* Mercurius . . . missus *in the next clause.*

381. tollunt ad sidera *Pont.;* volvunt ad litora *modern eds.*

382. sullato *Pont.;* curvato *modern eds.* subducta *V corrected manu Summontis from* deducta. descendimus *Pont.;* desedimus *modern eds.*

383. Paule Prassici *ed. 1507;* Francisce Poete *V added manu Summontis on a slip of paper pasted over* Paule Prassici. *See Note on the Text.*

384. coepit *ed. 1507;* cepit *V*

385. Paulo *ed. 1507;* Poeto *V added manu Summontis on a slip of paper pasted over* Paulo. *See Note on the Text.*

386. ac *V, corrected to* at *manu Summontis (Tateo 167).* At *is the first word in* Aeneid 9.503, *but the capital* T *of* Tuba *in the manuscript suggests that Pontano treated* tuba *as the first word of his quotation.*

387. intonuit *Pont.;* increpuit *modern eds.*

388. subito *Pont.;* subitus *modern eds.* diriguere *Pont.;* deriguere *modern eds.* Erinnis *V;* Erinnys *ed. 1507*

389. Solon quas Atheniensibus . . . cultumque dei maiorem *(at the end of the paragraph) V added manu Pontani*

390. ornatus *V, corrected from* ornatu(?)

391. excandescenter *V corrected manu Pontani from* irate

392. devexit, detrusit, insecuta est *V, all corrected manu Pontani from present tenses*

APPENDIX I

1. debebat *ed. 1507;* debeat *Prev.*

2. Syncerus *is Summonte's preferred spelling. Pontano uses* Sincerus.

3. Pontaniana *JHG;* Pontana. *ed. 1507*

Notes to the Translation

꧁꧂

CIL	Theodor Mommson, ed., *Corpus Inscriptionum Latinorum* 9 (Berlin, 1883)
DBI	*Dizionario biografico degli italiani* (Rome, 1960–). Online: www.treccani.it/biografico
Keil	Heinrich Keil, *Grammatici latini*, 7 vols. (Leipzig, 1857–80)
Pontano 2012	Giovanni Gioviano Pontano, *Dialogues*, vol. 1, I Tatti Renaissance Library 53, ed. and trans. Julia Haig Gaisser (Cambridge, MA, 2012)
Ramminger	Johann Ramminger, *Neulateinische Wortliste. Ein Wörterbuch des Lateinischen von Petrarca bis 1700.* Online: www.neulatein.de
Schad	Samantha Schad, *A Lexicon of Latin Grammatical Terminology* (Pisa and Rome, 2007)

ACTIUS

1. The dialogue opens with a brief comic scene in which the title of a cottage and pigsty is transferred from one rustic to another. The interlocutors are Caeparius ("Onion Grower"), a local notary who officiously presides over the sale, and the buyer, Segnitius Funestillus ("Funereal Lazybones"), a low-level traveling official. The seller, Pascutius Caulita ("Swineherd à la Cabbage"), does not speak. Other mute characters are mentioned; like the principals, most have "speaking names." The scene concludes with the appearance of the humanist interlocutors, who have been summoned to witness the sale. For the language in this scene, see Tateo, "Giovanni Pontano e la nuova frontiera," 58–61; see also Deramaix, "Exellentia et Admiratio," 195–200.

2. Pignatia Nigella: "Swarthy Pignatia." "Who himself buys it": Caeparius uses the archaic *ipsus* for *ipse* to give an official legal tone to the proceedings.

3. "And anterity (*anteritate*)": introduces a running joke playing on "posterity." The joke works in two ways. Segnitius takes "posterity" as referring to the back of the house; he wants to be sure of getting the front ("anterity"), too. But he is also buying the property not only for himself and his descendants ("posterity") but also for his ancestors ("anterity").

4. Segnitius breaks in here, and Caeparius finishes the sentence after the interruption. See Mariotti, "Per lo studio," 278.

5. "Eye-catcher" (*democulam*): a coinage by Pontano (note jingle with *domunculam*, "cottage"). Sueratus (cf. *sus*, "pig"), "Dear to hogs." "Little pigsty" (*harula*): a diminutive of *hara* ("pen" or "coop"), a neologism, perhaps coined by Pontano.

6. "Prophylactically" (*averuncate*), an otherwise unattested adverbial form of *averunco*, an ancient word used of averting bad luck. See Deramaix, "*Excellentia et Admiratio*," 200 n. 145.

7. "Old saying" (*vetuverbio*): apparently a coinage by Pontano; Summonte changed it to the more usual *proverbio*. Because a farm beside a river could be in danger of flooding, the notary quickly corrects the word "river" to "stream."

8. "Will make over" (*evincet*): Pontano uses *evinco* in this sense again in sections 3 and 5.

9. With "bloodless" (*cassus . . . sanguine*) Pontano sets up the next joke, on the name Cocleatius ("Snaily"). He is alluding to Cicero's riddling hexameter description of a snail (*cochlea*) in De divinatione 2.133: *terrigenam, herbigradam, domiportam, sanguine cassam* ("a bloodless earthengendered thing that crawls and bears its habitation on its back"; W. A. Falconer, trans.). Hordeatus Panicocta: "Barley Bread."

10. In the translation "with plenty of bread" I have taken some liberties with *triticatum* (from the rare verb *tritico*, "thresh," used of grain). Lardatius is pictured as rich in oil and wheat; *unctus* is often used colloquially for someone well-off, and *triticatus* seems to belong in the same semantic register.

11. "Mice" (*moires*). The form occurs only here. It perhaps suggests rustic or dialect usage. See Deramaix, "*Exellentia et Admiratio*," 200 n. 145; Ramminger, s.v.

12. "Purse" (*crumeram*). Perhaps an error on Pontano's part for the correct *crumenam*. See textual note *ad loc.*

13. "To be begotten": Pontano perhaps coined *egnatum* to make a jingle with *cognatum* a few words later. Tateo, "Giovanni Pontano e la nuova frontiera," 60.

14. *Unicabis* ("count out one by one"); a coinage by Pontano. For the meaning see Tateo, "Giovanni Pontano e la nuova frontiera," 60. *Digitulatim* ("on your fingers"): another coinage; see Ramminger, s.v.

15. An obvious impossibility, since the price is three ounces. For the coinage *duillabo* ("I will count by twos") and its meaning, see Tateo, "Giovanni Pontano e la nuova frontiera," 60.

16. For "to you" Caeparius uses the archaic form *tibe* (for *tibi*). See note 2 above on *ipsus*.

17. "Bedstead" (?): *bacem*, seemingly unattested elsewhere. Pontano's autograph (Vat. lat. 5984) reads *bacem grabatulum*, with *grabatulum* crossed out. *Bacem*, with or without *grabatulum*, seems to be an item of furniture.

18. St. Pedianus, described as both traveler and innkeeper, is a suitable patron for the traveling official Segnitius.

19. St. Verro (cf. Latin *verres*, "boar") is an appropriate protector for Pascutius, the grandson of the swineherd Sueratus; Mariotti, "Per lo studio," 266 n. 4.

20. For these humanists, see Appendix II.

21. Pietro (Compatre); Paolo (Prassicio).

22. "Swineherd" (*scrofarius pastor*): *scrofarius* is apparently a coinage by Pontano.

23. Ferrante Gennaro, or de Gennaro: a Neapolitan aristocrat who served Alfonso, duke of Calabria, as ambassador. He was named abbot of Santa Maria a Cappella in July 1489. See Monti, "Per la storia," 913 n. 1. Roberto Bonifacio (1465/6–1536): a Neapolitan aristocrat and an impor-

tant courtier of the Aragonese kings. He is perhaps mentioned here because of Sannazaro's ties with the Bonifacio family (on which see Carol Kidwell, *Sannazaro and Arcadia* [London, 1993], 4–8) or even as the brother of Carmosina Bonifacio, whom some have identified as Sannazaro's beloved. See Monti, "Per la storia," 930 n. 2; Guido D'Agostino, "Bonifacio, Roberto," *DBI* 12 (1971): 204–5.

24. Francesco and Domenico: St. Francis, founder of the Franciscan order, and St. Dominic, founder of the Dominican.

25. "What an age we live in! What morals!" Cicero, *Oratio in Catilinam* 1.2.

26. Pontano refers to the *Calamità d'Italia*, the invasion of Italy in 1494 by King Charles VIII of France to pursue the long-standing French claim to the throne of Naples. In February 1495 they took possession of Naples itself. For a succinct account, see Bentley, *Politics and Culture*, 3–46; for an account that discusses Pontano's bitter response to the disaster, see Hankins, *Virtue Politics*, 427–28.

27. At several points Azio's dream invites comparison and contrast with Cicero's *Somnium Scipionis* (*De re publica* 6.9–29). Azio emphasizes that his vision was not precipitated by his waking thoughts, which would have undermined their veridical status. Scipio, who had spent the evening talking and thinking about Scipio Africanus (the principal speaker in his dream), argues that "often our thoughts and conversations contribute something similar in a dream": *fit enim fere ut cogitationes sermonesque nostri pariant aliquid in somno tale* (*De re publica* 6.10).

28. "He departed. I was immediately released from sleep" (*discessit. Ego statim somno solutus sum*). Ferrante's departure recalls that of Africanus in Scipio's dream: *Ille discessit; ego somno solutus sum* (*De re publica* 6.29).

29. "Will dwell" (*diversatura*); see Ramminger, s.v. Azio endorses the orthodox Thomistic view that the soul after death remains incomplete until the resurrection of the body restores the full integrity of the human person.

30. Up to this point Azio has referred to the relation between soul (*anima*) and body, but now he changes to "mind" (*animus*) and body, following Cicero in the *Somnium* (see especially *De re publica* 6.15). But he sees

the relation very differently. In Cicero the mind at death is freed from the chains of the body, whereas the Christian vision of Azio longs for their reunion.

31. With "in this tiny speck that is called earth in the middle of such a vast expanse" (*in hoc perexiguo tam vasti aequoris meditullio quae terra dicitur*), Pontano recalls Cicero's *illum globum . . . in hoc templo medium . . . , quae terra dicitur* (*De re publica* 6.15).

32. "Very close friend": Pontano. Paolo seems to be assimilating the ancient gods to the angels of Christian theology, including guardian angels who impersonate ancient authorities and reveal the correct understanding of classical texts.

33. Paolo Prassicio was a canon of the cathedral of Aversa.

34. The friends have probably arrived at the place they called Porticus Antoniana, the traditional meeting place of their sodality under Antonio Beccadelli (Panormita). See note 67 below, and *Antonius* 1, Pontano 2012. But with his phrase "as our ancestors did" (*de more maiorum nostrum*) Pardo may also be invoking his philosophical ancestors, the Aristotelian Peripatetics, and their discussions under the colonnades of the Lyceum in Athens.

35. See section 11. Compatre introduces a discussion of the correct construction of *plenus* ("filled, full"). He complains that Paolo has used it with the ablative case (*oraculis, visionibus*). In the next sentence he will cite examples of it with the genitive (*rimarum, fidei, stultorum*), and Paolo will reply with an overwhelming number of cases using the ablative, effectively winning the argument. Martellotti, "Critica metrica," 371 n. 39, suggests that the target is Valla, both here and in the discussion of *etsi* and *quamquam, nedum,* and *instar.* The view that lighter topics dealing with philological questions are more appropriate after meals may reflect ancient literary banquets such as those depicted in Macrobius' *Saturnalia* and Aulus Gellius' *Attic Nights.*

36. Terence, *Eunuchus* 105; Cicero, *De senectute* 1 (quoting Ennius, *Annales* fr. 335 Skutsch).

37. Cicero, *Epistulae ad familiares* 9.22.4. The translation is that of D. R. Shackleton Bailey.

38. Cicero, *Epistulae ad familiares* 16.14.1; *Epistulae ad Atticum* 3.14.1; *Epistulae ad familiares* 10.16.1.

39. Tacitus, *Dialogus* 33.6. *Histories* 1.2 (book one was often called seventeen because the *Histories* immediately followed the sixteen books of the *Annals* in manuscripts). Pliny, *Naturalis Historia* 5.1.9; Cicero, *Epistulae ad Atticum* 7.4.1, 8.9a.2.

40. Compatre thinks that *nostrum* in Pardo's phrase *maiorum nostrum* (§12) is the genitive of the personal pronoun ("of us") and suggests that the possessive adjective *nostrorum* ("our") is preferable. In his reply Pardo will show that *nostrum* is not the pronoun but rather a contracted form of the adjective, winning the argument.

41. Sallust, *Historiae* 1.55.1, cited by Pardo as an example of the use of the genitive pronoun (*vestri*) instead of the possessive adjective *vestra* or *vostra* ("your"); modern editors, however, print *vostra*.

42. That is, the use of the genitive pronoun for possession.

43. Pardo's examples are all taken from Cicero, *Orator* 155–56.

44. Pardo follows Cicero in arguing that the contracted forms were a feature of old Latin, using examples from *Orator* 155. The first is Ennius, *Alexander* 37 (Jocelyn), the second Pacuvius, *Chryses* 80 (Ribbeck).

45. Compatre is thinking of the passages of *Orator* just invoked by Pardo. In *Orator* 155–57 Cicero argues against criticizing supposed irregularities in the language of older writers.

46. The forms *rhinocerontis* and *Aegocerontis* do not appear in modern texts of any author. *Minonis* is not found in Cicero, but it does appear in Sallust, *Historiae* fr. 2.7, and in Suetonius, *Tiberius* 70.3 and *Galba* 2.1.

47. "Ancient Latins" (*Prisci Latini*): the pre-Roman inhabitants of Latium. Bruttii: an ancient Italic people inhabiting the toe of Italy.

48. The word *erudituli* ("pedantically learned") appears only once in classical Latin, at Catullus 57.7, in a disdainful reference to the petty philological studies of Caesar and Mamurra.

49. Compatre is paraphrasing the ancient grammarian Q. Remmius Palaemon (fl. 35–70 CE): *Etenim studium fuit omnibus musicare latinitatem, et id addere quod in aures laberetur* (Keil 5.542, 13–16). Pontano discovered

Palaemon's work at some point before 1471; two manuscripts of it are preserved in the Biblioteca Nazionale in Naples. See Liliana Monti Sabia, "Due ignoti apografi napoletani dell' *Ars Palaemonis* scoperta dal Pontano," *Studi su Giovanni Pontano* 1: 87–100.

50. "Optative and subjunctive moods": Latin has no optative mood, but the ancient Latin grammarians, following their Greek predecessors, included it as a category. See Schad 278.

51. Since modern editions print not *reflaverint* (subjunctive) but *reflant* (indicative), the passage does not support Compatre's argument.

52. Modern editions print *habebam* (indicative), not *haberam* (subjunctive). In the next passage modern editions also have the indicative *negat*, not the subjunctive *negaret*.

53. "Although I know": a small jest on Compatre's part, for this time he uses *etsi* with the indicative (*scio*).

54. The use of *nedum* in the sense "not only" is very rare in classical Latin; the only examples from texts of Cicero are those cited by Compatre below. In *Epistulae ad Atticum* 10.16.6, it is a variant reading; in *Att.* 9.7a.1 it is used by Balbus writing to Cicero. It becomes much more frequent in medieval and Renaissance Latin. See J. B. Hofmann and Anton Szantyr, *Lateinische Syntax und Stilistik* (Munich, 1964), 618; Silvia Rizzo, "I Latini dell'Umanesimo," in *Il Latino nell'età dell'Umanesimo*, ed. Giorgio Bernardini Perini (Florence, 2004), 60. For *ne modo* see the following note.

55. Pontano seems to take *ne modo* to mean "not only"; its use in that sense is unattested in classical Latin. Modern texts of Livy print *non modo*; see note 64 on text.

56. The relevance of this example to Compatre's argument is not clear, since it does not contain the word *ne modo*. It is an addition to Vat. lat. 2843, but in Pontano's hand.

57. Here Pontano has deleted a page in Vat. lat. 2843. See textual note 70 and note to the text.

58. For the terms "copy" (*exemplum*), "exemplars" (*exemplaribus*), and "originals" (*originales, archetypis*), see Silvia Rizzo, *Il lessico filologico degli umanisti* (Rome, 1984), 318–19.

59. Puderico calls on Pardo, but it was Paolo Prassicio who discussed dreams (§§10–11). On "the vote Horace talks about," see Horace, *Ars poetica* 343: *omne tulit punctum qui miscuit utile dulci* ("he wins every vote who mixes the useful with the pleasant").

60. Playing on the double meaning of *somnio* as "I dream" and "I am talking nonsense."

61. In fact, it was Paolo who mentioned the visions and dreams of the Church Fathers (§11). Pardo here advances a view of the human cognitive powers of dubious orthodoxy, following an interpretation of Aristotle's *De anima* (110.18–28) similar to that of the pagan Aristotelian commentator Alexander of Aphrodisias. Alexander saw the active principle of mind as being separate from the human soul, being of divine origin, and having an illuminationist function in human cognition. The position was criticized as unorthodox by Thomas Aquinas, for whom active mind was a native power of the human soul. Alexander's position created difficulties for Christian defenders of personal immortality.

62. With his mention of "seers" (*vates*, used of divinely inspired poets with prophetic powers at least from the time of Horace) and *furor* (frenzy), Pardo hints at the poetic frenzy treated by Plato (*Ion* 533d–e, 535–36a) and promulgated by Marsilio Ficino in the introduction to his translation of the *Ion*. See *De furore poetico*, in Ficino, *Commentaries on Plato: Volume I, Phaedrus and Ion*, ed. and trans. Michael J. B. Allen, I Tatti Renaissance Library 34 (Cambridge, MA, 2008), 194–207. He slides away from the idea in the next paragraph, calling poets not *vates* but *poetae* (literally. "makers"), but briefly returns to it in section 22 when he urges Azio to talk about poetry. Azio, however, shows himself less interested in divine inspiration as a requisite for fine poetry than in artistry and craftsmanship.

63. "Purity" (*castitudo*): a very rare word, used only once in ancient Latin (Accius, fr. 585, cited by Nonius Marcellus).

64. Aristotle, *De somno et vigilia*; pseudo-Aristotle, *Problemata* 30.1.

65. Pontano seems to have coined *disputaces* (nominative *disputax*), translated here as "argumentatious."

66. "Sulla most fortunate" (*felicissimum*): a play on Sulla's agnomen, Felix. For Sulla on dreams, see Plutarch: "Lucullus called to mind the advice of Sulla . . . which was to think nothing so trustworthy and sure as that which is signified by dreams" (*Lucullus* 23.6, trans. Bernadotte Perrin, Loeb Classical Library translation); see also Plutarch, *Sulla* 6.6.

67. "This place": the Porticus Antoniana; see section 12 and note 34. Antonio Panormita (Antonio Beccadelli, 1394–1471) was Pontano's mentor and the first head of the Neapolitan sodality. He is celebrated in the dialogue *Antonius*. For his biography see Gianvito Resta, "Beccadelli, Antonio," *DBI* 7 (Rome, 1965): 400–406. "This old man of ours" (*hic noster senex*): an epithet for Pontano frequently used by his *sodales*. Cf. Sannazaro, *Elegy* 1.9.97–98: "Salve, sancte senex, vatum quem rite parentem / praefecit terris Delius Ausoniis" ("Hail, blessed old man, duly appointed father of poets / in the Ausonian land by Delian Apollo").

68. Compare the discussion in *Antonius* 20 of Cicero's description of the end of the orator: "dicere apposite ad persuasionem" (*De inventione* 1.5.6). In emphasizing admiration (*admiratio*) Pontano is probably thinking of Aristotle's remark "what excites wonder or admiration is pleasant" (*Rhetoric* 3.2.3); see Ferraù, *Pontano critico*, 48.

69. An acceptable means by which to pursue the "middle way" (*mediocritas*) is described in section 27. In the *Nicomachean Ethics* Aristotle famously defended his doctrine that human excellence lies in a mean between extremes of behavior.

70. For Pontano's discussion of metrics and rhythm, see Martellotti, "Critica metrica."

71. That is, the verse contains two elisions in close succession: *mult(um) ill(e) et*. Pontano uses several words for elision: here *collisio*, elsewhere such terms as *hiatus, contusio, concursus, detractatio, ademptio, extrusio, explosio*. See section 32 and Martellotti, "Critica metrica," 363 n. 25.

72. "And a weak one at that" (*eumque subinclinatum*); for the sense here of the very rare word *subinclinatus*, see Ramminger, s.v. The original phrase, *multum ille*, has two accents, one on the first syllable of each word. The elision of *-um* puts the two accented syllables next to each other; but in

the metrically equivalent *multumque*, the word accent is now on *-um*, the second syllable of the spondee, producing a flatter and weaker rhythm.

73. "You . . . yourself" (*tutemet*). The rare archaic form, *tutemet*, used twice by Lucretius (1.102, 4.915), is appropriate to didactic, as here, and appears in Pontano's autograph. See textual note *ad loc.*

74. "The combination that immediately followed": the elision *ill(e) et* with its two accents.

75. Modern scholars would not agree with Pontano that the *–que* in *quoque* is an enclitic (*inclinativa*).

76. That is, the full, open sound of the *o* in *obibat* counters the thinness of the preceding *-is* of *insignis*.

77. Both Pontano and the ancient grammarians treated *fluviorum* as quadrisyllabic and scanned it ⏑ ⏑ – –, considering that the verse began (anomalously) with an anapest rather than a dactyl; but in fact the *i* is consonantal and the scansion is – – –. See Martellotti, "Critica metrica," 370–71.

78. A "spondee unconnected and free" is one followed by diaeresis; see Martellotti, "Critica metrica," 367 n.33. The language is military here and in the next sentence, as if the poet is presented as putting his words into battle stations. Pontano has Sannazaro use *acies* ("line," "position") instead of the more usual *pes* ("foot"); *colloco* and *statuit* are both used of stationing troops.

79. The word *semiversus* in the sense "half verse" seems to occur only in *Actius*, here and below in section 63 (Ramminger, s.v.). The words have the rhythm of half of the pentameter of an elegiac couplet (– ⏑ ⏑ | – ⏑ ⏑ | –).

80. The military imagery continues (see n. 78). The word accents "sound at the same interval," falling as they do on alternate syllables: *bína mánu láto críspans.*

81. In both versions the word accent falls on the first syllable of each word, but in Vergil's the accent also coincides with the metrical ictus of the first two feet, whereas in the other version the accent falls on the first syllable of *furit*, the ictus on the second, making the accent ahead of the

metrical beat and the hypothetical poet "over hasty in accenting." For the rare word *accinendo* (accenting), see note 97.

82. Here again the word accent and metrical ictus coincide in the first two feet. One could reorder the words and keep the meter (*tempus erit Turno* and *fila legunt Parcae*), but again at the expense of making the word accent (érit, légunt) get ahead of the metrical ictus.

83. The last three feet of each line are the same: spondee, dactyl, spondee; each line ends with a disyllabic word.

84. Pontano's point is perhaps that the slowed rhythms of Catullus 64.6 would be inappropriate at the beginning of the narration; see Martellotti, "Critica metrica," 368.

85. The last word in the verse, *recepti*, goes with the beginning of the next line: *nequiquam cineres* (*Aeneid* 5.81).

86. In the line attacking Drances (*Aeneid* 11.378), as in *Aeneid* 1.313, 12.165 (see n. 80), the word accent falls on alternate syllables: *lárga quídem sémper Dránce tíbi*. As Martellotti notes ("Critica metrica," 369), the word accent conflicts with the metrical ictus until the fifth foot.

87. "Such an extraordinary display": the catalog of Turnus' troops at the end of *Aeneid* 7.

88. "Gaping" (*hiulcae*): i.e., in hiatus.

89. The four word accents fall like hammer blows: *Sigéa ígni fréta láta*.

90. "Assonance" (*convocalis sonus*); *convocalis* is very rare and may be a coinage by Pontano. See Ramminger, s.v.

91. "The combination": i.e., of *clamor* and *clangor*.

92. "Rough letter" (*litteram . . . asperam*): a periphrasis for the letter *r* borrowed from Ovid, *Fasti* 5.481.

93. The word accent of each word normally falls on the first syllable. According to ancient (and many modern) grammarians, the addition of the enclitic (*inclinativa*) shifts the accent to the syllable that immediately precedes it. Moreover, in both cases the shifted accent coincides with the metrical ictus, falling on the first syllable of its foot.

94. "Stand its ground" (*standum in acie*): for the military metaphor see note 78 above.

95. The middle way (*mediocritas*) in general was rejected in section 22, but with the suggestion that there might be some ways to observe it. See Martelloti, "Critica metrica," 361.

96. Four word accents in *Aeneid* 1.50 appear in close succession: *flammáto sécum déa córde*.

97. Azio reminds his audience that *accentus* is derived from *accino* and ultimately from *cano*. Cf. Diomedes (Keil 1.431.1): "Accentus est dictus ab accinendo, quod sit quasi quidam cujusque syllabae cantus" ("accent takes its name from singing because it is like a kind of singing of a particular syllable").

98. That is, in the verses "De Pristice" in *Urania* 4. The passage describes a whale hunt in which the whales are encircled by ships and attacked with spears.

99. Tingi (mod. Tangiers), also called Tingitana, was the capital of Mauretania in North Africa; Bocchus was a Mauretanian king. The region, sometimes called Gaetulian from its inhabitans, the Gaetuli, lies under Mars and the constellation Scorpio.

100. Latona's daughter is Diana, the moon. (The phrase *noctisque decus Latonia virgo* also appears at *Urania* 1.18.) The Lotus-eaters were a mythical people inhabiting North Africa. Bragrada, Cynips (or Cinyps), and Triton are rivers in North Africa. Masinisa (Masinissa) was a king of Numidia.

101. With *virginibus* as the first word, the rhythm is confused since the word accent falls on the first short syllable of the dactyl (*virgínibus*) and does not coincide with the metrical ictus; but since *ausa* and *maris* are both accented on their first syllable, the resulting dactyl has two word accents (*aúsa má-*). Pontano uses the term "circumflex" for an accent on a diphthong or long syllable, "acute" for that on a short syllable (as in *maris*). See also the discussion of Martellotti, "Critica metrica," 371–72.

102. In the revised word order the first three syllables are all accented: ét gúttas. Word accent falls on the syllables *et* and *gut-*; the metrical ictus falls on *-tas*.

103. At one time Pontano preferred *quid*; see textual note *ad loc.*

104. The verse is translated and discussed in section 26.

105. By "hard letters" Pontano means the gutterals *c* and *q*. By "stopping point" (*pausa*) he apparently refers to the junction between a word and an enclitic (*clamor-que, stridor-que*) or between syllables (*inse-quitar*). But see also note 111.

106. Azio quotes two verses, but he discusses only the first.

107. Azio quotes the whole passage a few lines below (*Aeneid* 1.441–45). Lines 441 to 443 all end with two-syllable words, each of which has the word accent on the first syllable: úmbrae, Poéni, Iúno. In line 444, the first half of the verse ends at the caesura with another two-syllable word accented on the first syllable: ácris.

108. *Monstrárat, cáput ácris équi, síc nám fóre béllo.* "As we have said"; see section 29.

109. Each verse has an elision in the third foot, *mari(a) ac* (*Aeneid* 1.58); *oppeter(e), o* (1.96); *vent(o) huc* (1.333).

110. "Hiatus" (*hiatus*): Pontano uses the term for a running together of vowels between words, whether elided or not. In his second version of *Aeneid* 1.333, there is hiatus and elision between *vento* and *et*; in Vergil's line, *vento* elides with *huc*, emphasizing the *u* sound in *huc*, and then cutting it off with the hard *c* sound at the caesura. See Martellotti, "Critica metrica," 364.

111. Pontano seems to use *pausa* to mean "stopping point," whether between a word and an enclitic, between syllables (see note 105), or between metrical feet, as here. This sentence and most of the following examples through *Aeneid* 1.99 are repeated in section 33; see note 141.

112. Hiatus and elision occur in the fourth foot, *pror(a) avertit*.

113. Hiatus and elision occur between the first and second feet, *ver(a) incessu*, and in the fifth foot, *ill(e) ubi*; there is hiatus without elision at the diaeresis (*pausa*) between the fourth and fifth feet, *dea ⌢ ille*.

114. In *Aeneid* 1.428 hiatus and elision occur between the third and fourth feet, *ali(i) immanis*; in 1.429 between the fourth and fifth feet, *decor(a)alta*.

115. Hiatus and elision occur between the fourth and fifth feet, *mari(a) omnia*.

116. Hiatus and elision occur in the fifth foot, *omni*(*um*) *egenos*.

117. Hiatus and elision occur between the first and second feet, *ub*(*i*) *Aeacidae*, and between the fifth and sixth feet, *ub*(*i*) *ingens*.

118. Hiatus and elision occur between the fifth and sixth feet, *agminaq*(*ue*) *armat*.

119. *Aeneid* 1.448 is hypermetric: *nexaeque* is elided with *aere* in line 449.

120. Hiatus and elision occur at the third-foot caesura, *membror*(*um*) *artus*, and between the fourth and fifth feet, *magn*(*a*) *ora*. *Aeneid* 5.422 is hypermetric: *lacertosque* is elided with *exuit* in 423.

121. Hiatus and elision occur in the first foot of *Aeneid* 7.160, *iamq*(*ue*) *iter*, and the verse is hypermetric: *Latinorum* is elided with *ardua* in 161.

122. Hiatus and elision occur between the fourth and fifth feet of *Georgics* 2.69, *foet*(*u*) *arbutus*, and the verse is hypermetric: *horrida* is elided with *et* in 70.

123. That is, in the hypermetric verses in the last four examples.

124. This passage is largely repeated in section 33; see note 146.

125. That is, the verses are not hypermetric and no elision takes place between the vowels in hiatus.

126. Aulus Gellius (6.20.1) relates the story that Vergil changed *Nola* to *ora* to punish the inhabitants of Nola for refusing his request to let their water run into his estate. But Gellius, like Pontano, likes the hiatus between *Vesaevo* and *ora*, which he says prolongs the *o*-sound in a melodious way.

127. When word breaks occur within feet, the feet are said to be linked, as in a chain (*complicati*), and the break is called a *concisio* (caesura). A word break between feet (diaeresis) leaves the foot separated (*solutus*) from its neighbors; Martellotti, "Critica metrica," 367 n. 33. The Greek terms count the number of half feet (one long or two shorts). Thus a trithemimeral caesura occurs after the third half foot (i.e., in the second foot), the hephthemimeral after the seventh (i.e., in the fourth foot), the enneamimeral after the ninth (i.e., in the fifth foot). Pontano's omission of the penthemimeral caesura (after the first long syllable of the

third foot) is odd since it is the most frequent caesura in the Latin hexameter.

128. The word *extrusio* ("pushing out") seems to be a Renaissance coinage; Ramminger, s.v.

129. Cicero, *Orator* 77: "habet enim ille tanquam hiatus et concursus vocalium molle quiddam." See also *Orator* 152; Quintilian 9.4.33–37.

130. There are two examples of *complosio*: *conatī imponere* and *Peliō Ossan*. (The *o* in *Pelio* is shortened by the Greek practice called "epic correption.")

131. "In the great Ionian sea" (*Aeneid* 3.211). Pontano seems to be thinking of *complosio* between *Ionio* and *in*; in fact, however, elision occurs there. The unelided vowels occur at the beginning of the verse: *insulae Ionio in magno*, where the diphthong in hiatus (*ae*) is shortened by epic correption.

132. "To Glaucus and Panopea and Ino's son, Melicertes" (*Georgics* 1.437), a famous line in antiquity (cf. Gellius 13.27), in which there are two examples of *complosio* (*Glaucō et* and *Panopeae et*): the *o* remains long in hiatus; the diphthong *ae* is shortened by correption. Pontano quotes the verse again in section 53. "To Dardanian Anchises" (*Aeneid* 1.617) with *complosio* between *-o* and *a*. "On Attic Aracynthus" (*Eclogue* 2.24) with *complosio* between *-o* and *a*.

133. "I am the one who once" (pseudo-Vergil, *Aeneid*, prooem. 1; *ill(e) ego*). "Then all Troy was freed from its long affliction" (*Aeneid* 2.26; *erg(o) omnis*). "The (winds) restlessly, with a great roar of the mountain" (1.55; *ill(i) indignantes*).

134. "Indeed, I believe, and my confidence is not unfounded" (*Aeneid* 4.12; *cred(o) equidem*). "Everything, indeed, to you, O king" (*Aeneid* 2.77; *cunct(a) equidem*).

135. "After they had entered" (*Aeneid* 1.520; *postqu(am) introgressi*). "Breathing out (flames) from his pierced chest" (*Aeneid* 1.44; *ill(um) expirantem*). "The Trojans (laughed at) him as he fell" (*Aeneid* 5.181; *ill(um) et*).

136. "Eight thousand soldiers" (Ennius, *Annales* 10.332). Pontano took his example from Priscian: "Vetustissimi non semper eam (sc. *m*) subtra-

hebant. Ennius in X. *Annalium*" Keil, *Grammatici Latini* 1.30. He perhaps also found the example of elision in *Aeneid* 1.44 just above on the same page.

137. See also Franz Bücheler and Alexander Riese, eds., *Anthologia Latina* (Leipzig, 1894), 1523. Pontano perhaps intended to include verses 3–6 and 11; see textual note.

138. Lucretius, *De rerum natura* 6.877. But *gelu* (or *gelus/gelum*) has forms from both the second and the fourth declensions; for Lucretius it belonged to the second.

139. As Pontano points out, the elided syllable, *ductoresqu(e) ipsos*, is not necessary for the meter — only for the rhythm and music of the line.

140. *praetere(a) aut.*

141. Repeated from section 31. See note 111.

142. Vergil's line has an elision at the beginning of the third foot, *mari(a) ac.* This version eliminates it.

143. The bracketed passage is repeated almost verbatim from section 31. See textual note *ad loc.*

144. Elision occurs at the beginning of the fifth foot, *tumid(a) aequora.*

145. In section 31 Pontano quoted only line 405. In 406 there is prodelision in the fourth foot, *fugientem (e)st.*

146. "As I have said": in section 31; see note 124.

147. There is "clapping" (hiatus without elision) between the verses in all the examples.

148. For Pardo's suggestion to sit in the portico, see section 12. At the end of section 21 he notes that the gathering is a quasi-formal meeting of the sodality.

149. The place is the portico where the sodales traditionally met. See notes 34 and 67.

150. Sannazaro did indeed venerate the reputed Tomb of Vergil in what is now called the Parco della Tomba di Virgilio in the Mergellina district of Naples. His own funeral monument in Santa Maria del Parto is placed in a direct line of sight with it.

151. "quantities" (*tempora*): see the discussion in Quintilian 9.4.46–47.

152. For Latin terminology on accent (which is largely derived from the very different Greek practice), see Schad 7–8; W. Sidney Allen, *Vox Latina. The Pronunciation of Classical Latin* (Cambridge, 1970), 83–88. The circumflex, "named after its sign in writing," is curved (*circumflexus*).

153. At this point Pontano has deleted two and a half folios in Vat. lat. 2843. See textual note *ad loc.* and Appendix III.

154. "a hundred at a time." The monster Aegaeon had a hundred arms.

155. Ajax had violated Pallas' temple in Troy, dragging away Cassandra, who had taken refuge there; see Vergil, *Aeneid* 2.402–6, 6.840.

156. *véla dábant laét(i) ét spúmas sális aére ru*ébant (*Aeneid* 1.35)

157. *Aeneid* 1.37, 1.39. Each phrase is followed by a strong caesura.

158. The unusual Greek patronymic *Oilei* gives the line an exotic ring. It is pronounced as a trisyllable: *O-i-lei*.

159. *Aeneid* 1.52, 1.56. (In the passage quoted above Pontano does not include *Aeneid* 1.56: *circum claustra fremunt.*) In both cases the phrase concludes a sentence begun one or more verses earlier; the first ends at a diaeresis, the second at the masculine caesura.

160. In Claudian's twenty-two lines there is no hiatus or elision.

161. *Aeneid* 1.44 and 53. (There are also four spondees in 1.37.) *Aeneid* 1.44 is one of Pontano's favorite verses; it is also quoted in sections 32 and 54.

162. *Aeneid* 1.55 and 58, both quoted earlier. For discussion and translation see sections 31 to 33 and notes 133 and 141.

163. *Aeneid* 1.35, 1.56, 1.39, 1.50.

164. Placing a single monosyllable at line end creates a strong conflict between the metrical ictus and the word accent: the ictus falls on the first syllable of the final spondee, the word accent falls on the monosyllable. For a good discussion with more examples, see R. D. Williams, ed., *P. Vergili Maronis Aeneidos Liber Quintus* (Oxford, 1960), 135.

165. Lucretius, *De rerum natura* 2.615. Most hexameter lines have a dactyl in the fifth foot. Lucretius has a spondee so that his verse ends with four long syllables, including the monosyllable *sunt* at the end.

166. The rhythm of this verse is discussed in section 30, where the text reads *monstrarat*; see also notes 107 and 108.

167. The second monosyllable, *tu*, is elided with *urbem*.

168. The verse has three monosyllables.

169. Of necessity there is a word break, or diaeresis, before a final spondee formed by two monosyllables.

170. Pontano added this example as an afterthought in the margin of Vat. lat. 2843 (fol. 43v), perhaps overlooking the fact that its two monosyllables (*i . . i*) are not placed next to each other.

171. There are two elisions in *Aeneid* 2.102, *un(o) ordin(e) habetis*, but at this point Pontano is interested in elisions involving words of three syllables. In 2.68, *Phrygi(a) agmina*; in 2.11, *suprem(um) audire*.

172. For Pontano the three-syllable word *Danaum* and its enclitic *–que* are separate entities.

173. *Aeneid* 2.414, *collect(i) invadunt*; 2.415, *gemin(i) Atridae, Dolopumqu(e) exercitus*.

174. *Aeneid* 3.690–91. Pontano quotes the beginning of 691 to show that Vergil has actually put not just five but six trisyllables in a row.

175. The observation about assonance was an afterthought. Perhaps trying to be less severe, Pontano added it to the margin of Vat. lat. 2843, fol. 44v.

176. Cf. Horace, *Ars poetica* 388: *nonumque prematur in annum*.

177. There is a diaeresis (*solvatur*) between the fourth and fifth feet (*maris | et*). For the term see Martellotti, "Critica metrica," 367 n. 33.

178. For this and the next example see Martellotti, "Critica metrica," 372.

179. Quoted above in section 38.

180. By "dactylic word" Pontano means one with two short syllables next to each other. If the four-syllable word is of the shape – ◡ ◡ – and a word beginning with two long syllables follows, the second foot in the line will be a spondee. If the next word begins with two shorts, the second foot will be a dactyl.

181. Pontano treats the four-syllable word *Threiciam* and its enclitic *-que* as separate entities. See note 172.

182. The word *argumentum* has four long syllables; when the last is elided with *ingens*, the resulting combination produces two spondees at the beginning of the line.

183. The second, third, and fourth feet are all dactyls: *hinc glomer|antur O|reades* (the final syllable in *Oreades* is short).

184. Each of the four-syllable words (*Pallanteum* in *Aeneid* 8.54, *Orithyia* in 12.83, and *antennarum* in 3.549) is scanned as two spondees (the first three syllables of each are long, and the last is scanned as long at the end of the line).

185. The verse would scan with *vertimus*, but by using *obvertimus*, Vergil creates hiatus and elision, *velatar(um) obvertimus*. The *a*-sounds of *velatarum* are picked up by the last two syllables of *antennarum*.

186. Four of the six feet are dactyls.

187. By "clashing" (*assultatio*) Pontano probably means the elisions *tumescer(e) et* (*Georgics* 1.357), which produces diaeresis after the fourth foot, and *miscer(e) et* and *nemor(um) increbrescere* (1.359). He could also have pointed out the assonance of *tumescere, misceri, and increbrescere*.

188. The dactyl constituted by a monosyllable and a disyllable is *et pede*.

189. For the metrical and sound effects of the passage, see Williams, ed., *P. Vergili Maronis Aeneidos Liber Quintus*, 35–36.

190. Nine accents: *sí peritúrus ábis, ét nós ráp(e) ín ómnia técum*.

191. The genitive ending *-ai* (pronounced as two syllables) is the archaic form.

192. The form *indupedita* ("intertwined") is archaic; the prefix *indu-* (for *im-*), provides an extra syllable, as Pontano says, and was metrically convenient for poets such as Ennius and Lucretius.

193. The word *imperito* ("command") is a frequentative form of *impero* often used for metrical convenience.

194. "This rhythm": that is, the use of four- or five-syllable words at the end of the line. All the examples are Greek words or proper names.

195. Both this and the next example have five dactyls.

196. "Words of this kind": that is, words of five or six syllables. Ovid, *Metamorphoses* 1.190; *Aeneid* 3.708, 1.726, 3.111, 3.707. In *Aeneid* 1.726 the second syllable *aureis* is scanned as a diphthong; *altis* would also make a final spondee, but Pontano prefers the sound with the diphthong *ei* to that with the single long-vowel *i*.

197. The words are archaic forms of *imperator, ingredi,* and *impeditus.*

198. In *Aeneid* 11.252 *o fortunatae* is followed by the spondaic word *gentes*, producing a rhythm of seven long syllables; in *Georgics* 2.493 the combination *fortunatus et ille* is more dactylic (– – – ∪ ∪ – ∪). In *Aeneid* 7.410 the combination *Acrisioneis Danae* produces the rhythm – ∪ ∪ – – – ∪ ∪ –; in *Aeneid* 6.838 *Agamemnoniasque Micenas* produces a predominantly dactylic rhythm from the third-foot caesura to the end of the line: ∪ ∪ – ∪ ∪ – ∪ ∪ – –.

199. The first three feet are dactyls, the fourth a spondee.

200. Pontano suggests that the line would scan (though badly) without *ac* if *-eus* were pronounced as two syllables rather than a diphthong. The rhythm from *–eus* to the end of the line would be – – – ∪ ∪ – –. But *Briareus* is always trisyllabic, and in any case, the *e* would be short.

201. In both this and the next example the poet has added a short syllable by separating the prefix from its participle (tmesis) with the enclitic *-que* (*inque ligatus, Aeneid* 10.794; *proque voluta,* Lucretius 6.1264). The added *-que* in both cases also gives the line an accent it would otherwise lack (*ínque, próque*), since the *pausa,* or junction of prefix and participle, would have left the prefix without an accent.

202. The five-syllable word *servantissimus* begins the fourth foot with a spondee and fills the fifth with a dactyl.

203. The four-syllable word *fortissima* completes the spondee of the third foot and fills the fourth with a dactyl.

204. *inque valebunt* must be taken as an example of tmesis like those above (see n. 201; see also textual note *ad loc.*).

205. For the terminology see section 32 above and note 127. In section 36 Pontano used similar language for the continuous interlinking of *thoughts* in Claudian, a technique he considered tedious and overdone.

206. By "dactylic diaeresis" Pontano means that the word break occurs after a dactylic foot.

207. Pontano begins with diaeresis after the first foot and will continue with each position in the verse.

208. Modern scholars make a similar observation about the effect of diaeresis after a first-foot spondee, pointing out that it greatly slows the rhythm. Norden calls it "im kunstmässigen Hexameter unbeliebt." For discussion, see Eduard Norden, *P. Vergilius Maro Aeneis Buch VI* (Stuttgart, 1957), 435–36.

209. "Even in a case like this": diaeresis after a first-foot spondee. "The verse I have mentioned": *Aeneid* 3.697, quoted above.

210. In *Aeneid* 4.553 and 8.693 the opening rhythm is – – – ◡ with diaeresis after the first spondee and caesura in the second foot; in 3.697 above, the disyllabic word is followed by a three-syllable dactyl, so that there is diaeresis after both feet.

211. In both 11.445 and 10.879 there are diaereses after each of the first two feet; in 11.445 the second foot is a spondee (*inter*), in 10.879 a dactyl (*haec via*).

212. There are diaereses after each of the first three dactyls: *scilicet* | *omnibus* | *est labor* |; the four-syllable word *impendendus* contains a spondee and the first two syllables of a dactyl, which is completed by the monosyllable *et*.

213. There is diaeresis after *domus, et,* and *atria,* but the line has no strong caesura. "The effect is a metrical picture of a vista, stretching far into the distance"; R. G. Austin, *P. Vergili Maronis Aeneidos Liber Secundus* (Oxford, 1966), 189.

214. The second half of *Aeneid* 2.125 is quoted and discussed in section 39.

215. There is diaeresis after *velit,* followed by two spondees.

216. *Aeneid* 4.461 is quoted and discussed in section 38.

217. In both verses the second-foot diaeresis occurs after two dactyls formed by a five-syllable word and a monosyllable. The diaeresis in Vergil is followed by a dactyl and a spondee, that in Lucretius by two spondees.

218. Diaeresis occurs after *seges* in the third foot and after *ensibus* in the fourth. The fourth foot "is free" (*solvitur*) because it is between two diaereseis. See also note 222 on *Aeneid* 2.691.

219. Pontano does not point out that the verse also has a striking diaeresis after the first foot.

220. Pontano does not note that the final monosyllable creates an unusual conflict of metrical ictus and word accent at the end of the line: *fides ést*.

221. With the phrase, "as I might say" (*ut ita dixerim*), Pontano may be hinting that he has coined the word *affabrefactus* ("artfully put together"). See Ramminger, s.v.

222. The fourth foot, *atqu(e) haec*, "goes free" (*liber incedit*) because it is between two diaereseis. See note 218 on *Aeneid* 7.526.

223. The verse has several features more common in Greek poetry. It has five spondees (only the first foot is a dactyl), and there is hiatus after both *matri* and *Neptuno*. The presence of spondees in both the fourth and fifth feet is highly unusual.

224. A diaeresis after the fourth foot (the so-called bucolic diaeresis) occurs very often in Greek hexameters and in Catullus 64, but it is much less frequent in Vergil.

225. If the text is sound, Pontano means that there is diaeresis also after the third foot, although earlier he describes a free verse as one between two diaereseis; see notes 218 and 222. It is possible that he meant to refer to the *fourth* foot, *in medi(a)*, which is between two diaereseis.

226. The fourth foot begins with the second syllable of *cava* and ends in *trabe*. Pontano seems to mean that weight (*pondus*) results from the alternation of accented and unaccented syllables from the caesura to the beginning of the fifth foot that results from the placing of two bisyllables before the diaeresis: *cá-va trábe | cúrr-*. With a bisyllable preceded by a word of more than two syllables as in his next examples, the alternation is weakened (e.g., *Týri-is dúce | lé-*; *Aeneid* 1.696). On the other hand, in his third group of examples, weight is produced by the presence of a

monosyllable in the fifth foot, which produces three accents in the last two feet (e.g., át mémor ílle; *Aeneid*.1.719).

227. A strange line: there are two accented syllables in the fourth foot, none in the third: *-is Furi-ár(um) égo*.

228. This verse was quoted earlier, to illustrate the elegant use of two-syllable words. See section 39.

229. The final monosyllable in this verse was noted in section 38.

230. The verse was quoted in section 42 in a general discussion of diaeresis and wordplay. See note 187.

231. *Aeneid* 6.186 has five spondees. *Aeneid* 6.310 begins with two dactyls, but the elision and paired monosyllables in the third foot slow the initial light dactylic rhythm. The verse has a diaeresis after both the third and the fourth feet.

232. "Depending on the nature of their quantities" (*pro natura temporum*): i.e., whether the syllables are long or short.

233. Pontano seems to have coined the word *alliteratio*. Remigio Sabbadini, *Il metodo degli umanisti* (Florence, 1922), 55–56; see also Tateo, "Per l'edizione critica," 188–89.

234. *Aeneid* 1.295, 3.183, 2.84, 5.866, 1.124, 4.526.

235. Lucretius 6.719–20.

236. The comedy has no character named Poenulus; the speaker is a slave named Milphio.

237. *Aeneid* 2.125, 10.503, 8.239, 8.318, 9.66, 8.393, 3.656, 11.351, 6.462, 11.284, 4.604. *Aeneid* 2.125 is quoted in sections 39 and 46, *Aeneid* 10.503 in section 24.

238. *Aeneid* 4.461 is quoted in sections 38 and 46. The Lucretian example, an addition by Pontano in Vat. lat. 2843, fol. 55r, is described as "inopportuno" by Tateo ("Per l'edizione critica," 176 n. 17) since it does not have the same alliteration in both verses.

239. A favorite with Pontano; he has quoted the verse twice before. See sections 42 and 47 and notes, 187 and 230.

240. There is wordplay on the near homophones *oro* ("beseech") and *ore* ("mouth"). The verse is quoted above in section 39.

241. "Striking or clapping" (*complosio*). Pontano uses the same word to describe the effect of unelided vowels in hiatus. A similar gulping or jerky effect is caused by a succession of the same sounds (e.g., *Ocea<u>no</u> <u>no</u>x*, discussed earlier in §§38 and 47).

242. At *Georgics* 1.281 and *Aeneid* 5.261 the unelided long vowel is shortened in the Greek manner by epic correption. *Georgics* 1.281 is quoted in section 32, and see note 130.

243. There are two elisions in *Aeneid* 5.552: *port(a) advers(a) ingens*.

244. "Ingeniously done" (*affabrefacta*): Pontano used the same coinage earlier; see note 221.

245. All these examples are full of jarring consonant combinations; most famous is 8.596 (*quadrupendante putrem*, etc.), which imitates the sound of a galloping horse.

246. The whole verse is quoted and discussed below in section 52.

247. The verse is discussed in section 27.

248. There are ten words in the line, each with an accent. The verse is quoted in sections 46 and 51: in 46 on diaeresis, in 51 on alliteration.

249. Pontano quoted this passage earlier (§27). This verse also has ten accents.

250. As his examples indicate, Pontano considers the diphthong *ae* equivalent to *e*.

251. Quoted above in section 39.

252. The three words beginning with vowels are *et, et* (both after unelided vowels), and *Inoo*. Pontano treated the hiatus in this line in section 32 (and see n. 132).

253. Both passages are examples of not only alliteration but also epanalepsis (the repetition of a word from the end of one line to the beginning of the next for pathetic effect). *Aeneid* 10.822 is quoted in section 44.

254. All the examples feature internal rhyme, whether of participles like *stringentem* and *secantem* (*Aeneid* 8.63), verb forms like *misere* and *dedere*

(*Aeneid* 2.566), or adjectives and their nouns like *imas* and *umbras* (*Aeneid* 6.404).

255. This differs from the previous examples, for the chiming is stronger between the verses than within them. The last words of the first two lines rhyme with each other and with the word before the caesura in the third (*vomentem, rigentem, ingentem*), and there is strong assonance between *galeam* (620) and *loricam* (621), which is perhaps also felt in *sanguineam* (622), even though its last syllable is elided.

256. The following verses are taken from *Aeneid* 1.34–54, translated and discussed in section 37.

257. The verse is treated in section 32 in a discussion of elision (see n. 135) and in section 37 in a discussion of spondees (n. 161).

258. The verse is treated in section 27 in a discussion of accents and disyllabic words (see n. 96) and again in section 37.

259. The verse is treated in section 37 in a discussion of caesura and diaeresis (see n. 159).

260. The word *submulceo* ("gently caress") may be a coinage by Pontano. See Ramminger, s.v.

261. Cf. Vergil, *Eclogue* 5.49: *tu nunc eris alter ab illo*. Through the speaker Azio, Pontano is making a claim of poetic succession. In the *Eclogue* the shepherd poet is promised that he will be a second Daphnis (the greatest of all shepherd poets); Pontano/Azio aspires to be a second Vergil. Pontano expressed his intention to hold a place in the poetic tradition as early as the *Parthenopeus* (see especially *Parth.* 1.28), and in *Antonius* he presents himself as a successor to Vergil. See Pontano 2012, xxi; Gaisser, "Succession and Inheritance"; Deramaix, "*Exellentia et Admiratio*," 180.

262. Antonio: see notes 34 and 67.

263. For Summonte's demand, see section 34.

264. Semivowel: ancient grammarians classified consonants as either semivowels or mutes (Quintilian 1.4.6). Since both *m* and *n* were called semivowels (e.g., Priscian 1.3), perhaps Pontano should have said that the semivowel *m* was assimilated to the semivowel *n*.

265. Pontano perhaps coined *anniculare* ("to store for a year") as a back formation from the medieval Latin *anniculatus* ("a year old").

266. Cf. Varro, *De re rustica* 1.2.14: "Rustici etiam nunc quoque viam veham appellant propter vecturas et vellam, non villam, quo vehunt et unde vehunt."

267. Cf. Isidore, *Origines* 10.128: "Inbecillus, quasi sine baculo fragilis et inconstans."

268. The primary meaning of the Greek word *historia* is "inquiry" or "investigation," but Pontano is probably thinking more along the lines of Cicero's description: "History . . . bears witness to the passing of the ages, sheds light upon reality, gives life to recollection and guidance to human existence, and brings tidings of ancient days" (*De oratore* 2.36, trans. E. W. Sutton, Loeb translation).

269. Cf. Quintilian 10.1.31: "Est (historia) proxima poetis et quodammodo carmen solutum."

270. Although a work on Empedocles by Sallust (no longer extant) is mentioned by Cicero (*Epistulae ad Quintum Fratrem* 2.9.3), its author was almost certainly not the historian. Much of Cicero's translation of Aratus' *Phaenomena* is preserved.

271. Cf. Quintilian 9.4.74. The word *semiversus* (half verse) seems to appear only in *Actius*; see section 24 and note 79. But the quotation here is not half of a hexameter, but extends to the fourth-foot caesura (– – | – ∪ ∪ | – ∪ ∪ | –).

272. Pontano marked this passage in his manuscript of Livy (Naples, Biblioteca Nazionale, ex-Vind. Lat. 33, 81v/a). Monti Sabia, "La mano del Pontano, 123.

273. With Pontano's reading *ingentemque*, the line can be scanned as the last five feet of a hexameter (– – | – ∪ ∪ | – – | – ∪ ∪ | – –); with *ingentem* as in modern editions, the metrical segment begins with the second syllable of *fugam* and supplies three feet (– – | – ∪ ∪ | – –).

274. *Aeneid* 3.191 is quoted and discussed in section 47 (see n. 226).

275. Pontano discusses this passage extensively in *Antonius* 38–53 and imitates it in his epic poem on Sertorius (*Antonius*, metrum ix.127–34 and

metrum xi.357–69 in Pontano 2012, 290, 338). See with earlier bibliography, Gaisser, "Succession and Inheritance."

276. Livy, 21.1.2, 21.2.1, 21.7.8, 21.43.12, 22.5.4, 22.4.4, 21.10.3, 21.10.11, 21.46.6, 22.50.10, 23.5.7. The last two examples are dactylic in rhythm. *Haec ubi dicta dedit* (22.50.10), which appears eight times in Vergil, but only here in prose before Petronius, is the first half of a hexameter. *Cum poenis . . . suscipiatur* (23.5.7) is a full hexameter.

277. The dictum is from the speech of the orator Antonius, who says that since the poets speak in a foreign tongue, he does even not touch their work. Instead, he prefers to read of historical events (*res gestas*) or to read orations or works that do not demand great learning to be understood.

278. Cicero, *De oratore* 2.51–54 (the speaker is also Antonius). Cicero expresses similar views in *Brutus* 228 and *De legibus* 1.6–7.

279. Pontano probably found all these compounds in contemporary poetry: *spumivomus* can be found at least twice (see Ramminger, s.v.); the combination *fluentisono . . . litore* appears in Catullus 64.52 and may have been used by Renaissance imitators. Sources for the others have yet to be identified.

280. See section 64.

281. "A poem is like a picture" (*ut pictura poesis*, Horace, *Ars poetica* 361).

282. The source of the first quotation is unknown. The others are from *Bellum Iugurthinum* 60.2 and 51.1.

283. "Those who wrote annals": like Ennius. Sallust, *Bellum Catilinae* 60.1; *Bellum Iugurthinum* 99.2, 98.2, 100.5. In 100.5 replacing *temporibus* with *diebus* produces a hexameter if the last syllable in *Marius* is treated as long at the caesura.

284. Pontano quoted the passage at greater length in section 63.

285. Each of the rephrasings breaks up a long sequence of long syllables.

286. Roscius: a famous actor commended by Cicero as a model for orators because of his high standards of perfection and ability to move an audience (*Brutus* 290; *De oratore* 1.129–30, 258).

287. Cicero, *Orator* 153. The popular etymology of Ahala, the cognomen of Brutus' maternal ancestor C. Servilius Ahala, derived it from *Axilla*.

288. Pontano is playing with the philological and philosophical senses of *elementum* (both "letter" and "element").

289. Cf. Quintilian 1.4.16.

290. "As if from treading with the feet": the bolts of ancient Roman doors (*pessuli*) fastened into the threshold or door sill.

291. An interesting series of etymologies, all related rightly or wrongly to *pes* (foot). The comment on destroying the double-*s* sound in *pessimus* in favor of *x* suggests that *peximus* for *pessimus* was accepted by Pontano's circle; see Tateo, "Per l'edizione critica," 160–61.

292. Cf. Quintilian 1.4.16.

293. "to undergo some experience." That is, the words are passive in sense: "lovable," "capable of being wounded," etc. But the late Latin *nabilis* is an exception since it means not "swimable" but "able to swim."

294. *penetrabile frigus: Georgics* 1.93. *telum exitiabile:* Silius Italicus, *Punica* 14.306.

295. The examples, although found elsewhere, all occur in Boethius. *First Commentary on Porphyry's Isagoge* 1.8.21: *nam cum dixeris 'hinnibile' vel 'risibile' illud est equi proprium, illud hominis* (when you say *hinnibile* or *risibile*, the one is the property of a horse, the other of a human being). *Second Commentary on Porphyry's Isagoge* 3.4.210: *sensibile animal.* The phrase *sensibile animal* does not occur in Lucretius, but he makes sensation the property of living things (e.g., *De rerum natura* 2.973).

296. Vergil, *Georgics* 3.311, 1.494; Cicero, *Orator* 170.

297. "Cut short" (*decurtatae*): cf. Cicero, *Orator* 178.

298. Cf. Isidore, *Origines* 11.1.34: *Vultus vero dictus, eo quod per eum animi voluntas ostenditur.*

299. Cf. Columella, *Res rustica* 1. praef. 24.

300. Cf. Isidore, *Origines* 11.1.144: *Foetus autem nominatus, quod adhuc in utero foveatur.*

301. Cf. Isidore, *Origines* 10.53: *Clientes prius colientes dicebantur,* a colendis patronis.

302. The connection between *casta* and *castitas* asserted by Servius on *Aeneid* 3.519 is later quoted by Isidore, *Origines* 9.3.44: *dicta autem 'castra' quasi casta, vel quod illic castraretur libido; nam numquam his intererat mulier.*

303. Summonte also discussed *veho* in section 60.

304. Cicero, *De oratore* 2.52.

305. Cf. Cicero, *De oratore* 2.52–54; *Brutus* 228; *De legibus* 1.6–7.

306. Cf. Cicero *De oratore* 2.64; *Orator* 66.

307. "Rambling" (*diffluentia*), apparently a Renaissance coinage. Pontano uses it in *De sermone* 3.15.2 to mean something like "wasteful excess" (Ramminger, s.v.).

308. Pontano probably expected his readers to remember Horace's next words: *ut cito dicta / percipiant animi dociles teneantque fideles; / omne supervacuum pleno de pectore manat* ("so that receptive minds may quickly grasp your words and hold onto them faithfully: everything in excess runs out of a mind filled too full"): *Ars poetica* 335–37.

309. Cf. Cicero, *Brutus* 66; *Orator* 30.

310. Cf. Cicero, *De officiis* 1.1.3, comparing the vigor of his oratorical style with the *aequabile et temperatum orationis genus* of his philosophical works.

311. "Convolutions" (*contortus*): apparently a coinage by Pontano to parallel *ambitus* (periphrases).

312. For Sallust's brevity (deemed appropriate in a historian, but not in an orator), see Quintilian 4.2.45 (*illa Sallustiana . . . brevitas*); 10.1.32 (*illa Sallustiana brevitas*). For a comparison of Sallust's rapidity (*illam Sallustii velocitatem*) with Livy's more leisurely pace, see Quintilian 10.1.102.

313. Cicero makes a similar observation about Thucydides (*Brutus* 66). See Gray, *History and Rhetoric*, 290 n. 17.

314. The contrast between the eloquent and the merely accomplished speaker and much of the language are drawn from Cicero, *De oratore* 1.94.

315. Marcellinus: the fourth-century historian Ammianus Marcellinus, often criticized for his turgid style.

316. Horace, *Ars poetica* 23: *denique sit quidvis, simplex dumtaxat et unum.*

317. When Amphion and his brother were fortifying Thebes, Amphion played his lyre and the stones moved into place at the sound. The story is often alluded to in classical literature, but Pontano may be thinking of Propertius 3.2.5–6: *saxa Cithaeronis Thebas agitata per artem / sponte sua in muri membra coisse ferunt*. In his manuscript (Berlin, Deutsche Staatsbibliothek MS Lat. fol. 500, folio 36r), he glosses *per arte* (his reading) with the words *cantu Amphionis*.

318. The phrase "treachery more than Punic" reflects a Roman stereotype of the Carthaginians that goes back at least to the time of Plautus (cf. *Poenulus* 112–13, 991).

319. "Vigorous gait of a senator": a reference to the fact that Sallust was a Roman senator.

320. "Not similar enough to this one in Livy": that is, for comparison. For the description see Sallust, *Bellum Catilinae* 5.

321. For Cicero on brevity as "unadorned and lucid," see *Brutus* 262 (*nihil est enim in historia pura et illustri brevitate dulcius*). Pontano calls it "straightforward and clear" (*aperta et clara*) in section 74.

322. "Caterpillar" (*involvolum*): a very rare word that Pontano has taken from a passage in Plautus' *Cistellaria* (4.2.63–64) that also refers to convoluted speech: *involvolum, quae in pampini folio intorta implicat se; / itidem haec exorditur sibi intortam orationem*.

323. The source is unidentified. Pontano is perhaps quoting from his own work.

324. Marcus Fabius : that is, Quintilian. Pontano paraphrases Quintilian's comment on Livy: *Ideoque immortalem illam Sallustii velocitatem diversis virtutibus consecutus est* (10.1.102).

325. "Magnifier" (*magnificatrix*), "exalter" (*sullevatrix*): both Renaissance coinages. See Ramminger, s.v.

326. Marcus Tullius: that is, Cicero.

327. "Exceedingly copious" (*perhuberem*): probably a coinage by Pontano.

328. Sallust, *Bellum Catilinae* 31.3, quoted above in section 76.

329. Livy, 21.4.9, quoted in 75. "Conscience": *religio*, which Pontano probably takes as simply "religion."

330. Cf. Cicero, *De oratore* 2.63. In section 73 Pontano quoted Cicero's first law of history, that it be truthful and impartial (*De oratore* 2.62). Here he has in mind Cicero's next words: *Haec scilicet fundamenta nota sunt omnibus; ipsa autem exaedificatio posita est in rebus et verbis* ("These [truthfulness and impartiality] are known to all; but the edifice itself rests on events and language").

331. Cf. Sallust, *Bellum Iugurthinum* 5.3: *pauca supra repetam, quo ad cognoscendum omnia illustria magis magisque in aperto sint*. Micipsa (148–118 BCE) was king of Numidia.

332. Sallust, *Bellum Catilinae* 5.9.

333. Livy 21.10.

334. "In debate" (*altercatim*): perhaps a coinage by Pontano; see Ramminger, s.v.

335. Sallust, *Bellum Catilinae* 51–52.

336. Pontano is drawing again on *De oratore* 2.63, where Cicero insists that the historian must describe not just the actions of his principal figures but also their life and character (*vita atque natura*).

337. Livy 21.4.3–9; Sallust, *Bellum Iugurthinum* 6.1; *Bellum Catilinae* 5. The passages on Hannibal and Jugurtha are quoted and discussed in section 75.

338. Hannibal's dream: Livy 21.22.6–9. Catiline's letter: Sallust, *Bellum Catilinae* 35.1. Scipio's letter: *Bellum Iugurthinum* 9.1–2 (but Pontano seems to be in error: the letter is to Micipsa). The prophecy on Cannae by the famous Roman soothsayer Marcius is reported at Livy 25.12.2–6; Sallust reports the prophecy about the Cornelii but attributes it to the Sibylline books (*Bellum Catilinae* 47.2).

339. "Formed in a square" (*quadrato agmine*): a line of march in which the army proceeds through dangerous territory with a guard on all four sides.

340. Monti Sabia notes that Pontano marked this passage in his manuscript of Livy (Naples, Biblioteca Nazionale IV C 20, fol. 128v) and added it to Vat. lat. 2843 fol. 90v; "La mano del Pontano," 133–34.

341. Livy 39.50.9–10.

342. In this sentence Pontano recalls two passages of Cicero. For nature's gift to man of superiority over other living things, cf. *De officiis* 1.97: "nobis autem personam imposuit ipsa natura magna cum excellentia praestantiaque animantium reliquarum." For the power of speech, cf. *De oratore* 1.8.30, especially: "mentes allicere, voluntates impellere quo velit; unde autem velit deducere."

343. "After telling of disasters of this kind": the phrase does not take into account the passage just quoted on the celebration after Gracchus' victory over Hanno, which was added as an afterthought (see textual n. 343).

344. Monti Sabia notes that Pontano marked this passage in his manuscript of Livy (Naples, Biblioteca Nazionale IV C 20, fol. 20r) and added it to Vatican City, Biblioteca Apostolica Vaticana, Vat. lat. 2843, fol. 92v; "La mano del Pontano," 132–34. Livy supposes that Thaumaci took its name from Greek *thauma*, "marvel"; Pontano calls it *Thaumati*, following the spelling in his manuscript, as Monti Sabia observes.

345. "Even in these rhythms": the passage begins with a very heavy rhythm. Of the thirty-two syllables in the first sentence, twenty-seven are long; the first seven are all long (and the number grows to fifteen with elision of those ending in *–um* with the following *aut*).

346. Monti Sabia notes that Pontano marked this passage in his manuscript of Livy (Naples, Biblioteca Nazionale IV C 20, fol. 49v) and added it to Vat. lat. 2843, fol. 93r; see "La mano del Pontano," 133.

347. The "town mentioned a little while ago" is the Numidian fortress described in section 83.

348. Monti Sabia notes that Pontano marked Livy 23.18.12–13 in his manuscript of Livy (Naples, Biblioteca Nazionale ex-Vind. Lat. 33, fol. 98v); see "La mano del Pontano," 123.

349. Cf. Cicero, *De oratore* 2.36: "Historia vero . . . magistra vitae."

350. "As it has been said": section 79.

351. "Est enim finitimus oratori poeta" (Cicero, *De oratore* 1.70).

352. See textual note *ad loc.*

353. For the exemplary function of history, see especially Livy, *Praefatio* 10: "Hoc illud est praecipue in cognitione rerum salubre ac frugiferum, omnis te exempli documenta in illustri posita monumento intueri." ("This is especially beneficial and useful in the study of history: that you see the lessons of every example placed on a conspicuous monument.")

354. On history as the guide of life, cf. section 85.

355. Cf. Cicero, *Brutus* 262: "voluit alios habere parata, unde sumerent qui vellent scribere historiam."

356. Curtius: Quintus Curtius Rufus (ca. 1st century CE) wrote a history of Alexander the Great, of which much is lost. "Different in style" (*diverso⟨s⟩que in dicendi genere*). For the different styles of Sallust and Livy, see sections 68, 74–75. See also Quintilian 10.1.73 and 10.101–2.

357. Trogus: Pompeius Trogus probably wrote in the Augustan period. Almost nothing of his *Historiae Philippicae* is preserved. Much more of Tacitus is extant, although much of both the *Historiae* and the *Annales* is lost. A major portion of the *Annales*, books 1–6, was unknown to Pontano, for it arrived in Italy only in 1508, five years after his death. See Robert W. Ulery, Jr., "Cornelius Tacitus," *Catalogus Translationum et Commentariorum* 6 (Washington, D.C., 1986): 87–174, especially 89–95.

358. See section 22, where Azio cites winning admiration as the purpose of poetry and attributes the principle to Pontano ("our old man").

359. Cicero, *De oratore* 1.70, referred to by Altilio in section 86.

360. Pontano is misquoting or misremembering Cicero, whose comment refers to orators, not poets (cf. *Brutus* 333 and *De oratore* 1.8–11). But see *De oratore* 11.

361. Bavius is criticized as a bad poet by Vergil (*Eclogue* 3.90). Maximianus was a late Latin poet (fl. 6th? century CE) whose elegies appeared in elementary school texts in the Middle Ages. The "Delian prophet" is Apollo, divine patron of poets. For poets as the only ones qualified to judge poetry, see Pontano 2012, *Antonius* 39 and 51; Gaisser, "Succession and Inheritance," especially 102–5.

362. "Urania so greatly venerated by our old man." Urania is the muse of astrology; Pontano used her name as the title of his poem on the heavens.

363. Pontano conflates lines 516–17 in *De hortis Hesperidum* 2.537: *audiit et Triviae longe lacus, audiit et Nar.*

364. Pontano borrows the line in *De hortis Hesperidum* 2.538, changing *et* to *ac.*

365. The "dread sisters" are the Furies.

366. Vergil mentions neither a sacrifice to Juno at Lacinium nor Aeneas' being driven to Drepanum by a storm (for the latter see Dionysius of Halicarnassus, *Roman Antiquities* 1.52.1). For Vergil's treatment of Aeneas' wanderings, see Robert B. Lloyd, "*Aeneid* III and the Aeneas legend," *American Journal of Philology* 78 (1957): 382–400.

367. "Sail-winged sea" (*mare velivolum, Aeneid* 1.224). "Shaggy forests" (*silvas comantes;* cf. Valerius Flaccus, *Argonautica* 1.429: *silvasque comantes*).

368. Sections 66 and 68.

369. "Maeonian": Homeric. According to ancient tradition, Homer was the son of Maeon.

370. Plutarch, *Solon* 3.4.

371. Plutarch, *Solon* 8.1–3.

372. Empedocles (5th century BCE) argued that the universe consisted of the four elements (fire, air, earth, and water); some fragments of his poetry are preserved. Dorotheus of Sidon (late 1st or early 2nd century CE) wrote an influential astrological poem that was subsequently translated into Persian and from there into Arabic. See *Dorothei Sidonii Carmen Astrologicum,* ed. David Pingree (Leipzig, 1976).

373. "With less envy" (*invidenter*); a rare word that occurs only once or twice in medieval Latin.

374. Azio closes with an encomium of poetry in the form of a classical hymn of praise, beginning with the repeated salutation "Hail" (*Salve . . . salve*) and continuing with repeated direct address in the second person (the "*Du stil*"): *tu . . . tu . . . per te . . . per te . . . per te.* For the style, see Eduard Norden, *Agnostos Theos: Untersuchungen zur Formengeschichte religiöser Rede* (Leipzig, 1913), 149–60.

APPENDIX I

1. For Summonte and Puderico see Appendix II.

2. For the posthumous publication of Pontano's works by his friends, see Introduction, pp. vii–viii. Their first publication was a volume of his poetry printed in Naples by Sigismondo Mayr in September 1505. (Aldo Manuzio had already printed the poetry in Venice in August 1505.) Their second volume, also printed by Mayr, contained *Actius, Aegidius,* and *Asinus* (Naples, 1507).

3. For Suardo Suardino see Appendix II. The phrase "spur on a willing horse" was a cliché in antiquity; see Cicero, *De oratore* 2.186.

4. Cf. Acts 1:1: *Primum quidem sermonem feci de omnibus, o Theophile, quae coepit Iesus facere et docere.*

5. Azio Sincero (Actius Sincerus) is the academy name of Jacopo Sannazaro. See Appendix II and Introduction pp. viii–ix.

6. Horace uses the phrase *emunctae naris* ("of clear nostrils," literally, "with nose well blown") to describe the keen discernment of his predecessor Lucilius (*Satire* 1.4.8). For judging with the "tip of the nose" (*summis naribus*), see Erasmus, *Adagia* 1.10.64.

7. After the final French conquest of Naples in 1501, Sannazaro accompanied King Federico into exile in France. He returned to Italy after Federico's death in November 1504. See Carlo Vecce, *Iacopo Sannazaro in Francia: Scoperte di codici all'inizio del XVI secolo* (Padua, 1988); Carlo Vecce, "Sannazaro in Francia: orizzonti europei di un 'poeta gentiluomo,'" in *Iacopo Sannazaro. La cultura napoletana nell'Europa del Rinascimento. Convegno internazionale di studi. Napoli, 27–28 marzo 2006*, ed. Pasquale Sabbatino (Florence, 2009), 149–65. Pontano refers to his exile in *Aegidius* 35.

8. Francesco Elio Marchese; see Appendix II.

9. The Aedui and Turones were ancient Gallic tribes inhabiting what is now central France. "The territory of the Aedui" may refer to Blois, where Sannazaro wrote a letter to Puderico announcing his discovery. "Turones" probably refers to Tours, the city in which Federico spent

much of his exile. Sannazaro's letter to Puderico is lost, but the letter Pontano wrote to Sannazaro on February 13, 1503 to congratulate him is extant. It is printed in Pontano, *Actius* etc. (Naples 1507), fol. L3r; Erasmo Percopo, ed., *Lettere di Giovanni Pontano a Principi ed Amici* (Naples, 1907) 65–66. For Sannazaro's manuscript discoveries, see especially Vecce, *Iacopo Sannazaro in Francia*; see also Remigio Sabbadini, *Le scoperte dei codici Latini e Greci nei secoli XIV e XV*, 2 vols. (Florence, 1905), 1:139–40.

10. The epigrams Summonte mentions are those of the *Anthologia latina*.

11. Sannazaro's manuscript of Solinus is apparently lost; it cannot be identified with any of the extant manuscripts. Vecce, *Iacopo Sannazaro in Francia*, 89.

12. Ovid mentions the *Cynegeticon* of Grattius in *Epistulae ex Ponto* 4.16.34. Grattius' poem and most of the other works listed in this sentence were included in Sannazaro's greatest find, an exemplar of the Carolingian *Florilegium Thuaneum*, whose principal extant witnesses are Paris, Bibliothèque Nationale de France, MS lat. 8071 (late ninth century) and Vienna, Österreichische Nationalbibliothek, MS Lat. 277 (the oldest section of which dates to the late eighth century). For the *Florilegium* and its complex history, see Vecce, *Iacopo Sannazaro in Francia*, 92–158.

13. In fact, it was many years before any of the texts discovered by Sannazaro were printed (Vecce, "Sannazaro in Francia," 157; Vecce, *Iacopo Sannazaro in Francia*, 56–62).

14. According to Plutarch (*Camillus* 23–29), the Roman hero Marcus Furius Camillus, after suffering exile, returned as a hero and recovered the gold that the invading Gauls had demanded as the price of leaving the city. Summonte sees Sannazaro's return from France and his recovery of Roman texts as a similar achievement.

15. In antiquity the oak-leaf crown (*querna corona* or *corona civica*) was awarded to one who saved the lives of his fellow citizens. Summonte's omission of the word *corona* has no ancient parallel. For the full phrase, see Ovid, *Fasti* 1.614; *Tristia* 3.1.36.

16. Sannazaro's Latin poetry includes epigrams in both elegiac and lyric meters, elegies, the *Piscatoriae Eclogae*, and his masterpiece, *De partu virgi-*

nis. Michael C. J. Putnam has translated his Latin poetry for the I Tatti Renaissance Library [ITRL 38] (Cambridge, MA, 2009). Sedulius (fl. 435) and Prudentius (348–after 405) were important early Christian poets with many imitators.

17. Enrico Puderico (Erricus, or Herricus Pudericus, died between 1472 and 1475) was an interlocutor in *Antonius.* See Pontano 2012, 362 n. 4

18. Summonte used a similar expression in the Neapolitan *princeps* of Pontano's poetry (1505): *Denique hoc non tacuerim: Felices nos omnino nec sine invidia iudicatum iri, quibus vivum obtigerit Pontanum videre.* See Giovanni Parenti, *Poëta Proteus alter: Forma e storia di tre libri di Pontano* (Florence, 1985), 9 n. 19.

19. Jacopo Sannazaro, *Epigram* 2.8.

Bibliography

EDITIONS OF PONTANO'S WORKS

Actius de numeris poeticis & lege historiæ. Aegidius multiplicis argumenti. Tertius dialogus de ingratitudine qui Asinus inscribitur. Naples: ex officina Sigismundi Mayr, 1507. [Edited by Pietro Summonte.]

I Dialoghi. Edited by Carmelo Previtera. Florence: Sansoni, 1943.

Dialoge. Translated by Hermann Kiefer and others. Introduction by Ernesto Grassi. Munich: W. Fink, 1984. [With Previtera's Latin text.]

Baiae. Translated by Rodney G. Dennis. I Tatti Renaissance Library 22. Cambridge, MA: Harvard University Press, 2006.

Dialogues, Volume I: Charon and Antonius. Edited and translated by Julia Haig Gaisser. I Tatti Renaissance Library 53. Cambridge, MA: Harvard University Press, 2012.

On Married Love. Eridanus. Translated by Luke Roman. I Tatti Renaissance Library 63. Cambridge, MA: Harvard University Press, 2014.

Actius de numeris poeticis, de lege historiae. Edited and translated by Francesco Tateo. RR, Saggi 76. Rome: Roma nel Rinascimento, 2018.

The Virtues and Vices of Speech. Edited by G. W. Pigman III. I Tatti Renaissance Library 87. Cambridge, MA: Harvard University Press, 2019. [*De sermone libri VI.*]

MODERN LITERATURE

Altamura, Antonio. *L'Umanesimo nel Mezzogiorno d'Italia: Storia, bibliografie e testi inediti.* Florence: Bibliopolis, 1941.

Arnaldi, Francesco, Lucia Gualdo Rosa, and Liliana Monti Sabia, eds. *Poeti latini del Quattrocento.* Milan and Naples: Riccardo Ricciardi Editore, 1964.

Bentley, Jerry H. *Politics and Culture in Renaissance Naples.* Princeton: Princeton University Press, 1987.

Black, Robert. "The New Laws of History." *Renaissance Studies* 1 (1987): 126–56. Reprinted in Black, *Studies in Renaissance Humanism and Politics.* Farnham, Surrey: Ashgate Variorum, 2011, essay I.

de Nichilo, Mauro, ed. *I Poemi astrologici di Giovanni Pontano. Storia del testo.* Bari: Dedalo libri, 1975.

Deramaix, Marc. "*Excellentia et Admiratio* dans l'*Actius* de Giovanni Pontano. Une poétique et une esthétique de la perfection." *Mélanges de l'École française de Rome* 99 (1987): 171–212.

Ferraù, Giacomo. *Pontano critico.* Messina: Università degli studi di Messina, Facoltà di lettere e filosofia, Centro di studi umanistici, 1983.

Furstenberg-Levi, Shulamit. *The Accademia Pontaniana. A Model of a Humanist Network.* Leiden and Boston: E. J. Brill, 2016.

——. "The Fifteenth-Century Accademia Pontaniana." *History of Universities* 21.1 (2006): 33–70.

Gaisser, Julia Haig. "Succession and Inheritance in Pontano's *Antonius.*" *Studi di erudizione e di filologia italiana* 2 (2013): 85–118.

Grafton, Anthony. *What Was history? The Art of History in Early Modern Europe.* Cambridge: Cambridge University Press, 2007.

Gray, Hanna Holborn. *History and Rhetoric in Quattrocento Humanism.* PhD diss., Harvard University, 1956.

Hankins, James. "Humanist Academies and the Platonic Academy of Florence." In *On Renaissance Academies,* edited by Marianne Pade, 31–46. Proceedings of the International Conference "From the Roman Academy to the Danish Academy in Rome." The Danish Academy in Rome, October 11–13, 2006. Rome: Danish Institute, 2011.

——. *Virtue Politics: Soulcraft and Statecraft in Renaissance Italy.* Cambridge, MA: Belknap Press, 2019.

Kidwell, Carol. *Pontano: Poet and Prime Minister.* London: Duckworth, 1991.

Mantovani, Alessandra. "Intorno ad alcune edizioni recenti dei *Dialoghi* di Pontano." *Studi e problemi di critica testuale* 96.1 (2018): 49–75.

Mariotti, Scevola. "Per lo studio dei *Dialoghi* del Pontano." *Belfagor* 2 (1947): 332–44. Reprinted with revisions in Mariotti, *Scritti medievali e umanistici,* edited by Silvia Rizzo, 261–84. Rome: Edizioni di Storia e Letteratura, 1994.

Martellotti, Guido. "Critica metrica del Salutati e del Pontano." In *Critica e storia letteraria: studi offerti a Mario Fubini*, 2 vols., 1:352–73. Padua: Liviana, 1970.

Minieri Riccio, Camillo. *Biografie degli accademici Alfonsini detti poi Pontaniani dal 1442 al 1543*. Naples: F. Furchheim, 1881. Reprint, Bologna: Forni, 1969.

Monti, Salvatore. "Per la storia del testo dell'*Actius* di G. Pontano." *Rendiconti dell'Accademia di archeologia, lettere e belle arti di Napoli* 44 (1969): 259–92. Reprinted in Monti Sabia and Monti, *Studi su Pontano*, 2:909–45.

——. "Ricerche sulla cronologia dei *Dialoghi* di Pontano." *Annali della Facoltà di Letteratura e Filosofia, Università di Napoli*, 10 (1962–63): 247–311. Reprinted in Monti Sabia and Monti, *Studi su Giovanni Pontano*, 2:757–826.

Monti Sabia, Liliana. "Manipolazioni onomastiche del Summonte in testi pontaniani." In *Rinascimento meridionale e altri studi in onore di Mario Santoro*, edited by Maria Cristina Cafisse et al., 293–320. Naples: Società editrice napoletana, 1987. Reprinted in Monti Sabia and Monti, *Studi su Giovanni Pontano*, 1:257–92.

——. "La mano del Pontano in due Livii della Biblioteca Nazionale di Napoli (mss. ex Vind. Lat. 33 e IV C 20)." *Italia Medioevale e Umanistica* 39 (1996): 171–208. Reprinted in Monti Sabia and Monti, *Studi su Giovanni Pontano*, 1:101–38.

——. "La mano del Summonte nelle edizioni pontaniane postume." *Atti dell' Accademia Pontaniana*, n.s. 34 (1986): 191–204. Reprinted in Monti Sabia and Monti, *Studi su Giovanni Pontano*, 1:237–55.

——. "Pietro Summonte e l'*editio princeps* delle opere pontaniane." In *L'Umanesimo umbro*. Atti del IX Convegno di Studi umbri. Gubbio, 22–25 settembre 1974, 451–73. Perugia: Facoltà di lettere e filosofia dell'Università degli studi di Perugia, 1977. Reprinted in Monti Sabia and Monti, *Studi su Giovanni Pontano*, 1:215–35.

——. "Profilo biografico." In *Un profilo moderno e due* Vitae *antiche di Giovanni Pontano*, 7–27. Quaderni dell'Accademia Pontaniana 25. Naples: Accademia pontaniana, 1998. Reprinted with additions in Monti Sabia and Monti, *Studi su Giovanni Pontano*, 1:1–31.

Monti Sabia, Liliana, and Salvatore Monti. *Studi su Giovanni Pontano*. Edited by Giuseppe Germano. 2 vols. Messina: Centro Interdipartimentale di Studi Umanistici, 2010.

Pèrcopo, Erasmo. *Vita di Giovanni Pontano*. Naples: Industrie Tipografiche Editoriali Assimilate, 1938.

Tateo Francesco. "Giovanni Pontano e la nuova frontiera della prosa latina; l'alternativa al volgare." In *Sul latino degli umanisti*, edited by Francesco Tateo, 11–78. Bari: Cacucci, 2006.

———. "Per l'edizione critica dell'*Actius* di G. Pontano." *Studi mediolatini e volgari* 12 (1964): 145–94.

———. "La poetica di Giovanni Pontano." *Filologia romanza* 6 (1959): 277–303.

———. "L'unità e il significato dell'*Actius*." In Tateo, *Umanesimo etico di Giovanni Pontano*, 63–132. Lecce: Edizioni Milella, 1972.

Terzaghi, Nicola. "Attorno al Pontano." *Annali della Scuola Normale Superiore di Pisa: Lettere, storie e filosofia* 16 (1947): 200–210.

Index of Citations

ക്ഷ്ട്ക

439

General Index

જ઼ૢૺ

Publication of this volume has been made possible by

The Myron and Sheila Gilmore Publication Fund at I Tatti
The Robert Lehman Endowment Fund
The Jean-François Malle Scholarly Programs and Publications Fund
The Andrew W. Mellon Scholarly Publications Fund
The Craig and Barbara Smyth Fund
for Scholarly Programs and Publications
The Lila Wallace–Reader's Digest Endowment Fund
The Malcolm Wiener Fund for Scholarly Programs and Publications